The "Inward" Language

Anne Ferry

The "Inward" Language

Sonnets of Wyatt, Sidney, Shakespeare, Donne

The University of Chicago Press
Chicago and London

ANNE FERRY is professor of English, Boston College.
She is the author of *Milton's Epic Voice, Milton and
the Miltonic Dryden,* and *All in War with Time.*

The University of Chicago Press, Chicago 60637
The University of Chicago Press, Ltd., London

90 89 88 87 86 85 84 83   5 4 3 2 1

Library of Congress Cataloging in Publication Data

Ferry, Anne D.
    The "inward" language.

    Includes bibliographical references and index.
    1. Sonnets, English—History and criticism.
2. English poetry—Early modern, 1500–1700—History
and criticism.   3. Self in literature.   4. English
language—Early modern, 1500–1700.   I. Title.
PR539.S7F47   1983   821'.042'09353   83-1072
ISBN 0-226-24466-0

To Bunny

Contents

Acknowledgments

The interests which this book pursues grew out of discussions in a doctoral seminar in sixteenth-century poetry which I taught at Boston College in the spring of 1976. To the members of the seminar I am greatly indebted in ways that they will recognize, I hope approvingly, in these pages. I want to thank Professor P. Albert Duhamel of Boston College for his generosity in answering my almost daily questions out of his astonishing store of knowledge about the sixteenth century. Professor Andrew Von Hendy of Boston College helped me with his great gifts as a listener, and used his learning to show me many of the questions I ought to be asking. Elizabeth Ferry's knowledge of language is reflected in the choices of words explored in Chapter 1, and made her a valuable corrector of my inaccuracies. The introduction and first chapter also reflect my many discussions of philosophical issues about language with Stephen Ferry. He cleared up some of my confusions, and gave me confidence in my conclusions. David Ferry, Professor of English at Wellesley College, has improved this book by his readings of it, and by the example of his own writings. His criticism, his poetry, and all his ways of thinking have shown me what I hold to be true and important about the nature of inward experience.

Time to complete this book was provided by an American Council of Learned Societies Fellowship for 1980–1981, and a grant from the Mellon Foundation for 1981–1982. For this support and encouragement I am most grateful.

The poems contained in this volume are reprinted by permission: Reproduced from *Collected Poems of Sir Thomas Wyatt,* edited by Kenneth Muir and Patricia Thomson (Liverpool: Liverpool University Press, 1969); *The Poems of Sir Philip Sidney,* edited by William Ringler (Oxford: Oxford University Press, 1962); *John Donne: The Divine Poems,* edited by Helen Gardner (Oxford: Oxford University Press, 1966); *Tottel's Miscellany* (rev. ed.), edited by Hyder Rollins, Copyright, 1928, 1929, 1956, 1965, By the President and Fellows of Harvard College (Cambridge, Mass: Harvard University Press, 1965); *Petrarch's Lyric Poems,* edited and translated by Robert Durling, Copyright © 1976 Robert M. Durling (Cambridge, Mass.: Harvard University Press, 1976).

A. F.

Cambridge, Massachusetts

♦

Foreword

The question this book attempts to answer is whether sixteenth- and early seventeenth-century writers, without modern vocabularies for describing what we call the *real self* or the *inner life,* nevertheless conceived of inward experience in any sense to which our terminologies can intelligibly be applied. The question grew out of direct response to the speaker in Shakespeare's sonnets, who seems to be endowed with a more modern consciousness than can be explained by now long-familiar studies of Elizabethan psychology. The need to pursue the question was intensified by the fact that recent discussions of this poetry describe it in the current vocabularies of a number of contemporary disciplines grouped around concern with *the self.* It seemed a useful effort to get behind these vocabularies, with their inescapably modern assumptions, to discover and explore those of much earlier writers. This study of sixteenth- and early seventeeth-century poems therefore poses an alternative to the description of them principally in these contemporary terminologies. In measuring the distance between our language and the English available to poets of the earlier period, this book also enters from its own peculiar angle the critical discussion which is, for example, represented and sanely illuminated by Richard Poirier's "Writing Off the Self."[1] It examines the language of poets writing about inward experience before the term *the self* meant more than what we mean by *itself* or *the same.*

Because I could find no paradigms in literary scholarship for this undertaking, I chose other models that seemed to embody the kind of exploration on which I was embarked. One such model was an article known to me only by its title, "Primordial Black Holes and the Problem of Missing Mass." Whatever its actual meaning, to me it represented the kind of plunge into the unknown that seemed to be demanded by the fundamental question of this book. In trying to get behind our peculiarly modern language for inward experience. to define and interpret that of earlier writers, I was continually brought up short by their lack of terms. I seemed to be looking into holes in space, attempting (as the article's title seemed to propose) to measure what was missing. To find ways of exploring this problem, I tried to follow the example of my friend William Bromell, who builds ship models for maritime museums. Once he has studied the relevant historical documents, he constructs miniature tools scaled to the minuteness of the representation he then builds. These seemed procedures to follow. The process began with an attempt to discover as fully as possible—in documents ranging from theological treatises to phrase books for foreign visitors—what means, if any, for portraying the *inner life* or the *real self* were available in English of the sixteenth and early seventeenth century. What followed then was an effort to reconstruct as minutely as possible how poets used these means.

Because this book is in a sense about the state of English in the sixteenth and early seventeenth century, I have preferred to use unmodernized texts. Some, especially from the early part of the period, present difficulties by their remoteness from our language. Yet in that very strangeness they support one conclusion to which exploration of sixteenth-century writing has led: that English of that time was much more radically unlike modern English in character than is usually taken into account in literary studies. It differed in important ways not only in vocabulary, but in grammar, punctuation, and spelling, and again, not only as they were used, but as they were conceived. The very notions about language were significantly unlike our own, and therefore its uses were predicated on altogether different assumptions. These differences have been recognized in theoretical discussions, but not sufficiently in studies which examine the poetry written in this period. Such differences tend to be further diminished when we too readily describe it in our vocabularies, or read it in versions altered to resemble our habits of language. Inconsistencies were inevitable, however, even among the preferred choices of texts, because some essentially unmodernized editions contain certain small but often significant changes. For example, in the definitive Clarendon Press edition of Sidney's poetry, the editor has introduced types of punctuation—quotation marks and apostrophes for possessives—which were not in existence in English of this period, and which can substantially alter a text by their inclusion. Editions of Donne in the same series, however, do not introduce this modern punctuation. Editions of Wyatt's poems present still other problems of editorial consistency which are mentioned in footnotes. At the risk of such unevenness, and some obscurity, I have quoted the poems from editions with as few modernizations as possible, in order to show how poets used the extraordinarily fluid character of English in this period, within its extraordinary limitations. As a measure of their achievement, I have also preferred to leave unmodernized the prose examples of what language was available for them to work with.

Introduction:
the *inner life*, the
real self, and Hamlet

To measure some vital changes in sixteenth-century English poetry, let us begin by setting a poem of Wyatt's beside one of Shakespeare's sonnets. The earlier poem, although written between about 1520 and 1542, the year of Wyatt's death, was first published in 1557 in Tottel's *Songes and Sonettes* under the title "A renouncing of hardly escaped loue."[1] It was in this version that it was known to Shakespeare, whose allusions to the miscellany in his plays show that he was among its many readers:[2]

> Farewell the hart of crueltie.
> Though that with payne my libertie
> Deare haue I bought, and wofully
> Finisht my fearfull tragedy.
> Of force I must forsake such pleasure:
> A good cause iust, sins I endure
> Therby my wo, whiche be ye sure,
> Shall therwith go me to recure.
> I fare as one escapt that fleeth,
> Glad is he gone, and yet styll feareth
> Spied to be caught, and so dredeth
> That he for nought his paine leseth.
> In ioyfull payne reioyce my hart,
> Thus to sustaine of ech a part.
> Let not this song from thee astart.
> Welcome among my pleasant smart.

The poem consists of the lover's analysis of what is in his heart, which is also true of Shakespeare's Sonnet 62, first published in 1609, but probably written in the 1590s. Both poems depend on recognizable conventions of love poetry to dispense with explanation. Wyatt does not need to identify the source of "crueltie," understood to be the lady from whose painful service the lover claims, with mixed joy and pain, to have escaped. Shakespeare does not have to justify the introduction in the couplet of an

unidentified "thee," recognized to be the beautiful recipient of the poet's
"praise," whom he loves as his true "selfe":

> Sinne of selfe-loue possesseth al mine eie,
> And all my soule, and al my euery part;
> And for this sinne there is no remedie,
> It is so grounded inward in my heart.
> Me thinkes no face so gratious is as mine,
> No shape so true, no truth of such account,
> And for my selfe mine owne worth do define,
> As I all other in all worths surmount.
> But when my glasse shewes me my selfe indeed
> Beated and chopt with tand antiquitie,
> Mine owne selfe loue quite contrary I read
> Selfe, so selfe louing were iniquity,
>   T'is thee (my selfe) that for my selfe I praise,
>   Painting my age with beauty of thy daies.[3]

The poem by Wyatt will be shown to be representative of his love poetry
other than sonnets, and of early sixteenth-century verse in English. Sonnet
62, to be discussed in detail in Chapter 4, embodies characteristics of
many sonnets by Shakespeare which he adapted from Sidney, whose own
Sonnet 27 of *Astrophil and Stella* was the specific model for Shakespeare's
Sonnet 62. The distance between it and Wyatt's poem, and the routes by
which some poets of the sixteenth and early seventeenth centuries trav-
eled that distance, is the subject of this book.

Wyatt's speaker, in the poem as it is printed in Tottel's miscellany,
declares himself to be stepping out of a "tragedy" (a word not in the earlier
version in the Egerton manuscript, or suggested by it, unless the editor
understood "part" in line 14 as a term for play-acting).[4] No reader would,
however, liken this speaker to Hamlet, whereas the speaker in Sonnet 62
sounds in many ways like the hero of Shakespeare's tragedy, which is to
say that he speaks in a more modern voice. The meaning of the term
modern in such an application is not at all precise, and yet many readers,
critics, historians use it without uneasiness to describe Hamlet, and to
distinguish him for qualities that make him virtually a new kind of figure
in English literature. These qualities, shared by Hamlet and the speaker
in Sonnet 62, are themselves usually described by other words and phrases
not precisely defined but generally understood, and agreed to describe a
distinctively modern consciousness.

Hamlet and the speaker in Shakespeare's sonnet, by the ways in which
they analyze what is in their hearts, seem to display such qualities. They
therefore create the impression of being figures who are more like ourselves, or more like what our language describes ourselves to be. They
seem to be individuals with distinct personalities who appear to have an

inward existence which our present-day vocabularies about them assume to exist. When we watch the figure of Hamlet moving through the play, we are made to believe that he has thoughts and feelings distinct from what he shows when he gestures, acts, speaks, or stands silent. We think of him as carrying on a kind of internal monologue which is occasionally revealed in an aside. This theatrical device is given special prominence because it is used for Hamlet's first spoken words in the play, at once giving the audience a privileged view of his inward state, which is not knowable by the other characters from his outward show. The same intimacy is established when he announces "Now I am alone," and we are then allowed to hear a soliloquy, of which he speaks more than the protagonist of any other play by Shakespeare.[5] The relative newness of these devices for portraying inward experience is shown by the fact that Shakespeare developed them and exploited them fully in *Hamlet* before they had become familiar enough to have been given names: the nouns *aside, monologue,* and *soliloquy* had not yet entered the English language (although the *O.E.D.* records that one of St. Augustine's works was known in England by the title *Liber Soliloquiorum*).

At such moments in the play, the audience is allowed to hear Hamlet talking to himself, as the reader overhears the speaker in Sonnet 62 making what, at least until the couplet, sounds like a private confession of his inward state. We are therefore made to believe that Hamlet has a continuous inward existence, what in his first extended speech he alludes to as "that Within, which passeth show."[6] Again the existence of his interior experience is given prominence by being made the subject of this first long speech. Reminders are then given throughout the play, not only in asides and soliloquys, but in such hints as his words to Horatio in the final scene, "thou wouldest not thinke how all heere about my heart: but it is no matter."[7] This impression is also characteristic of the speaker in Shakespeare's sonnet as he evokes intimate moments when he privately studies himself in a mirror. He measures the distance between his outward show and his inward state by his triply intensified location of it "so grounded inward in my heart" that he can only "read" it in an imperfect reflection. By contrast Wyatt's speaker analyzes what happens in his heart in such a way that his words do not evoke a sense of internal experience at a distance from outward expression. He names each "part" of his inward state, and explains their relationships. Even in the second-to-last line, when the reader unexpectedly learns that this song is being sung within the lover's heart, it is not otherwise distinguished from public address, as if it were an aside, or a soliloquy, or an interior monologue. It sounds like formal declaration. An audience for it other than himself is evoked, for example, by the explanatory phrase "be ye sure." The apostrophes to his heart, as a listener not set apart except by name from this outside audience of "ye," do not point to recesses of experience that escape outward show.

The lover in this poem does not seem to have what could be called a private self, an inner life, or even an individuality—he puts himself easily in the category of "one" and "he"—such as Hamlet and the speaker in Sonnet 62 seem to have.

This vast difference in the impression created by these speakers is of course an effect of differences between Shakespeare's uses of language and Wyatt's in such a poem. It is an object of this study to trace as fully and as precisely as possible the evolution of these differences. To do so will be simultaneously to describe profound changes in the conception of human experience. For Shakespeare created a speaker who describes what is in his heart in ways reflecting a very different sense of his inner state and its relation to outward expression from what Wyatt's lover conceived. Both the nature of poetry about inward experience and the notion of what is in the heart rendered by it changed radically between Wyatt's lifetime and about 1600, when Shakespeare was writing *Hamlet* and shortly after he is thought to have written his sonnets, two of which appeared in print in 1599.[8] The precise nature of these changes is to be discussed in this book.

The fundamental question it attempts to answer is twofold, or can be asked in two forms. How did sixteenth-century English poetry develop in ways that enabled Shakespeare and other writers to render a new sense of what is in the heart? How did poets of the sixteenth century come to invent a sense of inward experience reflected in new uses of language in their poetry? It should be said at the outset that, although the central question of the book can be asked in these two forms, no causal arrangement of them can be made. That is, it cannot be clearly or singly argued that changes in verbal patterns altered poets' conceptions, or that new concepts generated different uses of language. The two kinds of change, like the two forms of question about them, appear to represent different ways of considering a single phenomenon, or inseparable processes which cannot be differentiated into cause and effect.

What can be argued, however, is an assumption on which this book is predicated, that literary history is created by and in works of literature. The student of poetry who wants to define its historical changes must trace them in the language of the poems themselves. That language may make direct connections with parallel changes in other forms of writing, or may suggest analogies with shifting historical patterns in other areas of experience. Yet such analogies and parallels can be substantiated for the history of poetry only by evidence in the poems themselves. Many cultural historians have located an all-encompassing revolution in the sixteenth century, arguing that it was the period when the "mental organisation of the individual of the modern Western world was created in England."[9] Such sweeping changes can in poetry ultimately be measured only by differences in uses of language, which are sometimes minute. Large shifts

in fundamental attitudes, such as have been traced in the altered economic, political, social, and religious institutions of the sixteenth century, are
in poems created by and reflected in changes in diction, grammar, punctuation, meter, as well as in shifting preferences among rhetorical devices
and the introduction of new verse forms. Often they can be discovered
only in details.

This fundamental assumption can be predicated about changes in the
literature of any period: its history consists in and is interpreted by means
of the language of the works of literature themselves. All literary histories
therefore in one sense involve some of the same essential procedures.
Love poetry of the sixteenth century, by its peculiar nature, presents the
historian with some more special problems, however. On the one hand
English was in a state of remarkable fluidity. Grammar, punctuation, and
spelling were unfixed to a degree that a modern reader finds hard to
realize—very different attitudes toward language must have made possible the seventy-three recorded variants in the spelling of Sir Walter Ralegh's
name—and vocabulary was expanding with unusual speed.[10] Yet on the
other hand the conventions of love poetry remain remarkably consistent
in sixteenth-century English verse. There are no obvious changes in actual
vocabulary, or in the areas of it from which imagery is drawn, to articulate
the fundamentally different assumptions about inward experience that
distinguish Shakespeare's rendering of what is in the heart from Wyatt's
in his song. That is, there is no shift from one area of language to another,
such as Wordsworth's poems accomplished by moving from social to
more privately meditative modes. Nor is there terminology introduced
from a newly systematized way of thinking, such as entered English at the
end of the seventeenth century largely through the formulations of Locke,
or in the early twentieth century with the growth of modern psychology.
The earliest dictionaries of hard and unfamiliar words in English, Robert
Cawdrey's of 1604 and John Bullokar's of 1616, do not include sets of
terms from any recently formulated discipline comparable, for example,
to the dozens of psychological definitions—from "affectivity" to the "un-
conscious"—listed among new words prefixed to the 1935 edition of *Webster's Collegiate Dictionary.*[11]

The special difficulties of tracing the vast historical changes in sixteenth-
century love poetry can be illustrated if the language for what is in the
heart used by a speaker typical of Wyatt's love poems is again compared
to the parallel language of the poet-lover in Shakespeare's Sonnet 62, or
now with Hamlet's first extended speech of the play:

> Seemes Maddam? Nay, it is: I know not Seemes:
> 'Tis not alone my Inky Cloake (good Mother)
> Nor Customary suites of solemne Blacke,
> Nor windy suspiration of forc'd breath,

> No, nor the fruitfull Riuer in the Eye,
> Nor the deiected hauiour of the Visage,
> Together with all Formes, Moods, shewes of Griefe,
> That can denote me truly. These indeed Seeme,
> For they are actions that a man might play:
> But I haue that Within, which passeth show;
> These, but the Trappings, and the Suites of woe.[12]

Neither this speech nor Sonnet 62 uses words for the lover's inward state—except the compounds of "loue" and "louing" with "selfe" in the sonnet—that were not already available in the early sixteenth century. Virtually all of them, including the locating word "inward," were in fact repeated frequently, almost obsessively, by the love poets represented in Tottel's miscellany, as were the sighs, tears, and dejected visage catalogued by Hamlet as the outward "show" of inward "woe" (a common rhyme in sixteenth-century love poetry). Even his metaphor of "actions that a man might play," while peculiarly appropriate to Hamlet's theatrical sense of his experience, is part of the stock-in-trade of complaining lovers, illustrated by the emendation of Wyatt's poem in Tottel's miscellany, which portrays the lover concluding his part in a "tragedy." The organizing distinction in Hamlet's speech between "is" and "Seemes" is itself also not new either in terminology or interest. It preoccupied poets throughout the century, among them Wyatt, whose association with this distinction is shown in a passage from the autobiography of the poet-musician, Thomas Whythorne, written about 1576. He makes the curious observation that in his day, by contrast with Wyatt's, "seeming" has come to be sometimes wrongly used as if it were synonymous with "being," whereas

> seeming to do a thing is rather not to do the thing than to do it. As Sir Thomas Wyatt the Elder saith in one of his sonnets (writing to one named John Poynz, a friend of his), that he was not then in Spain where one must him incline, rather than to be, outwardly to seem to be; he would not meddle with wits that were so fine. Whereby ye may perceive that there is a difference between seeming, and being or doing indeed.[13]

Since the vast differences represented in these examples between Shakespeare's portrayal of inward states and Wyatt's cannot be measured by differences in their vocabularies or sources of metaphor, the changes must consist in other verbal patterns, more difficult to point to. No separate fact of our experiences of reading can be isolated to explain the differences. No newly formulated set of concepts recognized from our later perspective can be applied, with the knowledge of hindsight, to describe a historical development. This absence either of a shift in key vocabulary or sources of metaphor, or of a new terminology, is no accident resulting here from the limited choice of examples. For, it will be argued, there were no theoretical formulations of the new assumptions about inward experience which evolved in some late sixteenth-century poetry. What systematic means existed in the period for analyzing internal experience remained essentially the same throughout the century, although the proliferation of translations made classical and continental writings on man's moral and physiological nature, as well as many religious works, more widely known. The expanding interest in treatises devoted to psychology in the tradition of Aristotle and Galen is an example. It shows in the multiplication of such texts in many reprintings, but not in either a new or a more consistent formulation of the nature of inward experience. In fact psychological thinking did not significantly alter between the first publication of Sir Thomas Elyot's *The Căstel of Helth* in 1534 and Thomas Wright's *The Passions of the minde in generall* in 1601. While the body of theory became more elaborate, it remained a collection of inconsistencies in which observations, concepts, superstitions garnered from many periods were bundled together indiscriminately.[14] One would actually have to look to John Locke's *An Essay Concerning Humane Understanding,* published in 1689, eighty years after Shakespeare's sonnets, for the earliest use of a vocabulary that defines in systematic philosophic terms something like the kind of modern consciousness we identify in Shakespeare's speakers.[15]

To Locke's vocabulary have since accrued others, which expand or make variations on his original ways of organizing our conceptions of internal as distinct from external existence. These are so embedded in our language that we use them concurrently or interchangeably, without remembering their different origins, or troubling about their possible inconsistencies or their conflicting implications. The reason for their often unquestioned acceptance is, I believe, that they are all associated with our now deeply held belief in the existence of an *inner life* or a *real self,* phrases so familiar, so rooted in our view of human nature, that we have virtually ceased to think of them as metaphors. They were not, however, in use in sixteenth-century English. All the reading for this book yielded only two uses of *inward self,* only one — in an early seventeenth-century translation of a French work — of *inward life.* In their contexts, moreover, these phrases will be shown to have meanings different from those habitually assigned to them in modern usage. If, therefore, some poets of this period held conceptions of internal experience comparable to those implied by our language about an *inner life* or a *real self,* they did not have our ways of phrasing them.

At issue is an underlying question which, it has already been said, this book does not attempt to answer, about the shaping relationship of language to thinking. It is beyond the limits of this study to attempt to theorize about the priority of concepts or language. Yet the characteristics of sixteenth-century English discussed in these chapters, and the prevalent attitudes in that period toward the nature and function of language, do point to the conclusion that most writers then would have affirmed the priority of conceptions to words. One sixteenth-century meaning of *invention,* for example, as discovering or finding truth in words, reveals an underlying assumption that meanings exist in created things, that the world is intelligible, and that the function of language is to interpret and comment on inherent meanings. Words, according to Michel Foucault's analysis of their function as it was conceived in this period, "form a thin film that duplicates thought on the outside," and language is "an art of naming":[16]

> In the sixteenth century, signs were thought to have been placed upon things so that men might be able to uncover their secrets, their nature or their virtues; but this discovery was merely the ultimate purpose of signs, the justification of their presence; it was a possible way of using them, and no doubt the best; but they did not need to be known in order to exist: even if they remained silent, even if no one were to perceive them, they were just as much *there.* It was not knowledge that gave them their signifying function, but the very language of things.[17]

Even sixteenth-century spelling habits reflect conviction that a prior reality which is meaningful exists, to which words are applied. The "seate of life" could be named the *heart, hert, herte, hart,* or *harte* interchangeably—reflecting regional accents or historical changes in the sound of the word, of which its spelling was thought to be a picture.[18] Yet such varieties in spelling did not cause or reflect confusions of meaning because the prior reality itself is stable and recognizable. If the same word was also the name for a forest animal—a kind of *dear, deare, deer, deere, diere*—that coincidence of meanings truly mirrors the correspondences written in the nature of things. For as one sixteenth-century writer on language, John Hoskyns, declares in his *Direccions for Speech and Style:*

> The Conceipts of the minde are pictures of things and the Tongue is Interpretor of those pictures; The order of gods Creatures in themselues is not only admirable & glorious but eloquent.[19]

In keeping with this view, the commonest term in sixteenth-century English for the contents of the heart, *secrets,* implies confidence that they have hidden meanings and that a key to them exists which, once found, makes it possible for them to be known and named in words corresponding to their natures.

In keeping with our own sense of inward experience, however, we apply distinct but overlapping vocabularies which did not exist in the sixteenth century to describe the kind of figure Shakespeare creates in the speaker of the sonnets or in Hamlet, representing a new kind of human being who, according to many historians, emerged in this period:

> ... men who are able to imagine themselves in more than one *role;* who stand as it were outside or above their own *personalities.* ... The great symbol and epitome of this new state of being in the Renaissance is Hamlet. His consciousness of playing a part which is in some sense alien to his *real self* finds innumerable echoes in contemporary literature. ... Montaigne is especially aware of the connection between *role-playing* and the *autobiographical persona.* ... Montaigne was not content to merely re-create his historical, *external self* in the *Essays;* he sought a *role* or *persona* which would convey something of the subtle, *internal* motions of his *personality.*[20]

This passage from Paul Delany's *British Autobiography in the Seventeenth Century* is representative of the vocabularies (indicated by my italics) commonly used to describe Hamlet as a new kind of figure in literature, what another historian calls the "prototype of modern man" by virtue of the insoluble conflicts in his "personality," and his habit of "introspection."[21] The quoted description of the new characteristics of men in the sixteenth century depends on Lockian terms for organizing distinctions between "external" and interior existence—"consciousness," "person"— around which are clustered loosely related words with different histories, which we habitually use concurrently to talk about inward experience.

Some of these terms belong mainly to the discourse of social psychology, especially "role," "role-playing," "personality." Some are used in that discipline, but with different definitions in others, particularly "self," which the quoted passage separates in two contrasting phrases, "real self" and "external self." This term has been given equal prominence but distinct contexts in studies from different disciplines. It appears in the titles of key texts in social psychology, for example, George Mead's *Mind, Self and Society,* where selves are defined as unique "beings that have become conscious of themselves," and Erving Goffman's *The Presentation of Self in Everyday Life,* which distinguishes "our all-too-human selves" from "our socialized selves"; with other associations derived from structural anthropology and linguistics in Jacques Lacan's *The Language of the Self;* in psychoanalytic studies by Heinz Kohut, *The Analysis of the Self* and *The Restoration of the Self,* which endeavor to separate the term in a "different theoretical framework" from those often loosely and simultaneously attached to it—*ego, id,* and *superego, personality, identity*—as a "generalization from empirical data" about the "inner life of man."[22] The peculiar force exerted by the word *self* as an embodiment of fundamental modern assumptions is illustrated especially in another title, *La Découverte de Soi* by Georges Gusdorf. The title of a work documenting the history of the concept, it is predicated on the assumption that the self is a phenomenon which has always existed, like an unexplored continent, though undiscovered until, according to the author's argument, the explorations of Montaigne.[23] This assumption continues to underlie many recent studies of sixteenth-century English poetry, even those influenced by structuralist analyses which have maintained that "the self is a construct," leading them, in Jonathan Culler's words, "to chip away at what supposedly belongs to the thinking subject until any notion of the self that is grounded thereon becomes problematic."[24] Notwithstanding, much current writing about sixteenth-century poetry represented, for example, by Stephen Greenblatt's *Renaissance Self-Fashioning,* is shaped by the various vocabularies clustered around *the self.*[25] These are added to the already mixed modern terms prominent in somewhat earlier discussions of Wyatt, Sidney, Shakespeare, and Donne: *psychological, introspective, personal, individual, self-conscious, dramatic.*[26]

Still other wording in the quoted passage used to describe the distinctively modern consciousness represented in Hamlet and Montaigne has more specifically literary origins. That is clearly true of "autobiographical," a name invented, according to the *O.E.D,* by Southey for the narration of one's own life, and here associated with the search for a "persona" through which to present the "self." The word *persona* was used in classical Latin for a theatrical mask, but in medieval theology for the persons of the Trinity, which led Tyndale in his translation of the Bible to call them "visours," according to his scornful critic, More, as if "they dawnce in a maske."[27] In current use in literary criticism the word has reassumed its character as a theatrical metaphor, often paired with or substituted for *mask,* while becoming involved with originally nonliterary conceptions of the self. This association is made in an immensely influential comment by Ezra Pound:

> In the "search for oneself," in the search for "sincere self-expression," one gropes, one finds some seeming verity. One says "I am" this, that, or the other, and with the words scarcely uttered one ceases to be that thing.
>
> I began this search for the real in a book called *Personae,* casting off, as it were, complete masks of the self in each poem.[28]

The mingling of such literary metaphors and nonliterary concepts illustrates something like the same pattern in current language for inward experience as does the overlapping use of terms from very different theoretical frameworks. The existence of an inner life or self is so compellingly "real"—both quoted passages use the word—that it gives language to describe it the force of that reality. Such words as *persona* have therefore continued to exert this power in studies of sixteenth-century poetry, even when they contradict or conflict in implied assumptions with other descriptive terms like *autobiographical* or *personal.*

When we use such language to describe the impression created by Hamlet or the speaker in Sonnet 62, as distinct from Wyatt's lover, we are applying terms belonging to conceptual frameworks developed long after these works were written. It is not an assumption in this book that this is an improper procedure, as long as it is adopted knowingly. William Empson, in his earlier controversy with Rosemond Tuve, argues a position applicable to the questions raised in this discussion:

> . . . if the Freudian theory is true, writers previous to Freud ought to illustrate it; the idea that it is unhistorical to suppose that Hamlet illustrates it merely takes for granted that it is not true.[29]

Supposing it were desirable to describe sixteenth-century poems which analyze what is in the heart only in terms familiar to their original readers, with the meanings available to them, such a procedure would be crippling, indeed impossible to follow. Even many words for inward states that we use freely in everyday speech, that do not seem traceable to any particular conceptual discipline, were virtually nonexistent in sixteenth-century English: *feelings,* for example. Meanwhile the singular noun *feeling* was used occasionally, but pertained almost always to touch—Shakespeare uses it that way in Sonnet 141—or sensation, or perception. It did not mean what we would call *emotion,* another word which did not acquire its present meaning until the late seventeenth century (the *O.E.D.* cites its occasional use earlier to mean political upheavals or migrations). One context in which the noun *feeling* might be understood in something like its modern sense is in religious controversy. William Tyndale, to the disgust of Sir Thomas More, defines the difference between historical belief and true faith which is written on the heart by the Holy Ghost as the difference between "opynon" and "a sure felynge":

> . . . not that a man hath goten and conceyued in hys harte by herynge of other men, but by ye playne experyence of his owne felynge.[30]

Elsewhere in the controversy, however, the "experyence" with which "felynge" is associated is shown to be closer to sensation than to emotion, or to ignore distinctions between the two. For Tyndale's elect are guided "by theyr owne sure secrete felynge, such as they fele when they burne theyre fyngers."[31] Shakespeare seems to come closer to equating "feeling" with emotional experience as he uses the noun in Sonnet 121:

And the iust pleasure lost, which is so deemed,
Not by our feeling, but by others seeing.

It is probably true, however, that no distinction was conceptualized between sensation and emotion: in a translation of a Senecan dialogue between *Ratio* and *Sensus,* the latter term is translated "Sensualyte," but in
meaning combines matter pertaining to both the senses and feelings.[32]

The common nouns nearest in habitual meanings to the modern words
feelings and *emotion* were *affections* and, more often in poetry, *passions,*
but unlike our parallel terms, these were not consistently distinguished
from mental operations. For while *passion,* especially in the singular, was
often placed in contrast to reason, *passions* could nevertheless be associated with mental powers. Wyatt's translation of Plutarch contains such
phrases as "the apasionate parte of the mynde" and "affections of the
mynde," while a widely read English treatise on psychology first published
in 1601 bears the title *The Passions of the minde in generall.*[33] With similar
disregard of distinctions commonly made in modern English between the
workings of the mind and the feelings, the service of Holy Communion
in *The Booke of Common Prayer* opens with the petition that God "cleanse
the thoughtes of our hartes."[34]

The word *feeling* was more often used with the function of an adjective.
When characterizing human attributes, as in a line from Daniel's *Delia* 35,
"In feeling harts, that can conceiue these lines," it referred to the capacity
for experiencing emotions.[35] Signifying the quality of something nonhuman, *feeling* meant vivid or lively, for example when Sidney in Sonnet 2
calls Astrophil's art "a feeling skill," meaning a technique capable of
stirring the reader.[36] Often such words, which we use to describe inward
states, then pertained exclusively to outward phenomena. For instance, in
the earliest English dictionary of 1604, *sensible* is defined as the property
of that which can be "easily felt, or perceived," whereas in modern use it
describes the inward disposition of a person.[37] Other words—*sincere* is an
example to be discussed—described tangible or intangible attributes of
outward or inward states indiscriminately.

The distance measured by these differences between sixteenth-century
and modern English is so great, because of such radical changes in fundamental assumptions about the nature of inward experience, that it would
be virtually impossible for us to think about what is in the heart in the
language of that time. On the other hand, in describing the impressions
created by poems of this period with much later vocabularies, bringing to
bear a whole body of assumptions, sometimes unanalyzed, usually inescapable, that are built into our language about internal experience, we may
impose predetermined answers to the very questions we ask about this
poetry. Even the most historically scrupulous studies of changes in
sixteenth-century English poetry have sometimes tended to obscure the

precise nature of these changes by talking about them in distinctively modern terms. These studies explore what Lionel Trilling calls the poets' "scrutiny of the inner life," without determining whether they had their own phrases for such a concept, or finding precisely how poets used their own language to create effects—if, indeed, they did—that we use much later vocabularies to describe.[38]

The traditional line of questioning about poetry of this period which has most articulately and consistently opposed this tendency is the approach which describes changes in the lyric poetry of the sixteenth century in terms of shifts in rhetorical emphasis. Rosemond Tuve, in her controversy with William Empson, argued this approach, and predicated upon it her own writing about sixteenth- and earlier seventeenth-century poetry. These investigations take as their point of departure the undeniable fact that the linguistic training of writers and readers of this period was predominantly rhetorical. Before either dictionaries of English vocabulary or treatises of English grammar were felt to be needed, works on rhetoric, both translated and native, abounded in numerous printings: between 1553 and 1595 there were at least eight editions of Thomas Wilson's *The Arte of Rhetorique,* to take only one example.[39] Critical writings of the period demonstrate a rhetorical conception of the art of poetry as do the poems themselves, not only in their prominent and self-conscious display of rhetorical devices, but in their many uses of the vocabulary of the handbooks. Sidney, in *Astrophil and Stella* 3, and Shakespeare using that poem as a model in Sonnet 21, parody affected styles for their elaborations of "Tropes," "problems," "similies," "ornament," "compare," which are nevertheless abundant in the verse of both poets, even in these two sonnets.

A rhetorical study would point out that, although there are no significant changes in the vocabulary or sources of imagery for what is in the heart in Shakespeare's Sonnet 62, by comparison with Wyatt's "Farewell the hart of crueltie," there are shifts in rhetorical emphasis which account for the differences between the two poems. Such changes have been described in a number of parallel and overlapping lines of argument in studies of sixteenth-century poetry, many of them directly inspired by Rosemond Tuve's *Elizabethan and Metaphysical Imagery.* Her now widely known thesis is that, while the nature of poetic imagery is "much of a piece from Marlowe (or Wyatt) to Marvell," the influence of Ramus wrought a shift in rhetorical emphasis.[40] This she describes most generally as a drawing together toward the "virtual identification of poetry with dialectic."[41] More specifically, she points to the Ramistic emphases on images as "arguments," on "specials" as statements of "generals," and on the importance of the "figure of difference."[42] These shifts in emphasis account for the differences she finds between Elizabethan and metaphysical poems.

More recent studies echo and vary this argument that a revolt occurred in England between 1574—the year of the first published translation of *The Logike of the most excellent philosopher P. Ramus Martyr*—and about 1600, against scholastic logic and traditional rhetoric.[43] One cause suggested for this changing taste is the influence of Puttenham's enthusiasm for deceptive tropes, especially the ironic figures of *sarcasmus, asteismus,* or *antiphrasis,* which adapt themselves to a "courtly code of dissimulation" inspired mainly by Castiglione, but associated also with the views of Machiavelli.[44] Other rhetorical analyses of the developments in sixteenth-century English poetry have focused on the growing sophistication in the creation of *personae* (a term adapted from modern critical writing which may itself impose notions not identical with those of earlier poets). Sidney is viewed as crucial in this development for his invention in Astrophil of the first persona in English poetry who controls "with recognizable voice and attitudes" the whole sequence, as Petrarch's poet-lover shapes his poems to Laura.[45] This creation has been said to result from greater emphasis on Aristotle's categories of *relativa, actio, passio, quando, ubi, situs, habitus* which gives Astrophil a fuller and more solid presence than supports the voices typical of earlier poems.[46] In more inclusive terms, the "greater effectiveness of vocal tonality and expression" in the personae of later sixteenth-century poetry and drama has been attributed to the introduction of new genres and the expansion of verbal resources, allowing writers subtler variety in applying the principle of decorum.[47]

Without in the least denying either the validity of this approach, or all that can be learned from its application in these analyses of changes in sixteenth-century poetry, such studies do not make the kinds of distinctions demanded by the line of questioning pursued in this book. Of course, many of the described changes create possibilities for presenting a greater range of more subtle feelings than is typical in early sixteenth-century poems. Yet only some poets, and those almost exclusively in sonnets, seem to have concerned themselves with what a modern writer would call the *inner life* or *real self.* The rhetorical studies, on the other hand, have described a broad range of characteristics shared by Wyatt's songs and sonnets, *Astrophil and Stella,* Ralegh's satires and love poems, sonnets of Shakespeare, Greville's *Cælica,* Donne's love poems and holy sonnets. Because it was in love poetry that writers faced most directly the issues involved in representing what is in the heart, this book works mainly in that body of sixteenth-century poetry. Because it is an argument to be traced in chapters to follow that the development of means for rendering inward states took specially significant directions in the sonnet, discussions will concentrate on poems in that form as it was first practiced by Wyatt, developed in the sequences of Sidney and Shakespeare, and carried in later directions by Donne.

The sonnet, which Wyatt introduced into English, is very different from other verse forms used by sixteenth-century poets. It is unique in demanding an especially complex interrelationship of structural units—single lines, groups of four, groups of eight and six, couplets—within the very strictly imposed limit of fourteen rhymed lines equal in length.[48] These demands, it will be shown, taught Wyatt to use language in new ways that distinguish his sonnets from virtually all his own verse in other forms, even from poems rendering the same traditional material in essentially the same conventional diction. To these possibilities the sonnet sequence, of which Sidney's is the first in English, added other opportunities. While retaining the effects of condensation or compression within the individual sonnet, the sequence allowed indefinitely expanded variations on it. Its matter could be explored, complicated, modified, revised, questioned, criticized, ridiculed without loss of focus on the figure of the poet-lover presented throughout. This made the sequence, as well as the sonnet form itself, a vehicle for some poets to complicate and expand their analyses of what is in the heart.

Both Wyatt and Sidney knew Petrarch's sonnets in Italian. Yet the extent of their direct influence on these two poets, and on the development of the sonnet in England, is difficult to measure. Paradoxically, it is as easy to overestimate as to underestimate it, for reasons to do with the nature of his poetry, and with the shape of the Petrarchan movement on the Continent and in England. A description of Petrarch's love poems by their most recent English translator, Robert Durling, suggests part of the difficulty:

> Petrarch's themes are traditional, his treatment of them profoundly original. From Propertius, Ovid, the troubadours, the *Roman de la rose,* the Sicilians, the dolce styl novo, Dante, Cino da Pistoia there comes to him a repertory of situations, technical vocabulary, images, structures. Love at first sight, obsessive yearning and lovesickness, frustration, love as parallel to feudal service; the lady as ideally beautiful, ideally virtuous, miraculous, beloved in Heaven, and destined to early death; love as virtue, love as idolatry, love as sensuality; the god of love with his arrows, fires, whips, chains; war within the self—hope, fear, joy, sorrow. Conceits, wit, urbane cleverness; disputations and scholastic precision; allegory, personification; wooing, exhortation, outcry; praise, blame; self-examination, self-accusation, self-defense; repentance, and the farewell to love. These elements of the world of the *Rime sparse* all exist in the tradition. Petrarch's originality lies in the intensity with which he develops and explores them, in the rich, profoundly personal synthesis of divergent poetic traditions, in the idea of the collection itself.[49]

Because his poems were such an amalgam of traditions, most of them already woven into native English verse, and also because his sonnets were first generally used as models by continental poets, whose versions of Petrarch then exerted influences on English writers inseparable from his original example, it is often impossible to isolate his direct effects on the development of the sonnet in England. It is also hard to determine precisely what, other than forms and motifs, can be learned by a poet from verse models in a language different from his own. It will be shown that many of the distinguishing uses of language in sonnets by Wyatt and Sidney were actually calculated departures from Petrarchan models, rather than assimilations from them. It is also true that some of their chief preoccupations—for instance, Wyatt's with *trust,* Sidney's with *show*— were not Petrarch's, while his absorption with metamorphosis, memory, and beautific vision were alien to the moods and concerns of both English innovators in the sonnet.

Nevertheless, Petrarch's direct influence on them was probably as profound as his originality in the presentation of traditional materials. It can be defined most precisely in Wyatt's translations, which taught him ways to structure a poem different from his practice in other forms, as well as new means for exploiting the metaphorical possibilities of language.[50] The precise effect of Petrarch on Sidney's sonnets is much harder to define, a difficulty which increases with still later poets, because more strands of influence continued to converge on the vastly expanding body of sonnet literature.[51] Petrarch's most distinct influence on Sidney might be singled out, however, in a pervasive quality peculiar to both their sequences: a tension between an undercurrent of anxiety and an elegant, urbane manner which uses wit and compliment to prevent that anxiety from destroying the decorum of the poetry.[52] In still more inclusive ways, Petrarch (greatly expanding on Dante's example in the *Vita nuova*) must have influenced all his imitators by providing the first and most famous example of a sustained sequence of related poems which reflect from many perspectives on inward experiences which are presented as the poet's own.

Because the Italian poet did not give a literary name to the speaker in his sonnets, his sixteenth-century imitators in English always refer to that poet-lover as Petrarch, for instance in a sonnet printed in Tottel's miscellany under the title "A praise of Petrarke and of Laura his ladie."[53] It apostrophizes him in the first line, "O Petrarke hed and prince of poets all," and names him again in the couplet concluding the tribute:

> But ther was neuer Laura more then one,
> And her had petrarke for his paragone.

This use of a biographical name points to an identification of the author with the lover speaking in his poems. Yet inconsistencies were common in uses of names both of authors and speakers, and in the formulation of titles for love poems. These show that sixteenth-century English writers did not always equate author and speaker, but also that they had not formulated a distinct conception of the relationships possible between them, or of their significance. That is to say, they seem not to have considered, in any terms comparable to those in recent studies of their verse, the issues clustered around the modern critical term *persona,* for which no parallel word or phrase existed in English.

In referring to the persona, the speaker, or the voice in a poem, sixteenth-century writers had a mixture of habits with conflicting implications, showing that they did not clearly define or conceptualize the ways in which poems are or are not to be thought of as directly reflecting their authors. One instance of such inconsistency can be seen in catalogues of authors' names. To illustrate, in Drayton's dedicatory sonnet to his sequence, *Ideas Mirrovr* of 1594, he lists the actual names of Desportes, Petrarch, and "Divine Syr Phillip" as famous authors of sonnets, but in the dedicatory poem to *Zepheria,* a collection of sonnets published anonymously in the same year, the names of "Roman *Naso,* and the Tuscan *Petrarch*" are catalogued with "high-mused *Astrophil.*"[54] Actual and invented names were commonly interchanged in this fashion, showing the absence of sharp or consistent distinctions between author and what would now be called persona.

The use of fictional names also has contradictory implications which do not appear to have troubled sixteenth-century writers or readers. It could be an announcement that the lover is to be understood as a literary representation without reference to the author himself. A fictional name would then be a kind of literary pose functioning like the title of Marlowe's song, "The Passionate Shepherd to His Love," which is clearly not intended to identify the actual author, or even the speaker in the poem, as a tender of sheep.[55] On the other hand, the use of a literary name, especially one verging on an anagram of the author's real name, like Sidney's Astrophil, or Philisides, a disguised lover in the *Arcadia,* could signal the deliberate disguise of the author's identity, a kind of mask like those often actually worn at court to hide, or pretend to hide, the wearer's face. A gesture toward such disguise was expected at least in pastorals, according to the model established in Virgil's eclogues and imitated by Sannazaro and Montemayor.[56] In a work intended for publication, a fictional name might show a wish to keep the author's involvement hidden from the uninitiated in his audience, a practice followed or at least claimed by some writers. George Pettie makes such an avowal in a prefatory letter to *A petite Pallace of Pettie his pleasure* of 1576, claiming that his tales

> touch neerely divers of my nere freindes: but the best is, they are so darkely figured forth, that only they whom they touch, can understand whom they touch.[57]

In writings like Sidney's, apparently composed for his own social circle,
an anagram on his name would more likely have been intended as a kind
of game. Certainly his allusions to Penelope Rich give themselves away,
although only to readers knowing about affairs at court. Many references
show that his contemporaries understood them, identifying Stella with
Lady Rich and Astrophil with Sidney, as they equated Surrey with the
lover of Geraldine in his poems.[58]

A similar mixture of signals about the relationship between author and
speaker exists in sixteenth-century titles for love poems, such as those
assigned to Wyatt's in Tottel's miscellany. Very often they identify a
category of person speaking: "The louer compareth his state to a shippe
in perilous storme tossed on the sea," or, within the category of lovers
more specifically: "The wauerying louer wylleth, and dreadeth, to moue
his desire."[59] Other categories of speaker existed conventional to other
types of verse, as in the title of a poem among those of uncertain authorship: "The repentant sinner in durance and aduersitie," or were devised
for the particular demands of the poem's matter: "A carelesse man, scorn-
ing and describing, the suttle vsage of women towarde their louers"; "The
ladye praieth the returne of her louer abidyng on the seas."[60] This kind of
title seems to point to a conception of the speaker in a poem as a chosen
representative of a category associated with certain conventional attitudes
and emotional states, and sometimes with types of situation, for instance
separation or absence. Such a speaker would therefore be thought of as the
invention of the author.

A further step away from identification of speaker and author is measured in titles which name the poem by the category to which it, rather
than the speaker, belongs. Love poems by Wyatt in the miscellany bear
such generic titles: "Comparison of loue to a streame falling from the
Alpes"; "Complaint for true loue vnrequited."[61] These concentrate on the
type of the poem itself as a rendering of love according to its own conventions, setting the author outside it, as seems to be done in the title given
to one of Wyatt's sonnets translated from Petrarch, "Description of the
contrarious passions in a louer," where substitution of *by* for "in" would
have clearly identified the lover as the describer of his own passions.[62] A
few titles of love poems merely announce a subject or theme, again with
the effect of concentrating on the poem, without reference to the voice in
it. Another sonnet translation by Wyatt from Petrarch is headed in this
fashion: "Of Loue, Fortune, and the louers minde."[63]

With contradictory implications, however, the same volume assigns
some love poems to the poet by his biographical name, seeming therefore
to equate author and lover. One such, called "wiates complaint vpon
Loue, to Reason: with Loues answer," is actually a translation of a can-
zone by Petrarch (a fact perhaps unknown to the editor of the miscellany),
making no references to particular circumstances which would explain the

identification of this lover with Wyatt.[64] The title may not have been intended to make precisely that equation, however, but to designate the poem as belonging to the genre of complaint, and Wyatt as the author of this example. Given that interpretation, the title ignores the autobiographical question, making it the poet's primary task to choose a genre in which to work, not to write about his own inward experiences. Yet another style of title further illustrates such inconsistencies in the conceived relationship between the author of the poem and the lover whose states it renders. These use "his," rather than either the poet's actual name or a noun categorizing the speaker conventional to the type or situation of the poem. Wyatt's complaint beginning "What rage is this?" is given such a title, "To his vnkinde loue," although it does not contain any particular references to circumstances of the poet's life that would make it unsuitable to be spoken by a representative complaining lover.[65] The title of the poem immediately preceding in the miscellany, "why loue is blinde," does not name a speaker to whom "his" in the next could refer, so that the pronoun does not attach clearly either to a category of lover, or to Wyatt, the author of the complaint.[66] It therefore suggests the absence of a clear distinction between them, or shows lack of articulation of the issues that would be involved in making it.

These inconsistencies are most evident in love poetry. The titles of other kinds of verse in Tottel's volume name the genre of the poem, "An epitaph of maister Henry williams," its stance toward its subject, "Against a cruell woman," or merely state its theme, "Time trieth truth."[67] They do not normally call attention either to author or to speaker, so that they do not show the same inconsistencies in conception of the relation between them. A relatively small number of sixteenth-century English poems were identified as autobiographical by references to actual circumstances in the poet's life, such as Wyatt's entitled in Tottel's volume "Of his returne from Spaine," or Surrey's called "Prisoned in windsor, he recounteth his pleasure there passed."[68] There are a few other poems of the period which make such an identification by using the poet's biographical name, for instance, "Gascoignes woodmanship," a verse epistle rehearsing the writer's worldly failures.[69] A vastly greater number of sixteenth-century poems aim at a generality that does not raise questions about whether the poem represents the biographical experience of the poet. An example is a poem of Wyatt's called in Tottel's miscellany by its theme, "Of the meane and sure estate."[70] It is a powerful statement of the Stoic ideal of the "life in quietnesse," "Vnknowen in court," in preference to that of the man in "hye astate," who "knowen is to all: but to him selfe." Its sententiousness, matching that of *The Quyete of Mynde* which Wyatt translated from Plutarch, would prevent speculation about it as a representation of Wyatt's own experience, who spent years trying to keep his slippery footing at court, whose retirements from it to the sort of "hidden place" praise in the poem were enforced.

In love poetry, however, the very existence of inconsistencies in the uses of names, and in the references to author or speaker in titles, suggests that the relation between them was an issue, though one not clearly formulated. Even when the lover's states are typically rendered in the poem in terms as generalized as Wyatt's praise of the quiet life, frequently there is some identification of the voice describing them, implying concerns not raised in other kinds of poetry. The presence of these considerations is evident also in comments by sixteenth-century writers on their own love poetry. These remarks were made particularly with reference to sonnet sequences, probably in part because of characteristics already mentioned. Such a collection of interrelated poems allows more varied presentation of inward states associated with a single figure who is both a lover and a poet, and that figure was traditionally identified with its author. The most widely known of sixteenth-century editions of Petrarch's sonnets, first published by Allesandro Velutello in 1525 and used by Wyatt, includes an account of the lives of Petrarch and Laura.[71] After the model of Petrarch, who himself alluded in his sequence to actual circumstances of his life, referring to some people associated with him by their biographical names, English poets made similar kinds of allusions in their sonnet sequences. Sidney's references to his family background and to the name of Lady Rich, Shakespeare's identification of the lover in some of his sonnets as Will, Spenser's many allusions in *Amoretti* to his circumstances and to his poems, follow this pattern, pointing to some kind of identification of author with speaker in sonnet sequences. This seems to have been true even when the poet-lover is given a fictional name which hides, or pretends to disguise, his actual identity, at least from readers outside his social acquaintance.

Samuel Daniel assumes this association in the dedication of his authorized version of his sonnets to *Delia,* printed in 1592, the year after twenty-eight of his sonnets had been published in the same pirated volume as Sidney's sequence. In a dedicatory epistle to the Countess of Pembroke, Daniel, who had carefully revised and expanded his collection of sonnets for this publication, nevertheless apologizes "for my selfe, seeing I am thrust out into the worlde, and that my unboldned Muse, is forced to appeare so rawly in publique."[72] In an expanded version of this identification of poet and poems he is more explicit in claiming to have written about his own experiences:

> . . . although I had rather desired to keep in the priuate passions of my youth, from the multitude, as things utterd to my selfe, and consecrated to silence: yet seeing I was betraide by the indiscretion of a greedie Printer, and had some of my secrets bewraide to the world, uncorrected: doubting the like of the rest, I am forced to publish that which I neuer meant.[73]

There is not much pressure here—or in the sonnets themselves—to make the autobiographical confession more literally believable than the polite reluctance to publish, and yet there was evidently a need to claim personal experience of love, because the author of a sonnet sequence was meant to be indentifiable with the poet-lover speaking in it. Similar gestures toward this traditional association are made in comments on their poems by authors of other sonnet sequences. Thomas Watson plays with such a confession first in the title, then in the prefatory letter to his collection, published in 1582 as a *Passionate Centurie of Loue, Diuided into two parts: whereof, the first expresseth the Authours sufferance in Loue: the latter, his long farewell to Loue and all his tyrannie:*[74]

> Yet for this once I hope that thou wilt in respect of my trauaile in penning these louepassions, or for pitie of my paines in suffering them (although but supposed) so suruey the faultes herein escaped, as eyther to winke at them, as ouersightes of a blinde Louer; or to excuse them, as idle toyes proceedinge from a youngling frenzie; or lastlie, to defend them, by saying, it is nothing *Præter decorum* for a maiemed man to halt in his pase, where his wound enforceth him, or for a Poete to falter in his Poëme, when his manner requireth it.[75]

With something like the same playful equivocation, Giles Fletcher prefaces his collection of sonnets, *Licia,* with a hint that he may be the lover in his poems:

> . . . for this kinde of poetrie wherein I wrote, I did it onelie to trie my humour: and for the matter of love, it may bee I am so devoted to some one, into whose hands these may light by chance, that she may say, which thou now saiest (that surelie he is in love) which if she doe, then have I the full recompence of my labour, and the Poems have dealt sufficientlie, for the discharge of their own duetie.[76]

Notwithstanding, in the same prefatory letter he lists among possible answers to the question "What my Licia is" such mistresses as "Learning's Image" or "'some College.'"[77]

For these poets the identification of themselves with the lover in their poems is clearly only an expected gesture, and yet the need to make it shows their recognition of an accepted association of sonnet sequences with the poet's actual experience of love. A claim to first-hand knowledge of such passions is a claim to be convincing, both to an audience of readers, such as these poets address in their prefatory letters, and to the lady who is understood to be the poet's own beloved. This is the critical issue on which Sidney focuses his remarks in *An Apologie for Poetrie* about the lack of genuine warmth in the "Lyricall kind of Songs and Sonnets" which he dismisses as unworthy to be included in his catalogue of English verse that may legitimately be called poetry:

> But truely many of such writings as come vnder the banner of vnre-
> sistable loue, if I were a Mistres, would neuer perswade mee they
> were in loue; so coldely they apply fiery speeches, as men that had
> rather red Louers writings, and so caught vp certaine swelling phrases,
> which hang together like a man which once tolde mee the winde was
> at North West, and by South, because he would be sure to name
> windes enowe,—then that in truth they feele those passions, which
> easily (as I think) may be bewrayed by the same forciblenes, or
> *Energia* (as the Greekes cal it), of the writer.[78]

This comment focuses on the efficacy of the writer's art in convincing the
reader by its skill and power, but in reference to sonnet sequences, such
persuasiveness also involves the genuineness of passion in the speaker,
who is both poet and lover. Since, in turn, that figure is associated with
the author himself, his sincerity becomes a relevant question. While many
sonneteers only acknowledged it in the manner of the quoted comments
by Daniel, Watson, and Fletcher, Sidney made the poet-lover's sincerity
the focus of *Astrophil and Stella,* beginning with the opening line, "Loving
in truth, and faine in verse my love to show," which echoes his demand
here that love poets write what "in truth they feele." Although Sidney
never uses the word *sincere*—an early sixteenth-century English coinage—
in any of its forms, he nevertheless evolves from his concern with sincerity
a new conception of poetry as an effort to represent what is in the heart.[79]

Sidney's ways of developing that conception are traced in Chapter 3,
along with its possible beginnings in his metrical and other experiments
with the sonnet form itself, and with the opportunities allowed by a
sequence of sonnets. It is also conceivable that Sidney's concern with the
relation between Astrophil's verse and what is in his heart derived from
his unusually close, even private association of the poet-lover in his sequence with himself. For in several sonnets this association goes beyond
conventional allusions to the author's circumstances, creating a kind of
autobiographical writing found elsewhere in sixteenth-century English
poetry only in some of Shakespeare's sonnets.

Following Petrarch, Sidney weaves into his presentation of the lover in
his sequence facts derived from his own life. In Sonnet 30, for example,
the catalogue of topical questions refers to one about "my father," alluding
to Sir Henry Sidney's political activities in Ireland. The tournament in
Sonnet 41 is a reminder of Sidney's participation in many such entertain-
ments (Philisides in the *Arcadia* takes part in a similar event). Sonnet 13,
which praises Stella in heraldic terms resembling the Devereaux coat of
arms, and the poems beginning with 24 which play on the name of Rich,
undoubtedly point to actual people known to Sidney, and recognizable by
at least his inner circle of readers. These references belong to a game which
is as much a part of Astrophl's courtly behavior as his "good maners" in
Sonnet 30, or his skill at martial sports in Sonnet 41, and is designed to

be shared with the same audience, as he does in Sonnet 37 (omitted in the 1591 printing of the sequence, almost certainly because its riddling references are so transparent):

> My mouth doth water, and my breast doth swell,
>> My tongue doth itch, my thoughts in labour be:
>> Listen then Lordings with good eare to me,
> For of my life I must a riddle tell.
> Towardes *Aurora's* Court a Nymph doth dwell,
>> Rich in all beauties which man's eye can see:
>> Beauties so farre from reach of words, that we
> Abase her praise, saying she doth excell:
>> Rich in the treasure of deserv'd renowne,
> Rich in the riches of a royall hart,
> Rich in those gifts which give th'eternall crowne;
> Who though most rich in these and everie part,
>> Which make the patents of true worldly blisse,
>> Hath no misfortune, but that Rich she is.

Addressed explicitly to a courtly audience, this riddle keeps no secrets, nor does it refer to or even hint at anything in the "life" of either Sidney or Astrophil. It recites praise of a nymph on behalf of "man" and "we," in public and predictable terms. There is so little effort to charge the compliment with feeling that its subject seems to have been chosen more for the fact that her real name has also metaphoric possibilities as an adjective than because she is dear to the poet-lover.

By contrast Sonnet 93, which calls Stella by her allegorical name, is a far more personal, even private poem:

> O fate, ô fault, ô curse, child of my blisse,
>> What sobs can give words grace my griefe to show?
>> What inke is blacke inough to paint my wo?
> Through me, wretch me, even *Stella* vexed is.
> Yet truth (if Caitif's breath mighte call thee) this
>> Witnesse with me, that my foule stumbling so,
>> From carelesnesse did in no maner grow,
> But wit confus'd with too much care did misse.
>> And do I then my selfe this vaine scuse give?
> I have (live I and know this) harmed thee,
> Tho worlds quite me, shall I my selfe forgive?
> Only with paines my paines thus eased be,
>> That all thy hurts in my hart's wracke I reede;
>> I cry thy sighs; my deere, thy teares I bleede.

Although this shares many characteristics, even specific phrases, with other renderings of what is in Astrophil's heart, it differs so radically in

fundamental respects as to be another kind of poem. The distinction is in
the way Sidney expands on the occasion for this complaint, by comparison with many others in the sequence. They typically assume the cause
to be what he calls a lover's "case" (in Sonnets 31, 45, 46, 60, 64, 76, 106),
and therefore to need little explaining. A single line of such explanation,
like "But more I crie, lesse grace she doth impart" in Sonnet 44, can evoke
a constellation of associations that identifies Astrophil's case as a frustrated worshipper of a sovereign mistress proudly unmoved by his complaints. Sometimes a more specific occasion is evoked—Stella's absence,
or her sickness, or her appearance in a dream—but because these are
motifs conventional to love poetry, they need scarcely more elaboration
than the generalized woe of the complaining poet-lover. These occasions
themselves become categorized, as in Sonnet 106, when Stella's absence
causes Astrophil to grieve over his eyes' "famisht case." The occasion for
his suffering in Sonnet 93, by contrast with other complaints, is explained
at much greater length, and in more detail. Stella is "vexed" because
Astrophil has somehow "harmed" her, caused "hurts" to her heart. This
is not the conventional situation when, as in Sonnet 61, the lady is dis-
pleased by her suitor because "her chast mind hates this love in me." It
cannot therefore be conveyed by the shorthand of conventional diction
which makes explanation unnecessary to the poem's readers, to the lady
included in its audience, or to the poet-lover himself. Here Astrophil feels
the need to explain himself so strongly that he summons truth to "Witnesse with me," as in a courtroom. This occasion is described in language
making it at once more specific and less understandable than those of
other complaints. It seems to refer to a particular incident, but in veiled
hints which only the speaker and the lady, by line 10 addressed directly,
can understand. Neither "foule stumbling" nor "wit confus'd with too
much care" carry conventional associations, such as those which enable
the reader to interpret what would otherwise be unexplained phrases in
other sonnets, for instance "My mind bemones his sense of inward smart"
in Sonnet 44. In Sonnet 93, the reader is helpless to identify Astrophil's
stumbling, or confusion, or care, because familiarity with sixteenth-century love poetry provides no associations to fill out the meanings of the phrasing. The inward states evoked by the original incident also
expand beyond definition by such conventional categories as "griefe,"
"wo," "paines," "wracke." His sufferings cause Astrophil to blame himself, to feel guilty for the hurts he has caused, and to enter sympathetically
into Stella's feelings. Since the nature of the episode remains unexplained,
the reader is as if in the position of overhearing secrets in the middle lines
of this sonnet, rather than reading a complaint.

The qualities which distinguish Sonnet 93 as a different kind of
poem from many others in *Astrophil and Stella* are also characteristic of
Sonnet 33:[80]

> I might, unhappie word, ô me, I might,
> And then would not, or could not see my blisse:
> Till now, wrapt in a most infernall night,
> I find how heav'nly day wretch I did misse.
>   Hart rent thy selfe, thou doest thy selfe but right,
> No lovely *Paris* made thy *Hellen* his:
> No force, no fraud, robd thee of thy delight,
> Nor Fortune of thy fortune author is:
>   But to my selfe my selfe did give the blow,
> While too much wit (forsooth) so troubled me,
> That I respects for both our sakes must show:
> And yet could not by rising Morne forsee
>   How faire a day was neare, ô punisht eyes,
>   That I had bene more foolish or more wise.

Like Sonnet 93, this complaint opens with Astrophil seeking words to lament some specific event or situation in the past when he again "did misse." The first two quatrains elaborate on the nature of his error in oblique references hinting that he failed to recognize his happiness, identified by the associations of "blisse" and "heav'nly" with his deified beloved. Again his pained recollection leads the lover into explanation of the cause for his error. Once more he blames the confusion of his "wit," which "to my selfe my selfe did give the blow." Such castigation of himself, again a "wretch," attaches to this remembered occasion the same mixture of grief, remorse, self-hatred as Astrophil finds in his heart in Sonnet 93, and is described again as a guilty possibility in the opening of Sonnet 86, which seems also to allude to some specific episode:

> Alas, whence came this change of lookes? If I
>   Have chang'd desert, let mine owne conscience be
>   A still felt plague, to selfe condemning me:
> Let wo gripe on my heart, shame loade mine eye.

Because the original incident in Sonnet 33 is not fully disclosed, and because Astrophil shifts, as in Sonnet 93, from rhetorical exclamation through invocation of a personification to intimately addressing the lady, the reader seems again in th third quatrain to be in the position of over-hearing private speech in which the lover enters sympathetically into the lady's heart, as well as examining his own: "That I respects for both our sakes must show."

The qualities that distinguish these sonnets make them autobiographi-cal poems in a very different sense than those which contain references to the poet's circumstances and acquaintance. Their language, at once more specific but more veiled, seems to refer to actual incidents, known privately only to the lover and the lady involved in the episodes, who is intimately addressed by the ending. This knowledge is not shared with the reader in the poems themselves, or interpretable in the light of conventions familiar in sixteenth-century love poetry, or explained by the contexts of other sonnets or songs. Those surrounding Sonnet 93, for example, mainly expand on the motif of absence, while the context for Sonnet 33 is even less appropriate or explanatory. Why would Astrophil there blame himself for having lost Stella, when that confession is surrounded by complaints for her unattainability, tyrannical power, pride, and scorn, and when he continues to plead for her pity until he receives the first signs of grace almost thirty sonnets later? Because the occasions and inward states explored in these sonnets do not arise either from poetic convention or from the shape of the sequence itself, they seem likely to have originated in nonliterary matter, in autobiographical incidents. In these poems, Sidney seems to refer directly to some particular experiences of his own, not subsumed in a lover's case but creating an exceptionally close, even private identification of Astrophil with himself.

These sonnets are different in kind from the riddle on the name of Rich, and other poems of the sixteenth century which refer to the author's circumstances or acquaintance. They are also autobiographical in a different sense from Wyatt's sonnet modeled on Petrarch, "Whoso list to hounte," which has traditionally been thought to be about himself.[81] It is so if, as has been believed since his own time, Wyatt was Anne Boleyn's lover before she became queen, and if she is the "Diere" in the poem, who is unattainable by the lover because she belongs to Caesar. Without knowledge of that tradition, the reader would not necessarily feel that the poem required an autobiographical explanation of the kind demanded by Sidney's sonnets. The experience of reading is not like overhearing speech between lovers sharing intimate knowledge of a specific but undisclosed situation. Although it is charged with intense feelings, they do not need to be explained by the author's private identification of the lover in the poem with himself. These autobiographical sonnets of Sidney's also differ in kind from Wyatt's love songs, to be discussed in Chapter 2, which often include an oblique hint—"they change" or "some that vse to fayn"— suggesting a secret known only to the singer and some one listener in his audience.[82] These do not elaborate on the hinted matter, or on the poet's feelings about it, or allude to them in any but conventional terms, and so do not demand an extraliterary explanation. The only sixteenth-century poems that do so, other than Sidney's are several sonnets by Shakespeare.[83]

Shakespeare's sequence also includes poems of the type represented in Sidney's by the riddle on the name of Rich, referring to his real name of Will, and playing upon its meanings as a word.[84] Others seem to allude to actual circumstances of his life—his social position below that of a patron, or rivalry for his favor with other poets, for example. In addition to these types conventional to sonnet sequences, his also includes a few sonnets—36, 86, 111, 117 to 120—which are autobiographical in a more special sense. These share the specific but veiled language that distinguishes Sidney's sonnets in which he makes a private identification of Astrophil with himself from those which merely refer to his circumstances or acquaintance. The similarities consist in Shakespeare's use of language demanding explanation in nonliterary origins, in the nature of the occasions about which such language hints, and in its rendering of what is in the heart, the poet-lover's and his beloved's.

Sonnet 36 illustrates these as well as even more particular similarities:

> Let me confesse that we two must be twaine,
> Although our vndeuided loues are one:
> So shall those blots that do with me remaine,
> Without thy helpe, by me be borne alone.
> In our two loues there is but one respect,
> Though in our liues a seperable spight,
> Which though it alter not loues sole effect,
> Yet doth it steale sweet houres from loues delight,
> I may not euer-more acknowledge thee,
> Lest my bewailed guilt should do thee shame,
> Nor thou with publike kindnesse honour me,
> Vnlesse thou take that honour from thy name:
> > But doe not so, I loue thee in such sort,
> > As thou being mine, mine is thy good report.

The resemblances in kind and also in details to *Astrophil and Stella* 33 are many and various. Both sonnets allude to a separation which is not the kind conventional to love poetry, as the speaker in each feels the need to explain. Astrophil admits that he was not robbed of Stella by a rival, or by fortune, but by his own self-destructive behavior, which is not fully explained. Shakespeare's poet-lover also confesses that no division of their "loues" has separated him from his friend, but rather his own choice, for which the reasons are undisclosed. He admits "bewailed guilt," comparable to Astrophil's confession that "to my selfe my selfe did give the blow." Astrophil's command to his heart to "rent thy self" parallels Shakespeare's metaphor of "loues" which are "one," but divided in "twaine." The most detailed resemblance, perhaps constituting evidence that Sidney's sonnet sounded in Shakespeare's memory, is in his lover's argument that he and his friend must be publicly divided although "In our two loues there is but one respect." This seems a possible echo of Astrophil's admission that he brought the separation upon himself and his beloved because "I respects for both our sakes must show," a hint of public caution for the sake of reputation. While Astrophil now regrets having followed the dictates of discretion, whereas Shakespeare's speaker defends this practice,

both acknowledge a separation between what "must show" and what is
in the heart.
   Parallels of this kind also exist between Shakespeare's Sonnet 120 and
Sidney's Sonnet 93. There Astrophil seeks to "forgive" himself for the
"hurts" he has caused to Stella's heart by reading them in his own "hart's
wracke," and uttering them in his complaint: "I cry thy sighs; my deere,
thy teares I bleede." Shakespeare's poet-lover seeks forgiveness, from his
friend and from himself, for a similar "trespasse," by assimilating his
friend's sufferings into his own "wounded bosome":

> That you were once vnkind be-friends mee now,
> And for that sorrow, which I then didde feele,
> Needes must I vnder my transgression bow,
> Vnlesse my Nerues were brasse or hammered steele.
> For if you were by my vnkindnesse shaken
> As I by yours, y'haue past a hell of Time,
> And I a tyrant haue no leasure taken
> To waigh how once I suffered in your crime.
> O that our night of wo might haue remembred
> My deepest sence, how hard true sorrow hits,
> And soone to you, as you to me then tendred
> The humble salue, which wounded bosomes fits!
>   But that your trespasse now becomes a fee,
>   Mine ransoms yours, and yours must ransome mee.

These are complaints which again explode the boundaries of poetic convention, here one of the most common metaphors for the lover's case in
sixteenth-century poetry, the wounded heart. Both Shakespeare and Sidney seem to work through and beyond depiction of the lover's heart struck
first by Cupid's darts, then by the lady's scorn, to an exploration of "how
hard true sorrow hits" when lovers injure one another's feelings. Sidney
moves through this process by beginning with three lines actually echoing
other complaints in his own sequence, starting with the first sonnet, where
Astrophil seeks sobs mournful enough to "show," or ink black enough to
"paint" his suffering. Defined by the conventional category of "wo," it
predicts the plight of a devoted servant rejected by a sovereign mistress,
but line 4 overturns such expectations. Here Astrophil grieves instead
because it is he who has wounded Stella's heart. Shakespeare uses a parallel device by applying to the speaker rather than to the beloved the epithet
of "tyrant," making him the cruel wielder of sovereign power. Although
Shakespeare's poet-lover implicates his friend also in causing suffering, of
which Stella here is not accused, he imagines a reciprocity of cruelty, pain,
and succor which is a version of Astrophil's identification with Stella's
hurts. The religious language of confession, forgiveness, sacrifice, and
redemption resembles Sidney's, but in a cynical form. Both poets, by these

parallel means, transform the coventions of the complaint into very different explorations of what is in the wounded heart.

The particular but undisclosed nature of the episodes hinted as the occasions for these sonnets, their more than usual intimacy of address, their elaboration of the lover's involvement in causing pain to himself and to his beloved, their dramatization of his imaginative entrance into another person's heart, make these poems radically different in kind from a representative sixteenth-century complaint, such as the poem of Surrey's which opens Tottel's miscellany with the title "Descripcion of the restlesse state of a louer, with sute to his ladie, to rue on his diying hart."[85] These sonnets are intimate, private explorations of autobiographical material, Shakespeare's none the less convincingly so for having been influenced by Sidney's.

Autobiographical poems of this kind exist in sixteenth-century English verse only in the sonnets of Sidney and Shakespeare. Their presence shows that these two writers went beyond the expected association of the poet-lover in a sonnet sequence with its author. That kind of equation depended upon references to persons and circumstances known and recognizable by at least the poet's own social circle of readers. By contrast, Sidney and Shakespeare created a private identification of the speaker in some of their poems with themselves, based upon specific but unexplained incidents unknowable except to the lovers involved in them. It is perhaps at least in part because their own inward experiences were peculiarly equated in this very special way with those of the speakers in their sonnets, that they were the only two love poets to make central to their sonnet sequences the issue of showing in verse what is truly in the heart. Chapter 4 will demonstrate how profoundly Shakespeare assimilated this concern with the poet-lover's sincerity from Sidney, and how he followed his model in exploring, by means of the speaker in his sonnets, its implications for a new conception of inward experience. These implications, it will be argued, he expanded in the character of Hamlet.

Hamlet shows a sense of inward experience and the difficulty of denoting it truly which makes him a new kind of figure in English literature, and distinguishes him from the speakers in virtually all sixteenth-century verse, except the poet-lovers in the sonnet sequences of Sidney and Shakespeare. His opening aside, his first speech, his many soliloquys, his references to what is hidden in his heart all seem designed to present him as an individual aware of having what a modern writer would call an *inner life* or a *real self.* Yet almost none of the terms now used to describe Hamlet as a figure displaying a distinctively modern consciousness existed in the sixteenth century. Our ways of describing internal experience would have been as unfamiliar to Shakespeare as to Wyatt and his contemporaries. If, therefore, poets in the last decades of the period invented speakers who create the impression of fitting a modern sense of inward experience, they did so using verbal resources other than those at the disposal of much later writers. What means were in fact available in the English language to poets of the period for depicting what is in the heart will be the measure of their inventions. The nature of that *inward* language—the possibilities inherent in its vocabulary, metaphors, rhetorical devices, grammatical constructions—is explored in Chapter 1. How poets used those verbal resources will be the measure of historical changes in poetry designed to render what is in the heart. This is the subject of the other chapters on the sonnets of Wyatt, Sidney, Shakespeare, and Donne.

1.

the *inward* language

Everywhere in sixteenth-century writing there is evidence not only that the English language and its poetry were changing but that authors and their readers were aware that this was so and felt such changes were needed. Surrey paid tribute to Wyatt for having "taught, what might be sayd in ryme" and Tottel praised both poets for first showing English to be capable of matching the eloquence already achieved by Latin, Italian, and other foreign writers.[1] This view of Wyatt and Surrey as innovators and reformers of English verse and language was repeated throughout the century, as in George Puttenham's tribute to them in *The Arte of English Poesie* published in 1589. He praised them for having, by virtue of their familiarity with Italian poetry, "greatly pollished our rude & homely maner of vulgar Poesie, from that it had bene before."[2] Yet Sir Philip Sidney, writing *An Apologie for Poetrie* in the early 1580s, shows a strong sense that English lacked sufficient models for a poet to imitate. Surveying the whole canon of verse in the vernacular, he finds only four examples even partially worthy to be called poetry:

Chaucer, vndoubtedly, did excellently in hys *Troylus* and *Cresseid*; Of whom, truly, I know not whether to meruaile more, either that he in that mistie time could see so clearly, or that wee in this cleare age walke so stumblingly after him. Yet had he great wants, fitte to be forgiuen in so reuerent antiquity. I account the *Mirrour of Magistrates* meetely furnished of beautiful parts; and in the Earle of Surries *Liricks* many things tasting of a noble birth, and worthy of a noble minde. The *Shepheards Kalender* hath much Poetrie in his Eglogues: indeede worthy the reading, if I be not deceiued. That same framing of his stile to an old rustick language I dare not alowe, sith neyther *Theocritus* in Greeke, *Virgill* in Latine, nor *Sanazar* in Italian did affect it. Besides these, doe I not remember to haue seene but fewe (to speake boldely) printed, that haue poeticall sinnewes in them: for proofe whereof, let but most of the verses bee put in Prose, and then aske the meaning; and it will be found that one verse did but beget

another, without ordering at the first what should be at the last;
which becomes a confused masse of words, with a tingling sound of
ryme, barely accompanied with reason.[3]

The affectionate tribute to Chaucer nevertheless disqualifies him as a
model to be imitated because of the rude antiquity of his language to
Sidney's ears. Spenser, for his deliberate archaisms, is also not to be
imitated. The *Mirrour of Magistrates* is admired only in parts, leaving as
verse models in English the Earl of Surrey's "*Liricks,*" by which it is
possible that Sidney meant Tottel's miscellany as a whole. For in all
sixteenth-century editions only Surrey's name is mentioned on the title
page, lending aristocratic standing to the volume which is reflected in
Sidney's praise of its "noble" qualities.[4] Whether or not the contributions
of Wyatt and other poets to the miscellany were included in Sidney's
catalogue, its meagerness shows his sense that, although English verse was
already in a period of change, it was still much in need of enrichment.
Sidney saw the position of his generation of poets in the history of English
verse to be at once exciting and lonely. For in his view an English poet
in the later sixteenth century had great work to do, but virtually no one
who had written in his own language who could teach him how to do it.

There are many witnesses to the fact that the deficiencies in English
verse were attributed not only to the absence of models but also to inade-
quacies in the language itself. Complaints persisted throughout the period
that it lacked eloquence, and also that it actually did not have enough
words for what needed to be said. Wyatt, in his translation of Plutarch's
The Quyete of Mynde, apologizes for the absence in English of "plentuous
diuersite of the spekyng of it," making it "want a great dele of the grace"
of Latin.[5] The accuracy of his perception of these difficulties is confirmed
by any reader who compares Wyatt's awkward prose to the work of later
translators. Yet despite improved skills in the uses of the vernacular,
acknowledgments persisted throughout the period of the strains upon
expression caused by the limitations of English, especially its want of
words. Richard Mulcaster, Spenser's headmaster at the Merchant Taylors
School, though a defender of the vernacular, admitted to this sort of
deficiency. In a work published in 1582, about the time when Sidney was
lamenting in *An Apologie for Poetrie* the lack of verse models for English
poets, Mulcaster acknowledges the limits of vernacular vocabulary:

> The number of things whereof we write and speak is infinite, the
> words wherewith we write and speak, be definite and within number.
> Whereupon we ar driuen to vse one, and the same word in verie
> manie, naie somtime in verie contrarie senses, and that in all the
> verie best languages, as well as in English, where a number of our
> words be of verie sundrie powers, as, letters, wherewith we write, &
> letters which hinder: A bird flieth light, wheresoeuer she doth light:
> and to manie to stand on here.[6]

The linguistic neediness felt by English writers is confirmed also by the fact that the total vocabulary almost doubled in the sixteenth century.[7] This was accomplished by the combined practices of coining words, reviving archaisms, and especially borrowing foreign terms—by Mulcaster's account a practice much commoner in English than in other languages—to fill the need for richer resources.[8] As an aid to their naturalization, or in Mulcaster's term their "enfranchisement," Robert Cawdrey printed in 1604 the first dictionary of words in the vernacular, so that native speakers of the language might "better vnderstand many hard English wordes, which they shall heare or read in Scriptures, Sermons, or elsewhere, and also be made able to vse the same aptly themselues."[9] John Bullokar bears witness to the continuing sense of linguistic constraints on vernacular writers in prefatory remarks to the second English dictionary, published in 1616, the year of Shakespeare's death:

> . . . it is familiar among best writers to vsurpe strange words, (and sometime necessary by reason our speich is not sufficiently furnished with apt termes to expresse all meanings).[10]

Yet despite remarkable changes in English, especially its growth in vocabulary, it can be shown that there were not in fact very significant additions or other changes in the actual words used to describe inward experience, from which writers could draw. Poets toward the end of the sixteenth century used virtually the same linguistic resources as Wyatt and his contemporaries, to represent what is in the heart, but used them in new ways with radically new implications about both inward experience and language. Those verbal means available in English are explored in this chapter. Their application by Wyatt, Sidney, Shakespeare, and Donne are discussed in the chapters which follow.

individuum

Of the terms with which a reader steeped in post-Lockian, post-Romantic, and modern psychological vocabularies might describe the impression of an *inner life* or *real self* created by Hamlet or the speaker in Shakespeare's Sonnet 62, scarcely any existed in the sixteenth century, and those few which did had different meanings.

The word *individual,* for example, was very rarely used, and then never with the meaning from which the nineteenth-century coinage, *individualism,* derives. Many scholars have argued that it was in the sixteenth century that Europeans, and especially Englishmen, began to think of themselves as individuals. Citing economic, political, and social causes, the rise of Puritanism, and the spread of literacy, historians have collected varieties of satisfyingly concrete evidence in support of this claim, at least for the small group whose changed living arrangements, education, manners, funeral customs, and other details of existence were recorded.[11] Lionel Trilling summarizes the kinds of evidence leading historians to conclude that "at a certain point in history men became individuals":

> Taken in isolation, the statement is absurd. How was a man different from an individual? A person born before a certain date, a man— had he not eyes? had he not hands, organs, dimensions, senses, affections, passions? If you pricked him, he bled and if you tickled him, he laughed. But certain things he did not have or do until he became an individual. He did not have an awareness of what one historian, Georges Gusdorf, calls internal space. He did not, as Delany puts it, imagine himself in more than one role, standing outside or above his own personality; he did not suppose that he might be an object of interest to his fellow man not for the reason that he had achieved something notable or been witness to great events but simply because as an individual he was of consequence. It is when he becomes an individual that a man lives more and more in private rooms; whether the privacy makes the individuality or the individuality requires the privacy the historians do not say. The individual looks into mirrors, larger and much brighter than those that were formerly held up to magistrates. The French psychoanalyst Jacques Lacan believes that the development of the "*Je*" was advanced by the manufacture of mirrors: again it cannot be decided whether man's belief that he is a "*Je*" is the result of the Venetian craftsmen's having learned how to make plate-glass or whether the demand for looking-glasses stimulated this technological success. If he is an artist the individual is likely to paint self-portraits. . . . And he begins to use the word "self" not as a mere reflexive or intensive, but as an autonomous noun referring, the *O.E.D.* tell us, to "that . . . in a person [which] is really and intrinsically *he* (in contradistinction to what is adventitious)," as that which he must cherish for its own sake and show to the world for the sake of good faith. The subject of an autobiography is just such a self, bent on revealing himself in all his truth, bent, that is to say, on demonstrating his sincerity.[12]

Yet the virtual absence of the word *individual,* or its equivalent, cautions against attributing to sixteenth-century Englishmen what a modern writer would mean by a sense of *individuality,* a word itself not in use, according to the *O.E.D.,* until 1645, and then with the meaning of inseparability. To sharpen conclusions about such shifts in the conception of human nature, the concrete evidence collected by historians can be measured in turn by evidence in sixteenth-century language.

Individual in its very rare occurences referred to that which is one in substance or essence, indivisible, or that which is inseparable from a whole. It did not have the meaning now given to the word as signifying a sense of self-identity, for which the *O.E.D.* cites the first use in 1633. Even with its earlier meanings, the term was seldom used. More often writers made do with the clumsy word *individuum,* which by its very form shows that it had not been fully naturalized from its Latin original, *indiuidium,* so listed in the Latin vocabularies of their Latin-English dictionaries by Sir Thomas Elyot in 1538 and Thomas Cooper in 1584.[13] Bullokar, however, claims it is as an English word which he defines as a term from logic meaning a particular:

> . . . when we directly expresse, and seeme to point to that thing which we speake of: as in saying, This horse, That man: For although the words Horse, or Man, may bee applyed to any horse or man, yet being so expresly pointed at, they cannot then be drawen to signifie other then those two.[14]

There is evidence that this meaning was understood even outside logical contexts by pairings elsewhere of the terms "*indiuiduum* or *particular.*"[15] In the first English version of *The Confessions of the Incomparable Doctour S. Avgvstine* the translator uses "my *Indiuiduum*" where most modern translations say "my being," but the term occurs in a sentence explicitly defining it as "a kind of picture in litle, of the most secret vnity of thy Essence from whence I am deriued."[16] Such an epitome is particular to each human creature but unindividualized. The individuum of a man therefore designated him as a particular in a category without in any way attributing to him a sense of his own unique identity, or his real self.

The nature of English autobiographical writing of the period supports this distinction between particular and what is now meant by individual. The lives in verse and prose—the term *autobiography* was not coined until the early nineteenth century—that began to be written in the later sixteenth century show growing interest in particular human beings, but not in what would now be called their individuality. The autobiographical narratives written in verse in the mid-1570s by Thomas Tusser and Thomas Churchyard, the latter's with the generic title *A Tragicall Discourse of the Vnhappy Mans Life,* recount their authors' adventures and especially misadventures, only occasionally in detail, as in Tusser's description of an illness.[17] Neither includes any analysis of what is in the writer's heart. Autobiographical narratives in prose are characteristically told at an even greater distance from inward experience. The *Memoirs of his own life, 1549—1593* by Sir James Melville gives a first-person account of his service in the Scottish court containing no references to himself other than to his part in episodes and conversations involving public figures.[18] In *The life of Sir Thomas Bodley, written by himself* the author summarizes his principal actions in a volume totaling sixteen pages.[19] Simon Forman's autobiography is told in the third person, and although his diary for the

same period of 1564 to 1602 is written in the first person, it is no less
simply anecdotal, no more revealing of inward experience.[20] In the three
hundred pages of Henry Machin's diary, concerning the years from 1550
to 1563, his third-person account makes almost no references to himself.
Twice he mentions his birthday, once he refers obscurely to an occasion
when he made public penance during a sermon at St. Paul's Cross, and
once, surprisingly, he describes still in the third person what must have
been a memorable time in the early morning when "monser the Machyn
de Henry, and mony mo," sitting on hogsheads, enjoyed by candlelight
half a bushel of oysters, along with onions, red ale, malmesey, and other
wines at a seller's in Anchor Lane.[21]

Biographies of this period are similarly lacking in personal matter, even
when the subject was intimately known to the writer. The most maddening example is *The Life of the Renowned Sr Philip Sidney* by Fulke Greville, who was his friend from the time of their attendance as children at
Shrewesbury Grammar School. In the entire biography there is virtually
no more personal material than a mention of overhearing Sidney's father
refer to his son in Latin as the light of his family, and an account of a
challenge to a duel in defense of his honor when insulted by the Earl of
Oxford. This episode concludes with a comment which turns it into an
example of public virtue, "Wherin he left an authentical president to after
ages," of a subject's proper manner to his prince.[22]

Of the dozen autobiographical lives surviving from the period before
1600, the only one that has with some justice been called "introspective,"
and therefore "modern" in the sense that the author makes "full use of
self-analysis," is the autobiography of Thomas Whythorne, written about
1576.[23] This first-person account of the experiences of a musician in a
succession of households in which he was employed is much more revealing of precisely the sort of personal matter omitted from other recorded
lives of the period. Whythorne announces his intention to reveal to the
friend for whom he claims to be writing "all my private affairs and secrets."[24] He habitually describes such inward experiences as the "imagina-
tions and debatings of the matter with myself" on specified occasions.[25]
Yet characteristically he sees his experiences as fully representative of
general truths preached in the Bible, in ancient authors, and in everday
proverbs.[26] For example, he recounts at more than usual length an episode
in which he was "turmoiled in this labyrinth of unkindness" by the malice
of someone to whom he was then reconciled. His reflection immediately
following the account of the incident translates it easily into the experience
of a representative Christian "he" who then stands for the condition of
"the body" and "the soul":

Nigh about this time I had read in a place of St. Ambrose, that better
is he that condemneth injuries than he that sorroweth and fretteth

at it. For he that condemneth it, he passeth it away as though he felt nothing thereof; but he that sorroweth or fretteth at it is therewith tormented as though he felt it. Also, like as grief is a disease of the body, so is malice a sickness of the soul. Wherefore upon the consideration of our reconciliation, and upon the reading of those foresaid sentences, I made this sonnet following:

> He that condemneth injuries, his state will better appear soon,
> Than he who frets maliciously, till he revenge offences done.
> For as malice torments his heart, and all his health doth
>   straight unwrest,
> The other, not forcing thereof, returneth soon to quiet rest.[27]

Referring again to this troubling episode, Whythorne shows the same tendency to see himself not as a unique individual but as a particular instance of the general condition of man, this time as he read it expounded by a classical moralist:

> ... much troubled with the doubt of the feigned friendship of the tutor aforesaid, and having at this time read in Marcus Aurelius that the suspicious, the hasty and jealous man liveth ever in much sorrow, I did cast that care away from me now.[28]

Following that reflection he says that he wrote another so-called sonnet in which the reader can "soon see in each estate" a general representation of his particular experience. Whythorne's kind of sententiousness, characteristic of a great deal of sixteenth-century verse in English, embodies this interest in the exemplary. In rhetorical handbooks it is given formal recognition and explanation, for example by John Hoskyns in his *Direccions for Speech and Style* of about 1600:

> *Acclamacon* is a sententious clause of a discourse or report such as Daniell in his poems concludes with ppetually. It is a generall instruccion for euery man comonly for his paines in reading any historie of other men lookes for some private vse, to himselfe like a teller whoe in drawing great somes of other mens money, challendgeth somewhat in the pound for his owne ffee.[29]

Whythorne's poems, and the prose narration of episodes which according to his account occasioned the verse, resemble the pattern of Wyatt's poem previously quoted from Tottel's miscellany, "Farewell the hart of crueltie." Both equate what is in the speaker's heart with the generalized experience of a representative "he." Each understands himself as a particular instance within a category. The fact that the poems eliminate precisely what would distinguish the individual from the generalization shows very clearly the priority given to the category over the particulars within it, because, as the proposition is stated in Ramus' *Logike,* the "vniuersall excellethe in dignitie, by reason it containthe the cause."[30]

The very existence of lives and diaries in the late sixteenth century is evidence for some growing awareness of distinctions within humanity of importance to the understanding and conduct of life. Similar signs appear in other kinds of writing, both religious and secular. In the earliest sixteenth-century collections of prayers, for example, differentiations appropriate to spiritual circumstances and occasions are made, but not distinctions among the users of devotions.[31] By contrast, Thomas Becon's *The Pomander of Prayer,* first published in 1558 and then in at least five more editions within twenty years, separates prayers according to the status of the petitioners: magistrates, clergy, subjects, masters, servants, husbands, wives, fathers, mothers, children, pregnant women, maids, bachelors, and householders.[32] In the same period courtesy books make distinctions in the manners and conversation appropriate to such groups in human society. The title page of the 1581 edition of *The Civile Conversation of M. Steeven Guazzo,* an Italian work naturalized in George Pettie's widely read translation, promises to teach the conversation "to bee observed in companie between young men and olde, Gentlemen and Yeomen, Princes and private persons, learned and unlearned, Citizens and Strangers, Religious and Secular, men and women."[33]

Implied is a heightened awareness of distinctions within humanity, differences sometimes phrased as what is *particular* within a *general* category, or *proper* to one rather than *common* to all, or *private* as distinguished from *public.* Yet this awareness actually works away from defining a person as an individual with a unique identity to be discovered by detailed exploration of what is in his heart. For in the lives written in the later sixteenth century, the experience of the particular subject is always treated as exemplary (if it is not merely recounted) of general truths, a habit of mind which limits the usefulness of very detailed self-examination. There is no passionately elaborated exploration of inward experience comparable to what Sir Toby Matthew describes in his preface to the earliest English translation of St. Augustine's *Confessions,* published in 1620. With an emphasis suggesting the unusual, he calls the reader's attention to the minute care with which his subject did "euen ferret and search into euery little corner of his hart, for the true vnderstanding of his sinne, in that robbing of the Orchard."[34] The very fact that this work was not made available in English earlier, despite widespread respect for Augustine as a theologian, could suggest that his kind of exploration of inward experience was not in fact in great demand among sixteenth-century writers and readers. For other theological and devotional works by St. Augustine, as well as a number wrongly attributed to him, did exist in English translations made during the sixteenth century. One of the rare mentions of the *Confessions* showing actual familiarity with the contents occurs in *A Booke of Christian Exercise* published in 1596. There the author recommends it to readers of Latin, especially the account of Augustine's conversion in Book VIII, which is to be read for its general lesson in "this marvellous example of this famous mans conversion."[35]

Augustine's *Confessions* were not known to sixteenth-century autobiographical writers, whose presentations of their experience took very different forms. Whythorne alone among them actually mentions the work, but in a reference which shows that he had not read it.[36] His own announced intention in the conclusion of his autobiographical presentation is not to explore every little corner of his heart, but to "show" himself as a particular instance of a social category like those newly differentiated in collections of prayers and in courtesy books:

> I do add unto my name the title of a gentleman, so I mean to show myself to be one, as well in the outward marks as in the inward man; of the which inward man the music, with the ditties and songs and sonnets therewith joined, shall show to the sufficient judge in that respect.[37]

The verses in fact show the inward man as a representative of a generalized self.

know thy self

The word *self* of course was in common use: it occurs eight times in Shakespeare's Sonnet 62. *The self* meant itself or the same, as in a line from Wyatt's Psalm 102: "But thou thy sellff the sellff remaynist well."[38] It was not used in the sense now current in everyday speech which, according to the *O.E.D.*, was introduced in the late seventeenth century: "That which in a person is really and intrinsically *he* (in contradistinction to what is adventitious)." In the sixteenth century *self* was sometimes a simple synonym for the human soul, the definition Sidney jokes about in Sonnet 52 of *Astrophil and Stella* when the lover grants to his personified rival, "*Vertue*," the possession of Stella's "selfe" if only he can have her body. Occasionally the word designated the body rather than the soul, apparently the sense in which Spenser uses it in *Amoretti* 4, picturing how spring "warnes the Earth with diuers colord flore, / to decke hir selfe, and her faire mantle weaue."[39] Much more often the word included the whole human creature, body and soul together, as it is meant in the Anglican service of Holy Communion when the priest offers to God on behalf of the congregation "oure selfe, our soules and bodies."[40] This seems to be the primary meaning in Shakespeare's Sonnet 62: there the self which loves itself consists of "all my soule, and al my euery part."

In one of the earliest grammars of the English language, Butler's of 1633, the author writes in the section on pronouns: "Personals & Possesiv's are soomtim' compounded with Self: which sygnifieth a bodi's own person."[41] The phrasing of this definition can itself be misleading if it seems to stress a sense of individual identity intrinsic to a human being. For the word *person* did not acquire its general philosophic meaning of a self-conscious or rational being until the mid-seventeenth century. In Butler's definition of pronouns compounded with *self,* it distinguished a particular man from other particulars in the category of human beings rather than things (the rare term *personality* also designated the quality of being a person rather than a thing).

Compounds of *self* with nouns began to appear more frequently in the later sixteenth century, *self-love* being one of the most common. Sidney, in the opening paragraph of *An Apologie for Poetrie,* delivers with mock gravity the lesson "that selfe-loue is better than any guilding to make that seeme gorgious wherein ourselues are parties."[42] Used seriously, most often in theological contexts, it was said to be a sin such as the speaker confesses in Shakespeare's Sonnet 62.[43] Other combined forms also appeared: "selfnesse" is used by Sidney in *Astrophil and Stella* 61, and by Fulke Greville in his biography of Sidney, where he condemns those who trade in the "market of selfnesse," an earlier form of the mid-seventeenth-century coinage, *selfishness.*[44]

Even as it was used in its most highly charged context in the sixteenth century—the imperative to *know thy self*—the word did not stand for a modern conception of individuality or of unique inward experience. The classical formula was a favorite title, chapter heading, or opening text for sixteenth-century writers on religion, ethics, manners, health, or virtually any other subject of human affairs. The collection of "Godly lessons for Chyldren" included for translation in the most widely used Latin grammar of the period opens with the sentence "It is the fyrst poynte of wysedom to knowe thy self."[45] English writers knew the classical origins of this imperative—Wyatt, translating Plutarch, calls it the "poesy of Appollo"—and gave ancient philosophers credit for acting wisely upon it, but often God is said to have inspired it, and Solomon to have preached it in verses from the Canticles frequently quoted on title pages:

> If thou know not thy self, O fayrest among women, goe foorth and follow the steps of thy flocks, and feede thy kiddes by the tabernacles of Shepheards.[46]

Both Luther and Calvin exhorted man to "descend to loke into himselfe" where he would discover the misery of his fallen condition, which is the knowledge of himself necessary for repentance.[47] In the contexts in which theologians used this argument it is altogether predictable that each self is representative of the universal human condition, an embodiment of each man's sinfulness and his need for salvation. Throughout the period writers whose function it was to teach humility continued to phrase their own or any man's self-knowledge in general terms that could be brought home to every human breast, for if a sinner be led to "knowledge of himselfe, then followeth true repentance."[48] One such author, John Frith, published in 1533 a book called *A Myrrour or glasse to know thy selfe.* In it he does not perceive any particulars of his experience, any characteristics, acts, or inward states distinguishing him as an individual with a unique identity. Instead he sees and describes in the first person a generalized image of a representative sinner marked by the "imperfection of my nature," the "unstablenesse of my flesh being prone to all synne," the "poyson of the old serpent and hell." This knowledge of his own self leads him to the same conclusion as Solomon, that without exception or differentiation, "Euery man liuing is nothing but vanitie."[49] Sir Philip Sidney, in a letter dated 1580, begins his advice to a friend with the traditional imperative:

> The knowledge of our selves no doubte ought to be most pretious vnto vs; and therein the holy scriptures, if not the only, are certainly the incomparable lanterne in this fleshly darkness of ours: For (alas) what is all knowledge? if in the end of this little and weerisome pilgrimage, Hell become our school*master.*[50]

The ease with which Sidney assumes *know thy self* to be a Christian axiom about the need to recognize one's own sinfulness as representative of the universal condition of human frailty and misery shows that way of thinking to have been habitual. Sidney's exposition of the familiar text has at once an automatic quality and a ring of conviction that often characterizes the repetition of profoundly held and unanalyzed assumptions. His association of it with the Bible, although he well knew its classical origins—in a letter of 1578 he links the imperative with "playing the stoic"—is itself evidence that he thought of its application in the most general terms.[51]

    In contexts where the writer's intention is not primarily to inspire Christian sentiments of humility, penitence, dependence on God and his revealed word, the knowledge of one's self nevertheless led away from a sense of individuality and of unique interior experience. An early example is a passage in *The Boke Named the Gouernour,* first published in 1531, where Sir Thomas Elyot urges the imperative to self-knowledge among the precepts of reason and society for the formation of a just ruler. Although Elyot was more interested than a theological writer like Frith in its classical origins—he quotes the formula first in Latin, "*Nosce te ipsum,* whiche is in englysshe, know thy selfe"—and more influenced by ancient philosophical interpretations of it, he nevertheless shares with theological writers the view that self-knowledge leads directly to identification with the

general nature of man.[52] His discussion moves from what at first seems
to be an emphasis on the distinct, individual, personal nature of a man's
own self to an argument against such a view:

> For a man knowinge him selfe shall knowe that which is his owne
> and pertayneth to him self. But what is more his owne than his soule?
> or what thynge more appertayneth to hym thanne his body? His
> soule is undoughtedly and frely his owne. And none other persone
> may by any meane possede it or clayme it. His body so pertayneth
> unto him, that none other without his consent may vendicate therein
> any propretie. Of what valour or price his soule is, the similitude
> where unto it was made, the immortalitie and lyfe euerlastynge, and
> the powars and qualities therof, abundantly do declare. And of the
> same mater and substaunce that his soule is of, be all other soules
> that now are, and haue ben, and euer shall be, without singularitie
> or preeminence of nature. In a semblable astate is his body, and of
> no better claye (as I mought frankely saye) is a gentilman made than
> a carter, and of libertie of wille as moche is gyuen of god to the poore
> herdeman, as to the great and mighty emperour. Than in knowinge
> the condicion of his soule and body, he knoweth him selfe, and
> consequently in the same thinge he knoweth euery other man.[53]

The very fact that Elyot turns the imperative to self-knowledge into an
argument against "singularitie or preeminence" is evidence that he thought
there might be a tendency, at least among great men, to see themselves
as apart from general humanity. Yet he did not conceive of them as
mistaking self-knowledge for any distinction other than that of social
position and power. He uses the classical imperative to remind them that
in their "selfe," composed of soul and body, they are inseparable from less
privileged humanity.

The movement of this passage typifies interpretations of the ancient
precept made throughout the century. Even later writers, who stress more
than Elyot the differences among men—qualities "that concerne them
particularly"—the pursuit of self-knowledge does not end in consciousness of an individual self. The following passage from a translation of the
popular treatise *Of Wisdome* by Montaigne's friend, Pierre Charron, demonstrates the prevailing habit of mind. It moves directly, and without
explanation or apology, from urging examination of each man's "priuate,"
"simple," "peculiar," "proper," "naturall," "particularly" distinct self to
a conclusion about the undifferentiated condition of "man." The argument is that to know one's self:

> it is necessarie that we know all sorts of men, of all aires, climats,
> natures, ages, estates, professions, (to this end serues the traueller
> and the historie) their motions, inclinations, actions; not only pub-
> licke, (they are least to be regarded, being all fained and artificiall)

but priuate, and especially the more simple and peculiar, such as
arise from their proper and naturall iurisdiction; as likewise all those
that concerne them particularly, for in these two their nature is
discouered: afterwards that we conferre them all together to make an
entire bodie and vniuersall iudgement; but especially that we enter
into our selues, taste and attentiuely sound ourselues, examin euery
thought, word, action. Doubtlesse we shall in the end learne that
man is in truth on the one side a poore, weake, pitifull, and miserable
thing, and we cannot but pitie him; and on the other we shall find
him swollen and puffed vp with wind, presumption, pride, desires,
and we cannot but disdaine and detest him.[54]

At precisely the point where the author urges us to "enter into our selues"
by examining particulars, he leaps to a view of the generalized condition
of fallen humanity described in the third person.

In the course of the sixteenth century, writers tended more and more
often to define the knowledge a man ought to have of his own self in other
than scriptural or theological terms although, like Charron, they frequently passed from secular distinctions into generalizations assuming a biblical view of the human condition. Often the knowledge they associated
with self-examination belonged to other ways of analyzing experience.
These were of increasing familiarity and interest to Englishmen as more
classical and continental writings, such as Charron's (first published in
English less than a decade after the earliest French edition of 1601), were
made available in English translations. For example, a translation from
Latin published in 1581 of a work called *The Touchstone of Complexions,*
with *Nosce teipsum* printed on its title page, equates self-knowledge with
attention to the balance of humors which makes up the healthy complexion of body and mind.[55] The use of terminology—anatomical, physiological, psychological—from such treatsies in the tradition of Aristotle and
Galen gradually spread during the sixteenth century. Translation of moral
writings especially expanded the use of classical interpretations of self-
knowledge. In *The French Academie* by de la Primaudaye, published in
English in 1586, Lactantius is said to have defined man's knowledge of
himself as "knowledge wherefore and to what end he is borne."[56] In *The
Quyete of Mynde,* translated by Wyatt in 1527, he who obeys Apollo must
"take aduyse of his own nature & as she ledeth to take an order of lyfe,
rather than passyng from one to another to force & constrayn his nature."
Similarly, in Nicholas Grimald's translation of *Marcvs Tullius Ciceroes
thre bookes of duties* published in 1558, to know one's self is to recognize
one's true "disposition." The context defines this to mean the ability to
choose the style of conduct suited to one's attributes:

For that becommeth eche man, whiche is moste of all eche mannes
owne. Let euery man therefore know his owne disposition: and let

him make him selfe a sharpe iudge both of his vices, and of his
vertues: lest players may seme to haue more discretion than we. For
they do choose not the best enterludes, but the fittest for them selues.
For who upon their voices be bolde, they take Epigones, and Medea:
who upon gesture, do take Menalippa. . . . Shall a player then see this
in the stage, that a wise man shall not se in his lyfe?[57]

Such identifications of self-knowledge with playing a part appropriate to
one's capacities were common in texts of this period. Another passage
from *Of Wisdome* makes a similar equation between knowing one's self
and decorous conduct defined as playing a consistent part:

Socrates was accounted the wisest man of the world, not because his
knowledge was more compleat, or his sufficiencie greater than others, but because his knowledge of himselfe was better than others;
in that he held himselfe within his owne ranke, and knew better how
to play the man.[58]

Montaigne seems to have thought in terms similar to those used (perhaps
under his direct influence) by Charron. For Montaigne self-knowledge is
repeatedly said to be instruction in the conduct of a man's life. At least
twice in Florio's first English translation of the *Essayes* published in 1603,
the same Stoic formula is used to link self-knowledge with that which will
teach "how to live, and how to die well."[59] Like other writers of the period,
Montaigne habitually uses theatrical metaphors to describe this decorous
conduct made possible by self-knowledge. Urging recognition of the diverseness and changeability of "our selves," he concludes: "*Magnam rem
puta, unum hominem agere. Esteeme it a great matter, to play but one
man.*"[60]

The widespread use of play-acting metaphors to define self-knowledge
in this fashion cautions against imposing now current conceptions of
acting a *role* (a term used by Montaigne—*rolle*—but not in sixteenth-
century English either in the theater or as a metaphor for social behavior)
behind which is hidden a private self. As they were actually used, theatrical metaphors often worked toward defining a very different sense of
man's essential nature, as another passage from Florio's translation of
Montaigne illustrates:

But when that last part of death, and of our selves comes to be acted,
then no dissembling will availe, then is it high time to speake plaine
English, and put off all vizards: then whatsoever the pot containeth
must be shewne, be it good or bad, foule or cleane, wine or water.[61]

Here the "selves" which we know by acting our final "part of death" are
not, despite the metaphor of stripping off masks and disguises including

rhetorical ones, exclusively private or inward. For they will be revealed in our speech and other outward signs as we continue to act a part on a visible stage before witnesses (not, in this context, God, before whom no dissembling would ever avail). To this audience our "selves" as we face death "must be shewne." The metaphor equating each man's self with the part he plays in the "last act of his comedie" has therefore the effect of merging or blurring distinctions between inward and outward experience, and of incorporating each man's identity with our common mortality, as another quotation from the *Essayes* shows:

> It is not only for an exterior shew or ostentation, that our soule must play her part, but inwardly within our selves, where no eyes shine but ours: There it doth shroud us from the feare of death, of sorrowes and of shame: There it assureth us, from the losse of our children, friends and fortunes; and when opportunitie is offerd, it also leads us to the dangers of warre.[62]

Even Montaigne, for all his awareness of human differences—leading many historians to claim for him the discovery of human individuality—did not, as Florio understood him, formulate a conception of an intrinsic self separate from the common "part" that "our soule" must act in the face of mortality. This passage follows a pattern that will be shown also as characteristic of much poetry of the sixteenth century. It sets up apparent contrasts between "exterior" behavior and what is experienced "inwardly," only to blur the distinction between them by appropriating terms from the outward sphere to characterize what is inward. It also merges inward distinctions into a generalization applicable to ourselves as representative human beings by attaching the singular noun "soule" to the plural pronoun "our."

the closet of the heart

Most terms now in use to distinguish a sense of continuous internal being as distinctively modern did not exist in the sixteenth-century writer's vocabulary, for instance, *awareness* or *consciousness*. The noun closest in meaning, as well as in derivation, was *conscience* (from *conscientia,* commonly used by classical moralists).[63] It most often referred to the faculty that pronounces moral judgments upon one's own acts and inward states, but occasionally retained a meaning closer to its literal root (*con* with *scire*), as in Wyatt's phrases translated from Plutarch, "the consciens of thyne owne affection," "a naughty conscience in the soule."[64] In that sense it overlapped with the adjective *conscious,* a notorious coinage of the late sixteenth century. The phrase "Conscious mind" was mocked by Thomas Nashe as one of Gabriel Harvey's inkhorn terms, and by Jonson satirizing

Marston, but Jonson himself in "On My Picture Left in Scotland" uses
the phrase "conscious feares," meaning fears which are secret, known only
to one's self.[65] Yet the word was not compounded with *self* until the end
of the seventeenth century. The significant difference between these words
and the modern term *consciousness,* first given a conceptual framework
by Locke, is that the sixteenth-century uses always occur in contexts
defining knowledge of particulars, of discrete *states, moods, thoughts,
passions, affections, intentions, secrets.*[66] Although *experience* was in use
to mean accumulated knowledge from one's own observation, it does not
appear in contexts that would associate it with an inner life. No term
referring to a continuous internal awareness appears to have existed.
No metaphors were in use with connotations like those of William
James's invention, "stream of consciousness" which has become so im-
bedded in our everyday speech that it has almost ceased to be thought of
as metaphorical.[67]

Nor does there seem to have been a word for the process of examining
one's inward experience. *Introspection,* according to the *O.E.D.,* was not
used to mean examination of one's own thoughts until 1695, although Sir
Thomas Elyot lists *introspicio* with the translation "to loke in" in his
Latin-English dictionary of 1538. There were, however, several metaphors
which appeared with as much regularity as (and often in connection with)
the formula *know thy self,* to describe the act by which each man examines
the state of his heart or soul, mind, thoughts, bosom, breast, or reins
(literally the kidneys or loins, but in biblical language a term for the seat
of the affections).[68]

Sixteenth-century descriptions of examining one's internal state were
most commonly based on metaphorical comparisons to entering a room
in a house: a chamber, closet, or cabinet. It is clear that this metaphor
derived at least in part from physiological terminology. A translation of
a medieval Latin text familiarly referred to by its English title, *Batman
vppon Bartholome,* describes how "feeling"—here synonymous with sensation—emanates from the "most subtile Chambers of the braine," which
was more specifically thought to be divided into "foure little chambers or
ventricles."[69] The *O.E.D.* cites a quotation in which a heart is also said to
have chambers. Common phrases like "chambers in the ear" show that
the meaning of physical cavity was still generally understood, but in
metaphors for self-examination, the terms *chamber, closet,* and *cabinet*
had specific architectural reference.[70] To make that figurative meaning
especially clear, writers often paired *chamber,* the term most susceptible
of literal, physiological interpretation, with one of the other names. An
illustration of this practice occurs in the first English translation of St.
Augustine's *Confessions:*

Then in that great quarrel of my spirituall house, which I had stifly made against my selfe, in the chamber and closet of my hart.[71]

The first architectural phrase is a direct translation of the original: *interioris domus meae*. The second phrase—the Latin reads *in cubiculo nostro, corde meo*—is in the English version made more prominently a reference to rooms by the doubling of terms, which seems to serve no other purpose than to insist on the architectural nature of the metaphor.

These words referred to parts of a house (the noun *room* almost always meant space or accomodation rather than an architectural division) which writers of this period urged man to enter in order to know himself. He was exhorted to withdraw "in the most secret closet of his minde," or to examine what "lyeth secretly closed vp within the closet of the heart," to look into "his inward part, his priuy chamber," to search within himself in "so many cabinets and blind corners," or to retire into the "cabinet and innermost with-drawing chamber of the soule."[72] These three architectural terms had overlapping histories and meanings. The earliest was *chamber,* in use after 1300 to describe a separate room or apartment within a large house, most often a bedroom. In sixteenth-century English translations of the Bible, "chamber" was used in Matthew vi, 6, where Wycliffe had translated "couch," and where the 1611 version substitutes "closet," as the place designated for private devotions:

But thou, when thou prayest, enter into thy closet, and when thou hast shut thy doore, pray to thy father which is in secret; and thy father which seeth in secret, shall reward thee openly.[73]

Chaucer uses "chaumbre" for Troilus' bedroom, where he habitually retires so that no one can hear as he "of his deth roreth in compleynynge."[74] In other scenes, however, Criseyde is described withdrawing alone "into a closet, for to avise hire bettre."[75] *Cabinet,* as a synonym for closet, came into English usage in the later sixteenth century. All three terms referred to a room in a house in which members of the family could sometimes be alone.

Social and architectural historians have collected evidence that the existence and use of such rooms was increasing in the sixteenth century, which in turn they interpret as a sign of growing interest among Englishmen in their own individuality, to be enjoyed in privacy and explored by introspection.[76] This conclusion seems to be supported by the frequency with which writers used retirement to such rooms as a metaphor for self-examination. Henry Parker, Lord Morley makes this equation in the opening lines of a poem addressed to his posterity:

> Never was I less alone than being alone
> Here in this chamber. Evil thought had I none,
> But always I thought to bring the mind to rest,
> And that thought of all thoughts I judge it the best.[77]

The association of this conventional metaphor with the literal arrangements of his house is made in the title: "Written over a chamber door
where he was wont to lie at Hallingbury."

Yet the evidence does not point simply to such a conclusion as historians have drawn. First the signs suggest that people were still in fact very
rarely by themselves. Most worked, prayed, ate, and even slept in the
presence of others, and those few privileged to have a separate chamber
seem nevertheless to have been surrounded by servants and visitors, as
in earlier centuries. Chaucer's Troilus sends away his men and closes all
the doors and windows of his chamber in order not to be overheard in his
complaining.[78] Yet his solitude is on many occasions interrupted by in-
truding visitors, and he can manage private meetings with Criseyde only
by elaborate subterfuge. In sixteenth-century literature similar living arrangements are portrayed. The speaker in Wyatt's "They flee from me"
remembers ladies "With naked fote stalking within my chamber," evoking an atmosphere of dangerous intrigue conducted with difficulty behind
the public rooms and courts of great houses.[79] Whythorne's autobiography
and Gascoigne's possibly autobiographical *A discourse of the aduentures
passed by Master F. I.,* first published in 1573, show the continuation of
these social arrangements in the sixteenth century in their descriptions of
lovers sneaking about castles and great houses, in and out of each other's
chambers, under the eyes of rivals and spying servants.[80] *Hamlet* shows
the same world.

Withdrawals to private rooms and interludes of solitude were excep-
tional, occasional, usually brief, and subject to interruption unless elaborately protected. William Roper's *The Lyfe of Sir Thomas Moore, Knighte*
describes how his subject, desiring

> for godly purposes sometimes to be solitary and sequester himself
> from worldly company, a good distance from his mansion-house
> builded he a place called the New Building, wherein there was a
> chapel, a library, and a gallery. In which, as his use was upon other
> days to occupy himself in prayer and study together, so on the
> Friday, there usually continued he from morning till evening, spend-
> ing his time only in devout prayers and spiritual exercises.[81]

There he achieved the privacy otherwise limited precariously to the chamber or closet. Montaigne in loving detail describes a tower of his house
containing a chapel, a chamber "where I often lie, because I would be
alone," a wardrobe, a cabinet, and at the top his treasured library:

... which pleaseth me the more, both because the accesse unto it is somewhat troublesome and remote, and for the benefit of the exercise which is to be respected; and that I may the better seclude my selfe from companie, and keepe incrochers from me: There is my seat, there is my throne. I endevour to make my rule therein absolute, and to sequester that only corner from the communitie of wife, or children and of acquaintance.[82]

The suggestion that this retreat is a rare achievement is confirmed by Montaigne's following contrast between his arrangements and those he imagines in other men's houses:

Miserable, in my minde is he, who in his owne home, hath no where to be to himselfe; where hee may particularly court, and at his pleasure hide or with-draw himself.

The comparisons of self-examination to withdrawal into such rooms suggest that exploration of what is in the heart was considered to be a specialized activity which was occasional, set apart for certain times as well as places, not implying a consciousness of a continuous inner life. This interpretation is also supported by the kinds of activities associated with such withdrawals.

Closets or cabinets, where treasures and account books were hidden, were used for financial reckoning, which took place of necessity—in a period without banks, vaults, or safes—behind closed doors. Some great establishments even practiced a custom called "secret house" at the time of the yearly audit; most of the household was sent away while the lord shut himself up with his auditors to review the accounts.[83] The actual practice of withdrawing to a closet to perform a financial audit was combined with biblical language about keeping spiritual accounts to create a frequently used metaphor for examining what is in one's own heart. It was so familiar as to demand no explanation or elaboration in such instances as its appearance in *A Booke of Christian Exercise:*

Consideration is the key which openeth the dore to the closet of our hart where all our bookes of accounts do lie.[84]

The author immediately attaches to this another traditional metaphor implying a further equation between auditing the heart's account books and examining one's face in a mirror:

It is the looking glasse, or rather the verie eie of our soule, whereby she seeth hir selfe, & looketh into all hir whole estate: hir waie she walketh in, hir pace she holdeth: and finally, the place and end which she draweth unto.

The mirror was traditionally associated with self-knowledge, often appearing in titles like Frith's *A Myrrour or glasse to know thy selfe,* or as an emblem on title pages such as that of Charron's *Of Wisdome,* sometimes also bearing the motto *nosce teipsum.* In sixteenth-century texts, mirrors were also associated with rooms apart. For, like treasures and financial records, looking glasses were kept in chambers and closets rather than in public rooms. This may have been partially due to the fact that mirrors of real glass were themselves valuable possessions and still exotic, as one learns from John Florio's *Second frutes,* published in 1591 for the verbal instruction of foreigners. In a scene designed to teach the vocabulary for shopping, a buyer who asks the price of a looking glass is told: "It is faire, bright, cleane, and true glasse, and made at Venice. . . . The furniture alone is worth two duccats."[85] More likely, however, mirrors were kept in chambers, closets, or cabinets because they were usually small. To look in a mirror was therefore an intimate act, performed in privacy and on occasions apart, as Spenser shows in his description of Britomart examining her "selfe" in a looking-glass:

> One day it fortuned, faire *Britomart*
>   Into her fathers closet to repayre;
>   For nothing he from her reseru'd apart,
>   Being his onely daughter and his hayre:
>   Where when she had espyde that mirrhour fayre,
>   Her selfe a while therein she vewd in vaine;
>   Tho her auizing of the vertues rare,
>   Which therof spoken were, she gan againe
> Her to bethinke of, that mote to her selfe pertaine.[86]

When the speaker in Shakespeare's Sonnet 62 uses looking in a glass as a parallel to confessing a sin, he suggests the intimate nature of both acts, making them suitable metaphors for exploration of his inward state. A similar parallel is drawn in *Hamlet* when the hero visits his mother in her closet, a room where both activities were habitually performed. There he commands Gertrude to examine herself in the mirror in order to discover what is grounded inward in her heart:

> You go not till I set you vp a glasse,
> Where you may see the inmost part of you.[87]

Having thus bared her soul to view, he commands: "Confesse your selfe to Heauen."[88] Both mirrored reflections and confessions were vehicles for and expressions of self-examination, a double metaphor compressed in the title of a poem translated from French by Queen Elizabeth as *The glasse of the synnefull soule.*[89] Confession and other forms of private devotions were habitually practiced in "a secrete Closet, or some solitarie place" as distinguished from public or common worship in churches.[90] The performance of such devotions was a source of tension when not of open controversy throughout the sixteenth century, first between Roman Catholics and reformers, later between spokesmen for the official Anglican position and those whose puritan tendencies they feared.

The early reformers stressed the inward rather than the institutional performance of devotions, and therefore defended private worship. Their differences with the Roman Catholic tradition were focused in Tyndale's translation of the Bible, which began to be published on the Continent in 1524, particularly his rendering of *confessio* by the English word "knowlege." To Sir Thomas More, attacking the translation, this word epitomizes Tyndale's bad etymology and worse theology:

> And as for this worde knowlege is very farre from the greke word *exomologesis* & as farre from the latine word *confessio* and yet mych more from the very mater selfe, that is to wyt from the sacrament of penaunce. For bothe the greke worde and the latine, do sygnifye an openyng and a shewyng of ye thyng and ye mater selfe meaneth a willyngly offered declaracyon of ye secrete hyd synne and this englyshe word knowledge is ambyguose & doutefull.[91]

Tyndale, defending his translation, in turn condemns the papists for equating confession with "shrift in the eare," and for teaching men:

> . . . thou must first shriue thy selfe to us of euery sillable, and we must lay our handes on thine head and whistell out thy sinnes and enioyne the penaunce to make satisfaction.[92]

Arguing in similar terms against their equation of prayer with outward forms, he accuses them of teaching "that no man can pray but at Church, and that it is nothing els but to say *Pater noster* unto a post."[93] He insists, on the contrary, that true prayer is grounded inward in the heart:

> It is the hart and not the place that worshippeth God. The kitchen page turning the spit may haue a purer hart to God then his master at church, and therefore worship God better in the kitchen then his master at church.[94]

Because the Church of England did not retain confession as a sacrament, stressing instead its voluntary practice, contention over its meaning and practice subsided, but the existence of other forms of private devotions continued to be a troubling subject. Uneasiness shows, for example, in this exhortation from the official sermons designed—the first book originally issued in 1549 and the second in 1562—to be preached in all Anglican churches:

> Let us ioyn ourselues together in the place of common praier, and
> with one heart, begge at our heauenly father of all those thinges,
> which he knoweth to bee necessary for us. I forbid you not priuate
> prayer, but I exhort you to esteeme common prayer as it is worthie.[95]

In a passage from one of Donne's sermons he gives similar recognition to
existing practices of private devotions while continuing to urge the priority of public worship:

> Chamber-prayers, single, or with your family, Chamber-Sermons,
> Sermons read over there; and Chamber-Sacraments, administered
> in necessity there, are blessed assistants, and supplements; they are
> as the almes at the gate.[96]

The true feast, however, is to be enjoyed in the common worship of
church goers. Evidence that such uneasiness might have grounds in the
devotional practices of some families survives in the diary of Lady Margaret Hoby for the years 1599 to 1605, in which virtually every entry begins,
"After I had praied priuatly," or "After priuat praier."[97] To counter such
tendencies toward singularity (*singular* often being paired disapprovingly
with *private*), the English Church put forth by authority a series of vol-
umes of prayers suitable for recitation in the home on many occasions
from rising to bedtime.[98]

The existence of devotions performed at home in the chamber or the
closet was not the only embarrassment to defenders of institutional worship, however. For in Matthew vi, 6 Jesus commands men to pray "in
secret" behind the closed doors of their solitary chambers. A summary of
traditional apologies for that passage occurs in Pettie's translation of *The
Civile Conversation*:

> I will not graunt you that it is a matter of necessitie, that wee should
> be ever alone when wee pray, for where our Lorde saide wee should
> enter into our chamber to make our prayers, it was spoken onely to
> reprehend hypocrites, which used to kneele praying openly at the
> endes of streetes, and with their solemne and counterfeite devotion,
> to make the people returne to beholde them, to admire them, and
> to repute them for men of a holy life. For wee see that God hath
> appointed the Churche for Christians to assemble in.[99]

The use of chambers, closets, and cabinets for confession and other
forms of devotion might itself be evidence for a growing individualism
among sixteenth-century Englishmen. Their habit of comparing performance of these activities in such rooms to self-examination encourages the
conclusion that a conception of a private self leading an inner life was
emerging. Yet differences in language as well as customs between sixteenth-century and modern English usage again modify that conclusion.

The word *private,* as distinguished from public, was frequently used in contexts which define it simply to mean domestic. Etiquette books like Pettie's translation of Guazzo, for example, provided rules and models for what they called "private conversation," by which they meant domestic discourse among family members at home "within doores," rather than in "companie, out of their own houses."[100] The language of these conversations lacks characteristics that could distinguish sixteenth-century English as it was spoken in chambers and closets from public language of the period.

Similarly collections of what were called private prayers consisted of devotions suitable for recitation by families and their servants at home in the chapels or closets of "priuate houses" rather than in church.[101] They did not otherwise differ from public prayers in greater intimacy of style, or closer application to individuals, or more detailed scrutiny of the heart. One such prayer in the authorized volume of 1578 dictates what is to be said while putting on one's clothes, an act likely to be performed with relative lack of publicity. It moves from reminders that "we" come into the world "clothed" with original sin, to petitions—switching between first-person singular and plural—that Christ become our "clothing and apparel."[102] This style seems to have been characteristic even of private confessions, if Thomas Wythorne's are typical of the period. One paragraph of his autobiography begins with the first-person but otherwise ritualistic formula echoing the "generall Confession" in *The Booke of Common Prayer*—"I am A most manifold and grevows sinner"—and then slips easily into the liturgical "we" of public worship.[103]

There is even considerable evidence that private devotions were usually, like church prayers, recited aloud, not only by family groups in common worship but by single members by themselves. References to silent prayer are extremely rare and perfunctory, while the practice of solitary recitation aloud received much more attention, as in a passage from the Homilies:

These bee the two sortes of priuate prayer. The one mental, that is to say, the devoute lifting up of the minde to God: And the other vocall, that is to say, the secrete uttering of the griefes and desires of the heart with wordes, but yet in a secrete Closet, or some solitarie place.[104]

What is more, the few mentions of silent prayer tend to stress its resemblance to outward expression, "if not with the mouth, yet with the hart and harty sighs," or with "unspeakable gronings of the heart."[105] Praying aloud in solitude had been the custom earlier, as Chaucer shows when Pandarus, overhearing Troilus groaning in his chamber, mistakes the lover's complaint for "some devocioun."[106] One piece of evidence that such practice survived occurs in Richard Whitford's *A Werke for Housholders,* published in 1530. The author anticipates an objection of his audience in a passage which shows both the circumstances and the forms he imagined for the nightly chamber prayers of his readers:

> But yet some of you wyll say. Syr, this werke is good for religious persones, and for suche persones as ben solytary and done lye alone by them selfe, but we done lye. ii. or .iii. somtyme togyder and yet in one chambre dyvers beddes and so many in company, yf we shuld use these thynges in presence of our felowes, some wold laugh us to scorne and mocke us.[107]

The objection is that only those privileged to have a chamber to themselves could properly perform private prayers, because they were expected to be recited aloud, in a special posture with accompanying gestures. A later piece of evidence from a sermon by Donne, who was so privileged, shows in its incidental details the continuation of these practices, even in solitary prayers recited in private rooms:

> I throw my selfe down in my Chamber, and I call in, and invite God, and his Angels thither, and when they are there, I neglect God and his Angels for the noise of a Flie, for the ratling of a Coach, for the whining of a doore; I talke on, in the same posture of praying; Eyes lifted up, knees bowed downe.[108]

In such a context, in addition to meaning domestic, the word *private* refers to devotions performed in a solitary place, but not to prayer which is internal or otherwise different in form from public worship. The distinction is that this kind of praying takes place in the chamber, not that it occurs solely in the heart.

When applied to opinions or affections, *private* was usually synonymous with singular, meaning peculiar to a particular person rather than common to all, and therefore likely to be troublesome. This is the meaning given by the translator of Theodore Beza's *A briefe and pithie some of the christian faith,* published in 1566. He wishes to avoid controversy by asking his readers to "put a syde disdaine, contempt, and all singular and priuate affections."[109]

As a description of persons, *private* most often meant someone not holding public office or living in the public eye, the meaning given to it by Fulke Greville when in his biography he laments that Sidney had only a "private fortune" without "proper stages to act any greatness."[110] The earliest use of the word cited in the *O.E.D.* referring to a person alone is Shakespeare's description of lovesick Romeo, who steals from the cheerful light of day, "And priuate in his Chamber pennes himselfe."[111] *Privacy,* a term also new in Shakespeare for withdrawal from public action, was not used in the modern sense to describe either an external or an inward condition; instead writers relied on phrases suggestive of occasional withdrawals such as Romeo's.[112] Habitually these are associated with brief intervals in chambers and closets. Emphasis is given to the absence of company and the performance of special acts rather than to the internal nature of the experience, as this passage from *The Civile Conversation* illustrates:

> ... solitarinesse of place, is the chamber or privat dwelling which everie one chooseth of purpose to sequester him selfe from the companie and conversation of others. Here we have to consider that men settle themselves in this solitarinesse of place for divers respects, some to the intent to raise their thoughts from worldly vanities to the contemplation of God ... some to get with studie and speculation the fruit of learning, some to discourse with them selves publike or private affaires.[113]

The very phrase "to discourse with them selves" illustrates characteristic lack of a sharp distinction more fundamental than solitude in a chamber between private and public experience. The verb *to discourse* in this period had its present meaning, to communicate by speech, but the same verb also described the mental act of passing from premise to conclusion, the process of reasoning. This is Hamlet's meaning when he laments that his widowed mother has mourned less than a beast that lacks "discourse of Reason," a phrase in use at least since the early fifteenth century.[114] The lack of distinction between the two possibilities shows assumptions profoundly different from modern conceptions of internal experience: that thinking is identical with utterance in all but sound, and that a person alone thinks or talks aloud to himself in a formal pattern that differs significantly from speech to an outside listener only in the respect that it is not overheard.

secrets

To describe these rooms and the activities performed in them, writers often linked "secret and priuat," or used them interchangeably in similar contexts.[115] In Hoby's translation of Castiglione's book of *The covrtyer* published in 1561, for example, the courtier is advised not to "presse into the chamber or other secrete places where his Lord is withdrawne," but if once admitted "secretly in chamber with him," to change out of his ceremonial coat.[116] Such pairings and substitutions prove that the terms could be thought of as synonyms. In other uses the adjective *secret* and the noun *secrets* (very rarely used in the singular) had stronger suggestions than *private* of hidden matters, which were in some special contexts associated with divine mysteries kept from profane ears. The Secret, for example, was the name for a prayer in the Roman Catholic mass (not adopted in the English liturgy) said by the priest in an inaudible voice.

When writers urged the imperative to know one's self, they typically phrased it as a need to explore what Sidney calls the "secretest cabinet of our soules."[117] As often, and frequently in the same contexts, they reminded men that the secrets of those hidden recesses are clearly visible to God. No withdrawals into private places can escape the divine scrutiny, John Woolton warns readers of *The Christian Manuell* published in 1576:

> Which lesson let every christian man learn, and think himself, as the troth is, that when he is most alone, he hath many witnesses and eyes watching and beholding him: for into what secret place soever he withdraw himself, he hath present with him the living God, his holy angel, his own conscience, from whom it is not possible with any policy to hide and keep secret his cogitations and actions.[118]

The prime importance of this belief to the way Englishmen of the sixteenth century understood human nature is shown by the fact that they were continually reminded of it in the very opening words of the service of Holy Communion in *The Booke of Common Prayer*:

> Almightie God, unto whom all hartes bee open, and all desyres knowen, and from whom no secretes are hid: clense the thoughtes of our hartes, by the inspiracion of thy holy spirite: that we may perfectly loue thee, and worthely magnifie thy holy name.[119]

Here the secrets hidden in the hearts of men are clearly assumed to be sinful, since they are in need of cleansing. This was a common assumption among theological writers. Reminders that wicked thoughts and desires cannot be hidden from God were therefore intended to teach repentance and amendment of life, as were the frequent threats that the Judgment Day will bring to light what is "hidden in darknes, and will make manifest the thoughts of mens harts."[120]

A further assumption commonly made in theological writings was that these hidden matters are particular secrets. This is implied by the fact that the word in noun form is almost always plural—*secrets of all hearts*—and in adjective form commonly attaches to a plural noun: *secret thoughts, secret intentions*. One of the very rare instances when the noun was used in the singular occurs in Psalm 51 in the Geneva version: "Beholde, thou louest trueth in ye inwarde affections: therefore hast thou taught me wisdome in the secret of myne heart."[121] The King James version replaces "secret" with "hidden part," suggesting that *secret*, when used as a singular noun, was unfamiliar and needed explanation. Evidence for this assumption that the heart's secrets are particular is even stronger in the ominous words of the service of Holy Matrimony when the couple is enjoined to reveal, as at the Last Judgment, any knowledge of hidden matters detrimental to their union:

> I require and charge you (as you will aunswere at the dreadefull daye of iudgemente, when the secretes of all hartes shalbee disclosed) that if either of you doe knowe any impedimente, why ye maie not bee lawfully ioyned together in matrimonie, that ye confesse it.[122]

The kinds of "secretes" that the couple is cautioned to tell before they are opened at the final day of reckoning are hidden pieces of knowledge about their lives which, if disclosed, will be recognizable facts.

In secular contexts, the heart's secrets are not necessarily assumed to be sinful thoughts and desires or wicked knowledge, but they are still thought of as hidden particulars. Whythorne uses both noun and adjective forms with this kind of reference several times in explaining his intentions to the friend for whom he claims to write his autobiography:

> ... because that you did impart unto me at our last being together some of your private and secret affairs past, and also some of the secret purposes and intents the which have lain hid and been as it were entombed in your heart, I, to gratify your good opinion had of me, do now lay open unto you the most part of all my private affairs and secrets, accomplished from my childhood until the day of the date thereof.[123]

Later in the same passage he explains his reasons for commenting in detail on his poems:

> ... to open my secret meaning in divers of them, as well in words and sentences, as in the whole of the same, lest you should think them to be made to smaller purpose than I did mean.

Here "secret" certainly refers to matters which are specific as well as hidden. For Whythorne's plan is to explain the particular circumstances and motives of which each poem gives a general representation. Such awareness of specific secrets hidden in each man's heart cannot, however, be equated with a continuous consciousness of an individual interior life. They are thought of as discrete particulars exemplifying general categories. Only on extremely rare occasions where *secret* is used with the function of an adjective, when the noun is understood but not directly attached, does it seem to refer to a category of inward experience rather than a particular. Such an instance occurs in the translation of Charron's *Of Wisdome* in a list of paired terms summarizing "all that is in man, *Spirit, bodie, naturall, acquired, publike, priuate, apparent, secret.*[124] As the paired opposite of what is "apparent," defined by Cawdrey to mean "in sight, or open," "*secret*" must here refer to all within man which escapes show, which is visible only to God.[125]

Furthermore, since, according to the view which all Christians of the period shared, these secrets "cannot lye hyd, or unespyed of God," they are in this sense already known.[126] What is hidden in the hearts of men is therefore not necessarily widely distanced from what is apparent. Some writers argued that the secrets of the heart are knowable in outward signs, merely debating by what vehicle they are most clearly known, the eyes or the tongue. According to one position, the eyes alone give "infallible signes of our secretes," while opponents debated that "although the eies are after a sorte in deede expounders of our conceits, yet the tongue neverthelesse is bestowed upon us as a keie, to open the secret thoughts of our minde."[127] Both positions assume that what is hidden in the heart can by nature be made visible. Other writers insisted that the thoughts and desires hidden in men can be discovered only by the most patient and intrepid observer, who stands over them with the suspicious eyes of a watchman that "watcheth & prieth into them to discouer all those things which they would gladly hide if they could."[128] Very often a writer held several such views simultaneously. For example, in *The Passions of the minde in generall* Thomas Wright declares that "Words represent most exactly the very image of the minde and soule . . . for in wordes, as in a glasse may be seene, a mans life and inclination," and also that "question-less wise men often, thorowe the windowes of the face, behold the secrets of the heart," although of course not as immediately as they are revealed in God's sight.[129] In the same work he argues with less consistency that what is grounded inward in the heart is by nature wholly invisible, and yet readily knowable:

> Love lyeth secretly closed vp within the closet of the heart, which is inaccessible to any mortall eye: yet Love like hidde perfumes, muske, and other odoriferous smelles, casteth a sente though not seene: for wordes, eyes, deedes, gestures, are morall messengers, and daily discoverers of a loving minde.[130]

It is not uncommon for a writer to argue directly contradictory positions on this theme. In *Of Wisdome* Charron is translated as arguing the position that "we haue no cleerer looking-glasse, no better booke than our selues, if as we ought we doe studie our selues."[131] These metaphors are predicated on the assumptions that the secrets of our hearts are open and visible to our own scrutiny and that their meanings are intelligible, clearly readable in our own language. Only two pages later in the translation, however, he argues an almost contradictory view of our inward nature:

Now if we will know man we must take more than ordinary paines
. . . taking him in all senses, beholding him with all visages, feeling
his poulse, sounding him to the quicke, entring into him with a
candle and a snuffer, searching and creeping into euery hole, corner,
turning, closet, and secret place, and not without cause. For this is
the most subtile and hypocriticall couert and counterfait of all the
rest, and almost not to be knowen.[132]

The fact that these notions were commonly set side by side in this fashion
without uneasiness is evidence that they were unquestioned assumptions.
The ease with which any contradictions among them were overlooked
also suggests that they were not in fact radically antithetical. For the
secrets of the heart were not conceived to be widely distanced from outward expression in words, eyes, deeds, gestures, and — in love poetry especially — in tears and sighs which are endlessly catalogued as the betrayers
of hidden passions. The separation could be bridged if each man upon
occasion examines himself, as if auditing his account books, looking in a
mirror, or making a confession in which he acknowledges his secrets by
uttering the names by which they are already known to God. Even when
those hidden thoughts are buried in the "most secret corners and innermost places . . . conueyed by many crooked byways and windings," they
can be found out and given names which truly express them.[133]

inward and outward

In both theological and secular contexts, *secret* was sometimes used as
a synonym for *inward,* as in phrases like the "inward and secret thoughts
of the heart."[134] There, because they are attached to a plural noun, both
terms designate particular thoughts. Like *secret, inward* is very rarely
attached to a noun which could suggest a consciousness of continuous
internal existence. All the texts used for this book supplied only one
instance of it associated with *life,* and then in a context illustrating yet
again that writers of this period, even when they used words and phrases
current in today's language for what is in the heart, characteristically
understood them differently. The phrase occurs in *Of Wisdome* in a discussion of the moral choices and temptations in the three categories of
human life which are first defined:

. . . one priuate of euery particular man within himselfe, and in the
closet of his owne heart, where all is hid, all is lawfull: the second,
in his house and family, in his priuate and ordinarie actions, where
there is neither studie nor art, and whereof he is not bound to giue
any reason: the third is publike in the eyes of the world.[135]

Phrasing such as "within himselfe" and "of his owne heart" suggests a sense of internal experience which is then modified because "priuate" is used to describe both what happens in the closet of a man's heart and within the actual walls of his house. This repetition makes the two categories of life alike rather than distinct. Then as the argument continues, the distinguishing quality of the "inward" life is further blurred:

> Now of these three liues, inward, domesticall, publicke, he that is to leade but one of them, as Hermits, doth guide and order his life at a better rate, than he that hath two, and he that hath but two, his condition is more easie, than he that hath all three.[136]

By identifying the "inward" life with the conduct of hermits, the writer defines it to mean a solitary, secluded existence withdrawn from society. This equation moves away from awareness of continuous internal existence different in kind from outward. The hermit's life is "inward" in that it is private in the sense of solitary, that it is conducted away from human witnesses.

The same body of reading that turned up this one use of "inward" attached to "liues" provided only two instances of it joined to *self.* Sidney uses the phrase in *An Apologie for Poetrie* to praise Aeneas as a heroic model "in his inward selfe, and . . . in his outward government," meaning "selfe" as a likely synonym for soul or parts, and "inward" probably as the opposite of public.[137] Spenser uses the phrase in *Amoretti* 45, where the context defines the "inward selfe" as the heart, a truer mirror than the outward self, the face or body, which is all that can be seen in an actual looking glass:

> Leaue lady in your glasse of christall clene,
> Your goodly selfe for euermore to vew:
> and in my selfe, my inward selfe I meane,
> most liuely lyke behold your semblant trew.
> Within my hart, though hardly it can shew
> thing so diuine to vew of earthly eye:
> the fayre Idea of your celestiall hew,
> and euery part remaines immortally.[138]

The one frequently used expression which might seem to connote a continuous internal existence is the Pauline phrase *inward man,* sometimes translated as *inner man* or *hid man.* The passage cited most often as a source is Romans vii, 22–23:

> For I delight in the Lawe of God, after the inward man. But I see another Lawe in my members, warring against the Lawe of my minde, and bringing me into captiuity to the Law of sinne, which is in my members.

The other verses commonly cited are II Corinthians iv, 16: "but though our outward man perish, yet the inward man is renewed day by day," and Ephesians iii, 16: "bee strengthened with might, by his Spirit in the inner man." These texts use the phrase to describe man's spiritual nature as distinct from the flesh, leading to the common identification of the *inward man* with an invisible, immaterial part, as in I Peter iii, 16. There "the hidden man of the heart" is "that which is not corruptible, even the ornament of a meeke and quiet spirit." "Of the inner man, the soule" is a chapter heading in *Batman vppon Bartholome,* while in Matthew's translation of Augustine's *Confessions* the phrase is glossed with the marginal note "The Mind." In *The Christian Manuell* Woolton equates it with the heart.[139] This kind of translation, making the noun *man* stand for some one of his parts, shows that the word could be understood in these phrases somewhat arbitrarily. It could be made to stand for soul, mind, or heart by the attachment of *inward,* but for body when described as *outward.* In other comparable biblical phrases it is still more arbitrarily used in a metaphor of clothing, as in Ephesians iv, 22–24. There followers of Christ are exhorted to "cast of" the "olde man," and to "put on the new man," showing characteristic inattention both to the metaphorical implications of clothing, a temporary covering of the surface of the body, and to the ordinary meanings of the noun *man.* As a result, its actual meaning was not exploited as these phrases were habitually used. It was not thought of as identifying within each human being a consciousness of leading a continuous internal existence distinct from the experiences of his outward man. The biblical phrases were commonly taken as a whole to stand for something immaterial. The fact that such uses did not demand explanation shows that they must have had the unquestioned familiarity of convention. They did not therefore define a conception unlike that associated with other words and phrases naming inward parts, for which they could so easily be substituted.

Like *secret,* the word *inward* was virtually always used to refer to particulars (except when referring to a single part: heart, mind, soul). Also like other commonly used terms in sixteenth-century English for what is in the heart, *inward* occured in physiological as well as theological vocabularies. In addition, it was used both literally and metaphorically, often in ways which make it difficult or impossible to distinguish which uses are literal and which are figurative.

The human body was said to be divided into "outward parts," such as limbs and features, and "inward parts," the organs—including powers such as the will, which are no longer thought of anatomically—of which there are none "inwarder then the heart and Reynes."[140] The terms themselves show that these divisions must have been thought of literally, that is, anatomically and spatially, as were further subdivisions of man's inward and outward attributes. While these spatial terms describe inward and outward relations among man's parts, in other contexts "outward, or inward " distinguish external from internal phenomena. The terms function this way in Timothy Bright's definition of the heart in *A Treatise of Melancholie* of 1586:

> The hart is the seate of life, and of affections, and perturbations, of loue, or hate, like, or dislike; of such thinges as falle within compasse of sense; either outward, or inward; in effect, or in imagination onely.[141]

Even the soul is given its location, for example, in *Batman vppon Bartholome,* where it is described in a comparison with a spider

> that sitteth in the middle of the web, and feeleth all manner of mouing, and toucheth the webbe either within or without: So the soule, abiding in the middle of the heart, without spreading of it selfe, giueth lyfe to all the bodie, and gouerneth and ruleth the mouing of all the lims.[142]

Because this is a simile, and because it is used to describe an immaterial part, this passage appears to be a figurative definition while it was probably intended to be literal, or to be wording which is not exclusively in either mode.

This ambivalent character is typical of many phrases used in the sixteenth century to describe what is in the heart, for example, the phrase "inward hert" itself, which Wyatt uses in his translation of Psalm 51 where the authorized version of 1611 has "inward parts."[143] Since man has no outward heart from which to distinguish his inward, here the modifying word must be in one sense a kind of intensifier with a meaning something like the wording of one of Thomas Watson's love poems, "In secrete seate and centre of my hearte," or from Hamlet's speech when he vows to treasure Horatio "In my hearts Core: I, in my Heart of heart."[144] The "inward hert" must be at once literally the innermost part or chamber and figuratively the hidden center.

The possibility of using modifying words in this way partly depended on the fact that adjectives were not considered to be a separate part of speech, but to belong to one of two categories of noun: *De Adjectivo* or Noun Adjective, as distinguished from *De Substantivo* or Noun Substantive. As Ben Jonson makes clear in *The English Grammar,* English was thought to have virtually the same parts as Latin, adding only the article.[145] The earliest English grammars—William Bullokar's of 1586, Paul Greaves' of 1594, Charles Butler's of 1633—all record the same categories that must have been taught throughout the period: a noun is either substantive, with an article before it, or adjective.[146] The only definition of an adjective comes then under the category of a Noun Adjective: "An

Adjectiv' implyeth a qualiti belonging to a Substantiv'.''[147] As Wyatt's expression follows this definition, inwardness is a quality belonging to the heart. The whole phrase, "inward hert," must therefore have been thought of as a category without implying any necessary antithesis to what is outward.

Such expressions are common in which *inward* is attached as a quality belonging to interior parts of man or internal states which have no outward counterparts from which to be distinguished: soul, mind, thoughts, passion, affections, griefs. In these instances the modifier acts almost exclusively as an intensifier. Elsewhere, it has been shown, it may simply be synonymous with hidden or secret. Often, when an implied opposite would make no sense—thoughts or griefs which are outward, for instance— the phrases suggest that inward means the antithesis of uttered.

One kind of evidence for this use is the fact that the words *utter* and *outward* were pronounced alike. What is more, when *utter* functioned as an adjective, it could be interchangeable in meaning with *outward,* a use which, according to the *O.E.D.,* was very common from 1400 to about 1620. There the adjective is defined:

> That which is farther out than another (implied or distinguished as *inner*); forming the exterior part or outlying portion; relatively far out, outward, external, exterior; also, indefinitely remote.

The phrase *utter man* is also cited for this period in religious contexts, in contrast to the inner man, for example in a distinction made by Bishop Jewel between what things in the Bible are to be "applied to the Inner Man, and what to the Vtter."[148] For poets the likeness of *utter* to *outward* was a frequent inducement to verbal play, like Shakespeare's in Sonnet 69. There it is incorporated for sarcastic purposes into an extended contrast between outward show and inward truth:

> Those parts of thee that the worlds eye doth view,
> Want nothing that the thought of hearts can mend:
> All toungs (the voice of soules) giue thee that end,
> Vttring bare truth, euen so as foes Commend.
> Their outward thus with outward praise is crownd,
> But those same toungs that giue thee so thine owne,
> In other accents doe this praise confound
> By seeing farther then the eye hath showne.
> They looke into the beauty of thy mind.

Samuel Daniel, in *A Defence of Ryme* of 1603, exploits the likeness in a pun worked into the familiar pattern of architectural metaphors for outward and inward parts:

> When we heare Musick, we must be in our eare, in the vtter-roome
> of sense, but when we intertaine iudgement, we retire into the cabi-
> net and innermost withdrawing chamber of the soule.[149]

Further evidence that *inward* was in some contexts a synonym for unuttered, unexpressed, exists in many verse catalogues mixing tears, sighs,
sobs, groans, complaints, with the names for categories of inward states.
A clear instance occurs in Wyatt's translation of Psalm 38, which lists
David's "inward" experiences known only to God in alternation with
modes for expressing them in outward signs:

> O Lord thou knowst the inward contemplation
> Off my desire, thou knowst my syghes and plaintes,
> Thou knowst the teres of my lamentation
> Can not expresse my hertes inward restraintes.[150]

In this sense the song quoted previously from Tottel's miscellany, "Farewell the hart of crueltie," which Wyatt's lover bids not to "astart" from
his heart, is an example of inward thoughts or griefs, and was probably
intended as a rendering of what is literally in the heart. It differs from a
song that is uttered only in the single respect that it is not expressed out
loud, as "discourse of reason" differs from speech in the same way.

Still other phrases abound, especially in love poetry, in which *inward*
attached to a noun may make the phrase literal, or signal that it is figurative. Typical are instances where *inward* is joined to words that can refer
to physical states: *wound, sore, smart, hurt, pain, heat.* The combined
phrase may create a metaphor by talking about inner states in terms of a
physical phenomenon, or it may be a way of differentiating an actual
condition in man's inward parts from its parallel in the outward parts. The
likelihood is that the distinction between literal and figurative phrasing
was not a consideration.

Occasionally, however, *inward* seems to be inserted when a phrase is to
be read as figurative. This is the way the word usually works in the phrase
inward man, as an indication that the noun cannot carry its literal meaning, but must be understood as standing for some other noun that could
name an inward part. Sidney creates a similar effect in one of the poems
included in his collection of *Certaine Sonnets,* when the speaker refers to
his mind:

> Whose clowdie thoughts let fall an inward raine
> Of sorrowe's droppes.[151]

In this instance "inward" may be intended to distinguish unexpressed
sorrow from tears, but it may also be used to signal that the noun is
figurative. A phenomenon from the physical world is appropriated to

stand for an experience in man's inward parts. Therefore it is the noun "raine" that is the metaphorical term. Yet because the adjective attached to it cannot be thought of as a quality belonging to rain, the phrase calls attention to itself as a comparison rather than a category. By contrast "cloudie thoughts" does not do so to the same degree, because the slight metaphorical suggestion is carried by the adjective, while the noun is not made to stand for anything other than itself. The adjective describes qualities which may more easily belong to thought than rain may literally occur in the inward parts of man. By attaching "inward" to "raine," Sidney shows freedom from uneasiness about arbitrary uses of language. Rain can be made to stand for an experience in the heart and then given the quality of inwardness because outward and inward are closely parallel modes of experience, as literal and figurative are modes of language that can be mixed or identical.

An odder, but for that reason clearer, instance of this use of "inward" to make the name of a physical object stand for what is in the heart occurs in one of Sidney's early sonnets from the *Arcadia*. The lover both addresses his heart and analyzes what is in it:

> In vaine, my Hart, now you with sight are burnd,
>   With sighes you seeke to coole your hotte desire:
> Since sighes (into mine inward fornace turnd)
>   For bellowes serve to kindle more the fire.[152]

Here "inward" attached to a furnace must be a means of pointing to the figurative function of the noun, to the fact that it stands for the heart or breast. The figurative substitution needs such a marker because it is more forced, more arbitrary, and less familiar than such conventional noun adjectives as "hotte desire," which in fact may have been thought of as a literal rather than a figurative phrase, or as a noun adjective not belonging exclusively to either mode. For treatises of this period on physiology, for instance Elyot's *The Castel of Helth*, use similar language, as in catalogues of "Hote thynges conseruynge a colde Harte," or "Confortatiues of the Harte hotte."[153] There meanings must be intended literally, but in other lists physical operations and intangible states are included without distinction. A catalogue of symptoms of "The harte sycke," for example, combines "Feuers" and "Colde" with "Griefe about the hart."[154]

These mixed types of phrasing used in poems and in other kinds of writing to describe what is in the heart all have similar implications. For they show that inward experience was not conceived as necessarily antithetical to outward, or radically different in kind, or widely distanced from it. The same nouns—*heart, smart*—could characterize either, or terms from one area—*rain, furnace*—could be appropriated to describe the other merely by attaching *inward*. The very lack of consistent distinctions between literal and figurative uses of language for what is in the heart shows

that man's inward and outward experiences were viewed as closely parallel and that no great separation was consistently or systematically conceived to exist between them.

To be sure, in contexts where things inward are explicity distinguished
from outward, they are often seen as divided and in opposition. Many
passages in the Bible encourage such a division, as in St. Paul's terms of
conflict between the law in the inward man and the law of the members.
Religious writing commonly echoed such terms, for example, the Homilies authorized to be preached in all Anglican churches, in defining true
faith:

> This is the true lyuelie, and unfaigned Christian fayth, and it is not
> in the mouth and outward profession onelie: but it liueth, and stir-
> reth inwardlye in the heart.[155]

Because the Church of England defined a sacrament as an outward and
visible sign of an inward and spiritual grace, "that setteth out to the eyes
and other outward senses, the inwarde working of Gods free mercy," its
spokesmen obviously could not make a consistent equation of outward
forms with false show, although the definition of faith in the Homilies
does tend in this direction by adding "unfaigned" to "true" when characterizing inward faith in the heart.[156] In many religious texts, nevertheless,
such a distinction is made explicitly. For example, in a collection of
"priuate prayers for housholders to meditate vpon, and to say in their
families," Edward Dering entreats his readers

> that we may euen from the bottome of our heartes, examine and trie
> out thoughtes, before thy presence, that they bee vpright and vnfained,
> not hypocriticall in outwarde shewe onely, and appearance.[157]

Henry Lok phrases the division in literary terms in his preface to the
reader of his *Sundry Christian Passions Contained in two hundred Sonnets*
published in 1593. There he defends his verse for having "rather followed
the force of mine own inward feeling, then outward ornaments of Poeticall
fictions or amplifications, as best beseeming the naked clothing of simple
truth."[158]

Yet it is very frequently true in writings of this period that even
when things inward are explicitly distinguished from outward, the divisions between them blur, and the separation narrows as terms shift
and mix. A passage from *The Touchstone of Complexions* illustrates this
pattern:

> And not only in the inward mynd of man, do these ornamentes
> and giftes of nature appeare and expressely shew, out themselues
> but even in the outward shew, shape and behauvour of the body

there is euidently descryed and perceyed a comly grace and portly dignitye.[159]

The transfer of "shew" and "appeare" along with "ornamentes" here to the inward side of the comparison obliterates its distinction from "outward shew." In this instance the word "inward" cannot even be synonymous with unexpressed, since the qualities of the mind as well as of the outward parts do "expressely shew" themselves. In a passage from a work instructing a woman how to be both honest and comely, the writer exhorts her not to paint her face, a notorious instance of false outward show. She is advised

> not so much to decke and tricke her selfe vp to the eye, as to haue her *inner man adorned* with holy skill and discretion.[160]

Here the phrase *"inner man"* is used with evident arbitrariness and indifference to precise meanings to stand for the woman's soul, or mind, or heart, as opposed to her outward man, or "selfe," here equated with her body. Yet by being *"adorned,"* it becomes less an antithesis and more a parallel to a woman's ornamented face and body. Both the arbitrariness with which such equations are made, and the ease with which metaphors transfer from one side of the contrast to the other, work against clear separation between what is outward and what is inward.

When an English poet of the earlier sixteenth century wished to portray what is in the heart, his language characteristically followed the patterns explored in this chapter, whereas Shakespeare in his sonnets, although he works with essentially the same vocabulary, uses it with far other effects. Some instances of the differences have already been discussed in Wyatt's "Farewell the hart of crueltie," by contrast with Shakespeare's Sonnet 62 and with Hamlet's first speech. A fuller demonstration can be made now, if another poem by Wyatt is compared to Shakespeare's Sonnet 113. Wyatt's poem was known in the sixteenth century by the version published in Tottel's miscellany under the title "The louer to his bed, with describing of his vnquiet state":[161]

> The restfull place, renewer of my smart:
> The labours salue, encreasyng my sorow:
> The bodyes ease, and troubler of my hart:
> Quieter of minde, myne vnquiet fo:
> Forgetter of payne, remembrer of my wo:
> The place of slepe, wherein I do but wake:
> Besprent with teares, my bed, I thee forsake.
>   The frosty snowes may not redresse my heat:
> Nor heat of sunne abate my feruent cold.

I know nothing to ease my paynes so great.
Ech cure causeth encrease by twenty fold,
Renewying cares vpon my sorowes old.
Such ouerthwart effectes in me they make.
Besprent with teares my bedde for to forsake.
    But all for nought: I finde no better ease
In bed, or out. This most causeth my paine:
Where I do seke how best that I may please,
My lost labour (alas) is all in vaine.
My hart once set, I can not it refrayne.
No place from me my griefe away can take.
Wherefore with teares, my bed, I thee forsake.

The lover describes his state in terms of a separation of what is inward
in his heart from his outward experience, or a dislocation of the usual
relationship between the two modes. This is also the burden of the lover's
complaint in Shakespeare's Sonnet 113:

Since I left you, mine eye is in my minde,
And that which gouernes me to goe about,
Doth part his function, and is partly blind,
Seemes seeing, but effectually is out:
For it no forme deliuers to the heart
Of bird, of flowre, or shape which it doth lack,
Of his quick obiects hath the minde no part,
Nor his owne vision houlds what it doth catch:
For if it see the rud'st or gentlest sight,
The most sweet-fauor or deformedst creature,
The mountaine, or the sea, the day, or night:
The Croe, or Doue, it shapes them to your feature.
    Incapable of more repleat, with you,
    My most true minde thus maketh mine vntrue.

The refrain of Wyatt's poem locates the lover alone in his chamber,
uttering his complaint. Here it is not said to be sung within his heart but
is addressed to his bed, explicitly making it a spoken farewell accompanied "with teares." Shakespeare's speaker addresses his friend, but because the sonnet makes clear from the start that the friend is not present
to the lover, he seems to speak to him only in his own mind, or in a poem
which is like a soliloquy rather than a public address.

The first stanza clearly illustrates the way language works in Wyatt's
poem. It is composed entirely of a catalogue of apostrophes which nevertheless serves as an explanation of why the lover forsakes his bed. The first
half of each line assigns an epithet to the bed as a traditional place of
solace; the second half names it according to its disquieting effects on
the lover's heart. The stanza appears therefore to be arranged, almost

spatially, to represent the separation between the lover's outward experience in an actual place where his body literally functions, and the inward
state of his heart. Yet the distinctions are not consistently drawn between
outward and inward, so that the separation between them narrows and
even at some points seems to disappear.

Each catalogue of epithets includes both literal and metaphorical categories. The bed is actually a place; metaphorically a salve. To wake is a
literal, bodily response of the lover to suffering; to name his bed as a foe
is to represent his inward states metaphorically by personifying an external object. Furthermore, the metaphors scarcely function figuratively.
Given the same amount of space in the line, and intermixed in each
catalogue with the literal categories, they are not distinguished in kind or
in effect from the other names in the lists. In some instances it is even
difficult to decide if a category is literal or figurative, as has been shown
to be commonly true of conventional nouns—*smart, pain, wound*—naming categories of suffering in the heart. Here a similar ambivalence also
attaches by different means to epithets like "Quieter of minde." Placed as
it is between a literal category and a personification, it can be read as
either. For a silent, solitary place can in fact induce quiet, but since the
epithet is parallel to "Forgetter of payne" in the next line, it can as appropriately be read as a personification. Even the lover's tears cannot be
clearly located as distinctively either inward or outward. They are physical; they sprinkle the bed, making it an unrestful place, and are listed in
the catalogue of epithets otherwise naming the bed as an actual location.
Yet they come from within the lover and, with his grief, accompany him
when he forsakes his bed. They are therefore visible signs of what is in his
heart, but do not measure a separation between outward and inward.
Instead the lover's tears draw them together. For his tears differ from his
smart, sorrow, woe, pain, grief only in being their outward expression.

The actual word *expression,* commonly used by Wyatt and other writers
throughout this period for the utterance of what is in the heart, describes
the relationship here of outward signs to inward states. Bullokar defines
it to mean "A wringing or squeasing out," making the word itself at once
literal and metaphorical,[162] which seems to be how it was considered in
Sidney's use of it in *Astrophil and Stella* 96: "Thy teares expresse night's
native moisture right." In either a literal or a figurative reading, *expression*
defines outward signs, like tears, as the emission of what is in the heart;
to utter also meant to emit or exhale.

In Sonnet 113, by contrast with Wyatt's poem, Shakespeare measures
a radical separation between the speaker's inward and outward experience, although using terms which were equally available to Wyatt. The
division is depicted in such extreme ways as to suggest a violation of
nature like blindness or bodily deformity. The eye departs from its "function," or only partly performs it, "Seemes seeing," while in effect is plucked

from its socket. Perhaps parodying verse which arbitrarily mixes literal and metaphorical language to portray inward parts, Shakespeare then transfers the speaker's outward sight to his mind, giving him a grotesquely physical inward eye. Yet far from creating a parallel between outward and inward parts, the device is used to sever all connections between eye and heart. Nothing outward reaches the inward eye, which is the mind. Or if it does, the mind remakes it so that it no longer resembles its outward form. The world itself in all its variety and extremes is obliterated, or transformed into a single image. The mind or inward eye and the outward eye thus belie one another, destroying the possibility of parallels between them, or even of antitheses. Outward signs cannot express what is in the lover's heart, but must inevitably change or distort it. The sonnet itself, which is an outward form, an utterance, is therefore called in question as an expression of the speaker's "most true minde." It too is "Incapable" of bridging the distance between outward and inward "vision," and therefore it too "shapes" untruly.

The verbal resources available to sixteenth-century poets for describing what is in the heart, it has been shown, did not change in ways that would account for the profound differences between Wyatt's poem and Shakespeare's. No new terminology or newly formulated conceptual framework explains this remarkable shift in the characterization of inward states. Yet poets learned to use their verbal resources in new ways, especially in exploring the possibilities of the sonnet form, introduced into English by Wyatt. The nature of these discoveries and their implications for a new kind of poetry is the subject of the following chapters about the sonnets of Wyatt, Sidney, Shakespeare, and Donne. They show what the first two poets learned individually as English innovators in the sonnet form and the sonnet sequence, what Shakespeare taught himself directly from *Astrophil and Stella,* and what Donne assimilated from the associations which the form had accumulated for him by the time he chose to work within it.

2.
Wyatt

Tottel's miscellany of *Songes and Sonettes* both reflected and shaped the interests of sixteenth-century poets and readers of English verse written in what the prefatory letter calls "small parcelles."[1] Of the 271 poems which make up the first edition, about three-fifths have something to do with love. Among Surrey's forty assigned poems, twenty-six are about love, while the section devoted to Wyatt consists of seventy-six love poems and only twenty of other kinds. The taste of these two poets is shared by the other courtly makers who contributed to the volume.[2]

This emphasis in Tottel's collection reflects actual social circumstances of sixteenth-century court and upper-class life which have been explored in recent historical studies, for example in Lawrence Stone's *The Family, Sex and Marriage*:

> Romantic love and sexual intrigue . . . existed in one very restricted social group: the one in which it had always existed since the twelfth century, that is the households of the prince and the great nobles. Here, and here alone, well-born young persons of both sexes were thrown together away from parental supervision and in a situation of considerable freedom as they performed their duties as courtiers, ladies and gentlemen in waiting, tutors and governesses to the children. They also had a great deal of leisure, and in the enclosed hot-house atmosphere of these great houses, love intrigues flourished as nowhere else.[3]

The character of court poetry in some sense mirrors these actual circumstances, even by its very artificiality. Love's games, as they are rendered in verse, were also actually played at court, and in the same style. Its combined qualities of secrecy and extravagance were represented, for example, in Wyatt's rumored intrigue with Anne Boleyn, and in his dedication of *The Quyete of Mynde* to Queen Catherine, to whom he signs himself "your most humble subiect and slaue."[4] Courtly poets, more often than other writers, wrote of love because it was of compelling interest in

their society, because writing was a social accomplishment like lute playing and dancing, and because their compositions could often be specifically
useful to them much in the same ways as hyperbolic dedications and other
forms of social compliment.

Yet there is a more inclusive explanation of this literary emphasis. Not
only court poets and not only writers early in the century persisted in
ringing changes on the themes and situations of love poetry, because love
itself by its very nature was thought to express itself in a style characterized by wit and extravagance. As this process is described by Wright in
The Passions of the minde in generall, the modes of expression attributed
to love sound very like the poetic devices preferred by contributors to
Tottel's miscellany:

> Love is sayd to be *Ingeniousissimus,* most wittie, for the thought of
> such matters as concerneth love, continually delighting the minde,
> and rolling daily and hourely in the fancie, suggesteth a worlde of
> conceites and inventions, to find out means and wayes, to nourish,
> preserve, and increase the Passion, insomuch, as they which love
> vehemently, are never well, but eyther with them whom they love,
> or solitary by themselves, coyning some new practises, to execute
> their inordinate love and affections.[5]

If love was thought of as generating wit and hyperbole, elaboration and
amplification, it was a subject suited to the taste of most sixteenth-century
poets and readers, and love poetry, as George Puttenham elaborately
explains in *The Arte of English Poesie,* allowed writers a uniquely rich
range of possibilities

> because loue is of all other humane affections the most puissant and
> passionate, and most generall to all sortes and ages of men and
> women, so as whether it be of the yong or old or wise or holy, or high
> estate or low, none euer could truly bragge of any exemption in that
> case: it requireth a forme of Poesie variable, inconstant, affected,
> curious and most witty of any others, whereof the ioyes were to be
> vttered in one sorte, the sorrowes in an other, and by the many
> formes of Poesie, the many moodes and pangs of louers throughly
> to be discouered: the poore soules sometimes praying, beseeching,
> sometime honouring, auancing, praising: an other while railing, reuil-
> ing, and cursing: then sorrowing, weeping, lamenting: in the ende
> laughing, reioycing & solacing the beloued againe, with a thousand
> delicate deuises, odes, songs, elegies, ballads, sonets and other dit-
> ties, moouing one way and another to great compassion.[6]

Sounding again very much like a description of the verse in Tottel's
volume, this passage gives an explanation of the continuing interest in the
miscellany throughout the century. It can also suggest something about

the intentions of the contributors to the volume, and of poets later in the period. In their love poems they attempt to render the range of "many moodes and pangs" with which the lover's "case" alone was traditionally associated in poetry.

Among the titles given to poems in Tottel's miscellany, complaint is one of the commonest categories named, complaining the quintessential activity of the speakers in love poems. This mode, later identified with the work of Petrarchan sonneteers, had also deep roots in the native English tradition reaching back to their common sources in troubadour poetry. A representative example is the first entry in Tottel's volume attributed to unknown authorship, entitled "The complaint of a louer with sute to his loue for pitye."[7] This is a seventy-line compendium in poulter's measure of the situations and language conventional to the complaint. The complaining lover is, in another among the poems of unknown authorship, compared to the English prototype of that figure, Chaucer's Troilus, described alone in his chamber uttering his "great extremitie":

> His chamber was his common walke,
> Wherin he kept him secretely,
> He made his bedde the place of talke,
> To heare his great extremitie.
> In nothing els had he delight,
> But euen to be a martyr right.
>   And now to call her by her name
> And straight therwith to sigh and throbbe:
> And when his fansyes might not frame,
> Then into teares and so to sobbe,
> All in extreames and thus he lyes
> Making two fountayns of his eyes.
>   As agues haue sharpe shiftes of fittes
> Of colde and heat successiuely:
> So had his head like chaunge of wittes:
> His pacience wrought so diuersly.
> Now vp, now downe, now here, now there,
> Like one that was he wist not where.[8]

The styles identified in these lines with the complaint—extremity and diverseness, or "sharpe shiftes" of opposite states—are the commonest modes used in English love poems of the earlier sixteenth century to portray what is in the heart. Their association with Troilus shows that the tradition was well established before it met with the conventions of the Petrarchan sonnet sequence; both trace back to their common roots in troubadour poetry. The description of Troilus recalls the many episodes in Chaucer's poem in which Pandarus, slipping into the lover's chamber, overhears him making his solitary bed the "place of talke." The complaint was clearly conceived as a spoken form, even when uttered "secretely," following established conventions, associated with recognized styles.

We cannot know if the complaint was thought of as literally rendering the actual pattern of inward states, much as the literary mode of "stream of consciousness" in earlier twentieth-century writing intended to represent, or came to be thought of as representing the actual flow of internal experience. Yet there is some evidence that the complaint was so conceived. Since no distinctions, other than in occasion and audience, were made between private and public language, and since people by themselves actually spoke out loud, for example in prayer, such forms as the complaint and the soliloquy may then have seemed less remote from actual inward processes than they do in our way of thinking. Furthermore, reading was, if not always actually performed aloud, still thought of as declamation. Punctuation marks were, in the words of Mulcaster, "helps to our breathing, & the distinct vtterance of our speche," so that writing must still have been much more closely identified with spoken than with silent thoughts.[9] Silent thought itself, moreover, was the "discourse of reason."

A complaint of Wyatt's embodies many devices of style most commonly used to represent extremity—the violence, intensity, inescapability of the lover's inward states:

> Alas the greiff, and dedly wofull smert,
> The carefull chaunce, shapen afore my shert,
> The sorrowfull teres, the sighes hote as fyer,
> That cruell love hath long soked from myn hert,
> And for reward of ouer greate desire
> Disdaynfull dowblenes have I for my hiere!
>
> O lost seruis! O payn ill rewarded!
> O pitiful hert with payn enlarged!
> O faithfull mynde, too sodenly assented!
> Retourne, Alas, sethens thou art not regarded;
> Too great a prouf of true faith presented
> Causeth by right suche faith to be repennted.
>
> O cruel causer of vndeserued chaunge
> By great desire vnconstantly to raunge
> Is this your waye for prouf of stedfastnes?
> Perdy you knowe—the thing was not so straunge—
> By former prouff to muche my faithfulnes:
> What nedeth, then, such coloured dowblenes?
>
> I have wailed thus weping in nyghtly payne
> In sobbes, and sighes, Alas! and all in vayne,
> In inward plaint and hertes wofull torment;
> And yet, Alas, lo! crueltie and disdayn

Have set at noght a faithfull true intent
And price hath priuilege trouth to prevent.

But though I sterue and to my depth still morne,
And pece mele in peces though I be torne,
And though I dye, yelding my weried goost,
Shall never thing again make me retorne:
I qwite th'entreprise of that that I have lost
To whome so euer lust for to proffer moost.[10]

Exclamations—"O," "Alas," "lo"—and hyperboles are grouped in catalogues so that exaggeration is enhanced by amplification. The lists consist of nouns which designate categories. They are names for inward states,
such as "grieff" or "smert," or inward parts of the lover, his "hert" or
"mynde," which are acted on by those states, or outward modes for
expressing them, especially "teres," "sighes," and "sobbes" which love
has "soked" out of his heart. In the catalogue of stanza 4, the lover also
lists "inward plaint and hertes wofull torment" as accompaniments to the
wailing utterance exemplified in his complaint. Here "inward" is synonymous with unuttered, making the "plaint" in his heart identical with the
poem in all respects but outward expression. The effect of this catalogue
of mixed categories is to obliterate distinctions between interior monologue, the lover's language when he speaks a soliloquy aloud in his solitary
chamber, and public address.

Composed of such catalogues, the structure of the poem is additive: the
length and even the order of lists do not seem to be controlled inevitably
by the sequence either of logic or narrative. The main effect must be
intended to be cumulative, as the last stanza best illustrates. It is a catalogue of dire endings for the lover, which are redundancies rather than
distinct alternatives. Their combined effect is to express the great extremity of his inward states. Similarly, the almost ritualistic doubling of modifiers
to make a compound noun adjective, as in "faithfull true intent," works
more as an intensifying device than as a means of making distinctions.
The reader does not pause to contemplate subtle differences between an
intention which is merely faithful and one which is also true—the two
words were in fact more nearly synonymous in the sixteenth century than
now—because the noun adjective is conceived as a whole, and made such
by predictable coupling. This effect is particularly noticeable when the
catalogued noun adjectives are alliterative—"Disdaynfull dowblenes," "cruel
causer."

For Wyatt this is a relatively crude effort, but it is not at all unrepre-
sentative of sixteenth-century English love poetry before *Astrophil and
Stella*. A more skillful complaint by Wyatt shows the same associations
of love with extremity, and uses virtually the same kinds of language to
express it:

What rage is this? What furour of what kynd?
What powre, what plage, doth wery thus my mynd?
Within my bons to rancle is assind
    What poyson, plesant swete?

Lo, se myn iyes swell with contynuall terys;
The body still away sleples it weris;
My fode nothing my faintyng strenght reperis,
    Nor doth my lyms sustayne.

In diepe wid wound the dedly strok doth torne
To curid skarre that neuer shalle retorne.
Go to, tryumphe, reioyse thy goodly torne,
    Thi frend thow dost opresse.

Opresse thou dost, and hast off hym no cure,
Nor yett my plaint no pitie can procure,
Fiers tygre fell, hard rok withowt recure,
    Cruell rebell to love!

Ons may thou love, neuer belovffd agayne;
So love thou still and not thy love obttayne;
So wrathfull love with spites of just disdayne
    May thret thy cruell hert.[11]

By putting the opening catalogue in the form of questions, Wyatt charges it with a wider range of tone than the uniform wailing of the first complaint. Here the rapid accumulation of questions about what is in his heart makes the lover sound bewildered, baffled, angry, as well as pained, so that the opening prepares for the more bitterly humorous vengefulness of the last stanza. These differences imply a greater sense of love's complexity. The lover experiences a category of feeling such as "rage," but cannot tell what kind, cannot readily attach to it the modifiers which come so easily to the complaining lover in the other poem. Implied is the existence of a more bewildering variety within each category listed in the catalogue of questions, while the nouns themselves also name more diverse types of extremity.

The lines from the poem in Tottel's volume which describe the "extreames" of Troilus' complaint also associate utterance of what is in the heart with "diuersly" experienced effects. This aspect of love "What rage is this?" amplifies in its catalogue of questions, or condenses in the oxymoron "poyson, plesant swete." Such diverseness is both the subject and the stylistic mode of another complaint by Wyatt:

            It may be good, like it who list,
            But I do dowbt: who can me blame?
            For oft assured yet have I myst,

And now again I fere the same.
The wyndy wordes, the Ies quaynt game,
Of soden chaunge maketh me agast:
For dred to fall I stond not fast.

Alas! I tred an endles maze
That seketh to accorde two contraries;
And hope still, and nothing hase,
Imprisoned in libertes,
As oon unhard and still that cries;
Alwaies thursty and yet nothing I tast:
For dred to fall I stond not fast.

Assured, I dowbt I be not sure;
And should I trust to suche suretie
That oft hath put the prouff in vre
And never hath founde it trusty?
Nay, sir, In faith it were great foly.
And yet my liff thus I do wast:
For dred to fall I stond not fast.[12]

The lover describes his state, fearfully subject to "soden chaunge," like the fits attributed to Troilus. Here, however, the diverseness of love is more complexly defined as the impossible effort to "accorde two contraries." These are then illustrated in catalogues of paradoxes and antitheses in stanzas 2 and 3, each leading up to the same last line. That refrain condenses the precariousness and futility of the lover's contradictory experiences and, by its repetition at the end of each stanza, confirms his assertion that he treads "an endles maze." For the poem points toward a conclusion which its structure then denies. The lover has not learned a sure lesson such as is implied by the title given the poem in Tottel's miscellany, "The louer taught, mistrusteth allurementes."[13] For the last refrain leaves him in the same perilous posture he describes in stanza 1, impossibly poised between the contraries of standing and falling.

Certain assumptions about what is in the heart and the capacity of poetry to represent it are implied by the styles conventional to the complaint. Diverseness clearly aims at rendering variousness and complexity of inward states. Its antitheses are used to portray sudden alternations and contrasts; its paradoxes and oxymorons compress conflicts and contradictions to indicate simultaneous opposites. Extremity in style, embodied in hyperbole, amplification, repetition, seems most pointedly designed to represent the intensity and endurance of the lover's inward experiences. Yet such uses of language to render extremes are also designed to represent variety and complexity, as the catalogue of questions in "What rage is this?" has shown. That is to say, a catalogue of nouns in a typical complaint, listing grief, smart, pain, desire, while it may focus attention on the accumulation rather than the differentiation of these categories, still suggests that the lover's inward states are various as well as numerous, which defining them only by the single name "love" would not.

Both diverseness and extremity of style, while intended to represent complexity of inward states, nevertheless imply that what is in the heart is expressible and recognizable in outward manifestations, such as sobs and sighs, but especially in the verbal utterance of the complaint. The common device of the catalogue most clearly embodies this view by assuming that inward states can be described by names for categories carrying fixed and recognizable meanings, like names for physical phenomena such as tears and sighs. This assumption can be seen at work in the opening catalogue of questions in "What rage is this?" The nouns listed without distinction in kind are: "rage," "furour," "powre," "plage," "poyson." The first two name inward states, the third a force which may be physical or intangible, the fourth a physical phenomenon, and the fifth a concrete object used with figurative suggestions. Even the oxymoron created by the use of "plesant swete" to modify "poyson," while it puts together opposites in paradoxical combination, is nevertheless a form of name combining definable elements with recognizable meanings. Behind this catalogue lies the assumption that love is various, contradictory, baffling, but not inexpressible. Those very qualities can be represented by accumulations and combinations of names typical of the styles conventional to the complaint.

The association in the tradition native to earlier sixteenth-century poets of love with complaining, and of the complaint with extremity and diverseness, can explain the initial accessibility of some of Petrach's sonnets for Wyatt. He could find in the Italian sequence virtually all the familiar situations and attitudes of the complaining lover, expressed in a style suitable to the conventions already established in English poetry for describing what is in the heart. For example, Petrarch's Sonnet 224 clearly had a special appeal for Wyatt, since it is the only model on which he based two of his own sonnets, one a close translation and one a loose adaptation (departing from the original after the first six lines).[14] The Italian sonnet consists of a catalogue of extremes experienced by the complaining lover, organized by the easily adapted logic of an if-then proposition:

> S' una fede amorosa, un cor non finto,
> un languir dolce, un desiar cortese,
> s' oneste voglie in gentil foco accese,
> un lungo error in cieco laberinto,
>
> se ne la fronte ogni penser depinto,
> od in voci interrotte a pena intese
> or da paura o da vergogna offese,

s'un pallor di viola et d'amor tinto,

s' aver altrui più caro che se stesso,
se sospirare et lagrimar mai sempre
pascendosi di duol d'ira et d'affanno,

s' arder da lunge et agghiacciar da presso,
son le cagion ch' amando i' mi distempre:
vostro, Donna, 'l peccato et mio fia 'l danno.

If faithfulness in love, an unfeigning heart, a sweet yearning, a courteous desire—if chaste desires kindled in a noble fire, a long wandering in a blind labyrinth—
if to have all my thoughts written on my brow, or barely understood
in broken words, or cut off by fear or shame—if a pallor like the
violet's, tinted with love—
if to love another more than oneself—if to be always sighing and
weeping, feeding on sorrow and anger and trouble—
if to burn from afar and freeze close by—if these are the causes that
I untune myself with love, yours will be the blame, Lady, mine
the loss.

Wyatt's version parallels the original more closely than many of his other
translations, perhaps because he found this portrayal of the lover's extremity especially familiar. It is very like his own in his love poems other
than sonnets, as is the structure, which is essentially additive. For the
sonnet consists of a catalogue of inward states, of the inward parts of the
lover on which they act, and of the outward modes by which he expresses
them:

> Yf amours faith, an hert vnfayned,
>   A swete langour, a great lovely desire,
>   Yf honest will kyndelled in gentill fiere,
>   Yf long errour in a blynde maze chayned,
> Yf in my visage eche thought depaynted,
>   Or els in my sperklyng voyse lower or higher,
>   Which now fere, nowe shame, wofully doth tyer,
>   Yf a pale colour which love hath stayned,
> Yf to have an othre then my self more dere,
>   Yf wailing or sighting continuelly
>   With sorrowful anger feding bissely,
> Yf burning a farr of and fresing nere
>   Ar cause that by love my self I distroye,
>   Yours is the fault and myn the great annoye.

Wyatt's changes are minor compared to those in some of his translated
sonnets, and virtually all of them are substitutions or additions of single

words which work toward heightening the extremity of the lover's inward state. Rather than wandering in a blind labyrinth, he is "chayned" in it; his color, "pale" rather than delicate as a violet's, is appropriately "stayned" instead of tinted; his sighing is accompanied by "wailing," more vehement than weeping; his shame is "wofully" affecting, and he feeds "bissely" on his own state. All these changes prepare for a more violent conclusion. The speaker does not metaphorically untune himself with love, but claims with almost literal force to "distroye" himself. These changes heighten the extremity of the complaint by more violent language, as is habitual to Wyatt, without fundamentally altering the original in other ways.

The accessibility of some attributes of poems by Petrarch for Wyatt, and for English poets throughout the sixteenth century, is especially demonstrated in Petrarch's Sonnet 134. It too is a catalogue, this time of the contraries experienced by the lover. The continuing association of such diverseness with the complaint is shown by the efforts of numerous poets to turn this sonnet into English. One of them, Thomas Watson, printed in 1582 with his translation a commentary identifying its "contrarieties" with the insignia of the lover:

> The sense contained in this Sonnet will seeme straunge to such as neuer have acquainted themselues with *Loue* and his Lawes, because of the contrarieties mentioned therein. But to such, as Loue at any time hath had vnder his banner, all and euery part of it will appeare to be a familier trueth. It is almost word for word taken out of *Petrarch.*[15]

Wyatt must also have recognized in the Italian model some familiar truths about love, because it resembles poems of his own such as "It may be good," in that it consists of a catalogue of contraries:

> Pace non trovo et non ò da far guerra,
> e temo et spero, et ardo et son un ghiaccio,
> et volo sopra 'l cielo et giaccio in terra,
> et nulla stringo et tutto 'l mondo abbraccio.
>
> Tal m'à in pregion che non m'apre né serra,
> né per suo mi riten né scioglie il laccio,
> et non m'ancide Amore et non me sferra,
> né mi vuol vivo né mi trae d'impaccio.
>
> Veggio senza occhi, et no ò lingua et grido,
> et bramo di perir et cheggio aita,
> et ò in odio me stesso et amo altrui.
>
> Pascomi di dolor, piangendo rido,
> egualmente mi spiace morte et vita.
> In questo stato son, Donna, per vui.

Peace I do not find, and I have no wish to make war; and I fear and hope, and burn and am of ice; and I fly above the heavens and lie on the ground; and I grasp nothing and embrace all the world.

One has me in prison who neither opens nor locks, neither keeps me for his own nor unties the bonds; and Love does not kill and does not unchain me, he neither wishes me alive nor frees me from the tangle.

I see without eyes, and I have no tongue and yet cry out; and I wish to perish and I ask for help; and I hate myself and love another.

I feed on pain, weeping I laugh; equally displeasing to me are death and life. In this state am I, Lady, on account of you.

Wyatt's translation retains Petrarch's definition of love by contraries (itself derived from a tradition stretching back at least as far as Catullus' *Odi et amo*), and in that respect shows continuity between some of Wyatt's sonnet translations and his other love poems.[16] Yet his version is by no means taken word for word from its Italian model. It makes significant departures which resemble reworkings of Petrarch in other sonnets by Wyatt, as well as his uses of language in his original sonnets. These show new directions for poetry in portraying what is in the heart, which for Wyatt will be shown to have developed out of his work in the sonnet form.

The significant departures in Wyatt's version of Petrarch's Sonnet 134 follow a pattern, point toward a unified effect, as do his changes in details in "Yf amours faith." Yet there the alterations consist merely in substitutions of stronger verbs and nouns, or the addition of heightening modifiers, whereas here more elaborate departures create more significant changes in meaning, showing interests different from Petrarch's:

> I fynde no peace and all my warr is done;
>   I fere and hope I burne and freise like yse;
>   I fley above the wynde yet can I not arrise;
>   And noght I have and all the worold I seson.
> That loseth nor locketh holdeth me in prison
>   And holdeth me not, yet can I scape no wise;
>   Nor letteth me lyve nor dye at my devise,
>   And yet of deth it gyveth me occasion.
> Withoute Iyen, I se; and withoute tong I plain;
>   I desire to perisshe, and yet I aske helthe;
>   I love an othre and thus I hate my self;
> I fede me in sorrowe and laugh in all my pain;
>   Likewise displeaseth me boeth deth and lyffe;
>   And my delite is causer of this stryff.[17]

The second quatrain of Wyatt's translation is a sustained revision of the original. It omits any reference to the god of love, and avoids the pronoun *his,* with the result that the power which acts upon the lover by contraries is never defined more precisely than as "That" and "it." No details elsewhere in the translation invite the reader to think of the unspecified force as Cupid, so that its source remains ominously ambiguous. It could be the power of the lady, who is never immediately present, but whose existence and cruelty are assumed by the conventional nature of the complaint. Or it could be the force of the lover's contrary inward states which make him feel as if imprisoned by outside coercion which is actually within himself. The calculated indefiniteness suggests that both readings are intended simultaneously, especially since the last line of Wyatt's translation alters the original to the same effect. For it makes the cause of the lover's contrary state "my delite," which can refer to the lady, who is explicitly named as the cause in the Italian original, or to his own inward states, making them again the cause of his imprisonment in contraries. Both readings are allowed to exist simultaneously, as their parallels exist in the second quatrain of this sonnet. The combined effect is to make the lover's inward experience more difficult to interpret or define because it is more ambiguous. He feels in the grip of forces he cannot name either as a single category or in a cumulative list of noun adjectives. Instead he uses wording which has more than one possibility of interpretation simultaneously. It is not an oxymoron, which names a single category combining paradoxical properties, but a noun having more than one reference, with the implication that it cannot be singly defined. It represents what can only be suggested by ambiguities.

These changes in "I fynde no peace" cannot be attributed either to the exigencies of turning the original into English or solely to the fact that Wyatt, as was his consistent practice, alters the rhyme scheme so that the sonnet ends in a couplet. Watson's translation, for example, also rhymes the last two lines, but creates no ambiguities about the force controlling the lover:

> Twixt death and life, small difference I make;
> All this deere *Dame* befals me for thy sake.[18]

Yet some pressure exerted by the couplet ending to reflect on the preceding lines, or to give a complicating twist to them, must have been felt by Wyatt. For other sonnets of his, both translated and original, create similar kinds of ambiguity in the final line, with effects like the complication introduced here by the substitution of "my delite" for explicit naming of the lady. This, it will be seen, is his characteristic response to the special demands of the sonnet form, and one which distinguishes his work in it from virtually all his other love poems.

In "My galy charged with forgetfulnes," Wyatt for thirteen lines follows relatively closely Petrarch's Sonnet 189, but changes the original line 14: *tal ch' i' 'ncomincio a desperar del porto* ("so that I begin to despair of the port"). A literal translation could easily have been fitted into Wyatt's line;

by changing the verb he creates a double meaning that reshapes the presentation of the lover's inward state in the sonnet as a whole: "And I remain dispering of the port."[19] The last line of Wyatt's version can be paraphrased: "I continue to despair of reaching the port." This reading focuses on the extremity, the sameness, the inescapability of the lover's inward state. He is permanently "dispering" in the timeless immediacy of a present participle. By this interpretation, the revision of the ending intensifies the extremity of the lover's feelings, as was true of the changes made by Wyatt in the translation of "Yf amours fayth." The last line of Wyatt's translation can also be read: "I stay where I am, in the same situation, while despairing of the port." In a poem which, until this line, has been built out of a sustained comparison between the lover's inward state and a ship passing dangerously between rock and rock on a course steered by a hostile pilot, the possibility of this reading heightens the contradictions in the plight of which the lover complains. He feels as if he were in violent motion, propelled along a perilous course by an enemy outside himself, while he simultaneously feels as if he were unmoving, going nowhere, always fixed in despair where he began. The metaphor of a motionless voyage in a dark ocean is therefore, by the ambiguous verb "remain," turned into a representation of an inward experience which is simultaneously like treading an endless maze and like being chained in a labyrinth. The ambiguity of the last line makes the whole sonnet render what is in the lover's heart to be bafflingly paradoxical, not easily susceptible to definition because difficult to interpret.

Neither one of the possible readings of Wyatt's last line turns the sonnet into a presentation of the lover's inward state that is altogether unlike its definition in Wyatt's other love poems. Nor does their simultaneous existence altogether change that definition. The speaker in this sonnet experiences the extremes and contraries that are habitually associated with the lover's complaint. Its familiar nouns naming love's effect on the speaker and his modes of expressing them are woven into the comparison of the lover to a storm-tossed vessel. One important difference, however, is Wyatt's introduction in the last line of the sonnet of ambiguous wording that demands to be read in different ways simultaneously. This use of language is significantly unlike the devices of style characteristically used to represent extremity and diverseness in the other love poems. It implies ultimately different assumptions about the nature of what is in the heart and the capacity of poetry to express it. These assumptions can be defined more clearly through explorations of other sonnets in which Wyatt creates ambiguities such as those in the last lines of "I fynde no peace" and "My galy charged."

One of Wyatt's sonnets which is not a translation uses the couplet in similar fashion. It complicates the whole presentation of the lover's inward state by again introducing double meanings in the last line:

Ffarewell, Love, and all thy lawes for ever;
   Thy bayted hookes shall tangill me no more;
   Senec and Plato call me from thy lore,
   To perfaict welth my wit for to endever.
In blynde errour when I did perseuer,
   Thy sherpe repulce that pricketh ay so sore
   Hath taught me to sett in tryfels no store
   And scape fourth syns libertie is lever.
Therefore, farewell; goo trouble yonger hertes
   And in me clayme no more authoritie;
   With idill yeuth goo vse thy propertie
And theron spend thy many britill dertes:
   For hetherto though I have lost all my tyme,
   Me lusteth no longer rotten boughes to clyme.[20]

Here the complicating reflection is not introduced by a noun of unspecified reference like "my delite," or a word having more than one
meaning like "remain," but by ambiguous syntax. For the last line is
constructed grammatically so that it can be read to interpret the lover's
inward state in different ways simultaneously. It can be paraphrased: "I
no longer desire to climb rotten boughs," but also: "I desire to climb
rotton boughs no longer." The first reading confirms what the speaker has
previously asserted about his inward state. He has claimed that his sufferings have definitively "taught" him to see as trifling what the seductions
of love and his youthful error once tricked him to desire. In lines 1 to 13
his judgments have been absolute, his renunciations final. Meanwhile the
second reading calls this assurance in question by showing the lover to be
caught in the painful paradox of desiring to stop desiring what he still
desires, even while he sees its rottenness. This reading makes the previous
assertions sound like protestations. It calls attention to the fact that although the speaker bids a grand farewell to love "for ever" in the first line,
he still feels the need to dismiss it again in line 9. The second paraphrase
also alerts the reader to the sequence of negatives—"no more," "no store,"
"no more," culminating in the last line in the ambiguously placed "no
longer"—which shows the lover's continuing need to thrust away what he
claims to have renounced.

   In this sonnet the last line therefore again makes a complicating reflection on the lover's inward state, using a device not associated with the
complaint in Wyatt's love poems other than sonnets. It does so by ambiguous wording which implies that the lover's feelings are multiple and
difficult to define, so that he himself may be unable to name them clearly.
He may feel simultaneously liberated and trapped, or he may believe that
he is free from desires that are in fact still enticing him. Or he may be using
language as a way of fending off feelings rather than naming them. The
ambiguity in the couplet of this sonnet therefore creates a dramatic structure unlike the typically additive pattern of Wyatt's other love poems.

The fact that this practice can be found at work both in his translations of sonnets by Petrarch and in Wyatt's original sonnets is a particularly convincing sign of its deliberateness. Translations offer one kind of evidence, in that they show clearly and in precise detail a specific and limited set of choices open to the poet. If he makes a substitution, omission, or radical departure, we have the original by which to measure its significance. Poems which are not based on a specific model provide a different kind of evidence by showing what language the poet uses when his choices are limited only by the verbal resources available to him, by the conventions in which he works, and the formal elements of his poem.

In Wyatt's sonnets the conventions of the complaint are those operating also in his other love poems, but the formal structure sets different kinds of limits and opens new possibilities. These must in themselves have been of interest to Wyatt. For, in adapting sonnets by Petrarch, he almost always chose to restrict himself to fourteen rhymed lines of equal length, whereas in his translations of poems by Petrarch other than sonnets, he transposed their meanings into English without restricting himself to the same number of lines or the same stanza forms. In "Myne olde dere En'mye," for example, he translated into 147 lines of rhyme royal a poem of 157 lines divided into ten stanzas of fifteen lines with a concluding one of seven lines.[21] "So feble is the threde" renders in one hundred lines of poulter's measure an original of 120 lines divided into seven stanzas of sixteen lines and an eight-line conclusion.[22] Moreover in *Troilus and Criseyde* he had the precedent of the only version of a sonnet by Petrarch in English earlier than his own translations. Chaucer translated Petrarch's Sonnet 132, turning it into a stanzaic poem characteristic of complaints in the native tradition. Petrarch's sonnet becomes Troilus' song, composed of three seven-line stanzas.[23] To duplicate the form of the original, even of a sonnet, was therefore not demanded of a translation. The fact that Wyatt did translate sonnets into fourteen rhymed lines of equal length therefore proves deliberate choice; the fact that in every instance he nevertheless departed from his model in rhyming the last two lines together shows that such a conclusion lends itself to his special concerns. These are demonstrated also in other devices of language used repeatedly in the couplets of both his translated and original sonnets.

Wyatt's version of Petrarch's Sonnet 57 again makes no radical departure from the original until the last line. In the Italian sonnet it is a final comment on the conspiracy between Love and the lady: *Altro mai di lor grazie non m'incontra* ("Nothing else ever comes to me from their graces"). Wyatt's couplet reads:

> Any thing swete, my mouth is owte of tast,
> That all my trust and travaill is but wast.[24]

Wyatt's omission of the reference to the god of love in his wholly original last line recalls similar omissions in "I fynde no peace." His suppression of the lady's presence resembles the couplets of that translation and of "Yf amrous fayth," where he drops direct address to her, and in the latter names her by an ambiguous noun which can simultaneously refer to what is in the lover's own heart. Here both omissions focus the line on the speaker's inward state, and work with the ambiguous word "trust," introduced in Wyatt's substituted last line, to complicate the portrayal of what is in the lover's heart.

As a noun, "trust" could be defined as confidence or reliance in a quality or attribute of a person or thing, or in the truth of a statement, here the lover's trust, bitterly misplaced, in the righteousness toward himself of the lady and Cupid (mentioned in lines 10 to 11). It could be synonymous with the expectation of a better future which the lover calls "hope vncertain" in line 2, but which by the last line he sees as futile and empty "trust." The noun could mean the quality of being trustworthy, and so refer to the fidelity or loyalty of the lover himself. Used with a possessive, "trust" meant that which one puts one's trust in, but also the obligation with which one is entrusted, here the expectations or demands of loyalty imposed on the lover, adding further questions about the nature and cause of his sufferings. Wyatt's radical departure from the original last line of Petrarch's sonnet shows his own different concerns: the multiple meanings of "trust" complicate the speaker's inward states without resolving its ambiguous nature.

The noun *trust* with its multiple meanings seems to have been particularly suited to the interests developed by Wyatt in his sonnets, as distinct from his other love poems. There he uses the noun form of *trust* rarely, and not in contexts exploitive of its multiple meanings, although he uses forms of the verb more often, and although the meanings compressed in the noun *trust* as it is used in "Ever myn happe"—reliance on truth, fidelity, hope, the expectation or obligation of loyalty—are concerns in all of Wyatt's poetry.[25] By contrast, his sonnets, both translated and original, use the noun frequently. In two other sonnet translations from Petrarch, Wyatt substitutes "trust" where the original Italian could have been translated as hope. One example is from the second quatrain of Petrarch's Sonnet 140:

> Quella ch' amare et sofferir ne 'nsegna
> e vol che 'l gran desio, l'accesa spene
> ragion, vergogna, et reverenza affrene,
> di nostro ardir fra se stessa si sdegna.

She who teaches us to love and to be patient, and wishes my great desire, my kindled hope, to be reined in by reason, shame, and reverence, at our boldness is angry within herself.

In Wyatt's version, his choice of the more ambiguous noun complicates the lesson the lover is obligated to learn:

> She that me lerneth to love and suffre
> And will that my trust, and lustes negligence
> Be rayned by reason, shame, and reverence
> With his hardines taketh displeasure.[26]

Surrey, translating the same sonnet, seeks no such multiplicity of meanings; where Wyatt places "trust," he uses "doutfull hope."[27] In "Love and fortune and my mynde, remember," a translation of Petrarch's Sonnet 124, Wyatt's couplet intensifies but also complicates the lover's inward state in ways which depart from the direction of his model. Petrarch's speaker concludes his complaint:

> Lasso, non di diamante ma d'un vetro
> veggio di man cadermi ogni speranza
> et tutt' i miei pensier romper nel mezzo.

Alas, I see all hope fall from my hands, made not of diamond but even of glass, and I see all my thoughts break in half.

Wyatt's revisions make what is in the lover's heart characteristically more violent and, by the translation of *speranza* into "trust," more murky:

> Alas, not of steill but of brickell glasse,
> I see that from myn hand falleth my trust,
> And all my thoughtes are dasshed into dust.[28]

What crashes to destruction with the lover's thoughts is simultaneously hope, loyalty, fealty, belief in "Love"—standing at once for Cupid, the lady, and his own inward state.

The combined effects of all these combined devices of ambiguity can be seen in one of Wyatt's wholly original sonnets, where "trust" occurs characteristically in the last line, and also in line 9. Here the noun works with at least five other key words in the poem bearing more than one meaning. These are also given emphasis by repetition and likeness of sound in rhyme and alliteration. Their effect, combined with ambiguous grammar, is to make multiplicity of interpretation the focus of the reader's attention. Doubleness is therefore both the sonnet's stylistic mode and its subject, as diverseness or contraries in Wyatt's song "It may be good" is both subject and style:

There was never ffile half so well filed
  To file a file for every smythes intent,
  As I was made a filing instrument
  To frame othre while I was begiled.
But reason hath at my follie smyled
  And pardond me syns that I me repent
  Of my lost yeres and tyme myspent,
  For yeuth did me lede and falshode guyded.
Yet this trust I have of full great aperaunce:
  Syns that decept is ay retourneable
  Of very force it is aggreable;
That therewithall be done the recompence.
  Then gile begiled plained should be never
  And the reward litle trust for ever.[29]

This speaker (assumed to be a lover by the editor of Tottel's miscellany, who gave the sonnet the title "The abused louer seeth his foly, and entendeth to trust no more") complains of past mistreatment and plots revenge for it, using language altogether differently from the way the lover complains in Wyatt's song "What rage is this?" There, it has been shown, the speaker defines what is in his heart by listing names for his inward states, for the inward parts of himself on which they act, and for his modes of expressing them. He then repeats the same kinds of noun adjectives to describe how "wrathfull love" will revenge him with "just disdayne" to oppress the lady's "cruell hert." Such categorical names, even when they are listed in question form, declare that language defines inward states and that the speaker is using it to utter his by naming them in terms that have single and recognizable meanings. The impulse to complain may be to relieve his heart, or to win the lady's pity, or to gain sympathy from an audience, or all of these motives at once. Yet whether the lover has withdrawn to his chamber to make his bed listen to his complaint, or addresses it to his cruel mistress, or to a specific or general public—"Good ladies" or "all you that heare this plaint"—it is assumed that his utterance renders what is in his heart in all its extremity and diverseness.[30] This assumption is not embodied in the language of Wyatt's sonnet, "There was never ffile," which will be shown to operate according to very different principles.

Its most obvious feature to strike the reader is the repetition in the opening quatrain of *file,* first as a noun, then as a verb in the infinitive, then in past and present participle forms. Such word play is of a different kind from the alliterative patterns in catalogues conventional to complaints, such as those abounding in Tottel's miscellany:

    Ah piteles plante whome plaint cannot prouoke,
  Darke den of disceite that right doth still refuse,

Causles vnkinde that carieth vnder cloke
Cruelty and craft me onely to abuse,
Statelye and stubberne withstanding cupides stroke,
Thou merueilouse mase that makest men to muse,
Solleyn by selfe will, most stony stiffe and straunge,
What causeth thee thus causelesse for to chaunge.[31]

This passage is especially numbing , but not otherwise untypical in that such predictable patterns of sound tend to make the reader slide over distinctions, rather than calling attention to the choice of a particular word for its multiplicity of meanings. Even in the last line of this passage, the play on positive and negative verb and noun forms of *cause* does not lead to any question about how they are to be interpreted. The meaning of each is taken to be single and recognizable; the play on the variety of forms does not draw attention to any ambiguity in their uses.

The word play in the first quatrain of Wyatt's sonnet is on the sense as well as the sound of all the forms of *file*. As a noun it could name both a smith's tool for polishing, to which the speaker explicitly compares himself, or to a person who is worthless or cunning, artful, a deceiver. As a verb *to file* could mean the literal act of polishing metal, or could be synonymous with: to defile, to sully, dirty, dishonor; to deceive; to accuse or condemn; to arrange or elaborate. The present participle carried all these possibilities, to which the past participle added the sense of neatly finished off. With these meanings all working simultaneously in Wyatt's lines, his repetitions call attention to multiplicity of interpretation. The speaker chooses his words carefully in order to exploit their doubleness. They represent by their ambiguity the nature of his past experience of having been beguiled, and they also render his present ambiguous inward states brought about by that experience.

This stylistic device is sustained throughout the sonnet by repeated use of other key words bearing several meanings at the same time. "To frame," for example, is chosen to describe the speaker's own performance as an instrument for polishing, and as a deceiver, because this verb itself carried a bewildering number of meanings. It could signify: to further, execute, perform; to profit, to benefit another; to prepare, make ready for use; to furnish, adorn; to perform the work of building; to suit, fit; to shape the action of another person, or dispose another toward something; to put into words. In imagining his revenge, the speaker declares it to be "aggreable," therefore in some objective sense justifiable because suitable, fitting, corresponding, conformable. It will result in "gile begiled." Yet his revenge is also "aggreable" in the sense of being to his liking, pleasing to him because it will cause another pain. He is at once presenting an objective generalization about the nature of deceit and meanly savoring his private retaliation. The choice of this vocabulary forces the reader to make multiple interpretations, and in doing so to think about language itself as a vehicle capable of veiling or disguising as well as conveying meanings.

The way the stylistic mode of this sonnet works is best demonstrated by line 9: "Yet this trust I have of full great aperaunce." One editor's note in a recent edition offers this paraphrase, which the line certainly allows: "But I have one hope which looks very promising."[32] Yet "aperaunce" already also carried the meaning of semblance or illusion, and was commonly used to describe outward look or show as distinguished from reality or inward truth. Combining also the other meanings of "trust," and the grammatical alternatives that "full great aperaunce" may or may not modify "trust," the line invites very different, even partially contradictory paraphrases: "But I put my faith in deceiving outward show," and "But my loyalty consists in deceptive looks." These interpretations point toward the concluding line, which repeats "trust" to create its own bitter ambiguities: "And the reward litle trust for ever."

In a sonnet on deceit, in which the speaker complains of how it was worked upon him while confessing to his own manipulations of "trust," he uses a language which itself deceives. And it does so by its very nature, not its abuse. That is, the language of the sonnet acts as a file, not by telling lies but by its capacity to bear meanings which simultaneously reveal and disguise. Wyatt calls attention to this artfulness by the opening comparison of the speaker to an instrument for polishing, suggesting resemblances between the metal worker and an artist or poet. What is more, *filed* was frequently used to describe elaborately polished verse, what Shakespeare in Sonnet 85 dismisses sarcastically as "precious phrase by all the Muses fil'd." And the verb *to frame*, while generally associated with the work of building, also specifically meant to put into words and to invent or fabricate, as Wyatt means it in Satire I:

> My Poyntz, I cannot frame me tonge to fayne
> To cloke the trothe for praisse, withowt desart.[33]

The speaker in the sonnet uses a double vocabulary which is itself associated with the power of poetry to create semblances of reality. By doing so he implies that he is not uttering his feelings as in a complaint which catalogues them in names that have single and recognizable meanings. He suggests them in words which render them only ambiguously and can even simultaneously disclose and disguise them. This difference implies a sense of the greater complexity of both inward states and of language than is embodied in the styles of extremity and diverseness associated with the complaint. It also implies greater uneasiness about the relationship between what is in the heart and its portrayal in words.

Although "There was never ffile" depends so elaborately on word play

that it becomes somewhat like a puzzle or game, it is nevertheless different
in kind from a riddle-poem like Wyatt's "What wourde is that." Headed
"anna" in the Egerton manuscript, and given the title "Of his loue called
Anna" as it first appeared in the second edition of Tottel's miscellany, it
has traditionally been assumed to hint at Wyatt's relationship to Anne
Boleyn:

> What wourde is that that chaungeth not,
> Though it be tourned and made in twain?
> It is myn aunswer, god it wot,
> And eke the causer of my payn.
> A love rewardeth with disdain,
> Yet it is loved. What would ye more?
> It is my helth eke and my sore.[34]

While such a riddle may turn upon a pun—answer: Anne, Sir—it does not
demand multiplicity of interpretation so much as a knowledge of matters
outside the poem.[35] For the most part its words have distinct meanings
or references, some of which are, for the purposes of the riddle, kept secret.
Once known, they provide the key to its code.

The doubleness of language in "There was never ffile," in addition to
making the sonnet in some ways resemble a puzzle, gives it a secretive air,
since the reader is made to see so many possibly conflicting meanings that
he cannot be sure of the speaker's intentions. His language even seems at
times designed to hide one meaning behind another. Yet it is nevertheless
different in kind from the language of Wyatt's songs which hint at secret
knowledge. An example of this kind of oblique reference, common in
courtly poetry of the time, can be seen in the first two stanzas of "Blame
not my lute":

> Blame not my lute, for he must sownd
> Of thes or that as liketh me;
> For lake of wytt the lutte is bownd
> To gyve suche tunes as plesithe me;
> Tho my songes be sume what strange
> And spekes suche words as toche they change,
>   Blame not my lutte.
>
> My lutte, alas, doth not ofend
> Tho that perfors he must agre
> To sownd such teunes as I entend
> To sing to them that hereth me;
> Then tho my songes be some what plain,
> And tocheth some that vse to fayn,
>   Blame not my lutte.[36]

A particular reference is indicated by "they change," but then still more darkly alluded to in the oblique phrasing of "some that vse to fayn." To the public audience of "them that hereth" this song, such obscurity is intended to shroud affairs known only to the poet and the one or more guilty listeners whose secrets are spoken in such oblique language; it may aim at puzzling even a knowing hearer. That this kind of obscurity arose from the social circumstances surrounding court poetry has been most convincingly argued by John Stevens in *Music and Poetry in the Early Tudor Court,* and confirmed by comments of Thomas Whythorne on the calculated obscurity of one of his own poems:

> I made this song somewhat dark and doubtful of sense, because I knew not certainly how she would take it, nor to whose hands it might comen after she had read it. If she would take it to be written to herself, she might best do it . . . yet it is so made as neither she nor none other could make any great matter thereof.[37]

About another such poem he remarks on the advantage of musical accompaniment:

> If it were not to be well taken, yet inasmuch as it was sung, there could not so much hurt be found as had been in the case of my writing being delivered to her to be read.[38]

The greater safety of sung verse apparently consisted in its address to a general audience, and the fact that it left nothing incriminating in writing.

A song like "Blame not my lute" may have been an actual gesture in the game of love conducted at once publicly and secretively by elaborate codes such as love tokens and eye glances, as well as cryptic verses. Or the poem could be in imitation of such actual practice. Whichever is true of "Blame not my lute," its secretive language is based on assumptions closer to those embodied in the riddle than in "There was never ffile." Its obscurities are of a kind that could be cleared away if the reader were in possession of facts hinted in the poem. It therefore works on the same assumption as the riddle, in that it omits words which would define by their clearly recognizable meanings and references. The secretiveness of that language is not a function of awareness that what is in the heart is of an ambiguous nature demanding multiple interpretation. It therefore does not raise questions about the character of inward states or their rendering in language, or about the poet's manipulations of it to disclose and hide meanings simultaneously.

Even in "There was never ffile," Wyatt does not explicitly identify his speaker as a poet, or present him in the act of writing verses, or reciting them to the accompaniment of his lute, as is often true in his songs. Nor elsewhere in Wyatt's sonnets, either translated or original, is the speaker

identified as a poet-lover, the figure adapted from Petrarch by other English as well as continental sonneteers of the sixteenth century. Wyatt, for
instance, translates none of Petrarch's sonnets about the immortality con-
ferred by poetry on beloved and poet-lover. In "Myne olde dere En'mye,"
to avoid identifying his speaker as a poet, he departs most radically from
his model, Poem 360, when he reaches lines 110—120 where the god of
love describes the fame he has given to the poet-lover, whose history is
Petrarch's own:

> Sì l'avea sotto l'ali mie condutto
> ch' a donne et cavalier piacea il suo dire;
> et sì alto salire
> il feci che tra' caldi ingegni ferve
>   "il suo nome, et de' suoi detti conserve
> si fanno con diletto in alcun loco;
> ch' or saria forse un roco
> mormorador di corti, un uom del vulgo!
> I' l'esalto et divulgo
> per quel ch' elli 'mparò ne la mia scola
> et da colei che fu nel mondo sola."

"I had so carried him under my wings that his speech pleased ladies
and knights; and I made him rise so high that among brilliant wits
    "his name shines, and in some places collections are made of his
poems; who now would perhaps be a hoarse murmerer of the courts,
one of the mob! I exalt him and make him known by what he learned
in my school and from her who was unique in the world."

Wyatt omits all of this passage except the image in the first two lines of
the poet-lover carried under Cupid's wings to the heights of fame, which
his version totally transforms:

> I norisshe a Serpent vnder my wyng
> And of his nature nowe gynneth he to styng.[39]

Again social circumstances can explain this difference of emphasis. Writing poetry was not in itself acknowledged to be a means to fame and honor
for an English courtier, but a social accomplishment and a vehicle for
paying compliments. It was not thought of at court as a specialized activity
so much as one among many gestures suited to the courtly game of love.
In this sense, in fact, any lover would on occasion be a poet, and his
complaining, like Troilus' recitation of Chaucer's translation from Petrarch, would take the form of song or verse. Therefore the speaker in a
sonnet by Wyatt is a poet insofar as he is a lover. His complaint represents
the rendering in verse of what is in his heart, so that if the nature of his

language is called in question, then the questioning implicates the nature of poetry. This suspicion is implicit in Wyatt's original sonnet, "There was never ffile," and in two of his sonnets translated from Petrarch.

"Suche vayn thought" and "Bicause I have the still kept" are modeled on sonnets in which Petrarch's poet-lover is stricken mute when he attempts to utter what is in his heart. Wyatt's interest in these sonnets again shows continuity with his other love poems, where the speaker is wont to complain: "In faith I wot not well what to say," "My tong dothe fayle what I shulde crave," "I dare not loke nor speke."[40] Yet in these poems even the lover's moments of incapacity to express himself do not imply an essentially different sense of the nature of inward experience or of language than is assumed by the styles traditional to the complaint. In the opening stanza of "Suche happe as I," for example, the speaker sees himself singled out for misfortune hitherto unfelt, for which he therefore does not know the name:

> Suche happe as I am happed in
> Had never man of trueth I wene;
> At me fortune list to begyn
> To shew that never hath ben sene
> A new kynde of vnhappenes;
> Nor I cannot the thing I mene
> My self expres.[41]

The speaker is, however, able to assign his passion to the category of "vnhappenes," which is a way of defining it resembling the device of putting the catalogue of names for inward states into question form in "What rage is this?" For in both poems the lovers do believe that a word can name what is in their hearts more precisely. What they seek is a term to refine on a category by distinguishing diverse types—of "rage" or "vnhappenes"—within it. Proof of this assumption can be seen in the beginning of the next stanza of "Suche happe as I":

> My self expresse my dedely pain
> That can I well, if that myght serue.

The speaker has great confidence in the power to render inward states by expressing them, which would suggest that once he comes to know his new kind of unhappiness, he can find what to call it, and can then include it in a catalogue along with more familiar categories such as his conventional "dedely pain." For him, expressing inward states is actually synonymous with naming them.

In the sonnet translations in which the lover is unable to articulate what is in his heart, very different assumptions are at work, which can again be measured by Wyatt's departures from his Italian models. In Petrarch's

Sonnet 169, from which "Suche vayne thought" is translated, the poet-lover's muteness results from the fullness of his inward experience and his fear of the beautiful enemy to whom he wishes to disclose it:

> Pien d'un vago penser che me desvia
> da tutti gli altri et fammi al mondo ir solo,
> ad or ad ora a me stesso m'involvo,
> pur lei cercando che fuggir devria;
>
> et veggiola passar sì dolce et ria
> che l'alma trema per levarsi a volo,
> tal d'armati sospir conduce stuolo
> questa bella d'Amor nemica et mia.
>
> Ben, si i' non erro, di pietate un raggio
> scorgo fra 'l nubiloso altero ciglio,
> che 'n parte rasserena il cor doglioso;
>
> allor raccolgo l'alma, et poi ch' i' aggio
> di scovrirle il mio mal preso consiglio,
> tanto gli ò a dir che 'ncominciar non oso.

Full of a yearning thought that makes me stray away from all others and go alone in the world, from time to time I steal myself away from myself, still seeking only her whom I should flee;
and I see her pass so sweet and cruel that my soul trembles to rise in flight, such a crowd of armed sighs she leads, this lovely enemy of Love and me.
If I do not err, I do perceive a gleam of pity on her cloudy, proud brow, which partly clears my sorrowing heart:
then I collect my soul, and, when I have decided to discover my ills to her, I have so much to say to her that I dare not begin.

Wyatt, in his translation of this sonnet, reinterprets the speaker's incapacity to utter what is in his heart, so that the mood and meaning are very different from those of his model.

Departures from the original in the English version are many and various. Some are substitutions or additions of single words and phrases; elsewhere Wyatt takes suggestions from the Italian but reshapes them in keeping with his other changes; at several points he inserts clauses or whole lines which have no parallel in the original. Because such an elaborate variety of revisions works in a unified direction toward complicating the speaker's inward state, and increasing his difficulty in articulating it, they show some deliberation in Wyatt's choices. They are dictated by assumptions that seem to have emerged in the course of his work in the sonnet form:

Suche vayn thought as wonted to myslede me
   In desert hope by well assured mone,
   Maketh me from compayne to live alone,
   In folowing her whome reason bid me fle.
She fleith as fast by gentill crueltie;
   And after her myn hert would fain be gone,
   But armed sighes my way do stoppe anone,
   Twixt hope and drede locking my libertie.
Yet, as I gesse, vnder disdaynfull browe
   One beame of pitie is in her clowdy loke,
   Which comforteth the mynde that erst for fere shoke:
And therewithall bolded I seke the way how
   To vtter the smert that I suffre within,
   But such it is, I not how to begyn.[42]

In the octave of the translation, the substitutions, additions, and revisions have the effect of complicating the lover's inward state. In the first quatrain, for example, his thought is said to be "vayn," but then to work upon him simultaneously with "desert hope by well assured mone," a line not modeled on the original. Its introduction allows multiple interpretations. Taking the phrase "desert hope" as a parallel to "vayn thought," the reader first understands it as barren hope, or, because the lover's feelings lead him away from society, lonely hope. In these senses the adjective is understood as deriving from the noun meaning a barren, uninhabited wasteland. It could, however, be formed from a different noun meaning worthiness of recompense by merit or demerit. This possibility allows the phrase to be interpreted as deserved hope, which the context of the sonnet supports because the lover later thinks he sees a hopeful sign which comforts his mind. With the added phrase "by well assured mone," which has no parallel in Petrarch's sonnet, line 2 invites still other interpretations. Perhaps the lover's hope has been accompanied by his undoubted moaning. Yet it is also possible that his hope, either wasted or deserved, has been raised by the power of his own complaint, which itself might be either confident or presumptuous, other current meanings for "assured." The obscurity of what is in the lover's heart demands ambiguous language requiring multiple interpretation.

Such changes prepare for Wyatt's revision of the sestet, which enlarges on the difficulty for the lover of articulating what is in his heart. Where in the original sonnet the gleam of pity perceived by the lover encourages him to collect his soul, and makes him decide to reveal his woe to the lady, Wyatt's lover is much less certain and resolved. He can only "seke the way how" to speak, in a more confused and groping manner, and his search is frustrated by the difficulty of articulating inward states, as the revision of the last line shows. For this lover is mute, not because he does not dare to address his beautiful enemy, but because he does not know how. The introduction of "seke" with the repetition of "how" underline his uncertainty about the way "To vtter the smert that I suffre within." He can name it "smert," but at the same time cannot "vtter" it, because, "such it is," it frustrates his powers of expression.

This baffling paradox creates for the lover a problem of language which is different from the tongue-tied condition of Petrarch's lover, and which also differs fundamentally from the verbal difficulties that sometimes overcome the speakers in Wyatt's other love poems. A representative instance has been shown in the song "Suche happe as I." There the lover cannot utter his present suffering because it is so new and strange that he has not yet learned what to call it, whereas he can confidently express his familiar "dedely pain" by naming it with a noun adjective which places it in a category conventional to the complaint. In the sonnet as Wyatt revises it, his lover calls his suffering by a name which nevertheless is for him inadequate to "vtter" what is "within" him. The distance between the lover's language and his inward state is measured by some of the meanings available for the verb *utter*. It could mean the action of giving out audible sounds, but according to the *O.E.D.* it was used with special frequency from 1525 to 1590 to mean the act of disclosing something unknown, hidden, or secret. In the context of the sonnet, this meaning intensifies the speaker's difficulty. What he wishes to articulate is elusive and veiled, perhaps obscured even from himself.

Wyatt's sonnet departs from its model in taking as its argument a kind of uneasiness about the relationship of utterance to what is in the heart. This sense is also implied by its stylistic devices, which are common to his sonnets, both translated and original. Rather than confidently assuming a recognizable correspondence between inward states and their names, the speaker in this sonnet is stricken mute by his awareness of the distance between what is within him and what his language is capable of uttering. He seeks but does not find a more adequate mode of expression, and the frustration of his effort is not here due to the newness or strangeness of his feeling. It is attributed to the obscurity of his inward state, which no single name or accumulation of categories is adequate to portray. What is in the heart is therefore implied to be not only hidden, secret, but perhaps ultimately unknowable. No catalogue, then, however numerous and diverse its categories, could render the complexity and ambiguity of the lover's inward states. To name them is not to express them, as is assumed in complaints like "Suche happe as I," but possibly to distort or misrepresent them.

The nature of Wyatt's interest in the relation of outward modes of expression to what the poet-lover experiences inwardly is still more clearly shown in his translation of Petrarch's Sonnet 49:

Perch' io t'abbia guardata di menzogna
a mio podere et onorato assai,
ingrata lingua, già però non m'ài
renduto onor, ma fatto ira et vergogna;

ché quanto più 'l tuo aiuto mi bisogna
per dimandar mercede, allor ti stai
sempre più fredda, et se parole fai
son imperfette et quasi d'uom che sogna!

Lagrime triste, et voi tutte le notti
m'accompagnate ov' io vorrei star solo,
poi fuggite dinanzi a la mia pace!

Et voi, sì pronti a darmi angoscia et duolo,
sospiri, allor traete lenti et rotti!
Solo la vista mia del cor non tace.

Although I have kept you from lying, as far as I could, and paid you
much honor, ungrateful tongue, still you have not brought me honor
but shame and anger;
for, the more I need your help to ask for mercy, the colder and colder
you stay, and if you say any words they are broken and like those
of a man dreaming!
Sad tears, you also every night accompany me, when I wish to be
alone, and then you flee when my peace comes!
And your sighs, so ready to give me anguish and sorrow, then you
move slow and broken! Only my eyes are not silent about my heart.

Wyatt's translation follows the structure of the original very closely, while
making changes in many details. These in fact give his version new interests, almost a wholly different character, by implying again a very different
sense of the relationship between the lover's outward modes of expression
and what is in his heart:

Bicause I have the still kept fro lyes and blame
    And to my power alwaies have I the honoured,
    Vnkynd tong right ill hast thou me rendred
    For suche deserft to do me wrek and shame.
In nede of succour moost when that I ame
    To aske reward, then standest thou like oon aferd
    Alway moost cold, and if thou speke towerd,
    It is as in dreme vnperfaict and lame.
And ye salt teres again my will eche nyght
    That are with me when fayn I would be alone,
    Then are ye gone when I should make my mone;
And you so reddy sighes to make me shright,
    Then are ye slake when that ye should owtestert,
    And onely my loke declareth my hert.[43]

The first minute change, the insertion of "still" in line 1, is representative of Wyatt's revisions throughout. Where it is placed, it demands double interpretation. For the line may be read to mean that the lover has continually prevented his tongue from lying, but also that he has kept his tongue quiet and so prevented it from lying. The first reading parallels Petrarch's opening line, but the second allows possibilities of interpretation not invited by the original. It raises questions about the way the lover uses language by suggesting that, for him, speaking is almost synonymous with misrepresentation. For him it is not sufficient to keep continual watch over his language; to avoid lying, he must stop speaking altogether. His tongue, when it is silent, is "Vnkynd" (not *ingrata,* ungrateful). This epithet means it is unnatural as well as cruel; it violates its kind by refusing to speak for the lover when he wants to persuade. His intention in complaining is not to utter his feelings but to gain what he calls "reward," a substitution for the Italian *mercede,* translatable as *mercy.* Again this revision points to a use of speech different from that of Petrarch's poet-lover. For to plead for mercy is to use the language of prayer such as a humble and contrite petitioner would address to God; it redeems the request from the taint of calculated self-interest. To ask for "reward" is a more worldly demand, for a more tangible result, the acquisition of a prize or recompense. Like "deserft," one of Wyatt's additions with no parallel in the original, it raises the question of what the speaker calculates that he deserves and that he manipulates language to obtain. His unnatural tongue, by deserting him in this effort, has frustrated it. Instead of reward, it has rendered him "right ill," another insertion of wording requiring double interpretation. The phrase can be paraphrased: "you have poorly rendered me what I rightly deserve," and: "you have rendered me in an altogether ill manner." By inserting this ambiguous syntax, Wyatt complicates the issue of the lover's silence. His muteness can no longer be explained solely by the convention (on which assumption the Italian original is predicated) that the extremity of his passion overcomes his power of speech. For there is also the possibility that his manipulations of language have backfired, that his tongue has rendered him right, either by refusing to comply with his manipulations of language, or by playing tricks with speech as he has done. Such recompense of deceit, the speaker in "There was never ffile" calls "aggreable," that is, congruous, fitting. The lover in this sonnet has also, according to one possible interpretation, habitually used language for purposes other than to express what is in his heart, so that his speech has become a file, an instrument for polishing but also a deceiver. He can no longer control his utterance, or other outward modes of expression, to gain self-interested ends.

Wyatt's revisions in the sestet, describing the uncooperative behavior of the lover's sighs and tears, allow for an interpretation parallel to the meaning of the original Italian, while sustaining simultaneously the possibility of a very different reading consistent with the implications of earlier changes. In Petrarch's sonnet, for example, the lover's tears flee the presence of his peace, another reverential tribute to the lady's grace and power. Wyatt's line substitutes: "Then are ye gone when I should make my mone." Again the revision contains the suggestion that his lover habitually manipulates the expression of his feelings, and that again his calculations fail him. He cannot make tears come when he needs them, perhaps because his are not genuinely sad (*triste*) but merely "salt." Similarly Wyatt rearranges his description of the speaker's sighs to allow the suggestion that they too are instruments for persuasion rather than modes of expressing what is in his heart. "And you so reddy sighes to make me shright" can be paraphrased: "you sighs which are so ready to make me shriek," and also: "you so easily produced sighs which make me shriek," a reading sustained by the next line accusing them of slackness at the opportune moment when they "should owtestert."

Finally this lover does not even speak what is in his heart directly through his sight, because Wyatt characteristically substitutes the more ambiguous word "loke." The lover may declare his heart by the direction of his glance; he may also reveal or disguise it by the appearance of his countenance. As the last of so many revisions raising questions about the relation of outward expression to inward states, the final line cannot be read as identical in meaning with Petrarch's. Wyatt sustains to the end the added suggestions introduced by his many revisions throughout the sonnet. His lover's language cannot be trusted to express what is in his heart because words are at a distance from inward states, not commensurate with them. Language may even be double-edged, so that it can simultaneously reveal and disguise.

Wyatt's translations from Petrarch's sonnet sequence have been seen to share many interests with his other love poetry. Motifs that he adapted from Petrarch were also already established in the native tradition of the complaint; its styles of extremity and diversity are characteristic also of sonnets he chose for translation. Even the common device of the catalogue used in complaints to depict the intensity and variousness of love is incorporated into the total structure of three of Wyatt's sonnet translations from Petrarch: a list of the lover's contrary states in 'I fynde no peace"; catalogues of his modes of expressing them in 'Yf amours faith" and "Bicause I have the still kept." Yet many of the sonnets depart from Wyatt's practice in his other love poems by devices of language rarely used by him in other forms. Ambiguous syntax, words capable of having more than one reference or bearing more than one meaning, language therefore demanding multiple interpretation, can be found in abundance in Wyatt's sonnets, both translated and original, but seldom in his other poetry.

Instances there of such practices are very rare. "In eternum," in the phrase "and still to hold my pease," uses the same double meaning for "still" that functions in the sonnet translation "Bicause I have the still kept."[44] In "Though this the port," the refrain "en vogant la galere" may be literally translated as "while rowing in the galley," and also given its proverbial meaning, "come what may."[45] Yet such doubleness exists almost nowhere else in Wyatt's poetry other than his sonnets, with the single exception of his most famous love poem, "They fle from me."[46] Although not a sonnet, this poem is also distinct from much of Wyatt's other love poetry in that it is not a song. It does not catalogue the lover's inward experiences in an additive structure with a refrain at the end of each stanza. Instead it resembles more closely the structure of many of Wyatt's sonnets in that it develops dramatically, and by means of ambiguities of language also associated with Wyatt's sonnets. Characteristically, these multiple wordings cluster most thickly toward the end of the poem, so that the last stanza works toward effects parallel to those created by Wyatt's practice in the couplet endings of his sonnets:

> It was no dreme: I lay brode waking.
> But all is torned thorough my gentilnes
> Into a straunge fasshion of forsaking;
> And I have leve to goo of her goodeness,
> And she also to vse new fangilnes.
> But syns that I so kyndely ame serued,
> I would fain knowe what she hath deserued.

Especially the meanings of "kyndely" create effects like those habitual in the sonnets. Understood as benignly, the word combines with the lover's use of "goodeness" in describing the lady's behavior, of "gentilnes" to characterize his own. All three describe inward qualities but also manners, a suave conventionality that grates with the other definition of "kyndely" as meaning according to nature. Yet the two meanings exist simultaneously for the speaker. This doubleness creates the impression that the inward states involved in his recounting of his remembered experience are so complex, ambiguous, contradictory, that he cannot render them by naming them. It also allows the possibility that his language may reveal states that he does not recognize in himself. At the same time it points to the capacity of language for hiding one meaning behind another, as courtly conventionality can cover with "gentilnes" what is naked and wild in human nature. In these respects the poem is unique among Wyatt's nonsonnets.

Wyatt's love poems other than sonnets are concerned, even obsessed with truth, honesty, deceit, disguise, "coloured dowblenes," and the lover's efforts "To fassion faith to wordes mutable."[47] They show distrust of language insofar as it can be used for lying, and suspicion of it especially when it is elaborate or filed; the opposite of "plain" is "fals."[48] Yet these attitudes can be distinguished from those which the sonnets imply by their ways of complicating what is in the lover's heart and rendering it in ambiguous language. To make such a distinction, it is useful to set side by side a sonnet translation and a song in which Wyatt uses some of the same vocabulary for the relation of outward expression to inward states.

A three-part song on the theme of the opening line, "Lo what it is to love!" contains this stanza addressed to the slanderers of love:

> Ye graunt it is a snare
> And would vs not beware;
> Lest that your trayne
> Should be to playne
> Ye colour all the care;
> Lo how you fayne
> Pleasure for payne
> And graunt it is a snare![49]

Wyatt found in Petrarch's Sonnet 102 an exploration of the same conventional motif of a lover disguising his inward state by outward expression of its opposite. He translated it in some of the same key words he uses in the song:

> Caesar, when that the traytour of Egipt
>   With th'onourable hed did him present,
>   Covering his gladness did represent
>   Playnt with his teeres owteward, as it is writt:
> And Hannyball eke, when fortune him shitt
>   Clene from his reign and from all his intent,
>   Laught to his folke whome sorrowe did torment,
>   His cruell dispite for to disgorge and qwit.
> So chaunceth it oft that every passion
>   The mynde hideth by colour contrary
>   With fayned visage, now sad, now mery:
> Whereby, if I laught, any tyme, or season
>   It is for bicause I have nother way
>   To cloke my care but vnder spoort and play.[50]

This lover goes beyond the hints of the speaker in "Bicause I have the still kept" to open confession that he has manipulated outward looks to disguise what is in his heart. Although he uses many of the same terms for this process as the speaker in the song, his way of doing so here complicates both the nature of his inward state and the process of covering it, in ways that distinguish the sonnet from the song. The deliberateness of this complication is shown by the fact that it is achieved through a consistent pattern of departures from the original Italian sonnet.

After closely translating the octave of his model, composed of the two classical examples of dissimulation, Wyatt follows them, as does Petrarch, with a generalization about the process of disguising what is in the heart by contrary appearance, which the lover then applies to himself. In these lines Wyatt departs significantly from the sestet of the original:

> et così aven che l'animo ciascuna
> sua passion sotto 'l contrario manto
> ricopre co la vista or chiara or bruna.
>
> Però s' alcuna volta io rido o canto,
> facciol perch' i' non ò se non quest'una
> via da celare il mio angoscioso pianto.

and thus it happens that each soul covers its passion over with the contrary mantle, with a face now clear, now dark.
Therefore if at any time I laugh or sing, I do it because I have no way except this one to hide my anguished weeping.

Wyatt's characteristic substitution in the last line of a noun capable of more than one interpretation, "care," is the culmination of meanings introduced by his other changes. It could mean lamentation, the utterance of sorrow, and so be synonymous with Petrarch's *pianto*. The lover hides the true expression of his pain with falsely cheerful utterance. The word "care" could also describe his inward or unexpressed passion of sorrow, making the lover's state more secret and obscure. It could simultaneously define his state of mind, concern, heedfulness, serious mental attention, such as he gives but does not appear to give, to dissembling. These multiple meanings of "care," making it at once a category of passion and of mind, sustain ambiguities introduced earlier by Wyatt's revisions of lines 9 to 11. They are arranged so that the grammar is reversible: "mynde" and "passion" are interchangeable as subject and object, a reversal not allowed by the Italian original. There the poet-lover's soul has a kind of control over both his emotions and his countenance. In Wyatt's revised lines, however, while the mind (a characteristic substitution for soul in his translations) is understood to have power over passion, it is also true that every passion has power over the mind. One effect of this grammatical ambiguity is to complicate the generalization about inward experience. Different powers within the lover act upon one another simultaneously, so that they are not distinguishable like categories in a catalogue. Their effects cannot be rendered by listing them. The relation between the mind and the passions, the inward state of "care" and the process of disguising it, demand more than one interpretation. They therefore cannot be expressed simply by being named, as in the song. The workings of mind and passions are difficult to describe, as it is difficult to interpret a "fayned visage." This substituted phrase, by its own multiple meanings, further widens the distance between inward states and their outward expression. For "visage" could be synonymous with the simpler meaning of face, but was commonly defined as assumed appearance or outward show, so that feigning becomes a more conscious and sustained disguise than mere changes of facial expression. Furthermore, "visage" could also be defined as portrait or image, making the process by which mind and passions disguise each other analogous to the inventions of art, with which the words "fayned" and "colour" were also associated.[51] The process goes beyond lies or misleading facial expressions to the invention of an image more widely distanced from the lover's unexpressed or invisible "care." That inward passion and state of mind, and the process of representing it by false color or disguising cloak, require a far more complex rendering than the feigning of pleasure for pain in Wyatt's song. There no ambiguities demand multiple interpretation, so that words—even precisely those exploited for their doubleness in the sonnet—act as single definitions allowing simple recognition by the audience. The singer, as a further result, is not implicated in the process of feigning. No questions are raised about his uses of language, his representations of inward states, or his recognition of their true nature.

The uses of language which distinguish Wyatt's sonnet from his song were in this instance evidently not learned directly from the particular Petrarchan model he chose to translate. For the complicating and ambiguous devices are most often created by departures from the original rather than by strict imitation of it. In this respect they are representative of Wyatt's sonnet translations. Yet the fact that the distinct kind of language is used almost exclusively by him in sonnets shows that he must have developed it out of his work in that form, perhaps in the actual procedure of fitting his translation within the restrictions and possibilities set by the form to which he committed himself.

This development of a distinct kind of poetry can be explained in part by the formal elements of a sonnet in contrast to Wyatt's other love poems, which are commonly songs or poems in imitation of sung verse. Fourteen lines of interlaced rhyme demand a more sustained development than a typical song linking stanzas which are often shorter, with a simpler pattern of rhymes. An example is a five-stanza song to which the editor of Tottel's miscellany gave a title recapitulating its catalogue form: "The louer praieth not to be disdained, refused, mistrusted, nor forsaken":[52]

> Dysdaine me not without desert
> Nor leaue me not so sodeynly
> Sence wel ye wot that in my hart

I meane nothing but honestly.
    Dysdayne me not.

Refuse me not without cause why,
Nor thynke me not to be vniust;
Synce that by lot of fantasye
The carefull knot nedes knyt I must,
    Refuse me not.

Mystrust me not though some there be
That fayne would spot my stedfastnes;
Beleue them not, sins that ye se
The profe is not as they expresse.
    Mystrust me not.

Forsake me not til I deserue,
Nor hate me not, tyll I offend,
Destroy me not, tyll that I swerue;
But sins ye know what I intend,
    Forsake me not.

Dysdaine me not that am your owne;
Refuse me not that am so true;
Mystrust me not til al be knowen;
Forsake me neuer for no new:
    Disdayne me not.[53]

A sonnet is equivalent in number of lines to two stanzas of rhyme royal, one of the longest units in which Wyatt works and which he uses often in his love poems. Yet because a sonnet is not a stanzaic form, it does not invite the additive effect that songs encourage by the possibility of an undetermined number of stanzas—an additional stanza beginning "Betray me not" could be inserted without disturbing the structure of the quoted song—and a repeated refrain. By contrast, in the structure of a sonnet all the lines including the last must be interconnected but cannot repeat except in rhyming sounds. There is therefore a forward movement up to the last line, which simultaneously advances and concludes the development of interrelated and predetermined parts of the whole poem. One can measure this distinction in Wyatt's sonnet translation "I fynde no peace," which follows the essentially cumulative structure of songs insofar as it is a catalogue. Yet is uses the ending to make a conclusion which is neither the last item in a list nor a reiteration like "Dysdaine me not."

Wyatt's understanding of the difference between the typically cumulative structure of his songs and the development demanded by the sonnet form can be demonstrated most clearly if this or any other of his known sonnets is set beside an unascribed sonnet from the Devonshire manuscript. This poem has fourteen lines of interlaced rhymes ending, as was Wyatt's practice, in a couplet, but shows otherwise none of his awareness of the structural demands of this form.

> I abide and abide and better abide,
>   And after the olde prouerbe the happie daye;
>   And ever my ladye to me dothe saye
>   'Let my alone and I will prouyde'.
> I abide and abide and tarrye the tyde
>   And with abiding spede well ye maye;
>   Thus do I abide I wott allwaye,
>   Nother obtayning nor yet denied.
> Aye me! this long abidyng
>   Semithe to me as who sayethe
>   A prolonging of a dieng dethe
> Or a refusing of a desyrid thing:
>   Moche ware it bettre for to be playne,
>   Then to saye abide and yet shall not obtayne.[54]

The groupings of lines resemble more the additive effect of stanzas in a song with a repeated refrain than the relationship of octave and sestet, or of three quatrains and a couplet advancing a sustained development of interrelated but not repeated parts. Such structural differences in the sonnet form might encourage the kind of complication and ambiguity of language peculiar to Wyatt's sonnets by its greater complexity in the relationship of parts within a larger number of lines than song stanzas contain. By the practice of ending always with a couplet, Wyatt heightened this structural effect, because that device habitually coincides in his sonnets with the introduction of ambiguous language to reflect with a complicating twist on the sonnet as a whole.

The songlike quality of "I abide and abide," by contrast with Wyatt's sonnets, is also a product of the chanting cadence of its repetitions, especially in lines 1 and 5. Because they are evenly placed, their effect is more rhythmical than repetitions in "There was never ffile" (itself unusual among Wyatt's sonnets in pronounced use of repetition). Further resemblance to songs in "I abide and abide" is in its apparent breakdown in the middle into a shorter line. Wyatt's songs often use stanzas made up of lines with uneven lengths, repeated in the same pattern, which imitates musical form and contributes to the additive effect. In sonnets, however, Wyatt respects the principal of virtually equal line lengths supporting the relationship of parts demanded by the rhyme scheme.

The distinct nature of the sonnet as Wyatt understood it must in these ways have contributed to the creation of a language appropriate to the form. It may be also that the actual procedure of transposing the meaning of such a strictly limited number of lines from one language to another, within the further restrictions of rhyme and line length, alerted Wyatt to new possibilities. This, of course, is only speculation, but in support of it, it is useful to look again at Wyatt's translation of Petrarch's Sonnet 102 on the soul's power to hide inward states by the outward show of contrary passions. Wyatt here not only committed himself to the sonnet form, but to the structure of this particular model, which dictated the devotion of the first two quatrains to the two examples of dissimulation. He was then allowed only three lines for a generalization about the process of feigning, and three to confessing the lover's participation in that process. It seems possible that, fitting in the English words for Petrarch's original generalization, Wyatt may have been forced to move them around like pieces in a puzzle, and in doing so might discover, for example, that the equivalents of Petrarch's grammatical subject and object could be arranged so that they are reversible. Such an arrangement results in the kind of ambiguity virtually absent from Wyatt's other love poems. A discovery of this kind would reinforce the effects encouraged by the sonnet form as distinct from other types of verse, allowing greater complexity and ambiguity than the additive structure of songs and the catalogues typical of the lover's complaint.

There is a further difference between Wyatt's sonnets and most of his other love poems which also might have encouraged the distinctions in their uses of language. This is a difference in their actual or imagined mode of presentation. Many of the love poems were either designed to be accompanied by music, or were in imitation of poems that would actually be sung to the strains of the lute or other courtly instruments. This meant that they needed simpler verbal effects; it would be virtually impossible for an audience listening to sung poems to make the kinds of multiple interpretations that are demanded by Wyatt's sonnets and, among his other poems, almost uniquely by "They fle from me" (which, although stanzaic, is not in the style of a sung poem).

The uses of language so far identified as peculiar to Wyatt's sonnets may have developed in these ways out of his conception of the sonnet form and through the actual demands of translation within its strict dictates. They also may have been encouraged by other devices of language apparently learned directly from his chosen Petrarchan models. For a further distinction to be drawn between Wyattt's sonnets and his other love poems is their frequent rendering of what is in the heart through metaphors more extended and elaborate than any he uses elsewhere. This figurative language itself works toward a kind of suggestiveness which, like verbal practices demanding multiple interpretation, is fundamentally different from the declarative style of Wyatt's other love poems.

Earlier discussion in this chapter of the sonnet translation "My galy charged with forgetfulnes" focused on Wyatt's characteristic introduction in the last line of ambiguous wording creating more than one possible interpretaion of the lover's state. In the previous thirteen lines the translation follows in most details the comparison in Petrarch's Sonnet 189 of the lover's inward state to the journey of a ship. Perhaps Wyatt was drawn to this model because the comparison was already established in the native tradition—stretching back to its roots in troubadour poetry and ultimately in Ovid—of the complaint.[55] Wyatt himself uses it in one such poem, consisting of rhyme royal stanzas ending in a refrain, "en vogant la galere," which repeats the nautical comparison in its literal meaning, "while rowing in the galley."[56] Although scarcely developed, the metaphor is more extended than those characteristic of a Wyatt song. For they commonly consist in single phrases such as "poyson, plesant swete," or "wyndy wordes."[57] Often they are clichés which have virtually lost their metaphorical function. Others may not have been conceived to be figurative, but rather to be literal expressions of inward parallels to outward phenomena: "burnyng sighes."[58]

Nevertheless, the metaphorical functions of the comparison between what is in the lover's heart and a voyage are limited in the song even though the figure recurs in each stanza:

> Though this thy port and I thy seruaunt true
> And thou thy self doist cast thy bemes from hye
> From thy chieff howse promising to renew
> Boeth Joye and eke delite, behold yet how that I
> Bannysshed from my blisse carefully do crye:
> 'Helpe now, Citherea, my lady dere,
> My ferefull trust en vogant la galere.'
>
> Alas the dowbt that dredfull absence geveth;
> Withoute thyn ayde assurance is there none;
> The ferme faith that in the water fleteth
> Succour thou therefor; in the it is alone.
> Stay that with faith that faithfully doeth mone,
> And thou also gevest me boeth hope and fere,
> Remembre thou me en vogant la galere.
>
> By Sees and hilles elonged form thy sight,
> Thy wonted grace reducing to my mynde
> In sted of slepe thus I occupy the nyght;
> A thowsand thoughtes and many dowbtes I fynde,
> And still I trust thou canst not be vnkind
> Or els despere my comfort, and my chiere
> Would fle fourthwith en vogant la galere.
>
> Yet on my faith full litle doeth remain
> Of any hope whereby I may my self vphold,
> For syns that onely wordes do me retain,

I may well thinck the affection is but cold;
But syns my will is nothing as I would
But in thy handes it resteth hole and clere,
Forget me not en vogant la galere.

The recurrence of the refrain creates the structure of this song, rather than the metaphor of the voyage which, after the first two lines, otherwise surfaces only in line 10 and rather confusedly in line 15, where the coupling of "Sees and hilles" almost obliterates the image of a journey by water. The repetition of the refrain may suggest the tedious duration of the voyage, but otherwise the comparison is scarcely developed as a way of rendering the lover's inward state. By contrast, in "My galy charged with forgetfulnes," Wyatt imitates Petrarch's Sonnet 189 not only in developing the metaphor as a structural principle but also in exploiting the comparison for its suggestiveness:

My galy charged with forgetfulnes
　Thorrough sharpe sees in wynter nyghtes doeth pas
　Twene Rock and Rock; and eke myn ennemy, Alas,
　That is my lorde, sterith with cruelnes;
And every owre a thought in redines,
　As tho that deth were light in suche a case;
　An endles wynd doeth tere the sayll a pase
　Of forced sightes and trusty ferefulnes.
A rayn of teris, a clowde of derk disdain
　Hath done the wered cordes great hinderaunce,
　Wrethed with errour and eke with ignoraunce.
The starres be hid that led me to this pain;
　Drowned is reason that should me confort,
　And I remain dispering of the port.[59]

Details evoke the quality of the metaphorical experience, what it would be like to sail in a solitary vessel steered by a powerful enemy, through stormy waters in wet and wintry darkness. The lover's inward state is like that of such a traveler, driven but lost, buffeted, lonely, in great danger of being dashed to pieces or sinking into cold and violent depths. What is more, Wyatt's few departures from the original wording of the comparison work toward describing the journey in greater physical detail than suited Petrarch's more abstract treatment, so that what is in the lover's heart is represented more immediately. For instance, he substitutes "Twene Rock and Rock" for Petrarch's more distantly mythologized Scylla and Charybdis. Similarly Wyatt replaces Petrarch's allegorical phrasing in line 12, *Celansi i duo mei dolci usate segni* ("My two usual sweet stars are hidden"), with "The starres be hid," treating more literally the actual plight of a sailor lost in winter darkness with no signs to guide his course. By all these means he therefore makes greater use than in his song of the metaphorical voyage as a means of rendering what is in the speaker's heart.

In doing so he implies a different sense of the nature of inward states in relation to language than is characteristic of his love poems other than sonnets. That is, woven into the extended comparison are the names for categories of inward states conventional to the lover's complaint. Especially the second quatrain contains a familiar catalogue of causes of woe and the lover's modes of expressing it. But unlike "The sorrowfull teres, the sighes hote as fyer" of a poem like "Alas the greiff," which are simply listed, the sighs and tears of the lover in the sonnet translation are woven into the metaphorical design of the whole poem. His sighs are compared to winter wind which rips to useless shreds the buffeted sails; his tears are like freezing rain beating upon the fraying ropes. They are therefore associated with many qualities that are not explicitly named as categories in a catalogue, or paired with modifiers like "sorrowfull," defining the division to which they belong within the category of "teares." To ensure the full suggestive force of the comparison, Wyatt further imitates Petrarch in naming the metaphorical term first—wind before sighs, rain before tears, cloud before disdain, drowned before reason—so that the experiences of the journey are first evoked and then attached to the lover's inward state. This order invites multiple points of comparison, endowing the second term with a variety of qualities associated with the first term. By contrast a phrase such as "sighes hote as fyer" virtually limits the comparison to a single point of likeness, and also tends to reduce the metaphorical force of the second term. The phrase works more as a noun adjective—*burning sighs*—than as an evocative comparison, and may in fact not have been conceived as figurative. Its effect is to name, whereas Wyatt's uses of metaphor in this sonnet translation evoke multiple aspects of the lover's inward state and imply that their multiplicity cannot easily be defined, can only be suggested.

The choice of other models and the adaptations and revisions of them in Wyatt's sonnet translations show this interest in using extended metaphors to suggest rather than to name inward states. For example, Petrarch's Sonnet 19 extends a comparison between the lover in dangerous pursuit of the lady and animals who play with fire. Wyatt's translation follows the structure of his model, describing first the different ways that varieties of creatures respond to light and then applying the comparison to the lover so that multiple qualities are associated with his inward state:

> Som fowles there be that have so perfaict sight,
>   Agayn the Sonne their Iyes for to defend,
>   And som, bicause the light doeth theim offend,

Do never pere but in the darke or nyght.
Other reioyse that se the fyer bright
    And wene to play in it as they do pretend,
    And fynde the contrary of it that they intend.
    Alas, of that sort I may be by right,
For to withstond her loke I ame not able;
    And yet can I not hide me in no darke place,
    Remembraunce so foloweth me of that face,
So that with tery yen swolne and vnstable,
    My destyne to behold her doeth me lede;
    Yet do I knowe I runne into the glede.[60]

Set beside a typical comparison from Wyatt's songs, such as "sighes hote as fyer," this can be seen to be a far more elaborate use of the metaphorical possibilities of language. By following Petrarch in describing the actions of the animals before comparing them to the lover's inward state, Wyatt defines it by multiple qualities. Even the types of birds who are dismissed as unlike the lover actually attach associations to him: the need for defense against the power of brilliant light (the sun's and the lady's), or the longing for protection in dark and secret places. Then to heighten the evocative power of the metaphorical experience with which the lover's inward state is compared, Wyatt characteristically makes it more immediate and more violent. Where Petrarch in line 12 describes the lover looking at the lady's brilliance *con gli occhi lagrimosi e 'infermi* ("with tearful and weak eyes"), Wyatt evokes the physical discomfort of gazing into a glare "with tery yen swolne and vnstable." In the last line of the translation the lover does not pursue what burns him, but is compelled with more impulsive destructiveness to "runne into the glede." Like its Italian model, Wyatt's translation carries the central metaphor into the couplet, where he then characteristically exploits ambiguity of syntax and diction to give a complicating twist to the presentation of the lover's inward state. Line 13 is actually an exact transposition of the word order in the parallel Italian line: *mio destino a vederla mi conduce.* This syntax allows the line to be paraphrased: "My destiny leads me to behold her," and also: "My destiny, which is to behold her, leads me," a double interpretation making the lover doubly doomed. This ambiguity works in the same direction as his development of metaphor, toward complicating the presentation of the lover's inward state, which here can be suggested but not named, even by adding categories. It can be presented only in language demanding multiple interpretation. This instance shows therefore how the kind of metaphor Wyatt imitated in Petrarch works toward the same effects as his devices of ambiguous diction and syntax.

Wyatt's transformation of Petrarch's Sonnet 190 is a still more striking development of metaphor to suggest the multiplicity of inward states also achieved by the verbal ambiguities in his sonnets. Here the adaptation

becomes a poem almost wholly different in kind from the original. In the
Italian model, the poet-lover recounts a visionary appearance of a white
doe whose unattainable beauty he vainly follows, although warned away
by the jeweled inscription on her collar. Wyatt turns this allegorical pursuit into a metaphor of hunting a deer, a word with multiple meanings
which may themselves have shown him the suggestive possibilities of his
comparison.[61] For the word spelled "Diere" in the Egerton manuscript
was interchangeable with *deer* and *dear,* allowing the hunted creature in
his metaphor to be compared to a woman held precious by the speaker
simultaneously in the sense of being beloved, but also of being costly,
expensive, like the diamonds in her collar spelling out her unattainable
price:

> Who so list to hounte I knowe where is an hynde;
>   But as for me, helas, I may no more:
>   The vayne travaill hath weried me so sore,
>   I ame of theim that farthest cometh behinde;
> Yet may I by no meanes my weried mynde
>   Drawe from the Diere: but as she fleeth afore
>   Faynting I folowe; I leve of therefore,
>   Sithens in a nett I seke to hold the wynde.
> Who list her hount I put him owte of dowbte,
>   As well as I may spend his tyme in vain:
>   And graven with Diamondes in letters plain
> There is written her faier neck rounde abowte:
>   'Noli me tangere for Cesars I ame,
>   And wylde for to hold though I seme tame.'[62]

The multiple meanings of the word "Diere" work with the evocative
power of the metaphor of hunting—a type of "travaill" which is journeying as well as laboring and suffering—to present the lover's inward state
more suggestively than in any of Wyatt's love poems other than sonnets
(with the one usual exception of "They fle from me," which this sonnet
especially resembles). Ambiguous syntax contributes to the same effect
when the lover assures that any willing rival "As well as I may spend his
tyme in vain." Read to mean "as I do, in the same manner as I," the
phrasing supports the lover's claim to see the vanity of his ways, which
he has just renounced. The phrase may also be paraphrased, "as skillfully,
as effectively as I do," sarcastically extending the mocking picture of
himself as a proverbial fool catching wind in a net. Yet "as well as I" may
be read "in addition to me," revealing that the lover who claims to leave
the hunt has in fact no resolve to do so. He continues in the present to
spend his time in vain. For his "Diere" remains beloved to him even as
he recognizes the cost to him of hunting her, and her sale to a richer
bidder. He will pursue his exhausting course, taking bitter satisfaction

only in sharing its humiliation with equally unsuccessful rivals. The effect
of multiple diction and syntax is therefore to make the development of
the metaphor dramatic, and in doing so to raise questions about the
relation of language to inward states that would not be raised, for example,
by the lover's complaint to his bed. There the lover's capacity to catalogue
the causes and effects of his sufferings, however extreme and diverse, does
not invite the reader to ask if he actually understands what they are. Nor
does it raise the question whether, knowing them, he is nevertheless attempting to disguise them from himself to spare further pain, or hiding
them from an audience in order to protect them. These questions are
raised by the language of "Who so list to hounte," however, again marking
a radical distinction in kind between the style of Wyatt's sonnets and his
other love poems.

The metaphors in the complaint of the lover forsaking his bed have
been shown to be characteristic of Wyatt's verse other than sonnets in
their undeveloped and almost nonfigurative character. They are also representative because many of them are personifications in the form of
apostrophe, a common device in complaints not in sonnet form by Wyatt
as well as other poets of the period. The catalogues of "Alas the greiff,"
for example, include numerous vocatives in the second stanza:

> O lost seruise! O payn ill rewarded!
> O pitifull hert with payn enlarged!
> O faithfull mynde, too sodenly assented![63]

and in the third stanza: "O cruel causer of vndeserued chaunge." The
apostrophe is an obvious device for representing the extremity of the
lover's suffering. It shows him impelled to call out, and with such force
that his exclamations seem to charge the world with answering passion.
To multiply apostrophes by cataloguing them renders the diversity of
love, so that the device is suited to the traditional styles of the complaint.
Such use of apostrophe depends on the same assumptions as the reliance
on catalogues. What is in the heart can be expressed by names; inward
states are commensurate with their outward manifestations, including
complaining. Typically, the quoted sequence of apostrophes, like other
catalogues, mingles without distinction names for outward modes of expression, for inward states, and for the parts of the lover on which they act.
Another poem opens with a catalogue of apostrophes which virtually
identifies "plain," or complaining, with "pain," making utterance the
perfect mirror of what is in the heart:

> Resound my voyse, ye woodes that here me plain,
> Boeth hilles and vales causing reflexion;
> And Ryvers eke record ye of my pain.[64]

Wyatt's sonnets, on the other hand, although they often represent the extremity of love by the exclamation "Alas," virtually never use apostrophe.[65] Forms of personifications in the sonnet also differ from those typical of his other love poems. For personifications in his sonnets, both translated and original, share the qualities of extension and elaboration with such metaphors as the journey and the hunt, having the effect of exploiting their suggestive power. What the sonnets personify also distinguishes them from Wyatt's other love poems, which endow objects or places with human qualities in the same way that they personify the lover's inward parts, his passions, and his modes of expressing them. The sonnets, on the contrary, do not commonly describe in human terms things or places external to the lover, or even his own modes of expression such as sighs, tears, or complaints. The sonnets personify his heart and mind and passions, in characteristically extended and elaborate figures, like the other metaphors he apparently learned to develop in adapting Petrarch's sonnets. Often he carries them in directions showing interests very different from those of his models, but in keeping with the changes introduced by the verbal ambiguities in his other adaptations.

In Wyatt's translation of Petrarch's Sonnet 140, for example, he adapts the extended personification of love as a feudal lord, but by changes of detail gives greater emphasis to the identification of "love" with the speaker's inward state than with a god who rules over him:

> The longe love, that in my thought doeth harbar
> And in myn hert doeth kepe his residence,
> Into my face preseth with bold pretence,
> And therin campeth, spreding his baner.
> She that me lerneth to love and suffre
> And will that my trust, and lustes negligence
> Be rayned by reason, shame, and reverence
> With his hardines taketh displeasure.
> Wherewithall, vnto the hertes forrest he fleith,
> Leving his enterprise with payne and cry
> And there him hideth and not appereth.
> What may I do when my maister fereth,
> But, in the felde, with him to lyve and dye?
> For goode is the liff, ending faithfully.[66]

The changes in key details again turn what is essentially allegory in Petrarch's poem into metaphor, with effects which show most clearly when Wyatt's first question is compared with Petrarch's:

> Amor, che nel penser mio vive et regna
> e 'l suo seggio maggior nel mil cor tene,

talor armato ne la fronte vene;
ivi si loca et ivi pon suo insegna.

Love, who lives and reigns in my thought and keeps his principal
seat in my heart, sometimes comes forth all in armor into my fore-
head, there camps, and there sets up his banner.

Petrarch's opening word almost invokes the god of love as in apostrophe,
whereas Wyatt's version lifts "love" out of mythology by calling it "longe,"
restricting its reference here to the enduring passion harbored deep within
the speaker's mind and heart. The translation does not allow the comparison of love to a feudal lord, present in the Italian sonnet from the beginning, to emerge until the end of the second line, and in line 3 substitutes
for martial imagery a characteristically more physical detail, "Into my
face preseth," more directly evoking the force of passion which the lover
cannot hide.

Another departure from his model working toward parallel effects occurs in the beginning of the sestet. The original reads: *Onde Amor pavento-
so fugge al core* ("Wherefore Love flees terrified to my heart"). Wyatt
transforms the line: "Wherewithall, vnto the hertes forrest he fleith." The
focus shifts again from the allegorized figure of the god to the metaphor
of the lover's inward state as the "hertes forrest."[67] Though not extended
or elaborated like the other metaphors typical of Wyatt's sonnets, this is
nevertheless like them in creating multiple suggestions, and in this respect
differing in kind from the metaphors characteristic of Wyatt's other love
poetry. The noun adjective "stony hert" is representative of those figures,
in which the modifying word attaches a single metaphorical quality which
defines the division within the category to which the noun belongs: among
varieties of heart, this one is of the stony type.[68] The comparison of heart
to stone is so familiar and so undeveloped that it does not exploit the
suggestive possibilities of stoniness. Nor does it evoke qualities of the
lover's experience who exhausts or bruises or baffles himself by attempting to move or soften or leave a mark on such a heart. In its effects it could
be virtually interchangeable with another representative figure, "frosen
hert."[69] Similarly, the refrain of a stanzaic love poem by Wyatt illustrates
a differently constructed metaphor which nevertheless has virtually the
same effect: "the Iye is traitour of the herte."[70] The personification of the
eye as a betrayer logically makes the heart into a metaphorical figure as
well, but no other quality is attached by the phrase itself to the personified
heart other than the capacity to be betrayed. It is not, for instance, a once
mighty monarch whose rightful place has been stripped from him by an
usurper, or a criminal whose guilt is discovered by his own crime. The
deliberately limited nature of such a comparison is suited to sung poetry,
and in particular to this song, in which the refrain in one stanza may refer

to the lady's eye which betrays her faithless heart, and in another to the lover's which reveals his fidelity. In his best songs Wyatt shows great skill in shifting the references of the refrain in this manner. It is, however, a use of language different in kind from the devices in his sonnets demanding more than one interpretation simultaneously.

In "The longe love," by contrast, the metaphor of the lover's passion fleeing to the "hertes forrest" represents the style of Wyatt's sonnets, creating a multiplicity of effects inappropriate to sung poetry. It demands first the recognition of a metaphor-within-a-metaphor, because of the pun on heart-hart, which has a complicating effect on the workings of the comparison, as does the play on dear-deer in "Who so list to hounte."[71] It likens the inward part of the lover which harbors his passion to an untamed but gentle nonhuman creature, often hunted but elusive, swift of foot, and silent. The whole phrase also simultaneously compares the heart, the retreat to which love flees, with a forest, a dark, secluded, tangled, and enclosed place, which can both threaten and protect. The love itself is therefore also a fugitive creature fleeing for safety, hiding itself in solitude, where it cries silently. The metaphor is less logically clear than those typical of Wyatt's other love poems, giving it more ambiguous effects. Instead of naming, it suggests the lover's inward state by the multiple qualities attached through the metaphor of the "hertes forrest" simultaneously to his inward part and to the passion which acts upon it.

Among Wyatt's sonnet translations, the most extreme shift in focus to make figurative language suggest multiplicity of inward states is in his adaptation of Petrarch's Sonnet 98. The original is addressed by name to a nobleman who, the Italian sonnet itself seems to say, was prevented by sickness from taking part in a tournament:

> Orso, al vostro destrier si po ben porre
> un fren che di suo corso indietro il volga,
> ma 'l cor chi legherà che non si sciolga
> se brama onore e 'l suo contrario aborre?
>
> Non sospirate: a lui non si po torre
> suo pregio perch' a voi l'andar si tolga,
> ché come fama publica divolga
> egli è già là che null'altro il precorre.
>
> Basta che si ritrove in mezza 'l campo
> al destinato dì sotto quell'arme
> che gli dà il tempo, amor, vertute e 'l sangue,
>
> gridando: "D'un gentil desire avampo
> col signor mio, che non po seguitarme
> et del non esser qui si strugge et langue."

Orso, on your charger can be put a rein that will turn him back from
his course, but who can bind your heart so that it cannot get loose,
if it desires honor and abhors the contrary?
Do not sigh: no one can take away his worth even though you are
prevented from going, for, as public fame makes known, your heart
is already there, no other can precede him.
Let it suffice that he will be in the field on the appointed day, under
the arms he has from time, love, valor, and birth,
crying: "One with my lord, I burn with a noble desire, but he cannot
follow me and suffers and is sick that he is not here."

Wyatt follows his model in developing an extended personification of the
heart as a traveler who leaves his lord to enter the lists in pursuit of honor.
But the heart is the lover's own, so that the adaptation becomes a wholly
new poem, of a different kind from the original:

> Though I my self be bridilled of my mynde,
>   Retorning me backewerd by force expresse,
>   If thou seke honour to kepe thy promes,
>   Who may the hold, my hert, but thou thy self vnbynd?
> Sigh then no more, syns no way man may fynde
>   Thy vertue to let, though that frowerdnes
>   Of ffortune me holdeth: and yet, as I may gesse,
>   Though othre be present, thou art not all behinde.
> Suffice it then that thou be redy there
>   At all howres; still vnder the defence
>   Of tyme, trouth and love to save the from offence;
> Cryeng, 'I burne in a lovely desire
>   With my dere Maisteres: that may not followe,
>   Whereby his absence torneth him to sorrowe.'[72]

Whether it is the lover's mind which holds him back, as lines 1 and 2 seem
to say, or fortune named in line 7, the fact that the struggle is all within
himself, and that the lover directly addresses his heart from line 3, makes
the metaphorical pattern of bridling, journeying, and jousting more suggestive of his inward state. The speaker's tenderness toward "my hert" is
more intimate than the address of the poet to Orso, which is public
consolation and praise.

Wyatt's departures from his model in this adaptation can be a final
measure of differences between it and his characteristic love poems not
in sonnet form. An illuminating contrast is with his previously discussed
poem beginning with the lover's farewell to cruelty, followed by eleven
lines explaining—"be ye sure"—the lover's renunciation to an unidentified
audience.[73] Then in the last four lines the speaker addresses his heart,
concluding with a formal "Welcome" to balance the farewell of line 1.
Because the heart is merely named, not addressed in a manner which

would give it specific personified qualities or a definable human relationship to the speaker, it has scarcely any function other than to represent the
extremity of the lover's passions. By contrast in the sonnet the lover
speaks to his heart as his friend, to whom he gives comfort, encouragement, and advice. He knows his heart well enough to enter into its states
and to imagine a loving speech for it, and yet his heart has an existence
of its own about which the lover can only "gesse." The address to his heart
therefore suggests multiple and even indefinable qualities of his inward
experience, whereas in the song it has virtually no function except as an
exclamation point. There, because the heart has no personified identity,
it does not have a separate existence from the lover, as if what lies within
it may be unknowable even to the lover himself. It also does not represent
inward as distinct from or distanced from outward experience, because his
manner of speaking to it is identical with his other addresses in the poem
to an outside audience. These utterances are uniformly designed to express the extremity of love, and are assumed to be its true expression,
because inward and outward spheres are parallel and in close proximity.

Devices for rendering love's diversity also differ in these two poems.
The song uses the oxymoron "joyfull payne," which joins states commonly thought to be contradictory, as an indication of the contraries of love.
Yet it makes them into a category composed of a "part" previously called
"pleasure" and another named "woo." The oxymoron therefore expresses
love's diversity by naming it. In the sonnet, by contrast, contraries of
inward experience are not named but suggested. One means for doing so
is the developed personification itself. Another is the pattern of bridling,
traveling, and jousting metaphors, used to suggest the lover's simultaneous inward states of bondage and freedom, passivity and power, withdrawal and self-defense, fear and desire, exposure and secrecy. In
consequence of these uses of language, the sonnet creates the impression
that what is in the speaker's heart is more difficult to define, for the lover
cannot express it by naming it.

The poem is therefore predicated on assumptions about both language
and inward experience, and about the relation between them, which are
fundamentally different from those in other verse by Wyatt or by any
other poet writing in English before Sidney. For it implies a more radical
distinction between inward and outward experience. This separation points
to a new sense of distance between what is within the lover's heart and
his outward modes of expression, including the poem itself. It cannot
"vtter" what words naming categories like "smert" are inadequate to
define.

3.
Sidney

When Sidney in *An Apologie for Poetrie* praises Surrey's lyrics as virtually the only model for a poet writing in English in the late sixteenth century, his tribute may have been intended to refer to Tottel's miscellany as a whole.[1] His own verse, however, shows no signs of direct imitation of Surrey, or Wyatt, or the other contributors to the volume, although he repeats many of their traditional motifs, using virtually the same conventional diction in the same verbal patterns, in his earlier love poetry.

Sidney's interest in the sonnet form may have derived originally from his familiarity with examples in the miscellany. His own earliest sonnets in the *Arcadia* are metrically much more skillful, but otherwise very like many entries in Tottel's collection, and like much of the rest of his own love poetry. Often they have the additive structure of a catalogue: one is composed entirely of oxymorons, another of apostrophes to the lover's eyes, heart, reason.[2] Resembling songs with refrains, one ends with a line repeating its opening.[3] Even when Sidney develops a metaphor to structure the sonnet and to suggest what is in the speaker's heart, the poem typically turns into a list of names for the extremity and diversity of the lover's inward states. A sonnet which is a complaint of Gynecia follows this pattern. The first quatrain uses the actual cave where the verses are found in a figurative comparison to what is in the lover's heart. Yet it is the prose context rather than the sonnet itself that identifies the conventional "darke plight" as a cave, and by the sestet this metaphor is dropped altogether, to be replaced by catalogues naming inward states and their effects:

> Howe is my Sunn, whose beames are shining bright,
> Become the cause of my darke ouglie night?
> Or howe do I, captiv'd in this darke plight,
> Bewaile the case, and in the cause delight?
>
> My mangled mind huge horrors still doe fright,
> With sense possest, and claim'd by reason's right:

Betwixt which two in me I have this fight,
Wher who so wynns, I put my selfe to flight.

Come clowdie feares, close up my daseled sight,
Sorowe suck up the marowe of my might,
Due sighes blowe out all sparkes of joyfull light,
Tyre on, despaier, uppon my tyred sprite.
　　An ende, an ende, my dulde penn cannot write,
　　Nor mas'de head thinke, nor faltring tonge recite.[4]

Typically the catalogues mix inward and outward categories: sighs with fears, sorrow, and despair; thoughts with writings and utterance. The result is that the complaint in fact does precisely what the couplet disclaims. It does bewail the lover's inward state by closing the distance between outward expression and what is in the heart. To complain in this style is to present the "case" in the generalized terms common to earlier sixteenth-century love poetry. Only the prose context attaches a particular identity to the speaker, who within the sonnet itself is indistinguishable from countless other complaining lovers.

Sidney's Arcadian sonnets do not show that he learned directly from Wyatt's uses of extended metaphor, or from the other verbal practices that distinguish Wyatt's sonnets from virtually all the rest of his love poems. Many of those devices which create the need for multiple interpretations were in fact removed from Wyatt's printed sonnets, in the versions known to Sidney, by the editor of Tottel's miscellany. With a taste for order in meaning as well as in meter, that reviser often added punctuation or changed wording to eliminate ambiguities as well as metrical irregularities. In the last line of "My galley charged with forgetfulnesse," for example, he inserted a comma—"And I remayne, dispearying of the port"—marking a balanced pause while also excluding one of the original possibilities of interpretation: "I continue to despair of reaching the port."[5] In another sonnet translated from Petrarch, "Avising the bright beames of those fayre eyes," he cleared away all the multiplicity of meanings allowed in the second quatrain of Wyatt's poem as it is recorded in the Egerton manuscript:

And fynde the swete bitter vnder this gyse
　　what webbe he hath wrought well he perceveth[6]

To clarify the meaning of line 5, the editor excluded the oxymoron by rephrasing, "And bitter findes the swete," allowing the lover to discover bitterness that is disguised as sweetness, but not to find bitterness that is sweet.[7] Adding a comma marking a pause in line 6, "What webbes there he hath wrought, well he perceaueth," he again eliminated one possible interpretation by allowing "well" to modify "perceaueth" but not "wrought," as it can in the unpunctuated line.

These and similar changes in Wyatt's sonnets (they occur also in "They flee from me," where the previously discussed ambiguities demanding multiple readings are also eliminated) show that the editor of the miscellany did not associate the sonnet form with a distinct kind of language demanding a different mode of interpretation.[8] Sonnets in the collection by Surrey and Nicholas Grimald, as well as those by unknown contributors, point to the same conclusion. So do the sonnets by other poets whose work could have been read by Sidney before or during the time of his own first experiments: Gascoigne, Sackville, Tusser, Harington, Googe, Whetstone, Watson, and Spenser (in his early translations of DuBellay and of Petrarch in Marot's version).[9] Other than the evidence of these poems themselves, which often seem unaware of the distinct limits and opportunities in the form, there is little record in English of critical attitudes toward the sonnet in the sixteenth century. An exception is a comment by George Gascoigne in *Certayne notes of Instruction* published in 1575:

> . . . some thinke that all Poemes (being short) may be called Sonets, as in deede it is a diminutiue worde deriued of *Sonare,* but yet I can best allowe to call those Sonnets whiche are of fouretene lynes, euery line conteyning tenne syllables. The first twelue do ryme in staues of foure lines by crosse meetre, and the last two ryming togither do conclude the whole.[10]

While instructing his audience about rhyme and stress patterns, he says nothing to suggest any other distinguishing features of sonnets, or any special effects demanded or encouraged by the form. A later practitioner of the sonnet, Samuel Daniel, in his critical treatise of 1603 stresses order and limit as the distinguishing attributes of the form:

> Nor is this certaine limit obserued in Sonnets, any tyrannicall bounding of the conceit, but rather a reducing it in *girum,* and a iust forme, neither too long for the shortest proiect, nor too short for the longest, being but onely imployed for a present passion. For the body of our imagination, being as an vnformed *Chaos* without fashion, without day, if by the diuine power of the spirit it be wrought into an Orbe or order and forme, is it not more pleasing to Nature, that desires a certaintie, and comports not with that which is infinite, to haue these clozes, rather than, not to know where to end, or how farre to goe, especially seeing our passions are often without measure.[11]

These remarks show that he associated sonnets with the presentation of "passion," making such a set of controls more desirable than the additive patterns of other kinds of verse, where amplification is allowed free reign. Daniel's notion of the limits imposed in sonnets seems to focus on the length prescribed for the whole, and also perhaps for its lines, but not on other aspects of the form.

With the exception of a few sonnets by Wyatt which the editor of
Tottel's miscellany did not significantly alter, Sidney could have had no
models in English that used the form to work out fundamentally new
directions for poetry. When he wrote the Arcadian sonnets and most of
those included in the collection known (in the casual terminology frowned
on by Gascoigne) as *Certaine Sonets,* he followed earlier writers largely by
transferring motifs and uses of language traditional to love poetry into the
rhyme and meter of sonnets. He did not make other significant changes
that would differentiate them from the rest of his love poetry, as Wyatt
had done. Like those of other poets, Sidney's early sonnets develop along
the same lines as his work in other kinds of love poems.

The one exception is the last poem, a true sonnet, in *Certaine Sonets.*[12]
This is Sidney's one poem written probably before *Astrophil and Stella*
which shows him working in some of the same directions as had Wyatt
in his sonnets, although it does not seem to have been modeled on any
particular poem of Wyatt's. It belongs, however, to the same tradition of
the palinode as Wyatt's "Farewell, Loue, and all thy lawes for euer," which
Sidney undoubtedly read in Tottel's miscellany under the title "A renouncing of loue."[13] The printed version contains many revisions dictated
by the editor's taste for metrical regularity, but in this instance he did not
rewrite the last line, so that its syntactical ambiguity is retained as it was
printed: "Me lyst no lenger rotten bowes to clime." Previous discussion
of this sonnet has shown that the line demands more than one interpretation, reflecting on the whole of the poem so as to make dramatic its
rendering of what is in the speaker's heart. It can be read simultaneously
to mean that the speaker no longer desires to climb rotten boughs, and that
he desires to stop desiring such dangerous vanities (an interpretation
incidentally close to the final line of the sonnet immediately preceding
Sidney's palinode, "Desiring nought but how to kill desire").[14] The first
reading supports the finality of the speaker's renunciations, while the
second simultaneously shows that they are not absolute and that his
inward state is not susceptible of single interpretation or of simple definition.

In his palinode Sidney for the first time uses language in ways similar
to those which distinguish Wyatt's sonnets from his other love poems and
from other verse of the period, and with parallel effects:

> Leave me ô Love, which reachest but to dust,
> And thou my mind aspire to higher things:
> Grow rich in that which never taketh rust:
> What ever fades, but fading pleasure brings.
>
> Draw in thy beames, and humble all thy might,
> To that sweet yoke, where lasting freedomes be:
> Which breakes the clowdes and opens forth the light,

That doth both shine and give us sight to see.

O take fast hold, let that light be thy guide,
In this small course which birth drawes out to death,
And thinke how evill becommeth him to slide,
Who seeketh heav'n, and comes of heav'nly breath.
    Then farewell world, thy uttermost I see,
    Eternall Love maintaine thy life in me.

The essence of the poem is the speaker's sense that his experience demands multiple interpretation. This is compressed in the ambiguous wording of his opening address to "Love, which reachest but to dust," meaning that which aspires only to dust, stretches out to grasp it, but also that which only arrives at or ends in dust. He wishes to part from this "Love" but cannot himself take leave of it, cannot even renounce it by the name of desire or lust. He knows that it belongs among "What ever fades," which "but fading pleasure brings," yet things that can fade are alive, young, and beautiful, and what they yield he calls "pleasure," however evanscent or even because fleeting. He can urge his mind toward "higher things," and in so doing gain strength at last to leave the world behind. Yet his descriptions of what he aspires to derive their names from the very things of this world that he bids farewell. They are only distinguished by modifiers—wealth "which never taketh rust," "lasting freedomes," "that light," "heav'nly breath," "thy life"—phrases actually insisting on their likeness to their earthly counterparts. When he bids farewell to the world, he seems to explain that he does so because, having climbed above it, he can now "see" its "uttermost," meaning that he can see it utterly, and also see its outward show. Yet sight is a gift, like breath, and what it sees in the shining light of this world has a richness and life of its own. His final prayer for "Eternall Love" to enter into his heart therefore only seems to resolve the ambiguities of his inward experiences by simplifying them. In actuality it dramatizes their multiplicity. The difficulty of interpreting them is here represented by the parallels between the last line and the first, in that the "Love" he renounces and the "Love" he embraces have the same name.

Implied is an awareness of ambiguous and shifting relationships between words and what is in the heart. This is very different from the kind of arbitrariness exercised without apparent uneasiness by Sidney in his earlier poetry. Examples previously discussed are such noun adjectives as "inward raine" and "inward fornace," in which he confidently expresses what is in the heart by arbitrarily transferring nouns naming outward phenomena to the sphere of "inward" experience. This practice depends on the assumptions which are embodied also in catalogues mingling names for inward parts and states with outward modes of expression. These assumptions are that the two spheres are not widely distanced but closely

parallel, and that therefore inward experiences can be defined by words
with single meanings or referents like the names for outward phenomena.
The palinode is predicated on a very different view of language.

Sidney does not seem to have learned the devices he uses in "Leave me
ô Love" from imitation of any particular model, or from the act of transposing meanings into English within a strictly limited form copied from
a foreign original, the procedures which taught Wyatt in his sonnets a new
language for rendering what is in the heart. It may be that Sidney's own
experimentation in sonnets gave him a new sense of verbal possibilities
through his exploration of various structures, rhyme schemes, and especially metrical patterns. This development is suggested by John Thompson in *The Founding of English Meter* as part of his discussion of Sidney's
metrical experiments. He theorizes that Sidney learned to recognize what
earlier sixteenth-century poets in English did not, that metrical patterns
could be played off against spoken stress patterns which violate the meter,
as in the opening phrase of "Leave me o Lôve":

> . . . the recognition of an irreducible difference of form and substance
> in art must have been a profound experience, once. It seems to me
> that this difference must have led Sidney to the recognition of similar
> and equally profound differences. It is a recognition of the limita-
> tions of poetry. This of course is one of Sidney's themes.[15]

It cannot be proven that the uses of language demanding multiple interpretation in Sidney's palinode reflect such a recognition, but the sonnet
in these respects does resemble *Astrophil and Stella,* where the validity of
at least part of Mr. Thompson's hypothesis can be very clearly demonstrated. For in Sidney' sonnet sequence, explicit recognition of the limits
of poetry involves awareness of differences between outward expression
and what is in the heart.

In the quarter of a century between the publication of Tottel's *Songes
and Sonettes* in 1557 and the composition of *Astrophil and Stella* in the
early 1580s, a number of English poets tried their hands at sonnets, sometimes in paired or linked groups, which Gascoigne calls "sequences."[16] Yet
none produced a sequence in the sense in which the term is used to
describe *Astrophil and Stella,* and the many English sonnet cycles which
its first publication in 1591 inspired. Sidney therefore had no native models, nor were there English versions of any continental collections. Petrarch's was not translated in its entirety into English until the mid-
nineteenth century, and although some two hundred editions of it appeared on the continent between their first publication in 1470 and about
1600, not one in any language was published in England.[17] Some French
versions were known there, as were other continental sonnet collections,
to which English poets paid tribute. Although their poems allude most

often to Petrarch's sequence, they therefore did not necessarily have any firsthand knowledge of it. Yet a manuscript copy of it was in the library of Peterhouse College, Cambridge, as early as 1426, and in Lord Morley's introduction to his translation of Boccaccio's *De Claris mulieribus,* written between 1534 and 1544, he praises Petrarch's "swete ryme" in the vernacular, so esteemed in Italy that no prince or gentleman is to be found "withoute havynge in his handes hys sonnetes and hys 'tryomphes.' "[18]

Sidney did know Petrarch's sonnets in Italian: one of his own in *Certaine Sonets* uses in its title "this worde of *Petrarch: Non mi vuol e non mi trahe d'Impaccio.*"[19] The line is taken from Sonnet 134, *Pace non trovo,* chosen by Wyatt as a model in his translation, "I find no peace," and also translated into English by Gascoigne, Watson, and Southwell, by Spenser perhaps in *Amoretti* 25, and by Lodge imitating a version of Ronsard's.[20] Its attraction for so many poets may derive in part from its resemblance, previously discussed, to complaints in the native tradition which catalogue the contraries of love. Yet the existence of so many translations by different poets of the same sonnet suggests that the impetus to make them was also in part to imitate English models. For only a small number of Petrarch's sonnets were translated into English, only perhaps about fifty by 1625, and those (almost all from the first part of his sequence, said to be written in Laura's lifetime) repeatedly.[21] This pattern of selection shows that most of Petrarch's English translators were not interested in his sonnets as a model for a whole sequence. They probably had not read his in its entirety.

Sidney translated individual sonnets from different parts of Petrarch's sequence, as had other English poets. He was the first in England to follow the practice of continental imitators of Petrarch by adapting the form of a large collection of sonnets developed around a loosely suggested love story, containing some tightly linked smaller groups, and including other types of poems inserted at intervals. Such a work obviously allows more sustained exploration of his concerns than was possible when a translator adapted individual sonnets. Especially it encourages fuller presentation of a speaker whose voice is understood to be heard throughout the sequence.

Astrophil resembles the speaker in Petrarch's sonnet sequence in one fundamental respect pertinent to this discussion, that he is a poet-lover. Yet Sidney develops the conventional figure in ways which distinguish Astrophil both from the poet whose praising, *laudando,* immortalizes his beloved, *Laura,* and from Wyatt's lovers, who utter complaints. For Sidney does not make Astrophil such a poet as Petrarch describes in his Poem 360, translated by Wyatt as "Myne olde dere enmy." There, in the lines previously discussed which Wyatt omitted from his version, the lover in Petrarch's sequence is described as a famous poet whose name shines brighter than those of other wits because of his divinely inspired verse, collected and publicly praised in many courts. Throughout the sequence

Petrarch puns on Laura's name, both as a synonym for his own praise and for the laurel, reward of victorious poets as of emperors. His verses will win himself and his beloved the laurel crown of immortality. The identification of the speaker in the sequence with Petrarch, himself publicly crowned as poet laureate, is never forgotten.[22]

Astrophil is identified with Sidney, who is not a famous poet. He is a courtier who writes verses for the entertainment of a lady and their small circle of courtly acquaintances, professing the kind of nonchalance toward his compositions deemed suitable by Castiglione. Astrophil is not portrayed as reciting them publicly, or even singing them to the accompaniment of his lute on social occasions (a practice which Thomas Whythorne, writing his autobiography in the mid-1570s, describes as old-fashioned).[23] He shows the same aristocratic disdain as Sidney's of an amateur for vulgar professional poets. In *An Apologie for Poetrie* Sidney mocks the notion that he might aspire to the dignity of being "admitted into the company of the Paper-blurrers." For

> as I neuer desired the title, so haue I neglected the meanes to come by it. Onely, ouer-mastred by some thoughts, I yeelded an inckie tribute vnto them.[24]

Sounding like his inventor (who dismisses his defense of poetry as an "incke-wasting toy"), Astrophil calls his verse "Ink's poore losse," and mocks himself for struggling with it, in Sonnet 34:

> 'Art not asham'd to publish thy disease?'
> Nay, that may breed my fame, it is so rare:
> 'But will not wise men thinke thy words fond ware?'
> Then be they close, and so none shall displease.

He never vows that his verse will immortalize Stella or himself, although her allegorical name of star might invite the promise of such an elevation. Sidney pokes fun at this convention in the last paragraph of *An Apologie for Poetrie* when he urges sympathetic readers to believe poets who promise to immortalize them in verse:

> Thus doing, your name shal florish in the printers shoppes; thus doing, you shall bee of kinne to many a poeticall Preface; thus doing, you shall be most fayre, most ritch, most wise, most all; you shall dwell vpon Superlatiues.[25]

His closing words, by contrast, are a curse upon readers hostile to poetry:

> . . . that while you liue, you liue in loue, and neuer get fauour for lacking skill of a *Sonnet*; and when you die, your memory die from the earth for want of an *Epitaph*.[26]

Astrophil jokingly rejects the eternizing title of poet for his epitaph in
Sonnet 90. He seems explicitly to distinguish himself from Petrarch because he is young in praising, because he lacks wings to soar among
immortal wits, but also because—there is a cutting edge to his modesty—
he is not so ambitious as to "frame" for himself a crown of public praise:

> *Stella* thinke not that I by verse seeke fame,
>   Who seeke, who hope, who love, who live but thee;
>   Thine eyes my pride, thy lips my history:
> If thou praise not, all other praise is shame.
> Nor so ambitious am I, as to frame
>   A nest for my yong praise in Lawrell tree:
>   In truth I sweare, I wish not there should be
> Graved in mine Epitaph a Poet's name:
> Ne if I would, could I just title make,
> That any laud to me thereof should grow,
> Without my plumes from others' wings I take.
> For nothing from my wit or will doth flow,
>   Since all my words thy beauty doth endite,
>   And love doth hold my hand, and makes me write.

There are further complications to Astrophil's joking here which define
Sidney's figure of the poet-lover by contrast with the speakers in Wyatt's
sonnets as well as with Petrarch's poet. For while Astrophil distinguishes
himself from Petrarch as youthful amateur writing poetry only to please
his beloved, he does so in terms conventional to verse, even in echoes of
Petrarch's own Sonnet 293. There, with blatant disregard of his many
sonnets on fame, Laura's lover insists that in her lifetime he did not write
to gain public honor but only to unburden his heart. Astrophil, while
disclaiming the title belonging to poets, by imitation and allusion very
obviously associates himself with them. Although the lover claims to
write only for Stella, the sonnet itself is consciously addressed to sophisticated readers whose familiarity with the conventions of Petrarchan sonnets enables them to appreciate the wit of Astrophil's dissociations from
them. This very stance likens him to continental, especially French sonneteers—to Ronsard above all—whose playful anti-Petrarchan gestures were
also established conventions. Sidney himself knew their work, and in such
a sonnet as *Astrophil and Stella* 90, depends also on their familiarity for
his readers.[27]

Although Sidney's poet-lover is a courtier, not a professional man of
letters, whose skill in verse is merely one of his aristocratic accomplishments, he is nevertheless literary in the sense that Wyatt's speakers in his
sonnets, even in those which are translations of specific verse models, are
not. They utter complaints because they are lovers. They are not explicitly
presented as writing verse, and when they raise questions about language,

it is not specifically the language of poetry. Wyatt's lover who seeks but
cannot find the way to "vtter forth the smart I bide within" struggles with
the separation between his inward state and outward expression.[28] He
does not conceive of this effort as the love poet's struggle to show in verse
what is grounded inward in the heart.

"Loving in truth, and faine in verse my love to show" opens the first
poem in the first English sonnet sequence, and with that line changes
poetry in our language. This sonnet is the earliest poem in English to make
its central concern the relation between what may be felt "in truth" and
what may show "in verse," an issue explored and complicated throughout
Astrophil and Stella in ways which create new uses of language for portraying inward experience in a new kind of poetry.

A first reading of the sonnet, and one independent of its network of
connections with others following it in the sequence, might challenge such
a claim, because the poem seems most obviously to embody the traditional view of the plain stylist who rejects fine inventions for the unornamented truth of the heart:

> Loving in truth, and faine in verse my love to show,
> That the deare She might take some pleasure of my paine:
> Pleasure might cause her reade, reading might make her know,
> Knowledge might pitie winne, and pitie grace obtaine,
>   I sought fit words to paint the blackest face of woe,
> Studying inventions fine, her wits to entertaine:
> Oft turning others' leaves, to see if thence would flow
> Some fresh and fruitfull showers upon my sunne-burn'd braine.
> But words came halting forth, wanting Invention's stay,
> Invention, Nature's child, fled step-dame Studie's blowes,
> And others' feete still seem'd but strangers in my way.
> Thus great with child to speake, and helplesse in my throwes,
>   Biting my trewand pen, beating my selfe for spite,
>   'Foole,' said my Muse to me, 'looke in thy heart and write.'

The program of the plain-stylist seems to be advocated in the closing line
by Astrophil's Muse, in a tone of frank manliness associated with this
poetic preference, and the Muse is certainly allowed the last word in
Sonnet 1. The final imperative comes with the relief of a solution for all
the frustrated struggling built to a climax in the previous, tortuous thirteen. Its string of monosyllables attaches to it the credence traditionally
associated with the simplicity and directness it advocates. What would
then be expected to follow, if the Muse were dictating an aesthetic seriously proposed for Astrophil's poetry, would be a sequence in the plain style
uttered by a speaker like Wyatt's in his satire "to Iohn Poins," who defines
the "truth" of his words by their avoidance of falsifying eloquence, colors,
and fine wit.[29]

Yet the wit of *Astrophil and Stella* 1 is built upon recognition that "my Muse"—not the Muse—is itself the poet's invention, and therefore can have no more authority than its troubled author.[30] What is more, his Muse, though cocksure of how Astrophil should proceed, actually solves nothing, offers only a moment's relief. For although the episode recounted in the poem happened in the past—"I sought," "said my Muse"—the rhetorical pattern of prominently repeated present participles reenacts Astrophil's mounting frustrations in a continuously present retelling of the episode. The past difficulty of showing in verse his experience in truth has found no solution, as the sonnets which follow demonstrate.

Indeed Astrophil's problem in Sonnet 1 raises questions about poetry and implies attitudes toward it which actually are not identical with those of the plain stylists, although their attitudes are alluded to here and in other sonnets of the sequence. The Muse's conventional opposition between the heart's truth and inventions fine or stale is much simpler than the distinctions with which Astrophil struggles.

Sidney's opening sonnet defines Astrophil's poetic problem in terms recurring throughout the sequence, often in the same clusters:

> Loving in truth, and faine in verse my love to show . . .
> I sought fit words to paint the blackest face of woe.

The balance of *love* "in verse," with *loving* "in truth"—actually loving, faithfully loving—does not precisely oppose them but underlines a distinction between them. Loving is an inward experience, love a name for a passion or an epithet for the lady. Heightening this distinction between Astrophil's inward experience and his poetic term for it, line 1 on first reading does not make clear whether that term "love" is the direct or indirect object, whether Astrophil wants to show forth his love for Stella or her image in verse, or whether he wants to use his verse as a gesture to show *to* her something unspecified about himself. Ambiguous grammatical constructions of this kind occur often in the sequence, pointing to complications in the relationship between inward states and their verbal rendering. The device, apparently rediscovered by Sidney, resembles Wyatt's practice in his sonnets. As it is used in *Astrophil and Stella,* and in combination with other practices new to English poetry in Sidney's sonnets, it will be seen to widen still further the distance between outward show and what is in the heart.

The distinction between loving and its versified presentation is further defined by the verb "show," rich in meanings in the sixteenth century, and used with extraordinary frequency in *Astrophil and Stella,* almost always in the emphatic position of a rhyme word. It does not mean here what it sometimes means for Sidney (and usually for Shakespeare in his sonnets), to make a false appearance. Yet it also is not simply synonymous with the act of revealing, as it is in Wyatt's line "Thenne fere not the Iye to shewe the hert."³¹ For in this context Sidney's stress is on making love visible as a parallel to painting a picture (whereas Wyatt's line, based on the convention that love can simply be seen through the window of the eye, assumes a more direct, unmediated vision). Therefore "show" in Sidney's sonnet means the act of causing to be seen, in the sense of exhibiting or displaying, again implying a distinction between the lover's inward experience and the verbal form in which it is shown. Similarly "to paint" here means to depict, to represent in an image. It does not mean (as Shakespeare most often uses it, and as Sidney means in *An Apologie for Poetrie* when he condemns false diction as "a Curtizan-like painted affectation") to represent falsely, to cover with deceiving colors, or to cheapen with cosmetics.³² Yet as it is used here, "to paint" has different implications as the name for the process of uttering complaints than *to express*—"A wringing or squeasing out"—previously discussed as in common use in earlier love poetry.³³ For here what poetry paints is a face, giving the verb its meaning of portrait-making. Furthermore, here it paints the "face of woe" exaggerated in its "blackest" hue, perhaps like a tragic mask.³⁴ In this metaphor, painting woe cannot be equated with expressing it, an act of bringing out what is internal. Again a distinction is implied between what the poet makes visible and what the lover experiences inwardly: the poem portrays the visage of the inward state. The possibility that this image may be a calculated mask—in Sonnet 69 when Astrophil is granted Stella's heart he claims to set aside "all maskes"—is strengthened here by the parenthetical explanation in lines 2 to 4, as it were between "show" and "woe," of Astrophil's plan to use this painted face to move Stella.

His Muse's prescription of a plain style in place of inventions fine or borrowed does not resolve Astrophil's difficulties because it ignores the distinctions actually troubling him between the lover's inward experience and its presentation in poetry, and also because it assumes his inward state to be more simple and single than it is. Even as presented in Sonnet 1, "Loving" is a complex of worshipping, desiring, admiring, resenting, pleasing, self-serving, calculating, flattering; "love" a term both for that mixture and for its object, Stella. If Astrophil looks in his heart, he will find there more than Stella's image; he will find a tangled inward state his unsubtle Muse knows not of.

That his Muse cannot teach his inventor to write as he wishes is demonstrated in Sonnet 2. At first Astrophil's manner in describing himself as a reluctant lover and poet might suggest that he has mastered the monosyllabic bluntness and forthright tone of his uncourtly Muse. Yet his exaggerated style of manly English sportsman is immediately contrasted with hyperbolic complaining in line 2. The effect is therefore closer to parody of both styles than it is to imitation of them. Such use of contrasting styles and of parody will be seen here and throughout the sequence as a means of questioning the adequacy of Astrophil's poetic language to represent what is in the heart:

> Not at first sight, nor with a dribbed shot
>   *Love* gave the wound, which while I breathe will bleed:
>   But knowne worth did in mine of time proceed,
> Till by degrees it had full conquest got.
> I saw and liked, I liked but loved not,
>   I loved, but straight did not what *Love* decreed:
>   At length to *Love's* decrees, I forc'd, agreed,
> Yet with repining at so partiall lot.
>   Now even that footstep of lost libertie
> Is gone, and now like slave-borne *Muscovite,*
> I call it praise to suffer Tyrannie;
> And now employ the remnant of my wit,
>   To make my selfe beleeve, that all is well,
>   While with a feeling skill I paint my hell.

By declaring that his inward state is "to suffer," he allows it the simultaneous and unreconciled meanings of agonizing and permitting. By then calling this state of humiliating endurance "praise," he is willfully manipulating language, as the speakers in some of Wyatt's sonnets confess to doing. This issue is developed explicitly for the first time as a question specifically for the poet in Sidney's sequence (and still more guiltily by Shakespeare).

Here Astrophil calls his pain praiseworthy, perhaps to make it acceptable to Stella. He is also offering it in celebratory verse, for which "praise" is a formal term. Both verbal acts make the lover's inward state and its presentation in poetry more widely and explicitly distanced here than in Sonnet 1. What the poet will "paint" to persuade his audience (perhaps Stella but, since she is not directly addressed or even referred to, perhaps also his readers) does not coincide with his unversified persuasion of himself. It is not made clear whether his poetic depiction is truer than the cliché he tries to make himself believe, or whether verse has transformed "my hell" into Stella's "praise." According to this second reading, "paint" would have a more suspect meaning than in Sonnet 1, closer to covering over with colors of skillful rhetoric. The ambiguity is here allowed to remain unresolved, and so raises questions, to be discussed, about sonnets following. What is clear, however, is the distinction marked by 'While," a word occurring often in Sidney's collection with effects similar to those created here. "While" defines Astrophil's outward and inward actions to be simultaneous and divided. The division marks off what is painted in his verse from what is grounded inward in his heart.

These two sonnets are carefully placed to introduce Astrophil as a lover in the act of struggling to write poems about his love, and it is that struggle to which their order gives greatest emphasis. For the poem chosen to open the sequence tells a story about trying to show inward states in verse, not about loving. The second, although it does narrate Astrophil's struggle to resist conquest by Cupid, builds rhetorically to a climax in which he acts out the division between that experience and its presentation in poetry: "Not . . . not . . . not . . . Now . . . now":

> And now employ the remnant of my wit,
> To make myself beleeve, that all is well,
> While with a feeling skill I paint my hell.

Here the reader might expect Astrophil to pay some tribute, however mixed with resentment, to the lady as yet unmentioned in the poem, or to admit his heart's capitulation to Cupid's arrow, as in the second sonnet of Petrarch's sequence, to which the opening lines allude. Instead Sidney focuses on the difference between the sonnet's portrayal of Astrophil's state and what he is experiencing as a continuous inward monologue "While" he writes Sonnet 2 and others to follow.

In depicting the struggle to show inward states in poetry, the opening two sonnets demand that the reader think of Astrophil's loving as the matter for his invention. At the same time they point to a separation of his activity as a poet from his experience of suffering. This distance is further widened in Sonnet 2 when poetry-writing is defined as "skill," the technique of a trained artificer. Among all the terms for poetry in *Astrophil and Stella* or *An Apologie for Poetrie*, "skill" is the least susceptible to identification with the artist's own inward states, and elsewhere in the sequence Sidney uses it to stress its meaning as technical effort.[35] In Sonnet 12 the difficulty of winning Stella's heart demands "all the skill" of poetry, as distinct from all the "paine" felt by the lover. In Sonnet 15 Astrophil advises others how to win fame "both for your love and skill," again separating the love poet's inward experience from his writing.

Such divisions of Astrophil's acts into those of poet and of lover are a way of portraying his struggle to write truly about what is in his heart. This struggle itself then becomes a means of portraying his experience as simultaneously—but distinctly—outward and inward, public and private, visible and unseen, apparent and secret, uttered and unexpressed. These portrayals, absolutely central to *Astrophil and Stella,* are attempted by Sidney in a sustained way for the first time in English poetry.

Sonnet 1 uses terms recurring throughout the sequence for the act of writing—*show, paint*—which call attention to the relation between words and their referents. Both verbs have the innocent or neutral meanings of causing to be seen, or portraying, and are so used in the first and many other sonnets in Sidney's sequence as well as in *An Apologie for Poetrie*.[36] Verbs like *paint* which were associated with other arts than poetry were conventionally used in sixteenth-century verse for the act of writing, often as synonyms for the verb *to express*. Grimald, for example, praises Virgil for surpassing in skill other engravers and painters who could not "So graue, so paynt, or so by style expresse."[37] Such verbal equations show the kind of inattention to metaphorical possibilities of words previously discussed as characteristic of earlier sixteenth-century English verse. For if the qualities of engraving and painting—both marking or altering the appearance of a surface—are actually considered, they can only arbitrarily be equated with expressing, an act of emitting, bringing out. Painting was, however, used conventionally as a synonym for expressing, to describe outward shows of inward states, such as langor, blushing, palor. This equation illustrates another characteristic of the earlier poetry in that it tends to diminish or dissolve distinctions between inward and outward spheres, as a typical portrayal of a lover in Tottel's miscellany illustrates: "Lo, death is painted in his face."[38]

Both *show* and *paint* also had more suspect meanings that were widely used in the sixteenth century.[39] Examples abound in verse, as in lines from a poem in Tottel's collection entitled "Of the sutteltye of craftye louers":

And for to shew a griefe such craft haue they in store,
That they can halt and lay a salue wheras they fele no sore.[40]

In a poem by Surrey such a crafty lover complains:

But all to late loue learneth me,
To painte all kinde of colours new,
To blinde their eyes that els shoulde see,
My specled chekes with Cupides hewe.[41]

One all important difference in Sidney's use of these current terms is that he characteristically places them in such a way as to exploit their neutral and suspect meanings simultaneously. This practice raises questions, central to his sonnet sequence, about the poet's language not inherent in the kind of poetry represented by the examples from Tottel's miscellany.

Another formal critical term, *praise,* is introduced in Sonnet 2 and used throughout the sequence for a kind of poetic activity practiced by Astrophil. It also has an untainted meaning, extolling worth, making it complimentary here to Stella. Yet in Sonnet 2 Astrophil's admission to manipulating language simultaneously makes the term morally questionable. For one reason, it casts doubt on the virtue of his subject, here not "so true a Deitie" as he calls Stella two sonnets later, but a tyrant who has reduced a freeborn subject to slavery. This use of "praise" also casts suspicion on the relation of his poetry to his inward state. Whether different from it, inadequate to portray it, or deliberately falsifying it, his versified presentation is not commensurate with what is in his heart. All these terms defining the nature of poetic language therefore also imply inward experience for the poet-lover which is unexpressed, withheld, or disguised in his poetry.

More implications for the critical vocabulary of the opening sonnets can be seen as it is playfully applied to persuading Stella in Sonnet 45:[42]

> *Stella* oft sees the verie face of wo
>> Painted in my beclowded stormie face:
>> But cannot skill to pitie my disgrace,
> Not though thereof the cause her selfe she know:
> Yet hearing late a fable, which did show
>> Of Lovers never knowne, a grievous case,
>> Pitie thereof gate in her breast such place
> That, from that sea deriv'd, teares' spring did flow.
>> Alas, if Fancy drawne by imag'd things,
> Though false, yet with free scope more grace doth breed
> Then servant's wracke, where new doubts honor brings;
> Then thinke my deare, that you in me do reed
>> Of Lover's ruine some sad Tragedie:
>> I am not I, pitie the tale of me.

Here Astrophil builds his persuasion upon a contrast between his woeful countenance, which Stella sees unmoved, and a love story that stirred her to tears of pity. His argument appears to differentiate the true expression of his inward suffering in his face from the "show" of grief by Fancy, the author of the "fable" which succeeds in moving Stella. This personified rival has an unfair advantage in the pursuit of Stella's grace. For Fancy, less scrupulous than Astrophil, has appealed to Stella by exercising the "free scope" allowed to the poet by Sidney in *An Apologie for Poetrie*. There such "high flying liberty of conceit" is defined as virtuous feigning, but here its practitioner is resentfully accused of falsifying.[43] Astrophil, abandoning his losing position in the competition, then adopts the stratagems of Fancy in order to gain its moving power. He offers in place of his suffering countenance a generalized literary representation or "tale," a formal term which, in *An Apologie for Poetrie,* shares with "fable" the meaning of fiction.[44] He asks Stella to "reed," as if it were an invented story, the look of actual suffering she has grown accustomed to seeing without pity.

Yet this contrast between the lover's true rendering of his inward state with what Fancy shows in poetry is wittily complicated by Astrophil's claim that woe has been "Painted" in his face. Fancy, then, is not the only poet in the contest. Astrophil's face is itself a poem, in which he (or woe, or Nature, or perhaps even Love) has depicted an image of a visage other than his own. His own changeable, vulnerable countenance is represented by the generalized, tragic portrait or mask that, in Sonnet 1, he sought fit words to paint. Both Astrophil's ostensible contrast between himself and the poet Fancy, and his simultaneous admission to complicity in its actions, stress the distance between what is in the lover's heart and the forms in which it may be known. "I am not I" lays claim to what it wittily denies: that behind the pitiable "tale of me," admittedly false and calculated to move Stella, is an "I" with an identity distinct but unexpressed, held in reserve. Further, "my beclowdied stormie face" hints at a mutable individual represented by, but not identified with, the tragic mask of woe.

Divisions are thus emphatically marked between inward states and their literary portrayal. The lover is distanced from the general representations of art. The "verie face of wo" is not "my . . . face," but closer to the fictional categories of "a grievous case" or "some sad Tragedie." Unlike the lover in Wyatt's song in which the lover bids farewell to cruelty, Astrophil does not easily identify himself with a representative "one" or "he." On the contrary, he playfully assumes such an identification only in order to set himself apart from it. Beyond even these distinctions is Astrophil's sense of himself as separate from what can be shown through direct outward expression of inward states. For his troubled countenance makes visible only a portrait—and here such artistic images are "false"—of suffering. Undefined but implied by contrast with the verbal representations of "fable," "Tragedie," "tale," is something unspoken; by contrast with the vocabulary of painting and showing, something unseen but true to Astrophil's sense of being who "I am."

The speaker's struggle with the distinction between what is in his heart and the language of poetry is an explicit subject in many sonnets of *Astrophil and Stella,* far more than in any other English collection except that of Shakespeare. This subject is approached from a variety of perspectives, following different lines of argument. Some of Sidney's sonnets borrow attitudes toward poetry found in plain style verse, or adapt conventions associated especially with the Petrarchanism of earlier Italian, French, and English models. These adaptations, as Sonnets 1 and 2 have already shown, transform their borrowed matter to reveal new interests. Other sonnets in *Astrophil and Stella,* seeming more radically experimental, appear to try out wholly new approaches to the subject of writing poetry. The patterns of connection between these and the sonnets reshaping conventional matter point to Sidney's central concerns. They define his use of a speaker arguing the task of the love poet, or in the act of struggling to show his inward states in verse, to portray areas of inward experience and to explore their complexity. To that end he developed large motifs and many stylistic devices used in ways new to English poetry. As is true of Wyatt's sonnets, Sidney's in *Astrophil and Stella* provide two different ways of measuring his intentions. Those sonnets which set themselves in explicit relations to established conventions, like Wyatt's

translations, can be measured by their approximations and departures
from their chosen models. On the other hand, sonnets which strike out in
new directions point directly to new interests.

  Astrophil and Stella 6 is one example among a number of sonnets in
which allusions evoke attitudes toward writing familiar to Sidney's readers in other poems, but point them, as the plain-speaking Muse of the
opening sonnet is used, toward Astrophil's distinctive concerns:

> Some Lovers speake when they their Muses entertaine,
> Of hopes begot by feare, of wot not what desires:
> Of force of heav'nly beames, infusing hellish paine:
> Of living deaths, deare wounds, faire stormes and freesing fires:
>   Some one his song in *Jove,* and *Jove's* strange tales attires,
> Broadred with buls and swans, powdred with golden raine:
> Another humbler wit to shepheard's pipe retires,
> Yet hiding royall bloud full oft in rurall vaine.
>   To some a sweetest plaint, a sweetest stile affords,
>   While teares powre out his inke, and sighs breathe out his words:
> His paper, pale dispaire, and paine his pen doth move.
>   I can speake what I feele, and feele as much as they,
>   But think that all the Map of my state I display,
> When trembling voice brings forth that I do *Stella* love.

The first eleven lines reject the forced rhetoric and expensive ornament
of other lovers' verses for Astrophil's unornamented and therefore more
honest style of lines 12 and 13. These resemble the blunt, monosyllabic
manner of the Muse in Sonnet 1, or a speaker in the plain style such as
Wyatt's in his satire given in Tottel's miscellany the title "Of the Courtiers
life written to Iohn Poins":

> I meddle not with wyttes that be so fine . . .
> But I am here in kent and christendome:
> Among the Muses, where I reade and ryme.[45]

Astrophil's catalogue of criticisms would predict for Sonnet 6 a conclusion
similar to this of Wyatt's, in which he too would advocate an alternative
to affected courtly styles, one suited to an honest, independent critical
intelligence such as we hear in the voice of Wyatt's country gentleman.
Astrophil does in fact sound that way in lines 12 and 13—forthright,
confident, clear-headed—but not in line 14: "When trembling voice brings
forth that I do *Stella* love." This line alludes to a different tradition by
evoking a very different voice, known to Sidney in the sonnets of Petrarch.
Among them is Sonnet 170, for example, in which the speaker abandons
vain efforts to write verse because the god of love has made him so
trembling and so weak (*così m'à fatto Amor tremante et fioco*), whereas

the lover able to say how he burns is in but a little fire (*chi po dir com' egli arde è 'n piocciol foco*).

In Sonnet 6 Sidney has therefore evoked, in a combination itself original, attitudes toward writing familiar to his readers from other poetry. What these traditions have in common, of relevance to Sidney's concerns here, are speakers who contrast what is truly in their own hearts with false show in the poetry of others. Their terms of contrast, however, are not identical. Wyatt's satirist opposes plainspun country rhyme to fine verse because he distrusts courtliness in writing as in living. By contrast Petrarch's speaker, in Sonnets like 170, claims inward experiences that transcend poetry because powerful forces overcome the lover and render him mute. Sidney has put together allusions, therefore, which in their juxtaposition raise questions about their uses: Astrophil's attitudes toward himself as lover and poet cannot simply be identified with either tradition, as more extended comparisons will show. By putting them together Sidney modifies them, and makes them distinguish Astrophil's difficulties from those of Petrarch's lover or Wyatt's satirist, in showing truly in verse what is in the heart.

Astrophil's catalogue in lines 1 to 11 of courtly poetic affectations seems to repeat the critical attitudes of plain stylists, but his exaggerated manner goes beyond criticism to parody of such styles.[46] Loudest among parodic devices are the near-nonsense jingling of "wot not what"; the tricky alliterative patterns of lines 3, 4, and 11 especially; the heavy regularity and balance of hexameters approximating the monotony of poulter's measure. Added to these are verbal plays like the pun on "vaine"-vein, and the reversible grammar of "His paper, pale dispaire, and paine his pen doth move," which jokes about whether the moving force is in the lovers' passions or in their writing equipment.

Exaggerated in a spirit of mockery here, such patterns of sound and verbal plays actually have been used already elsewhere in the opening sonnets of *Astrophil and Stella,* and pervade the whole sequence. Furthermore, the language ridiculing others' poetic styles in Astrophil's catalogue makes many connections, both specific and inclusive, with his own language in other poems of *Astrophil and Stella,* especially those the reader has already encountered before the sixth sonnet. The consequence is that the catalogue which criticizes false poetic styles simultaneously parodies Astrophil's own poetry, with far-reaching implications to be discussed.

This pattern of connections with other sonnets in the sequence runs through the entire catalogue of Sonnet 6. Beginning with line 1, the category of lovers who "their Muses entertaine" must pointedly include Astrophil, for he begins the sequence with a plan Stella's "wits to entertaine," and in Sonnet 3 identifies her with his poetic inspiration, "no Muse but one I know." He is clearly one among these courtiers whose accomplishments and leisure are devoted to the art of pleasing. The hyperboles of such lovers' praises and plaints—"heav'nly beames," "hellish paine"—are not distant from his own when he calls Stella "so true a Deitie" in Sonnet 4, or paints his "paine" and his "hell" in the two introductory sonnets. Nor has his own sequence been free of the mythologizing he mocks in lines 5 and 6. In Sonnet 2 Astrophil describes loving as conquest by Cupid's arrow which, in the fifth sonnet, he confesses:

> An image is, which for our selves we carve;
> And, fooles, adore in temple of our hart.

Here "we" includes himself again among other lovers, and also specifically love poets who are the makers of images such as those he ridicules in the very next sonnet.

In his catalogue Astrophil then attacks the affected posturing of pastoral verse, of which he is not specifically guilty in his sonnet sequence. Yet his accusation that its pretense demands "hiding" a courtly identity reminds readers of his own allegorical name, announcing an assumed character (and one which was conventionally thought of as a shepherd).[47] To the circle familiar with Sidney, his *Arcadia* also would be called to mind, in which many courtly figures put on rural disguises. One such retires to rustic life behind the allegorical name of Philisides, like Astrophil an obvious anagram for Philip Sidney.[48] Rather than distinguishing his style from pastoral absurdities, Astrophil's mocking lines therefore call up resemblances. The remaining modes catalogued, sugared mellifluousness and hyperbolic complaint, are not much in evidence prior to Sonnet 6, but do not lack for prominent later examples. Sonnet 100 catalogues apostrophes to Stella's tears which rain upon flowers, her "honied sighs," and her sweetly breathed utterance:

> O plaints conserv'd in such a sugred phraise,
> That eloquence it selfe envies your praise.

Among other complaints, Sonnet 95 addressed to the lover's "deere sighs," which remain his only "true friends" when sorrow has killed his tears, could match the weeping and sighing mocked by exaggeration in Sonnet 6.

The pattern of connections between the absurd poetic styles parodied in the catalogue and Astrophil's own sonnets, and between him and the courtly makers of such love poetry, prevents an ending like that of Wyatt's satire. Astrophil cannot propose an alternative style of his own because he is not identified with one, does not seem here to believe in its possibilities.[49] Instead he casts doubt on the truth of poetry including his own, reminding readers of what preceding sonnets have made known: of his calculated plan to use verse in pursuit of Stella; of his admission to manipulating its terms; his complicity as love poet in the creation and worship of idols; above all, his distinction between what verse can show or paint and what is in his heart. Astrophil's distrust is not principally of fine inventions, but of poetry's power to "display" inward states. Like *show* and *paint, display* can have the innocent or neutral meaning of unfolding or exhibiting, but also the more suspect suggestion of ostentation. Both possibilities seem to be at work in Sonnet 6.

The evocation in lines 1 through 11 of attitudes associated with the plain style is therefore used to point up Astrophil's different sense of the relation of poetry to inward states in the last three lines. Echoing Petrarch's lover, Sidney again uses an allusion to poetic convention to distinguish Astrophil's concerns. For in sonnets like Petrarch's Sonnet 170, the figure of the speaker, his attitudes toward poetry, and the passions which incapacitate him from writing it, make revealing contrasts with Astrophil. Petrarch's poet-lover trembles breathlessly under the assault of his beloved's eyes; it is their power, and Cupid's, which render him inarticulate. He abandons versifying because her virtue defeats his most skillful efforts, and because the extremity of what is in his heart—desire, fear, pain, submission, awe—stops his voice. Astrophil's situation in Sonnet 6, despite his echoes of Petrarch's trembling voice, is presented very differently. No god rules this lover, and if, as other sonnets say, Stella's power commands him, he nevertheless has independent resources of attention and energy here to give to the subject of poetry. Though his inward states render him tremulous, they do not transcend all utterance as do those of Petrarch's lover, nor do they overwhelm him. He retains his powers of articulation and choice—"I can speake . . . and feele . . . But thinke"—and also makes a conscious decision about the form in which he will exhibit what is in the heart. In this important respect he differs from the lover known to Sidney in Tottel's version of Wyatt's sonnet, who seeks how "To vtter forth the smart I bide within." Astrophil will unfold a "Map," a conventional metaphor for the face, but also, as Samuel Daniel describes in *A Defence of Ryme,* a "superficiall Card" which shows in abstract representation a country "neuer seene, which alwayes proues other to the eye than the imagination forecast it."[50] He will therefore exhibit in diagram and epitome an inward "state" which remains distinct from its depiction. The effect is again to focus on the distance between what is in Astrophil's heart and what his poetry will "display." This is paradoxically far wider even than the distance between the unuttered smart of Wyatt's lover and his outward experience. As in Sonnet 2, the separation seems to be forced on Astrophil by the essential difference between loving in truth and what may be shown in verse. Yet there is also a hint here, as in Sonnet 45, of deliberate witholding, of choosing to keep in reserve what no utterance "brings forth" into the open, or in sight.

Questions about the adequacy of poetry, including Astrophil's, to paint,

show, display what is in the heart are raised in numerous other poems
structured like the sixth sonnet, and using similar stylistic devices. Sonnets 3, 15, 28, 74 all employ the mode of parodying styles which, in 55,
Astrophil explicitly identifies as having been his own. There he characteristically mocks himself in them:

> Muses, I oft invoked your holy ayde,
>   With choisest flowers my speech to engarland so;
>   That it, despisde in true but naked shew,
> Might winne some grace in your sweet skill arraid.
> And oft whole troupes of saddest words I staid,
>   Striving abroad a foraging to go,
>   Untill by your inspiring I might know,
> How their blacke banner might be best displaid.
>   But now I meane no more your helpe to trie,
> Nor other sugring of my speech to prove,
> But on her name incessantly to crie:
> For let me but name her whom I do love,
>   So sweete sounds straight mine eare and heart do hit,
>   That I well find no eloquence like it.

The parodies in these sonnets again make connections with his habitual
styles elsewhere in the sequence, so that he is repeatedly included in the
categories of lovers and love poets—"some," "them," or "you"—whose
styles he ridicules. For example, "You" in Sonnet 15 who sigh "poore
Petrarch's long deceased woes" can count among their company the author of many complaints echoing Petrarch in the sequence, although in
Sonnet 74 Astrophil jokingly vows that he is not one of such "pick-purse"
poets. In other instances, the wits whose "fancies" are "maskt" in sonnet
3, and the makers of "allegorie's curious frame" in Sonnet 28, are also
criticized for styles actually resembling his own, although there again
Astrophil disavows the likeness:

> I list not dig so deepe for brasen fame.
> When I say *'Stella,'* I do mean the same.

Since these very lines of Sonnet 28 are in the midst of a number of poems
punning on the real name of Lady Rich, they pointedly remind the reader
that, when Astrophil says *"Stella,"* he has in fact allegorized Penelope
Rich into a star. Because these parodies of others' styles are simultaneously self-parodies, they implicate Astrophil in poetic practices which he then
calls in question. In this sense they function in a parallel fashion to the
double language of Wyatt's sonnet comparing the speaker to an instrument for filing, who uses it to confess his own doubleness.

Nor is the reader allowed to trust the solutions posed as alternatives to suspect poetic styles in the conclusions of Sidney's poems. For again in Sonnets 3, 15, 28, 55, and 74, as in 6, the speaker seems to offer in place of fine, far-fetched, curious verse, the more trustworthy simplicity of unadorned speech. Yet because the endings of these sonnets are radical oversimplifications of Astrophil's struggles, they are themselves open to question. They solve no more than does his Muse's prescription in the last line of Sonnet 1. For example, Sonnet 3 concludes that the true poet's skill "But Copying is" like the humblest scribe's. This solution, however, is cast in doubt by Astrophil's immediately preceding admission in Sonnet 2 that praise in his verse at least manipulates, if it does not falsely paint over with the rhetorical colors of his skill, the true nature of what is in his heart. What must the reader be expected then to ask about the poem of praise immediately following this confession? We would seem to be alerted to hear with scepticism the poet's claim that he need only copy Stella's face to show in verse what in truth love is. Yet the questions about poetry are not those raised by the trembling voice of Petrarch's speaker in Sonnets like 170, where the extremity of love overpowers utterance.

Limits had also been imposed upon the power of poetry by sonnets in the tradition of Petrarch's Sonnet 247—"*Lingua mortale al suo stato divino / giunger non pote*" (" 'Mortal tongue cannot reach her divine state' ")—or Sonnet 20—*qual son poria mai salir tant'alto?* ("what sound could ever rise so high?"). There the issue is the inadequacy of human language to copy the transcendent truth and beauty written (by Nature, by Love, by God) in the lady's face. Sidney alludes to that motif in many sonnets of *Astrophil and Stella.* An example is Sonnet 50, where Astrophil again acts out the struggle to render the fullness of his thoughts in words:

> With sad eyes I their weake proportion see,
> To portrait that which in this world is best.

Yet as is characteristic of his other adaptations, Sidney develops this motif in ways which transform it to present Astrophil's different concerns. Although he claims that his subject exceeds his verbal powers by surpassing "all things" in Sonnet 19, by embodying "perfection" in 35, he is not principally troubled by the incapacity of his speech to transcend human limits. His questions are rather about the disinterestedness, even the credibility, of poetic language, and therefore about its portrayal of what is in the heart.

Sonnet 35, for example, opens with lines which may be read as a rhetorical question designed for witty compliment, but also as an expression of doubt about poetic praise:

> What may words say, or what may words not say,
> Where truth it selfe must speake like flatterie?

A first reading makes these lines resemble a tribute, in the vein of Petrarch's Sonnets 20 and 247, to the virtue of Stella, so absolute that when
described by the poet it arouses incredulity in mortal readers. Yet the
phrasing actually belongs to a worldly and social situation in which truth
does not occupy a transcendent position along with the lady's beauty and
virtue. Here in Sonnet 35 truth is personified as a courtly dissembler
compelled, by self-interest or fear, to use a style indistinguishable from
false compliment. In this world, poetic expression—what words may or
may not say—is determined by what can be credited. The focus of the
sonnet shifts then to what is in Astrophil's heart, the matter which he
seeks fit words to paint:

> Within what bounds can one his liking stay,
> Where Nature doth with infinite agree?
>   What *Nestor's* counsell can my flames alay,
> Since Reason's selfe doth blow the cole in me?
> And ah what hope, that hope should once see day,
> Where *Cupid* is sworne page to Chastity?

By following his complaint about the fires of passion with these lines
about hope, Astrophil reminds the reader that his words are not disinterested efforts to tell the truth but praise calculated to persuade. (The lines
must be included precisely for this remainder, since they do not quite fit
the logic of the preceding series of questions.) Astrophil then returns
explicity to the relation between flattery and the truth of poetic language:

> Honour is honour'd, that thou doest possesse
>   Him as thy slave, and now long needy Fame
>   Doth even grow rich, naming my *Stella's* name.
> Wit learnes in thee perfection to expresse,
>   Not thou by praise, but praise in thee is raisde:
>   It is a praise to praise, when thou art praisde.

For the first time in this sonnet the poet pays direct compliments to Stella,
but they do not locate her in a transcendent sphere. Honor is her "slave,"
a word debasing the relation of lover to sovereign mistress. Fame is a kind
of entrepreneur promoting her name for his own gain. Wit, in seeming
contrast to these base figures, is a poet inspired by divine powers in Stella
to praise her perfection, presumably in words more credible than those of
truth itself. Yet the moral power of poetry is undermined by the proximity
of "truth" which sounds like "flatterie," and "naming" for gain, to "praise,"
especially when that term is stressed five times in the last two lines. At
worst, praise is a corruption of truth, at least a witty game, like Astrophil's
disguise of his subject, Lady Rich, "raised" to the stars by what the reader
is again pointedly reminded here is the flattering and false name of Stella.

Suggesting both interpretations simultaneously, the sonnet implicates itself in the questionable nature of praise, which may also disguise what is
in Astrophil's heart. As in some of Wyatt's sonnets, language here may
hide one meaning behind another. For Sidney, however, this capacity is
specifically associated with the poet's skill.

In addition to literary allusion, parody and self-parody, and burlesque,
Sidney uses structural devices that also point to inner states as distinct
from their outward show in poetry. Sonnet 80, for instance, gives a different
shape to the game of flattery, or praise, but again plays with the issue of
its distance from what is in the lover's heart:

> Sweet swelling lip, well maist thou swell in pride,
>   Since best wits thinke it wit thee to admire;
>   Nature's praise, Vertue's stall, *Cupid's* cold fire,
> Whence words, not words, but heav'nly graces slide.
> The new *Pernassus,* where the Muses bide,
>   Sweetner of musicke, wisedome's beautifier:
>   Breather of life, and fastner of desire,
> Where Beautie's blush in Honour's graine is dide.
>   Thus much my heart compeld my mouth to say,
>   But now spite of my heart my mouth will stay,
> Loathing all lies, doubting this Flatterie is:
>   And no spurre can his resty race renew,
>   Without how farre this praise is short of you,
> Sweet lip, you teach my mouth with one sweet kisse.

The structural device for measuring the distance between the lover's inward state and his showing of it in verse is used by Sidney here, and
elsewhere in the sequence, for the first time in English sonnets.[51] The
device is a kind of frame, or poem-within-a-poem. That is, the opening
two quatrains are to be read as verses; the sestet as a spoken comment on
them directed to Stella in Astrophil's own voice. One effect, seen in sonnets previously discussed, is to juxtapose contrasting styles. Lines 1 through
8 burlesque hyperbolic, mythologized, sugared verse by even greater exaggeration than ornate literary styles are parodied elsewhere by Astrophil.
In the sestet he speaks in a simpler, and therefore seemingly more trustworthy manner; the metaphor of spurring a horse to race makes him a
manly sportsman, as in the opening of Sonnet 2, rather than a courtly
maker. Yet more distinctly than other such contrasts, the frame draws a
line between the lover who speaks the sestet, and his poem, which is the
octave. That is an object wrought by him, including what he decides it
should and omitting what he wishes to reserve. Attention is therefore
called to the limits of the poem, and to its distinction from what is in the
lover's heart. To insist on that separation, Sidney makes fun of the conventional relation between heart and mouth, making the mouth the plain

stylist who distrusts the literary ornateness of the heart. A further result
is to implicate Astrophil as both poet and lover in "praise" which is
indistinguishable from "lies." Astrophil's persuasive tactics are crude in
this sonnet, making the poem more silly than witty, but it shows clearly,
perhaps because of its unsubtlety, the function of the poem-within-a-
poem to measure the distance between heart and mouth, or inward states
and their outward show.

The distinguishing line is drawn whether the frame comes at the end,
as in the sestet of Sonnet 80 and at line 12 of sonnet 50—"And now my
pen these lines had dashed quite"—or at the beginning, as in Sonnet 37,
or both at the beginning and ending, in 34. Most successful of the sonnets
using this device is Sonnet 40, in which a poem of complaint and persuasion is introduced by one line of speech by Astrophil to himself:

> As good to write as for to lie and grone.
>   O *Stella* deare, how much thy power hath wrought,
>   That has my mind, none of the basest, brought
> My still kept course, while others sleepe, to mone.
> Alas, if from the height of Vertue's throne,
>   Thou canst vouchsafe the influence of a thought
>   Upon a wretch, that long thy grace hath sought;
> Weigh then how I by thee am overthrowne:
>   And then, thinke thus, although thy beautie be
>   Made manifest by such a victorie,
> Yet noblest Conquerours do wreckes avoid.
>   Since then thou hast so farre subdued me,
>   That in my heart I offer still to thee,
> O do not let thy Temple be destroyd.

Line 1 is outside the grammar of the poem-within-a-poem. Those thirteen
lines of verse have an elaborate shape, beginning and ending in balanced,
formal addresses to Stella, developed by extended, conventional metaphors—astronomical, political, military, religious—into a connected argument: "if . . . then . . . then . . . Yet . . . Since then." The first line, by
contrast, is only a fragment of a sentence, which therefore must be mut-
tered by Astrophil to himself, for he would need no explanation to fill out
its meaning. By contrast with his poem, it is casual, even colloquial. "As
good to write" has the sloppy, pragmatic quality it would have in daily
speech, "good" not referring to the power emanating from virtue's throne
but meaning something more like useful, effective, self-serving. This line
locates the speaker in a situation, alone and kept awake by love's pain
(deduced from the convention that the lover lies and groans aloud when
in his solitary chamber, and from the presence of two sonnets on sleepless-
ness immediately preceding). It creates an occasion for the poem, Astrophil's decision to do something instead of lying about in pain. It shows

his motives for writing, a desire to paint his sufferings in verse in order to alleviate them more effectively than by groaning, and to persuade Stella to grant him the grace he sought fit words to obtain in Sonnet 1.

Because this line spells out his situation and motives, and because its exaggeration consciously mocks the lover's posture, we see the speaker as aware of himself, moved by powerful passions but not wholly identifying himself with them, presenting them in his poem but exerting a shaping force so that they are distinct from his solitary groaning. That sense of his inward state would emerge from the character of his verses themselves, since their announcement of Astrophil's helpless prostration is belied by their witty control. Yet the presence of the frame makes much more marked than would the verses alone a distinction between his inward state and its show in poetry, by contrasting his poetic style with the language Astrophil talks to himself. As with other sonnets using a frame, the reader is made to think of Astrophil's verses as an object shaped by his skill, by contrast with his mind, which is "wrought" by Stella's power. They depict what he feels, but in a form involving prior selection and arrangement. They are uttered by a speaker who represents Astrophil, but cannot simply be identified with him as would be possible without the first line. They are written in a poetic style chosen by him, but different from the language he talks to himself.

The use of framing comments both at the beginning and end is somewhat clumsy in Sonnet 34, but its more uncertain experimentation is useful in showing some of the effects the frame may have been intended by Sidney to create:[52]

> Come let me write, 'And to what end?' To ease
>   A burthned hart. 'How can words ease, which are
>   The glasses of thy dayly vexing care?'
> Oft cruell fights well pictured forth do please.
> 'Art not asham'd to publish thy disease?'
>   Nay, that may breed my fame, it is so rare:
>   'But will not wise men thinke thy words fond ware?'
> Then be they close, and so none shall displease.
>   'What idler thing, then speake and not be hard?'
> What harder thing then smart, and not to speake?
> Peace, foolish wit, with wit my wit is mard.
> Thus write I while I doubt to write, and wreake
>   My harmes on Ink's poore losse, perhaps some find
>   *Stella's* great powrs, that so confuse my mind.

The phrases "Come let me write . . . Thus write I" frame a debate within Astrophil about the relation of poetry to what is in his heart. Debates of various kinds occur often in *Astrophil and Stella*. The lover's opponent is sometimes a personified abstraction, like Reason in Sonnet 10 or Patience

in 56, elsewhere a critical friend as in Sonnets 14 and 21. These debates
are acknowledged as a means of representing conflicts within the speaker,
as for instance in Sonnet 47 where a debate is concluded when Astrophil
admits that his eye, beholding Stella, "Doth make my heart give to my
tongue the lie" for denying his love for her. This kind of debate is, with
the metaphor of civil war within the lover's breast, among the most
common of means in sixteenth-century verse for representing such
conflicts.[53] What is peculiar to Sidney's concerns in Sonnet 34 is that here
the debate does not represent a struggle between such conventional opponents as "will and wit" in Sonnet 4, or "*Heroicke* minde" and "*Love*" in
25, or Virtue and Desire in 71. The debate here is between Astrophil's
conflicting attitudes toward poetry. With one voice he argues its usefulness to relieve his pain and to persuade the object of his desire. On the
other hand he shows aristocratic distaste for its public exposure of what
is in the heart, recalling some uneasiness over poetic "display" in Sonnet
6. Similar distaste can be heard in the financial metaphor of poetry as
"ware" to be traded for "fame," predicting the personification of Fame in
the next sonnet as a promoter growing rich by praising Stella. This critical
voice even doubts the private efficacy of poetry to alleviate the lover's
sufferings by expressing them, because words reflect inward states as in a
mirror continually holding them in sight. By contrast the defender of
poetry defines it in Astrophil's characteristic comparison to painting which
can picture forth inward states with a pleasing skill. This is the voice
which speaks the framing lines concluding the debate about writing. Unexpectedly the implications of the metaphor of writing as painting a picture become the focus of Astrophil's uneasiness, for the ending stresses the
distance between what may be shown in verse and what is in the speaker's
heart even *while* he writes.

Versions of this dramatic situation are acted out several times in the
sequence. It occurs first in the conclusion of Sonnet 2, previously discussed, where the contrast between Astrophil's published language and his
simultaneous inward monologue is stressed, and made an issue for the
sequence of poems to follow. Writing while doubting what he writes is
again Astrophil's situation in Sonnet 50:

> So that I cannot chuse but write my mind,
> And cannot chuse but put out what I write.

The struggle is also described in Sonnet 19:

> My best wits still their owne disgrace invent:
> My verie inke turnes straight to *Stella's* name;
> And yet my words, as them my pen doth frame,
> Avise themselves that they are vainely spent.

This situation dramatizes a conflict within Astrophil such as the conventional devices of the debate and the metaphorical civil war represent, but with the crucial difference that the struggle is focused on his power to "invent" poetry distanced from what is in his heart. Here the verb "invent," like *frame* previously discussed, characteristically associates with the act of writing verse the innocent or neutral meaning of composing, and also the possibility of false fabrication. Astrophil's uneasiness about this process is especially clear in the framing conclusion of Sonnet 34, "Thus write I while I doubt to write," but what is not clear is the relation, even the grammatical connection, of that statement to the closing phrases:

> Thus write I while I doubt to write, and wreake
> My harmes on Ink's poore losse, perhaps some find
> *Stella's* great powrs, that so confuse my mind.

Astrophil may mean that, while he struggles with writing, absorbed in his passions and words, others look directly to Stella where they "find"—sometimes a synonym for the act of inventing—what would resolve all his difficulties. Conclusions of other sonnets, for example 3, 15, 19, offer parallels to such a compliment. Astrophil's lines also may be read to mean that, while he recognizes the insufficiency of his verses, they nevertheless reflect, as in a mirror, something of his inward confusion and therefore, however imperfectly, testify to Stella's command over him. The grammatical weakness here is perhaps a sign that Sidney did not fully work out the conclusion to the debate of Sonnet 34, but it can nevertheless show something of his intentions. For in addition to sharing the effects of framing lines in other sonnets, it evokes the sense of a complex and confused struggle, carried on in a continuing inward debate for which poetry—"Ink's poore losse"—is an impoverished rendering.

The relation of words to what is in the heart is approached often in Sidney's sequence through explicit comment on the moving power of poetry. In Sonnet 45, previously discussed, Astrophil borrows what in 36 he calls "all sweete stratagems sweete Arte can showe" to turn himself into a tragic "tale" that Stella may pity him. Sonnet 44 speculates that his poems, though they portray his "sense of inward smart," fail to stir her to pity because when they enter her celestial mind they are transformed to hymns of joy. That motif is reversed in Sonnet 57, where Astrophil's "thorowest words, fit for woe's selfe to grone," instead of moving her, turn his woe to rejoicing when Stella sings them. Sonnet 58 recasts that occasion in the form of a pseudoclassical debate between alternatives weighed in the octave, which Astrophil then asks the reader to judge. The debated powers are "words" and "pronouncing":[54]

> Doubt there hath bene, when with his golden chaine
> The Oratour so farre men's harts doth bind,
> That no pace else their guided steps can find,
> But as he them more short or slacke doth raine,
> Whether with words this soveraignty he gaine,
> Cloth'd with fine tropes, with strongest reasons lin'd,
> Or else pronouncing grace, wherewith his mind
> Prints his owne lively forme in rudest braine.

Here the relative moving powers of words and their delivery are balanced with an impartiality that is only pretended, since "pronouncing grace" and "lively forme" attach to utterance much more dignity and force than the metaphors of clothing and ornament give to written words. This bias prepares for the sestet, in which Astrophil attributes greater powers of moving to Stella's recitation than to his own verbal skill:

> Now judge by this: in piercing phrases late,
> Th' anatomy of all my woes I wrate,
> *Stella's* sweete breath the same to me did reed.
> O voice, ô face, maugre my speeche's might,
> Which wooed wo, most ravishing delight
> Even those sad words even in sad me did breed.

Astrophil's way of describing his poetry as an "anatomy of all my woes" has his characteristic stamp. For an anatomy is a model representing, or a treatise dissecting, the structure of its subject, and therefore resembles the "Map" representing his "state" in Sonnet 6. Both are renderings in another form of their originals. The description is also characteristic in that it is phrased with an exaggeration—"all my woes"—shared by other such references to his verses: "thorowest words, fit for woe's selfe to grone" in Sonnet 57; "whole troupes of saddest words ... Striving ... How their blacke banner might be best displaid" in 55; "the verie face of wo" in 45; "all the Map of my state" in 6; "the blackest face of woe" in the opening sonnet. Such calculated exaggeration itself shows a detachment from his own efforts as lover and as poet. It acknowledges strong passions with which Astrophil does not wholly identify himself, and raises questions about poetry's anatomizing of them.

   Here in Sonnet 58 he endows verse with a persuasive force independent of his own motives and in explicit contradiction of his inward state, since what his sorrowful words recited by Stella cause him to experience is "most ravishing delight." That definition of poetry's effect resembles language used by Sidney in *An Apologie for Poetrie,* when he says of the Romans' name ("*Vates,* which is as much as Diuiner, Fore-seer, or Prophet") for the poet, "so heauenly a title did that excellent people bestow vpon this hart-rauishing knowledge."[55] There the defining phrase clearly has the religious meaning of transporting in ecstasy, as it does also in the Seventh Song of *Astrophil and Stella,* giving poetry a more than human power, like grace.[56] The same possibility is at work in Sonnet 58, where the "ravishing delight" of poetry is caused by Stella's graceful voice and face. Yet it has been shown that Sidney's other terms for defining poetry—*paint, show, praise, display, invent*—in both *An Apologie for Poetrie* and *Astrophil and Stella* have simultaneously innocent and tainted meanings. The same is true also of the phrase "ravishing delight" in Sonnet 58, where it is given its sexual meaning by association in an extended metaphor with "wooed" and "breed." Astrophil's poetry is personified as a seducer who, while pursuing "wo," inadvertently ravishes and even impregnates Astrophil himself. This inept bumbler (like the many seducers in literature of the period who are tricked into sleeping with the wrong women) is not controlled or trusted by Astrophil, who dissociates "sad me" from such an irresponsible fool as "those sad words." They therefore embody what in Sonnet 45 he calls the "tale of me," but not "I."

Astrophil and Stella begins with two sonnets clearly designed as an introduction to the sequence. They focus on the speaker's uneasiness about the distinction between loving in truth and love shown in poetry, a subject considered *explicitly* in approximately one-fifth of these one hundred and eight sonnets. Employed in this exploration are a variety of verbal devices which accumulate related effects. The first two sonnets introduce a vocabulary for writing poetry—*paint, show, praise*—that is repeated and developed in connection with other recurrent terms to distinguish what is in the lover's heart from his poetic representation of it. Used to similar ends are other words and grammatical constructions bearing different or conflicting meanings, allusions transforming attitudes traditionally associated with other poetry, stylistic parodies including self-parodies, the structural device of a frame around a poem-within-a-poem, and many other explicit comments by Astrophil on himself in the act of writing or on his poems as objects with an independent existence and moving power. The fact that the sequence focuses in its opening, and for the first time in English poetry, on the lover's struggle to write truly about what is in his heart, that it expands so often on this preoccupation, and that so many uses of language are employed to similar ends in its elaboration, make convincing evidence that Sidney's deepest concerns are involved in this struggle.

To explore the nature of these issues more fully (and as further signs of their significance for the poet), it is useful to see how the sonnets explicitly about writing love poetry provide ways of exploring inward states in other poems of the sequence which seem to originate in different situations and concerns.

Sonnet 40, "As good to write as for to lie and grone," is immediately

150

CHAPTER THREE

preceded by two sonnets which also depend on the situation of the lover alone in his chamber, evoked or explored again in Sonnets 31 and 32, and in the group extending from Sonnet 96 through 99. Models were known to Sidney in Italian, French, and English of sonnets in which the speaker is wakeful with desire, courts sleep as release, or dreams of his beloved, but the conventionality of these motifs does not in itself explain Sidney's reasons for elaborating upon them. For other motifs traditionally associated with the sonnet form are not treated at all in his poetry. The promise to immortalize the beloved in verse, as has been said, is never alluded to—not even parodied—in *Astrophil and Stella,* a pointed omission in a collection containing so many sonnets explicitly concerned with the power of poetry and its limitations. Experimental though *Astrophil and Stella* is, and designed to accomplish in English achievements comparable to those of continental sonneteers, it was evidently not intented to cataloque all the established forms and conventions of the sonnet sequence. The presence of a related group of motifs in nine nocturnal sonnets is therefore in itself evidence of their particular interest for Sidney.

Sonnet 40 provides a partial explanation for this interest. Nocturnal poems create a plausible situation for the lover to be alone, a rare occurrence taking place virtually only in chambers and closets. That situation carries associations of the chamber with experiences described as "inward" in all its sixteenth-century meanings. In Sonnet 40 the first line is understood as spoken by Astrophil to himself when no one can hear him. It is therefore like an aside, giving a momentary glimpse of what is in his heart, or a piece of a soliloquy, in that it illustrates the way he talks aloud to himself. It therefore provides a contrast with outward show, represented in the sonnet by the thirteen remaining lines, which are understood to be the poem he decides to write to Stella instead of continuing his private groaning. The special nature of Sidney's interest in nocturnal poems can also be explained in part by the pattern of connections between the sonnets presenting Astrophil alone in his chamber and the still greater number, previously discussed, which focus explicitly on his struggle with the discrepancy between loving and writing about love.

Sonnet 32, which plays with the motif of the lover visited in sleep by the apparent sight of his beloved, shares a vocabulary associated in other sonnets with writing verse. It also uses a mode of self-parody resembling Astrophil's manner elsewhere in describing love poetry, including his own. These connections show interest in the lover wakeful, sleeping, or dreaming, as a situation in which Sidney could explore the relation of images to actuality, the power of the image-making faculty, and its fidelity both to external fact and to inward states:

> *Morpheus,* the lively sonne of deadly sleepe,
> Witnesse of life to them that living die:

> A Prophet oft, and oft an historie,
> A Poet eke, as humours fly or creepe,
> Since thou in me so sure a power doest keepe,
>   That never I with clos'd-up sense do lie,
>   But by thy worke my *Stella* I descrie,
> Teaching blind eyes both how to smile and weepe,
>   Vouchsafe of all acquaintance this to tell,
> Whence hast thou Ivorie, Rubies, pearle and gold,
> To shew her skin, lips, teeth and head so well?
> 'Foole,' answers he, 'no *Indes* such treasures hold,
>   But from thy heart, while my sire charmeth thee,
> Sweet *Stella's* image I do steale to mee.'

Joking first about the power of dreams to act as prophet by foretelling the future or as historian by recounting the past, Astrophil then expands on the possibility of Morpheus as "Poet eke" (the archaic intensive exaggerating his mock amazement) whose high-flying power he questions. The vocabulary and manner used to characterize Morpheus' art is like the language describing Astrophil's own poetry in other sonnets. It can "shew" Stella's lovely face, in the bejeweled style of a blazon like Sonnet 9. Here the verb has the morally neutral meaning of depicting or causing to be seen, yet Morpheus' power of showing has deceiving possibilities as well. For what it makes visible is an "image," defined in Sonnet 5 as a false idol, which appears with all the liveliness of actual sight, Astrophil says, when "I with clos'd-up sense do lie." Like the verb "shew" here, "lie" has an innocent meaning, the primary one in this instance, of recline, but it also hints at the possibility of false-speaking here and in many other uses in Sidney's sequence.[57] For when he does "lie" dreaming, Astrophil sees Stella present to him although in fact she is not.

The association of sleep and dreams with "false fained" appearances, as in Wyatt's sonnet entitled in Tottel's miscellany "The louer hauing dreamed enioying of his loue, complaineth that the dreame is not either longer or truer," is traditional to nocturnal poems.[58] The motif was known to Sidney in continental as well as English models. What is special in his use of it is its association with writing, with art. Sleep and dreams, like poetry, may show what is in the heart, but what they show is only an "image." So the dream is at the same distance from inward experience, has the same capacity to alter it, as poetry. Although it was a commonplace of sixteenth-century psychological treatises to attribute dreams to the same image-making faculty—phantasy, fancy, imagination—as the feigned images of art, it was not a convention in nocturnal poems to use a specific vocabulary about writing.[59] This seems to have been Sidney's invention: to carry over to them from his sonnets explicitly about writing a vocabulary for that activity which characteristically bears neutral and suspect meanings simultaneously. In so doing he raises questions about the image-making faculty which are not asked in nocturnal poems by other writers, even when they borrow from Sidney's.

The suspect activity of poetry in Sonnet 32 implicates Morpheus, his father Sleep, and eventually Astrophil himself. For Morpheus accomplishes his thievery while his parent "charmeth" Astrophil. This is another verb used repeatedly by Sidney in *An Apologie for Poetrie* to define the power of verse, giving it magical properties which can be viewed as divinely elevating, or as the dangerously seductive spells of an enchantress or a siren.[60] The lover, victim of these base conspirators, is himself a carver of golden idols, like the gilded blazon of Stella in Sonnet 9, or her deification in Sonnet 4. Of such false worship Astrophil makes mocking confession in Sonnet 5, previously discussed, but that early recognition of his sin effects no permanent conversion. For in Sonnet 40, when he decides to write verse instead of lying in pain, what he invents in his poem and worships in his heart is an idol like the one vandalized in Sonnet 32 by Morpheus. Morpheus and Astrophil are therefore rival poets, as are Fancy and Astrophil in Sonnet 45. Yet in that poem it is Astrophil who helps himself to the stratagems of Fancy, whereas in Sonnet 32 Morpheus is the thief, vying with Astrophil for riches which surpass actuality—"no *Indes* such treasures hold"—by the powers of invention, meaning discovery and also perhaps false fabrication.

The vocabulary shared by Sonnet 32 with sonnets explicitly concentrated on poetry's powers of true representation appears in a variety of instances in the other sonnets where Astrophil lies alone in his chamber. In Sonnet 39 he offers a bribe to Sleep if it will come to him: "thou shalt in me, / Livelier then else-where, *Stella's* image see." In Sonnet 96 Silence "displaies," in 97 the moon "Shewes," in 99 the night "perswades," with powers like that of the poet. In Sonnet 98 Astrophil tosses in his bed:

> While the blacke horrors of the silent night,
> Paint woe's blacke face so lively to my sight,
> That tedious leasure marks each wrinckled line.

The lines referred to are simultaneously the tangles of the troubled lover's bedclothes, the wrinkles marked by long suffering on the imagined face of woe, and the verses painted by darkness to depict that tragic mask as a mirror reflecting Astrophil's own pain.

The pervasive presence of this vocabulary points to resemblances, of special interest to Sidney, between the situations of the poet struggling to show in verse what is truly in his heart, and the lover in his chamber alone with only images of his beloved. These, "wrought" by powers resembling his own art, are brought to him by sleep, dreams, silence, moonlight, night, darkness, or his own fancy, as in Sonnet 38, one of the most serious and sustained of Sidney's explorations of the nocturnal situation:

This night while sleepe begins with heavy wings
   To hatch mine eyes, and that unbitted thought
   Doth fall to stray, and my chiefe powres are brought
To leave the scepter of all subject things,
The first that straight my fancie's error brings
   Unto my mind, is *Stella's* image, wrought
   By *Love's* owne selfe, but with so curious drought,
That she, me thinks, not onely shines but sings.
   I start, looke, hearke, but what in closde up sence
Was held, in opend sense it flies away,
Leaving me nought but wailing eloquence:
I, seeing better sights in sight's decay,
   Cald it anew, and wooed sleepe againe:
   But him her host that unkind guest had slaine.

Except in the rather feeble last line, the mood of this sonnet is one of grave and troubled melancholy, closer to Petrarch's manner than is characteristic of Sidney. By contrast with the playfulness of his questions to Morpheus in Sonnet 32, Astrophil's reflections here are solemn as he relives a moment more like a flicker of vision than other appearances, and disappearances, of Stella's image. The vocabulary used to define the moral quality of his experience does not here seem mockingly exaggerated, as in so many sonnets where he comments explicitly on his own writing. Nor is it played off with parodic effects against a more blunt, pragmatic speech. The sustained metaphorical pattern of control and escape—"unbitted," "fall," "stray," "leave," "error," "closde," "held," "flies away"—makes a serious issue of the nature of Astrophil's powers once they "leave the scepter of all subject things."

Although in the situation of the sonnet that inward state is attributed to sleep's effect on the lover, many pointed parallels are drawn between sleeping or dreaming and writing, making the metaphors of control and flight pertain to the activity of showing love in poetry. For it is Fancy which is released when controls are lifted from the mind, a faculty associated elsewhere in the sequence and in *An Apologie for Poetrie* with the "high flying liberty of conceit" of the poet, "not inclosed within the narrow warrant" of natural objects, but "freely ranging onely within the Zodiack of his owne wit."[61] What this faculty brings to the sleeping lover is an "image," here "wrought" by Love personified as an artist (like Morpheus in Sonnet 32 and Fancy in 45) to whom Astrophil is rival or pupil. The "image" carved by this master craftsman is so finely made that it "not onely shines but sings." This vision is therefore "better" than the "sights" he can see with the open eyes of mere physical sense.

Yet the use of "image" raises questions about the morality of this vision by recalling its common meaning in *Astrophil and Stella* of false idol. Here it is also given its physiological definition (used again in Sonnet 66) as decayed sense impression, which tends to empty it of religious meanings. The use of "curious" to describe Love's art has a similar effect, since it personifies him as a courtly maker of fine inventions—like "allegorie's curious frame" in Sonnet 28—rather than as a divinely inspired bard. Other terms share Sidney's habit of associating with the activity of writing a vocabulary having both neutral and questionable meanings; "fall to" can mean begin, while "fall" must be associated with a sinful lapse; "error," though originating in the Latin verb meaning to wander, cannot escape suggestions of wrong thinking or falsity.

The image of Stella brought to sleeping Astrophil is not therefore "better" than actuality in any single or simple sense, but he nevertheless wishes to have "held" it. That is the desire of the lover who, when the image escapes, renews his wakeful groaning. Yet it is also the desire of the poet who laments that his moment of vision escapes, leaving him only "wailing eloquence," which is the husk of poetry. It is uttered, it is skillfully wrought, but it cannot hold inward experience. Astrophil's manner is more sorrowful than self-mocking, perhaps because here he does not accuse himself of manipulating language so as to widen the distance between his "wailing eloquence" and his unexpressed state. That is characterized here as a dream rather than as an unspoken poem, and therefore it is an "image wrought" by an art other than his own, which it escapes. The focus of the sonnet seems to be particularly on this sense of helplessness and loss. It dramatizes a special moment of brightness, false perhaps, but more vivid and precious than actuality. This dream the poet experiences inwardly, but cannot capture in his verse, despite the strength of his passion or the eloquence of his complaint.

Other possible interests for Sidney in the situation of the lover alone in his chamber are shown in Sonnet 40 by its contrast between Astrophil's casual language to himself—"As good to write as for to lie and grone"— and his formal style in the poem-within-a-poem addressed to Stella. Private speech is there distinguished from public utterance, internal monologue or soliloquy from verse writing. The situation of the sonnet encourages this because the chamber was traditionally a port of refuge from public curiousity, where the lover can complain unheard, or examine what is in his heart unobserved. This aspect of the situation conventional to nocturnal poems, the lover's "mazefull solitarinesse" as he calls it in Sonnet 96, is stressed by Sidney in a number of poems in which wakeful Astrophil confronts his own mind while all other men are sleeping.

This interest is elaborated most fully in Sonnet 99, in a mood of melancholy reflectiveness similar to that of Sonnet 38:[62]

> When far spent night perswades each mortall eye,
>   To whom nor art nor nature graunteth light,
>   To lay his then marke wanting shafts of sight,

Clos'd with their quivers in sleep's armory;
With windowes ope then most my mind doth lie,
    Viewing the shape of darknesse and delight,
    Takes in that sad hue, which with th'inward night
Of his mazde powers keepes perfit harmony:
    But when birds charme, and that sweete aire, which is
Morne's messenger, with rose enameld skies
Cals each wight to salute the floure of blisse;
In tombe of lids then buried are mine eyes,
    Forst by their Lord, who is asham'd to find
    Such light in sense, with such a darkned mind.

Here Astrophil's situation alone in his chamber is explicitly worked out as a metaphor for his inward condition. His mind is "darkned" so that it becomes an "inward night," but it is also a room "With windowes ope" to allow him a view of the surrounding darkness. Both night and chamber separate him from all other human beings. Their lives are ruled by "light in sense" which does not penetrate his darkened mind. This solitary and very private nocturnal experience has greater intensity for Astrophil than ordinary daytime existence. For when night successfully uses its art of persuasion to make all other men close up their powers of seeing, then is his mind "most" open. It is as if night grants him special gifts of vision, enabling him to view what is unseen. Astrophil therefore becomes a kind of fellow-poet who can paint his own inward state with the same "sad hue" as night. Yet the terms used in the second quatrain to describe this activity again show the lover's troubled sense of discrepancy between inward experience and outward expression. The pun on "lie" is inescapable here, suggesting that its applicability was another reason for Sidney's interest in the situation of the lover in his chamber. Astrophil's wakeful thoughts repose in darkness, and also falsify what they see. Uses elsewhere in the sequence of terms bearing both neutral and suspect meanings are recalled here also by "shape," definable as external form or contour, picture or image, phantom, and disguise. Other suggestions of falsifying are conveyed by the use of "mazde" (echoing "mazefull soliltarinesse" of Sonnet 96) to describe Astrophil's powers, which are therefore said to be overcome with amazement at what he views, but also artfully entangled like a labyrinth, perhaps concealing dangerous secrets. By contrast Sidney's Arcadian complaint of Gynecia describes how the dark cave has overwhelmed her "mas'de head" so that her pen cannot write, nor her tongue recite, yet without raising the issue of falsification. In the later sonnet the grammar of the second quatrain is itself so confused that Sidney seems not to have fully worked out the relationship of these multiple terms. Yet they convey more than the intensity of his inward state and his lack of control over it. He seems powerless to sustain the "shape," perhaps false as well as evanescent, of his inward experience, either in his mind or in a poem.

The sonnets in which Astrophil is alone at night in his chamber show the nature of Sidney's interest in that conventional situation by their many parallels and connections with sonnets dramatizing the speaker's struggle to write truly about what is in his heart. For the nocturnal sonnets provide other situations in which to explore the relations of images to actuality, and furnish metaphors like the chamber, night's darkness, and the dream to characterize the lover's inward state, and to contrast it with outward existence, his own and that of other men. Further parallels with these poems can be found in *Astrophil and Stella* in sonnets like 27, built around the situation of the lover who is again "alone," but "in greatest companie." Chaucer describes Criseyde several times in the midst of a group when "hire herte on oother thyng is, / Although the body sat among hem there."[63] To be in company and yet alone (*accompagnate et sole*) is one of love's contraries in such poems as Petrarch's Sonnet 222. Yet it was not a motif conventional to English or continental sonnets to present the lover in such a situation, as Sidney repeatedly does in *Astrophil and Stella*. Here his departure from tradition points directly to his new concerns.

In a number of poems Astrophil recounts a courtly appearance, as in the tournaments of Sonnets 41 and 53, or presents himself in a social scene, surrounded by courtly acquaintances: "curious wits" in Sonnet 23; "busie wits" in 30; "courtly Nymphs" in 54; "Envious wits" in 104. Their preoccupations and language are contrasted with those which fill his heart and mind *while* he is in their presence. Because the situation of the lover alone in company, unlike the nocturnal motifs, was not a widely established convention available in many models, its use is all the more revealing of Sidney's particular interests. This is especially true since he explores it so often, and in so many connections with other characteristic groups of sonnets in *Astrophil and Stella*. Particularly it seems designed to stress the simultaneity and distinctness of Astrophil's outward, social existence and his continuous inward experience, and to dramatize his consciousness of the distance between them.

Because these sonnets contrast Astrophil's inward states with the concerns of others around him, they suggest parallels with poems in which the lover is alone in his chamber with only images to occupy his darkened mind, while all other men lead a different existence ruled by light and physical sense. Because they show him isolated inwardly while surrounded by court wits and gossip, they make connections with sonnets in which Astrophil rejects the courtly love poetry of "daintie wits" in his effort to show in verse what is truly in his heart. They also resemble others where he confesses to painting his love as praise, while his inward monologue takes a very different form.

Some suggestion for this situation of the lover alone in company might perhaps have been found by Sidney in Petrarch's Sonnet 234, in which the lover contrasts his chamber, once a welcome hiding place, with his present escape from solitude in the refuge of the crowd:

O cameretta che già fosti un porto
a le gravi tempeste mie diurne:
fonte se' or di lagrime notturne
che 'l dì celate per vergogna porto.

O letticciuol che requie eri et conforto
in tanti affanni: di che dogliose urne
ti bagna Amor con quelle mani eburne,
solo ver me crudeli a sì gran torto!

Né pur il mio secreto e 'l mio riposo
fuggo, ma più me stesso e 'l mio pensero
che sequendol talor levommi a volo;

e 'l vulgo a me nemico et odioso
(chi 'l pensò mai?) per mio refugio chero,
tal paura ò di ritrovarmi solo.

O little room that used to be a port from my fierce daily storms, now
you are a fountain of nocturnal tears, which in the daytime I keep
hidden for shame!
O little bed that used to be a rest and comfort among so many labors,
with what sorrowful urns does Love bathe you, with those ivory
hands cruel only toward me, and so unjustly!
Nor do I flee only my hiding place and my rest, but even more myself
and my thoughts that used to raise me in flight as I followed them;
and I seek (whoever thought it?) the mob, inimical and hateful to me,
as a refuge: so afraid am I of being alone.

Sidney reverses the conclusion, emphasizing the lover's isolation in public. He also develops the situation differently, in that in a number of sonnets he attempts to dramatize it, rather than describing it or using it as a kind of allegorical figure. The result is to create a sense of contrasting but simultaneous outward and inward experience. These sonnets give the impression that Astrophil leads a conscious and continuous, hidden existence. The effect is to make him a figure more like Hamlet than like lovers in earlier sixteenth-century poems.

Connections between sonnets dramatizing the lover alone in company and those in which Astrophil seeks true language for what is in the heart are most evident in Sonnet 54:

Because I breathe not love to everie one,
    Nor do not use set colours for to weare,
    Nor nourish speciall lockes of vowed haire,
Nor give each speech a full point of a grone,
The courtly Nymphs, acquainted with the mone
    Of them, who in their lips *Love's* standerd beare;
    'What he?' say they of me, 'now I dare sweare,

He cannot love: no, no, let him alone.'
    And thinke so still, so *Stella* know my mind,
Professe in deed I do not *Cupid's* art;
But you faire maides, at length this true shall find,
That his right badge is but worne in the hart:
    Dumbe Swannes, not chatring Pies, do Lovers prove,
    They love indeed, who quake to say they love.

As in Sonnet 6, Astrophil ridicules by exaggeration the affected style, here not specifically of verse but deportment, of courtly lovers from whom he distinguishes himself. Yet again, in the light of other poems in the sequence like Sonnet 104, the reader knows him to participate at times in the very manner he mocks. This catalogue of affectations therefore works like the parody of courtly styles in Sonnet 6, which is also self-parody. The grounds of Astrophil's claims to difference are also familiar. He shows aristocratic distaste for public exposure of feelings; the vulgar lovers wave their "standerd" as he says in Sonnet 55 that he formerly displayed the banner of all his woes. Again he goes beyond that disdainful attitude to a more inclusive uneasiness about the distance between the inward experience of loving and its formulation in language. In a manner resembling the alternative plain style at the end of sonnets like the sixth, Astrophil swears, "Professe in deed I do not *Cupid's* art." Straightforward in manner only, this line is ambiguous in using the verb "Professe," yet another widely current term for a type of utterance bearing both innocent and tainted meanings: to acknowledge, to avow religious beliefs, but also to pretend to or falsely claim beliefs. What Astrophil then professes to his audience about the truth in his heart again cannot be simply equated with "love indeed," love which is a simple matter of fact, which is simply shown in deeds.

    Following a similar structure in Sonnet 30, Astrophil in lines 1 through 12 parodies in a catalogue of topical questions the manner of "busie wits."[64] They ply him with such questions, showing their self-important preoccupation with politics and affairs of state while he is "still"—silently, continually, in spite of all—lost in thoughts implied to be of far truer magnitude:

Whether the Turkish new-moone minded be
    To fill his hornes this year on Christian coast;
    How *Poles'* right king meanes, without leave of hoast,
To warme with ill-made fire cold *Moscovy,*
If French can yet three parts in one agree;
    What now the Dutch in their full diets boast;
    How *Holland* hearts, now so good townes be lost,
Trust in the shade of pleasing *Orange* tree;
    How *Ulster* likes of that same golden bit,

Wherewith my father once made it halfe tame;
If in the Scottishe Court be weltring yet;
These questions busie wits to me do frame;
    I, cumbred with good maners, answer do,
    But know not how, for still I thinke of you.

He makes metaphorical fun in Sonnet 51 of the weightiness of such
political language when used by court gossips who trouble him with their
news:

    Meane while my heart confers with *Stella's* beames,
        And is even irkt that so sweet Comedie,
        By such unsuted speech should hindred be.

In these sonnets Astrophil carries on intense inward experience, in 51 a
sustained monologue—"confers" and "Comedie" both involve continuous speech—while outwardly engaged in answering or fending off other
talk. This contrast between his internal and social existences then involves
further contrasts between his private state and public interests, and between ostentation (in the pomposity of his courtly acquaintances) and the
unuttered truth of the heart.

Astrophil is surrounded in Sonnet 104 by "Envious wits" who study his
"lookes," and interpret "each word, nay sigh" by which outward signs his
"sorrowe's eloquence" expresses the "hid meaning" they wring from his
heart. Far more often, however, his observers read his appearance wrongly
and so, as at the tournament of Sonnet 41, miss its "true cause." The
errors of their guessing increase the distance between their preoccupations
and the lover's, and emphasize the secrecy of his inward experience,
continuous, conscious, but unexpressed. He describes that hidden activity
in Sonnet 23 by a metaphor of a "race" without beginning or end:

    The curious wits, seeing dull pensivenesse
        Bewray it selfe in my long setled eyes,
        Whence those same fumes of melancholy rise,
    With idle paines, and missing ayme, do guesse.
    Some that know how my spring I did addresse,
        Deeme that my Muse some fruit of knowledge plies:
        Others, because the Prince my service tries,
    Thinke that I thinke state errours to redresse.
        But harder Judges judge ambition's rage,
    Scourge of it selfe, still climing slipprie place,
    Holds my young braine captiv'd in golden cage.
    O fooles, or over-wise, alas the race
        Of all my thoughts hath neither stop nor start,
        But only *Stella's* eyes and *Stella's* hart.

Here his secret thoughts are again contrasted with political affairs. Significantly they are also separated from his own poetry, which must therefore be understood to "addresse"—to direct speech toward, but also to arrange or dress—matters at a distance from the course of his inward activity. The lover is powerless to prevent hints of it from showing in his face, but chooses not to display its true nature in speech or verse.

The distance between the busy world of political talk or court scandal in which the lover moves, and his simultaneous inward experience is explored most seriously in Sonnet 27. Here the social atmosphere is more dangerous, and the false judgments of Astrophil are nastier, making more urgent the need to keep his thoughts hidden from his companions at court:

> Because I oft in darke abstracted guise,
>> Seeme most alone in greatest companie,
>> With dearth of words, or answers quite awrie,
> To them that would make speech of speech arise,
> They deeme, and of their doome the rumour flies,
>> That poison foule of bubling pride doth lie
>> So in my swelling breast that only I
> Fawne on my self, and others to despise:
>> Yet pride I thinke doth not my soule possesse,
> Which lookes too oft in his unflattring glasse:
> But one worse fault, *Ambition,* I confesse,
> That makes me oft my best friends overpasse,
>> Unseene, unheard, while thought to highest place
> Bends all his powers, even unto *Stella's* grace.

The exploration of Astrophil's situation alone in company is fullest here. Detailed descriptions of how he must "Seeme" widen the separation of his social from his inward experience. Just as his daily life is made up of many such occasions, his thoughts are habitually engaged in their own drama. To underline the simultaneity of these outward and inward existences, "oft" is repeated to describe both, but without narrowing the distance or blurring the distinction between them. His inward experience is also presented in more detail in this sonnet: through the metaphor of the soul examining itself in the mirror, and the formula "I confesse," enacting a scene in which the sinner recounts his faults to God. Both of these are private acts, taking place in the lover's chamber or closet, shut away from the great halls through which Astrophil moves unseeing and unhearing, with what in Sonnet 94 he calls "inbent eyes."

Yet the couplet gives Sonnet 27 a witty and unexpected turn. After widely distancing his outward and inward existence, Astrophil then appropriates social, even political language to describe the course of his hidden reflections. The sin he confesses to be "worse" than what his accusers suspect is in fact similar in kind. His admitted *"Ambition"* is not unlike what they judge to be his "pride." Instead of fawning on himself, he pays court to Stella, who occupies the "highest place" of sovereign mistress from which he aspires to receive grace. The wit is complimentary to Stella because it places her above all subjects and worshippers, commanding Astrophil more compellingly than the actual ruler whose court he attends. There is a tinge of bitterness to the wit, however. For it grants Astrophil no more control over the inner drama of his passions than he can exercise over his outward behavior. In this mood it resembles the ending of Sonnet 2, where Astrophil sees both his public act of praising in verse, and his internal self-delusion as the lot of a slave. Both the bitterness and the wit keeping it within the bounds of decorum may signal the closeness of Astrophil's social world, as it is presented in Sonnet 27, to Sidney's own. Its description resembles a letter dated 1586 to Sir Francis Walsingham, explaining a decision by Sidney not to act in a certain manner which

> in my absence thens might bring forth som mischeef and considering how apt the Queen is to interpret every thing to my disadvantage. . . . Therefore I pray yow know that so much of my regality is faln. I understand I am called very ambituous and prowd at home, but certainly if thei knew my ha[rt] they would not altogether so judg me.[65]

The command of Astrophil's Muse at the end of Sonnet 1 to "looke in thy heart and write" has been shown to silence his frustrations only until he begins to compose the next sonnet. It can offer a moment's relief because it is satisfyingly simple, but that kind of simplicity leaves out what has been seen to preoccupy Sidney's speaker throughout the sequence: his uneasy sense of the difficulty for the love poet of showing in verse the truth in his heart. His Muse's formula stands for very different assumptions about both art and inward states from those characteristic of Astrophil.

Writing, to the Muse, is an act comparable to, almost synonymous with, seeing. As the viewer sees immediately and effortlessly with his physical eyes whatever he looks at, the writer's words make their objects directly visible, almost as if words were like sight, identifying the object viewed with the act of viewing. His task is therefore accomplished by turning his gaze in the proper direction. If he is a love poet, that direction will be outward toward his beloved's face, on which is written true beauty, virtue, love, or inward where he will always find it mirrored in his own heart or mind. For Astrophil, however, writing is not like looking, but like showing, painting, praising, displaying, inventing, framing, addressing, professing, lying, dreaming, with all their multiple and even contradictory implications about the relation of poetry to inward truth. Nor are words for Astrophil like sights uniting viewer and object. They have in some

ways the opaque property of things in themselves, with a capacity to come
between the viewer and what he would see: like fine clothing which can
adorn or cover up in Sonnet 58; like pigment "to portrait" in true representation or poor imitation in 50; like banners to give signs or display
ostentatiously in 54 and 55. Words are not found by Astrophil through
looking but inventing, and his inventions are in another way unlike the
objects of physical sight because they are images, dreams, insubstantial
and evanescent, perhaps even false creations, idols.

   Astrophil's awareness that the love poet's right use of words is a far
more difficult task than his Muse would have him believe is demonstrated
everywhere in the sequence. The strongest evidence is its exploitation
throughout of the vocabulary bearing multiple or conflicting meanings to
define the relation of poetry to what is in the heart. This practice implies
that words are not commensurate with inward states as a copy corresponds to its subject, or as a name identifies its referent. Another sign is
the characteristic definition of Astrophil's internal experiences in grammatical constructions capable of being read in more than one direction,
as in the opening line of the sequence which initially leaves unclear whether
"love" is the direct or indirect object. This is a practice which, it has been
shown, Wyatt developed in his work with the sonnet form. Sidney appears
to have rediscovered it independently, but like Wyatt to have associated
it particularly with sonnets, for he does not habitually use such constructions in his other poems, not even the songs inserted in the sequence. The
effect of using grammar ambiguously is again to complicate the relation
of words to what is in the heart, so that they cannot be understood simply
to copy what the writer sees.

   Examples of this device can be found throughout *Astrophil and Stella*.
An instance is in the second sonnet when Astrophil recounts his defiance
of Cupid: "I loved, but straight did not what *Love* decreed." The grammar
compresses the reluctant lover's struggle by allowing two interpretations:
he did not do what Love commanded, instead refused to do anything; he
did, not what love ordered, but something contrary, acting independently.
The meter gives primacy to the first reading; the rhythm of Astrophil's
speech supports the second; the syntax allows both at once. Another line
in which Sidney's sentence structure acts out the struggle against love
occurs in Sonnet 54, where reversible syntax further complicates the multiple possibilities of meaning for the act of professing. "Professe in deed
I do not *Cupid's* art" can be read: "I do not profess Cupid's art in my
deeds, leaving open the possibility that I do in my words"; "I do not—
indeed!—profess Cupid's art" (line 14 offers another use of "indeed" as
an intensifier). If the metrical pattern of the line is stressed, it can even be
understood to say: "I do not indeed profess that art which is Cupid's, but
another art." The sentence structure therefore makes possible characteristic distinctions between what can be known of the lover by the professions
of his poetry, and what is going on in his heart. Another example of

reversible grammar occurs in Sonnet 31 where Astrophil resents proud beauties who "Those Lovers scorne whom that *Love* doth possesse." The arrangement of words, along with the different meanings of "possesse" used as transitive or intransitive verb, act out Astrophil's state: he is one among humiliated lovers possessed by Cupid, enslaved and driven mad by his arrows; he is one among proud lovers who possess ennobling passions.

Further evidence for Astrophil's awareness of the complex relationship of words to what is in the heart, and therefore of the difficulty of using them rightly, is his habit of pointedly repeating the same word while giving it different references or opposing meanings. Too often this rhetorical practice creates effects that seem merely frivolous, almost like the meaningless repetitions by other poets which he ridicules in Sonnet 74: "But (God wot) wot not what they meane by it." Typically his own poetry can furnish many examples of the very stylistic device he parodies, for instance in the last line of Sonnet 10, "By reason good, good reason her to love," or in the thirteen repetitions of "love" in Sonnet 62.

Multiple meanings possible for *love,* serving as both noun and verb, are most often exploited in *Astrophil and Stella,* beginning with the opening line of the sequence. In that prominently placed instance "love" has been seen to refer initially either to the speaker's passion or its object, Stella. The effect there is similar to what Wyatt achieves in one of his sonnet translations, "I find no peace," known to Sidney in Tottel's miscellany, where he substitutes for the lady's title the noun "my delight," with its double reference. The possibility of *love* as a name for Cupid is added in other instances, in Sonnet 62, for example, or far more effectively in Sonnet 31. Here the stylistic device of repeating a word but changing its reference or meaning is not frivolous, but witty and suggestive. It is another means of presenting Astrophil's complex inward state, and his difficulty in finding fit words to define it:

> With how sad steps, ô Moone, thou climb'st the skies,
>> How silently, and with how wanne a face,
>> What, may it be that even in heav'nly place
> That busie archer his sharpe arrowes tries?
> Sure, if that long with *Love* acquainted eyes
>> Can judge of *Love,* thou feel'st a Lover's case;
>> I reade it in thy lookes, thy languisht grace,
> To me that feele the like, thy state descries.
>> That ev'n of fellowship, ô Moone, tell me
> Is constant *Love* deem'd there but want of wit?
> Are Beauties there as proud as here they be?
> Do they above love to be lov'd, and yet
>> Those Lovers scorne whom that *Love* doth possesse?
> Do they call *Vertue* there ungratefulnesse?

Astrophil does not use the term *love* in the first quatrain, but in its place substitutes an irreverent epithet, "That busie archer," for the idol invented by love poets who, subjected by his imaginary arrows, adore him in their hearts. Then using "long with *Love* acquainted eyes" to "judge of *Love*" in the Moon's pale looks, he shifts from the image idolized by poets to the definition of love modish among courtly ladies (like the nymphs in Sonnet 54), or among rival wits (such as those in 104) who try to read Astrophil's heart in his outward behavior. He parodies their equations of love with such signs as wan cheeks and languishing postures, displays which—like Hamlet—he both ridicules and elsewhere at times exhibits. In the sestet Astrophil shifts to the frank, manly manner so often heard in sonnets previously discussed, in contrast to more elaborate, courtly styles. Now he speaks of "constant *Love*," as if to plain men like himself and the Moon the word could have only one, unchanging meaning. They recognize straightforward, honest love, however wordly sophisticates might judge such singleness of heart to be "want of wit." Yet we hear this blunt self-defense also as self-parody, because Astrophil next undercuts any such unmixed definition by wondering if "they above love to be lov'd," a jingle burlesquing empty or cynical uses of the term in fashionable conversation. Here the verb "love," attached to proud beauties, means nothing, or it means a mixture of cruelty, gratified vanity, desire for power, snobbery, while the past participle equates being "loved" with the ritual of courtship and praise relished by these ladies. By contrast, the last use of "*Love*" in the ambiguous syntax of line 13, previously discussed, refers simultaneously to the inward state which can ennoble the lover, and the god which can enslave and madden him.

Such repetitions of a word given different references or definitions act out implications raised explicitly by the question in the last line of Sonnet 31: "Do they call *Vertue* there ungratefulnesse?" The question can be read, as it were, both backwards and forwards. Do the proud beauties call their own ungratefulness (their ingratitude to their constant lovers) a virtue? Do they consider the virtue (of constancy) in their lovers to be ungratefulness in the sense of being unpleasing or distasteful?[66] The simultaneous possibility of both readings points the question toward the relation of names to inward states. The same word can be used in different and contradictory ways; terms can be manipulated to "call" what is in the heart by whatever name suits the calculations of the speaker. All language about inward states is therefore susceptible to the arbitrariness recognized by Astrophil in his own poetry when in Sonnet 2 he confesses, "I call it praise to suffer Tyrannie," or in 5, "What we call *Cupid's* dart, / An image is." Here in the last line of Sonnet 31 he is in fact calling "*Vertue*" (the lady's chastity) "ungratefulnesse" (lack of compliance with his desire). Characteristically he is implicated in the very practice he criticizes.

Similar devices point to Astrophil's awareness of the troublesome relationship of words to what is in the heart in Sonnet 5. Here repetitions of the words "true"—reiterated also throughout the whole sequence—and "Beautie" stress the difficulty of defining the lover's inward states in his poetry:

> It is most true, that eyes are form'd to serve
> The inward light: and that the heavenly part
> Ought to be king, from whose rules who do swerve,
> Rebels to Nature, strive for their owne smart.
>   It is most true, what we call *Cupid's* dart
> An image is, which for our selves we carve;
> And, fooles, adore in temple of our hart,
> Till that good God make Church and Churchman starve.
>   True, that true Beautie Vertue is indeed,
> Whereof this Beautie can be but a shade,
> Which elements in mortall mixture breed:
> True, that on earth we are but pilgrims made,
>   And should in soule up to our countrey move:
>   True, and yet true that I must *Stella* love.

The third quatrain makes especially clear the function of ringing changes on the same words, a practice combining various rhetorical devices illustrated in the handbooks under such categories as *conduplicatio, traductio, ploce, diaphora, antanaclasis.* "Beautie" is a name for that category of beauty which is virtue, or that virtue which is beauty; it is a name for that beauty which is virtuous in its deeds, or which is indeed—truly—virtuous. Again ambiguous grammar supports multiple interpretation. Yet the same word, when modified by "this," refers to a particular mortal beauty. This beauty is only a shadow or unsubstantial image of true beauty, but it is nevertheless experienced as beautiful (like the things of this world in "Leave me ô Love"). It is therefore describable truly by the same word. The effect of these lines is therefore to act out and intensify the issue of the whole sonnet, that Astrophil, as a poet writing about loving, must use the same term to refer to inward experiences which are multiple, conflicting, "and yet true." The strong stress on the last "true" emphasizes the simultaneity of these experiences. The imperative to love Stella does not overturn the other truths. It does not make them irrelevant to Astrophil, or make his adherence to them mechanical. The last line therefore does not undercut the rest, as is usually said to be the effect of Sidney's sonnet endings.[67] Instead it makes a complicating reflection on what precedes, which in turn comments on the conclusion. This has been shown to be a characteristic effect also of Wyatt's final lines in sonnets, themselves often dependent on conjunctions like "yet."

The intensity of Astrophil's passions in this sonnet, as he struggles with the difficulty of using words rightly, is communicated by the pattern of repetition. He uses "true" to assent to, almost to profess in the sense of publicly vowing belief in, a series of statements. It is as if he is attempting to verify or make credible his own feelings about them by formulating them as absolute definitions, "most true." The repetitions, intensifying as the poem develops, build the urgency of his attempts to make words define rightly and permanently what is in his heart. These affirmations of "true" statements might seem to belie Astrophil's sense, shown in other sonnets, that words have a certain arbitrariness. Yet the fact that the same words are used with different referents and changing definitions, even in assertions, makes them work very differently from names for categories catalogued in earlier sixteenth-century verse, and in Sidney's earlier poetry. What is more, there is a tinge of defensiveness in his tone, especially in the last line, as if he expects some challenge to his assertions. It is as if he alone knows, and therefore has the right to say, what is "true" of his loving, and as if it has a continuous existence and force exerted in his heart but difficult to show in words.

What the lover knows to be true of his inward experience is defended against false interpretations in Sonnet 14. The fact that the judgment he rejects here is not made by envious wits or gossiping courtiers, but by a friend whom he addresses intimately, intensifies the hidden nature of what is in his heart. It is uniquely his, not interpretable in categorical terms, not even by his intimates:

Alas have I not paine enough my friend,
  Upon whose breast a fiercer Gripe doth tire
  Then did on him who first stale downe the fire,
While *Love* on me doth all his quiver spend,
But with your Rubarb words yow must contend
  To grieve me worse, in saying that Desire
  Doth plunge my wel-form'd soule even in the mire
Of sinfull thoughts, which do in ruine end?
  If that be sinne which doth the maners frame,
Well staid with truth in word and faith of deed,
Readie of wit and fearing nought but shame:
If that be sinne which in fixt hearts doth breed
  A loathing of all loose unchastitie,
  Then Love is sinne, and let me sinfull be.

Astrophil argues that his inward state is different from what his friend calls "Desire." Yet the form of his argument challenges the friend's judgment by casting doubt on the adequacy of names to describe what is in the heart. In the pseudological form of conditional propositions leading to a conclusion, Astrophil repeats and redefines "sinne" until it loses any fixed meanings, but by interchanging it with the word "Love," he undercuts both terms. The conclusion seems like a flippant dismissal of Astrophil's efforts throughout the sequence to find a true language for love poetry. It accepts the arbitrariness of words by manipulating them to serve a witty argument. Yet the interchange of terms in the definition "Love is sinne"— allowing also that sin is love—is only an exaggeration of the habit of repeating a term while changing its referent or definition. Both devices point to the difficulty for Astrophil of finding words that he can trust to define in verse those inward states that only he can know, if indeed they can be known at all, or distinguished by names. This difficulty he describes most directly in the opening of Sonnet 72, where he confesses his inability to separate the categories interchanged in his argument with his friend:

> Desire, though thou my old companion art,
> And oft so clings to my pure Love, that I
> One from the other scarcely can descrie;
> While each doth blow the fier of my hart;
> Now from thy fellowship I needs must part.

The problem of distinguishing what is in his heart predicts the difficulty of following his Muse's dictate to look in it and simply copy what he sees.

If Astrophil's assumptions about the nature of language and the act of writing differ fundamentally from those of his Muse, so does his notion of the heart. To the Muse it is a transparent receptacle, easy to see through like a window, giving a direct sight of the beloved's image to the poet when he looks inward, and to the reader to whom he then shows this sight in verse. Astrophil sometimes claims to have such a heart, for instance in Sonnet 4:

> I sweare, my heart such one shall shew to thee,
> That shrines in flesh so true a Deitie,
> That *Vertue,* thou thy selfe shalt be in love.

Since questions have just been raised in preceding sonnets about Astrophil's ability to "shew" truly, about the disinterestedness of his praise, and the legitimacy of Stella's power, this claim is already suspect. Since Sonnet 5 immediately following defines the love-poet's image worship as idolatry, the reader cannot equate Astrophil's conception of his heart with his Muse's, even when they sound most alike. What lies in his breast he knows can be ambiguous, or even more suspect.

Elsewhere in sonnets previously discussed, Astrophil stresses the secret or hidden nature of his inward states, making them inscrutable to observers. In still others he has been seen to compare what is in his heart to a dark dungeon, night's blackness, a labyrinth, or fumes and cloudiness. These metaphors are conventional to the complaint, as Gynecia's from the *Arcadia* illustrates. Yet Sidney's uses of them to characterize Astrophil's inward experience have different implications more directly challenging to his Muse's notion of the heart.

The difference can be seen if the Arcadian sonnet is compared to *Astrophil and Stella* 94, where Astrophil's difficulty in finding words to show his inward state is attributed to his incapacity to see into his own murky breast:

> Griefe find the words, for thou hast made my braine
>   So darke with misty vapors, which arise
>   From out thy heavy mould, that inbent eyes
> Can scarce discerne the shape of mine owne paine.
> Do thou then (for thou canst) do thou complaine,
>   For my poore soule, which now that sicknesse tries,
>   Which even to sence, sence of it selfe denies,
> Though harbengers of death lodge there his traine.
>   Or if thy love of plaint yet mine forbeares,
> As of a caitife worthy so to die,
> Yet waile thy selfe, and waile with causefull teares,
> That though in wretchednesse thy life doth lie,
> Yet growest more wretched then thy nature beares,
> By being placed in such a wretch as I.

Whereas Gynecia's catalogue listing names which define her inward state ends only because despair has tired her, Astrophil cannot find any words to paint what is in his heart because he cannot pierce its obscurity. The style of Gynecia's complaint is predicated on the assumption that what is in the heart can be uttered because outward and inward phenomena are closely parallel. It therefore blurs the distinction between them in a catalogue mixing names for the lover's physical powers and inward parts, passions and modes of expressing them. By contrast Astrophil widens the distance between outward and inward experience. His "inbent eyes" can barely make out even a "shape," a word previously shown in Sonnet 99 to allow the kinds of multiple meanings characteristic of Sidney's vocabulary for what is in the heart. In this context its primary meaning of contour makes the darkness within Astrophil so dense that it almost obliterates even the outlines of his inward state. With the added meanings, of image and disguise, the word "shape" allows the possibility that what Astrophil can only dimly perceive in his heart may be an invention or falsification of its true nature. Meaning phantom, it prepares for the description of the sick blankness that possesses Astrophil's soul, "Which even to sence, sence of it selfe denies." For the ambiguous grammar of this line allows the extreme possibilities that Astrophil's soul is in a ghostly condition in which not only his inward state but even his physical sensations are obscured, or a condition in which even physical sense denies to itself the existence either of the sickness or of his very soul. The distance between inward and outward is so great as to constitute a disease, a violation of nature something like what Shakespeare's speaker experiences in Sonnet 113, when his outward eye delivers nothing of what it sees to his heart. In *Astrophil and Stella* 94 the lover's "inbent eyes" cannot see into his heart, so that he cannot know what is there in truth to show truly in his verse. This is the view of inward experience which Shakespeare in his sonnets learned from Sidney and carried to more radical conclusions about the capacity of poetry to render it.

4.
Shakespeare and Sidney

"O let me true in loue but truly write" is the plea of the speaker in
Shakespeare's Sonnet 21. The deliberate echo of the opening of *Astrophil
and Stella* is verified by the poem as a whole, which assimilates many
characteristic means invented by Sidney for representing Astrophil's struggle to show the truth of his love in verse. The issues involved in that effort
about the relation of poetic language to inward experience are first raised
in Shakespeare's sequence in this sonnet, which is so closely, complexly,
and successfully patterned after a characteristic Sidneian model as to
prove that Shakespeare there understood the issues in Sidney's terms, and
learned his means for exploring them.

In Sonnet 84 Shakespeare again borrows Astrophil's language about
writing love poetry, echoing his claim of Sonnet 3 to be a truthful tran-
scriber of love and beauty: "all my deed / But Copying is, what in her
Nature writes." Shakespeare's speaker adapts this metaphor to a prescription for the successful love poet:

> Let him but coppy what in you is writ,
> Not making worse what nature made so cleere.

At this point in the sequence, the issues playfully raised in Sonnet 21, and
by means apparently learned from Sidney, have become an obsession of
Shakespeare's poet-lover, who reinterprets borrowings from Astrophil's
language with implications about the relation of poetry to what is in the
heart—his own and his friend's—more radical because more bitterly felt.

Shakespeare's Sonnet 21 invites comparison with Sidney's verse by
echoing the opening poem of his sequence while also, it will be shown,
following in structure and in verbal detail *Astrophil and Stella* 3. That
Sidneian model establishes a pattern used again in his own Sonnets 6, 15,
28, 74: a catalogue of courtly styles dismissed for lacking "inward tuch,"
and then contrasted with the poet-lover's own style of "pure simplicitie,"
claimed to utter truly what is in his heart. These sonnets, the previous

chapter has shown, use the pattern in ways which implicate the speaker himself in the suspect poetic practices he dismisses, casting in doubt his claims to speak in verse with the true voice of passion. By imitating this model in Sonnet 21, Shakespeare there raises questions about the relation of what the lover experiences as "true in loue" to what as poet he may "truly write." They are virtually identical in nature with Astrophil's questioning in the opening sonnet, and in those patterned after Sonnet 3. The fundamental assumption implied, that there exists an inward identity for the speaker not revealed in his language, is the same.

Sonnet 21 is the only poem in Shakespeare's sequence modeled to these ends after the paradigm of Sidney's third sonnet. Shakespeare, in the lower-numbered sonnets of his sequence, is less consistently concerned than Sidney with the questions of how to write truly about what is grounded inward in the heart. Many of the lower-numbered sonnets ignore them for other interests. Some even articulate a very different conception of the nature and power of poetry, one which would rule out questioning of its truth to inward experience. Sonnet 18 ("Shall I compare thee to a Summers day?"), for example, predicates its promise to immortalize the beauty of the speaker's friend on the assumption of poetry's godlike nature and power. It vows to give eternal life by the inspiration of its divine breath. Though nowhere else so triumphant in their claims, there are many other sonnets in the first half of Shakespeare's sequence built on the conventional promise of the poet-lover to immortalize the beloved. Sonnets 15, 55, 60, 63, 65 postulate for poetry miraculous powers to transform timebound nature into an eternal golden world for the fair friend to dwell in. By contrast Astrophil, like Sidney in *An Apologie for Poetrie*, often ridicules associations of poetry with divine inspiration or power, for instance in Sonnet 74:

> Some do I heare of Poets' furie tell,
> But (God wot) wot not what they meane by it.

He never includes among his persuasions or praise any promise to immortalize Stella, or any prediction of eternal fame for his verse or name. Nor does Sidney in the sequence ever represent poetry as a force that can transform the mutable into a timeless world, although the most famous passage in *An Apologie for Poetrie* seems to state such a view, and in terms close to Shakespeare's in Sonnet 18. For Sidney argues there that Nature's "world is brasen, the Poets only deliuer a golden."[1] If this view is reflected at all in *Astrophil and Stella,* it is in the absence from the sequence of any consideration of time and its passage. Stella is beautiful, Astrophil young and passionate, and no reminders of fleeting time threaten them in the sequence. In all of *Astrophil and Stella* Sidney shows little interest in the sweets and beauties of nature, none in the ravages of time upon them or

his love, and therefore none in the efficacy of poetry to rescue them from
sad mortality.

It is perhaps for these reasons that his sonnet sequence has been traditionally believed to have offered little of interest to Shakespeare, beyond
a few motifs already established in the sonnet tradition. For many of the
sonnets encountered first in a reading of Shakespeare's sequence, those
also most often quoted or anthologized, focus on a struggle altogether
different from Astrophil's. They portray the poet battling "all in war with
Time" to immortalize his fair, young love.[2] These concerns liken them on
the one hand to Daniel's sonnets, twenty-eight of which were first printed
in the same volume as Sidney's in the 1591 edition of *Astrophil and Stella*.
Of these, twenty-three were then revised and reprinted the following year
in an expanded collection of fifty sonnets to *Delia*. Daniel's elegiac tributes
to the short glories of the morning dew and the blushing rose, used metaphorically to praise and persuade his sweet love, resemble in mood and
metaphor Shakespeare's to his fair friend.[3] On the other hand, Shakespeare's sonnets also resemble Spenser's in his *Amoretti,* published in
1595, which radiantly celebrate the eternizing gift of art.[4] Shakespeare's
may have been influenced by both these English contemporaries, who
themselves borrowed from continental models. Daniel learned especially
from Desportes, Spenser from Petrarch (in Marot's version) and DuBellay, whom he translated in experimenting with the sonnet form, and both
from Tasso.[5] The presence and power of the sonnets resembling Daniel's
and Spenser's in the lower-numbered poems of Shakespeare's collection
overshadow his interest there in Sidney's different questions about poetry,
which become much more insistent in the higher-numbered half of Shakespeare's sonnets. For the concerns of *Astrophil and Stella* are with the
efficacy of poetry exclusively in the human world as it is experienced by
the poet-lover simultaneously in his outward social existence, and his
inward states. Where Shakespeare shows interest in these issues in his
sonnets, and they become a focus for many in the higher-numbered part
of the sequence, the poems reveal that he assimilated their concerns directly from *Astrophil and Stella*.

Sidney's portrayal of Astrophil's struggle to write truly about loving
raised explicitly for the first time in English verse questions about the
adequacy of poetic language to portray what is in the heart. Shakespeare,
alone among English writers of love sonnets after Sidney, followed him
in making these questions a central concern, assimilating their most far-
reaching implications for what amounts to a new conception of human
nature. Other poets, by contrast, borrowed only details of phrasing from
Sidney, or imitated his motifs and manner, practices for which Drayton
is the most prominent example. His sonnet sequence, first published in
1594 under the title *Ideas Mirrovr,* begins with a dedicatory poem in
which he announces his originality by quoting *Astrophil and Stella* 74:

> Divine Syr Phillip, I avouch thy writ,
> I am no Pickpurse of anothers wit.[6]

In fact his borrowing here and elsewhere imitates Sidney's self-mocking tone without catching its fineness of wit, or its implications about his view of poetry. Typically Drayton copies phrases characteristic of Sidney, as in Amour 14: "Paynted the blackest Image of my woe."[7] Yet he appears not to have understood the crucial multiplicity of meanings in Sidney's language as he uses it to explore its adequacy for showing what is in the heart. Similarly, the sonnets of William Drummond of Hawthornden, first published in 1616, the year of Shakespeare's death, show indebtedness in details borrowed from Sidney. Examples begin with the mocking account of past efforts to write love poetry in the opening sonnet:

> I first beganne to reade, then Loue to write,
> And so to praise a perfect Red and White,
> But, (God wot) wist not what was in my Braine.[8]

Fulke Greville, who knew Sidney and his poems intimately, responded to some of them in his own love poetry, in part probably written during Sidney's lifetime. In *Cælica* 24, for example, art which is "Painting, the *eloquence of dumbe conceipt,*" is contrasted to a truer kind resembling that advocated by Astrophil's Muse:

> *But who, his Art in worlds of woe, would proue,*
> *Let him within his heart but cipher Loue.*[9]

In these and other collections of verse following the publication of *Astrophil and Stella,* English poets echo Sidney's phrasing and something of the manner characteristic of his poet-lover, without showing Shakespeare's understanding of his struggle to bridge the distance between what the poet can show in verse and what is truly in his heart.

Furthermore, Shakespeare alone followed Sidney in using this distinction in love sonnets as a means to portray experience itself as simultaneously outward and inward, public and private, apparent and secret, expressed and silent, readable and inscrutable. It is possible to argue that Shakespeare learned to present a speaker who, like Hamlet, gives the impression of leading a continuous inward existence distinct from his outward show, from imitating *Astrophil and Stella* in his own sonnets. One of them at least, Sonnet 33, will be shown by the nature of its borrowing to indicate that Shakespeare read Sidney's sequence in the edition of 1591, which was altered in some of its phrasing in the 1598 printing. This detail helps to confirm the traditional dating of the majority of Shakespeare's sonnets earlier than the period of the mature plays. It has

become the generally accepted view that they were written roughly between 1593 and 1597, a chronology based in part on resemblances in
wording between the lower-numbered sonnets and the narrative poems
and plays of this period, especially *Loves Labour Lost, Romeo and Juliet,
A Midsummer Nightes Dreame,* and *Richard the Second.* Others of the
sonnets, however, particularly in the higher-numbered half of the sequence, resemble more closely *Hamlet* and other plays of the period
around 1600.[10] Among those are a number modeled directly on sonnets
in *Astrophil and Stella.* Many more focus on precisely the issues explored
in a sustained way previously only by Sidney in his sonnet sequence. It
is therefore not only possible to argue that the invention of a speaker
resembling Hamlet in Shakespeare's sonnets grew out of his assimilations
from Sidney, but that this earlier development prepared for the expansion
of such a figure in the larger form of a play.

"O let me true in loue but truly write" imitates in Astrophil's characteristic manner the relationship in the opening line of Sidney's sequence
between showing "love" in verse and "Loving in truth."[11] Without precisely contrasting them, Shakespeare's Sonnet 21 draws a distinction like
Sidney's between the state of *being* (the verb implied in the first phrase)
"true in loue," and the effort to *write* "truly" about it. Inward experience
and its rendering in poetry are grammatically placed in a kind of balance,
but separated by a conjunction in distinct parts of the line, as in Sidney's.
This balance is then further complicated by devices also imitative of
Sidney. Shakespeare repeats a key word—"true . . . truly" parallels Sidney's "Loving . . . love"—in different grammatical forms, and with multiple possibilities of meaning, to make the lover's wish as susceptible of
various readings as Astrophil's desire to show his love. Stephen Booth has
paraphrased them:

> I pray that I, who am true in love (a faithful lover) and true in love
> (truly in love, genuinely feel the passion I report) may in love (for
> love's sake, in charity) but (only, do no more than) write truly (tell
> the truth) in love (about love, with regard to love).[12]

These complications make the balance of the line less simple than it
sounds, especially if one accepts an additional reading of "but" as nevertheless, even though: "I pray that I who am true in love may nevertheless
write poems that render my feelings truly, even though such a rendering
would seem incompatible with true love." The multiple ways in which the
seemingly balanced terms operate therefore imply that only to write truly
of what is in his heart, to do no more than that, or to do that despite
inherent incompatibility, is for the poet no easy effort.

Yet the intense frustration of Astrophil's struggle in Sonnet 1 is not
reenacted here. The speaker's tone—amused, argumentative, assured—is

closer to Astrophil's in Sonnet 3, which Shakespeare's poem also resembles in structure, and in many details as well. The octave catalogues examples of fancy writing dismissed by the speaker for a plainer style claimed as his own in the sestet:

> So is it not with me as with that Muse,
> Stird by a painted beauty to his verse,
> Who heauen it selfe for ornament doth vse,
> And euery faire with his faire doth reherse,
> Making a coopelment of proud compare
> With Sunne and Moone, with earth and seas rich gems:
> With Aprills first borne flowers and all things rare,
> That heauens ayre in this huge rondure hems,
> O let me true in loue but truly write,
> And then beleeue me, my loue is as faire,
> As any mothers childe, though not so bright
> As those gould candells fixt in heauens ayer:
>   Let them say more that like of heare-say well,
>   I will not prayse that purpose not to sell.

This structure, containing within it many resemblances also of details, is imitated after the model of *Astrophil and Stella* 3:

> Let daintie wits crie on the Sisters nine,
> That bravely maskt, their fancies may be told:
> Or *Pindare's* Apes, flaunt they in phrases fine,
> Enam'ling with pied flowers their thoughts of gold:
>   Or else let them in statelier glorie shine,
> Ennobling new found Tropes with problemes old:
> Or with strange similies enrich each line,
> Of herbes or beastes, which *Inde* or *Afrike* hold.
>   For me in sooth, no Muse but one I know:
>   Phrases and Problemes from my reach do grow,
> And strange things cost too deare for my poore sprites.
>   How then? even thus: in *Stella's* face I reed,
>   What Love and Beautie be, then all my deed
> But Copying is, what in her Nature writes.

The styles catalogued in the octaves of both sonnets are rejected on the same grounds in very similar diction for being fancy, expensive, and ostentatious. For both speakers such displays of opulence are also associated with exotic or far-fetched comparisons, to which each gives formal rhetorical terms, and with false claims to divine inspiration by the Muses. Both speakers mock such guarantees of truth by linking this pseudo-inspiration with deception, and in similar phrases: "bravely maskt" and "painted beauty." These phrases evoke a courtly world of affectation and dissimulation, though Shakespeare's is less gallant, more vulgar than Sidney's. They have also multiple possibilities of meaning which are parallel. For "painted" can have the meaning characteristic of Sidney's uses of it—depicted, represented in an image—making the "painted beauty" praised by the courtly poet a fabricated or borrowed image. The word can here also bear the meaning it sometimes has for Sidney of being covered over with colors, thus associating the rejected style with deceiving rhetoric. Or the poet may be stirred by the "painted beauty" of his subject, someone whose looks are falsified by cosmetics, a cheaper definition often given to painting in Shakespeare's sonnets. A model for these interpretations is provided by Sidney, who characteristically combines multiple meanings of both "maskt" and "fancies" with ambiguous grammar. That is, "fancies" can refer to the poets' powers of invention, or to their amorous objects, while "maskt" can mean either decked out or disguised. Simultaneously the grammar allows the phrase "bravely maskt" to describe the wits who use the claim of inspiration to ennoble or hide their fancies, but it can also describe the "fancies," allowing that these poets' imaginings or beloveds are either splendidly arrayed or hidden behind a disguise, a false face. Shakespeare, in Sonnet 21, has therefore adapted Sidney's characteristic kind of vocabulary for writing in order, like his model, to exploit its multiple meanings. In doing so he mocks the styles of courtly makers by the same means as Sidney uses in the octave of Sonnet 3, and others of the same pattern.

To these rejected styles both speakers then contrast a manner claimed as their own, credible because disinterested, not designed to "sell" their subjects or, in Astrophil's more playful innuendo, to satisfy their "thoughts of gold," meaning gilded notions but also preoccupations with money. The blunt protestation of Shakespeare's speaker—"And then beleeue me"— imitates Astrophil's—"For me in sooth" in simple manliness. Shakespeare's sonnet therefore seems to argue the platform of a plain stylist like that of the poet in Wyatt's satire, known to both Shakespeare and Sidney in Tottel's miscellany under the title "Of the Courtiers life written to Iohn Poins."[13] Yet that position is actually distinguished from Shakespeare's own by means that here also must have been learned from *Astrophil and Stella*.

Like Sidney, Shakespeare carries the mocking catalogue of courtly styles of praise beyond criticism to parody. He mimics their ransackings of heaven and earth in clichés, hyperboles, and fancy diction. Yet all of these practices can be found in many of Shakespeare's own sonnets, including poems the reader has already encountered in the sequence before hearing their styles parodied in Sonnet 21. To implicate even more pointedly the speaker's own verse, in parodying the poet who "euery faire with his faire doth reherse," he virtually quotes a line which occurs three sonnets earlier, "And euery faire from faire some-time declines." What he is therefore actually rehearsing is his own Sonnet 18, itself a "proud compare" using spring flowers and the gold complexion of the sun in heaven to praise his fair friend. Shakespeare's speaker, like Astrophil in sonnets following the pattern of the third, implicates himself in the styles he also mocks by making connections, both inclusive and specific, with his own poems. Such echoes in both sonnets turn parody into self-parody. In so doing each reminds the reader that its speaker is not committed to a single style, and that his verse can therefore nowhere be simply identified as a true voice of passion.

The plain speaking in the sestet cannot then be accepted as unquestioningly as Shakespeare's poet-lover pretends to expect when he asks the reader to believe him. He actually invites amused skepticism rather than credence by his way of comparing his love to "any mothers childe," as an example of his trustworthy plainness. For the homely diction is a rhetorical trick disguising hidden hyperbole: his love is as beautiful as anyone ever born, or ever praised as "faire" by other poets. A model for this device is Astrophil's claim that by "But Copying" what he sees in Stella, he can embody true love and beauty in his verse, because she is the original in which Nature has written them. The hidden or disguised nature of their compliments depends on each poet's disavowal of his own invention—"I will not prayse," "But Copying is"—as well as on his protestations of honesty in a manner untainted by courtly affectation.

These playful disavowals have effects similar to those of self-parody, calling in question whether it is possible to write truly. For unlike the plain stylist whose claims depend on a single manner of writing to which he is wholly committed, the speakers in these two sonnets are implicated elsewhere in the styles they here dismiss, and even in these very poems they invent compliments which they pretend are mere transcriptions of what is true. Each of these sonnets therefore wittily turns criticisms of hyperbole into hyperbolic praise of its own subject, by means of a speaker who adopts a voice we are not allowed to equate with his own. We are therefore made aware that each speaker has an identity behind a humble posture, without our knowing from these sonnets themselves whether that disguise is deliberate, or unavoidable by the very nature of poetry. The multiple possibilities of the vocabulary about art allow both inferences simultaneously. They therefore measure the distance perceived by Sidney between form and substance in art, which for the love poet is the distinction between outward expression and inward states. Sonnet 21 points in the direction in which Shakespeare followed Sidney.

To express his own sense of the relation between what verse can show and what is experienced inwardly, Shakespeare repeatedly turned to *Astrophil and Stella* for models. He adapted individual poems, sometimes borrowing simultaneously from more than one source in Sidney's sequence, or combining specific echoes with adaptations of devices more generally characteristic of Sidney's style. In Sonnet 21 the first line of Sidney's sequence is echoed in a poem otherwise modeled closely on the structure of his third sonnet. It also uses such generally characteristic devices as terms for art with both neutral and suspect definitions; grammatical ambiguities supporting multiplicity of meanings; hidden hyperboles; parody including self-parody. Their combined effects create a speaker like Astrophil, who claims credibility in a manner which cannot simply be identified as his own true voice, because he has playfully called attention to the fact that he has spoken in more than one. Implied then is the existence of private, inward experience not expressed by the poet in any of his modes of utterance, any of his poetic styles. Such a speaker represents a stage in the development of a figure like Hamlet, who has that within his heart which passes show.

In Sidney's sonnet sequence these issues are concentrated exclusively on the figure of Astrophil, as they are focused solely on the speaker in Shakespeare's Sonnet 21. It is the only one of his adaptations to resemble Sidney's poems in this respect. Elsewhere, and in sonnets indebted to his predecessor in other ways, Shakespeare widened his focus so that concerns shared with Sidney are brought to bear on the poet-lover, but also on the human subjects of his praise. Both speaker and subjects are portrayed as living in a public and social world while having a simultaneous inward existence distinct from what they show to that world, or what its representatives deem them to be. Because Shakespeare's poet reflects on this distinction not only in his own experience but in that of someone other than himself, his questions inevitably differ in some respects from Astrophil's.

They are differently adjusted also because Shakespeare portrays the public, social setting which speaker and subject inhabit as characteristically more cynical and vicious than Astrophil's society is usually pictured. In such sonnets as 27 and 35, both to be discussed as models for Shakespeare, Astrophil too is surrounded by the poisoned atmosphere of court intrigue and suspicion resembling the dangerous world evoked in Wyatt's poems. Yet the taint is more pervasive in Shakespeare's depiction of society. Especially in the higher-numbered sonnets, it resembles the vicious court of Denmark and the sterile promontory or unweeded garden that Hamlet perceives the world surrounding it to be. It therefore informs somewhat differently Shakespeare's portrayal of the poet-lover and his subject as they exist, he says in Sonnet 69, simultaneously in the "worlds eye," and in those inward parts of themselves now "showne" to it.

As a means of portraying this double existence, Sonnet 38 again contrasts true and false styles of verse by combining specific details borrowed from *Astrophil and Stella* 3 with other uses of language reminiscent of Sidney:

How can my Muse want subiect to inuent
While thou dost breath that poor'st into my verse,
Thine owne sweet argument, to excellent,
For euery vulgar paper to rehearse:
O giue thy selfe the thankes if ought in me,
Worthy perusal stand against thy sight,
For who's so dumbe that cannot write to thee,
When thou thy selfe dost giue inuention light?
Be thou the tenth Muse, ten times more in worth
Then those old nine which rimers inuocate,
And he that calls on thee, let him bring forth
Eternal numbers to out-liue long date.
　　If my slight Muse doe please these curious daies,
　　The paine be mine, but thine shal be the praise.

Following Sidney in Sonnet 3, Shakespeare presents his speaker here in the humble posture of a scribe, for whom his friend gives light to copy by. Like Astrophil he disclaims invention, as if his verse were merely the receptacle for the "sweet argument" written in his friend, the way love and beauty are written in Stella for her poet-lover to read and copy. Or he claims that the friend's worth can overcome the poverty of his invention. Even his "dumbe" powers or "slight" verses, like Astrophil's "poore sprites," can be made worthy by merely rendering their subject. Also like Astrophil, he claims to know inspiration only from that source, not from those "old nine" other Muses whom he dismisses with Astrophil's characteristic blend of irreverence and amused contempt. He therefore implies greater truth for his poetry as an accurate portrayal of its inspiring subject, by contrast with the rhymes of other poets who invoke worn out and borrowed sources of pseudoinspiration.

The couplet of Sonnet 38 then points in a different direction from the conclusion of *Astrophil and Stella* 3. Yet it recalls Sidney's own distinctions elsewhere, for instance in the couplet of Sonnet 2, between the poet-lover's interior monologue and what in verse he calls "praise." Shakespeare's last line makes a Sidneian contrast, seemingly balanced, between "paine" and "praise." Its neatness is then immediately complicated by multiple meanings for each term, having effects characteristic of Sidney's vocabulary about showing love in poetry. A first reading of the line might be: "the pains or effort of writing will be mine, yours the praise for having provided the invention, argument, inspiration." Yet in the singular, *pain* was not commonly used to mean pains in the sense of difficult effort, whereas when the singular noun was uttered by a lover in a sonnet, it would inevitably have suggested such suffering as Astrophil paints in Sonnet 2. Sidney himself, however, uses both possible readings of the word in the conclusion of Sonnet 12:

O no, her heart is such a Cittadell,
   So fortified with wit, stor'd with disdaine,
   That to win it, is all the skill and paine.

Oddly both meanings seem in Shakespeare's couplet initially irrelevant to the rest of the poem. For on the one hand Sonnet 38 has not previously hinted at the speaker's suffering, but neither has it acknowledged the pains of the love poet struggling to write truly. On the contrary, the poet's praise of his subject has consisted of his claim to be the mere copier of the argument written in the friend. The last line, if it is not merely feeble, must then hint at truths unspoken in the rest of the sonnet, a possibility which a rereading confirms. The glib compliment of line 14 hints that to write in praise of the friend may be more painful in the sense of difficult than previously admitted—either because writing is in truth not mere copying, or because the friend's "owne sweet argument" about himself does not coincide with what the poet truly sees in him. Then the praise which the poet paints to flatter his subject and please his public audience, like Astrophil's in Sonnet 2, may not show truly what is in his heart. There is a further hint that the very fact of pleasing "these curious daies," whose taste resembles but is more vulgar than that of the "curious wits" dismissed by Astrophil, is another source of pain to the poet.

The "bitter undertaste," as Stephen Booth describes it, in Shakespeare's Sonnet 38, has some parallels in Sidney's second sonnet where Astrophil resents his humiliating state as a slave who must praise his tyrant by disguising his pain. Astrophil's bitterness arises there from his position as lover and as poet, which is true also of Shakespeare's speaker. His distaste is more insulting, however, in a number of ways. It implicates the friend in actively encouraging poetry divorced from truth. For it accuses him of inventing an argument about himself for his flatterers to copy. In doing so he exacts a kind of praise not brought forth by the poet's labor to show his love truly in verse. The speaker accedes to these demands, but gives credit for his success sarcastically to his friend, who must thank himself if anything "Worthy perusal stand against thy sight," meaning "meet your eye," but also "take arms against or withstand your inspection."[14] Implied is the existence of unseen truths, which may be those about the friend omitted from his own presentation of himself. Or they may be unuttered truths about what is in the poet's heart that he has kept "dumbe." This is strongly hinted in the way metonomy—"if ought in me / Worthy perusal"—is used to equate the poet-lover with his verse, as if he had no other identity. Only the friend could uncritically use this equation, since his interest in the speaker is solely as author of praises to himself. The poet, however, knows what is within his heart but withheld from his verse.

Borrowings from Sidney are here reshaped to somewhat altered concerns about poetry as the representation of inward experience. Here questioning of its adequacy to portray what is in the heart is made to focus on the subject's as well as the poet-lover's. The skepticism is disguised, however, never openly acknowledged, but hidden behind a complimentary convention that the excellence of the love poem depends on the worth of the subject. By disguising other preoccupations behind this convention, Shakespeare widens the distance measured in *Astrophil and Stella* between what is felt by the poet-lover and what he shows in verse. Astrophil is troubled or frustrated by the difficulty of that task. At other times he suggests deliberate reserve, as if withholding his inward state from display, or draws a line between it and what may be known of him by his looks, behavior, or utterance. Astrophil does not—even in sonnets hinting like the second that Stella is tyrannical—go as far as Shakespeare's speaker in Sonnet 38 in hiding insult behind flattery. He pretends to write a conventional compliment which its subject, seeking praise, will read it to be, while the poet actually sees his beloved as an unpraiseworthy subject toward whom he directs uncomplimentary hints. By writing a poem which can be read as a kind of disguise or mask behind which the poet guards his unspoken states, Shakespeare carries the notion of arbitrariness in poetic language and its distance from what is in the heart to far more cynical lengths than Sidney, even in his sonnets most deeply tinged with bitterness. Shakespeare also strengthens the impression of both poet and subject having an identity and inward experiences not disclosed.

Shakespeare's adaptation and redirection of concerns found in *Astrophil and Stella* work in a similar direction in the connected group of poems beginning with Sonnet 33, which is itself a recasting of Sidney's Sonnet 22. The model is a courtly compliment to Stella as the most brilliant ornament of a courtly world. Shakespeare transforms it into another poem in which compliment veils insult. It therefore raises questions, explicitly discussed in Sonnet 35, about the capacity of poetry to hide one meaning behind another. For this issue Sidney's poem provides a starting point in its pattern of contrasts between faces hidden and unveiled.

The episode recounted in Sonnet 22 of Stella riding forth unmasked to vie in brightness with the regal sun supplied the structure as well as many details for Shakespeare's comparison of his friend to the sun personified as a brilliant sovereign. Yet when the poems are first set side by side, they seem so different that the reader could conclude Shakespeare's borrowings to be merely superficial, such as his echoes of phrasing from Henry Constable's sonnet sequence, *Diana,* of 1592, or from Marlowe's *Hero and Leander*.[15] His borrowings would then demonstrate nothing more than a detailed familiarity with the earlier sequence, like that shown by Drayton's echoes of Sidney, or Drummond's. Shakespeare's adaptation does radically transform Sidney's playful compliment into another kind of poem, but the direction of the transformation points to concerns that Shakespeare recognized as Sidney's elsewhere in *Astrophil and Stella*. Seen in that context, and also as part of a connected group including Sonnet 35, Shakespeare's reworking of his Sidneian model in 33 shows how profoundly he absorbed the central issue of the earlier sequence.

The sun as Sidney personifies it belongs to the same shining, courtly world as Stella, whose matching brightness can ride uncovered to meet the sun on its royal progress, can race or march unarmed against it as in a tournament:

> In highest way of heav'n the Sunne did ride,
>   Progressing then from faire twinnes' gold'n place:
>   Having no scarfe of clowds before his face,
> But shining forth of heate in his chiefe pride;
> When some faire Ladies, by hard promise tied,
>   On horsebacke met him in his furious race,
>   Yet each prepar'd, with fanne's wel-shading grace,
> From that foe's wounds their tender skinnes to hide.
> *Stella* alone with face unarmed marcht,
>   Either to do like him, which open shone,
>   Or carelesse of the wealth because her owne:
> Yet were the hid and meaner beauties parcht,
>   Her daintiest bare went free; the cause was this,
>   The Sunne which others burn'd, did her but kisse.

The courtliness of Shakespeare's personified sun is also brilliant, so that the comparison seems at first similarly complimentary to his subject:

> Fvll many a glorious morning haue I seene,
> Flatter the mountaine tops with soueraine eie,
> Kissing with golden face the meddowes greene;
> Guilding pale streames with heauenly alcumy:
> Anon permit the basest cloudes to ride,
> With ougly rack on his celestiall face,
> And from the for-lorne world his visage hide
> Stealing vnseene to west with this disgrace:
> Euen so my Sunne one early morne did shine,
> With all triumphant splendor on my brow,
> But out alack, he was but one houre mine,
> The region cloude hath mask'd him from me now.
>   Yet him for this, my loue no whit disdaineth,
>   Suns of the world may staine, when heauens sun staineth.

Yet there are suspicions of corruption—for instance, in the sequence of "Flatter," "Kissing," "Guilding"—even before the sun is openly accused of permitting baseness. The form of that accusation is adapted from Sidney's pattern of compliments likening Stella's "daintiest bare" to the sun "Having no scarfe of clowds before his face." In the version printed in the 1591 edition, Sidney's sun wears "no maske," showing that Shakespeare followed the wording of this earlier version very closely. He also made use of the fans carried by Stella's companions to shade their complexions, transforming them into a metaphorical mask hiding guiltiness from public show. When the comparison is applied to "my Sunne," Shakespeare's speaker implicates his friend in the corruptions of their society in ways which go far beyond suggestions anywhere in Sidney's sequence that Stella may not match Astrophil's praise. At times he complains that she scorns him because she shares the pride of beauties who prefer ritual courtship and display to an honest heart. Or he complains that she uses the stratagems of art to ensnare him, or worse, the unjust power of a tyrant to enslave him. Sonnet 35 hints that she may accept or even encourage false praise. Yet never is she so explicitly associated with what is "basest," or implicated in public shame or disgrace.

Recognition by Shakespeare's speaker of such ugly possibilities in his subject does, however, hint at gravely troubling questions recalling those raised—though less insultingly—in Sidney's second sonnet by Astrophil's confession to the arbitrariness of poetic language:

> I call it praise to suffer Tyrannie;
> And now employ the remnant of my wit,
>   To make my selfe beleeve, that all is well,
>   While with a feeling skill I paint my hell.

The poet can call his inward state by whatever name serves his own interest, either in flattering his subject or deceiving himself. His praise may therefore disguise the true nature of his subject, here a tyrant whose cruelty enslaves him. It may also disguise his own inward state, either by painting over it with the skillful colors of rhetoric, or merely by skillfully painting it in verse. Shakespeare does not openly acknowledge such arbitrariness in Sonnet 33, but his poem does call attention to its manipulations of language by the way the couplet comments on what precedes. The speaker declares that despite "this" hinted in the poem, his love for his friend is undiminished, and the reason or justification that he gives is his own simile. That is to say, because his own highly contrived comparison has made the subject like the sun, he is then excused for behaving as the poet has made the sun behave in his personification. This explanation is parallel to Astrophil's mock-philosophical analysis of the "cause" for the sun's tribute to Stella. Shakespeare's couplet is not designed to compliment, however, but to exonerate the friend to the audience of the poem, and also to persuade the speaker himself that, despite the ugliness he can see in his subject, he will continue to "love" him, and to praise him by comparing him to heaven's sun. Yet because the couplet can be read as insulting—the friend has been demoted from being the sole light of heaven to one among the "Suns of the world"—it extends the impression created throughout the sonnet that the speaker may be withholding what is in his heart, or disguising it as praise. Or, like Astrophil, he may experience conflicting inward states demanding representation in language which allows multiple interpretations at the same time. Unlike Astrophil in Sonnet 2, Shakespeare's speaker here does not admit to using his art for self-deception or false praise, so that the degree of his self-knowledge is part of the unuttered experience at which the sonnet hints.

Such a confession is made, for the first time in Shakespeare's sequence, in the octave of Sonnet 35:

> No more bee greeu'd at that which thou hast done,
> Roses haue thornes, and siluer fountaines mud,
> Cloudes and eclipses staine both Moone and Sunne,
> And loathsome canker liues in sweetest bud.
> All men make faults, and euen I in this,
> Authorizing thy trespas with compare,
> My selfe corrupting saluing thy amisse,
> Excusing their sins more then their sins are.

Coming so soon after Sonnet 33 as part of a connected group of poems, and commenting so explicitly on the falsifying power of comparison (specifically the likening of guilty behavior to the workings of nature), this confession points to conscious arbitrariness in the earlier simile of the sun. As the couplet of Sonnet 33 makes evident, it is the nature of his own comparison which makes it possible for the speaker to go on loving and praising his subject. Moreover, he has manipulated the way its terms work so that they are carefully aligned except at one crucial point. For while the personified sun is accused of actively permitting itself to be hidden, and of stealing guiltily from disgrace, the friend is said only to be masked by a cloud coming between him and the speaker. The parallel is set up but then not fully drawn. Both the nature of the comparison and the way its terms are manipulated therefore seem designed to hint at, but then to obscure, the friend's unworthiness from the public audience of the poem, and from its author. The poet himself is morally implicated more seriously than Astrophil, for praising a more unworthy subject. The debased parody of the Lord's Prayer in his confession of Sonnet 35 to "Authorizing thy trespas with compare" taints him with the corruption of a more cynical world than Astrophil's, who can use the word "hell" with its full force to confess his sin and punishment.

The association for Shakespeare of *Astrophil and Stella* with the issue of poetry's relation to what is in the heart is demonstrated in somewhat different ways by another sonnet adapted from Sidney. Sonnet 127 is a recasting of Astrophil's tribute to Stella's black eyes in Sonnet 7. This is one of the few debts to Sidney's sequence that has been frequently noticed by commentators on Shakespeare's sonnets. Their remarks have concentrated on the resemblance of motif in the two poems, however, usually concluding that it is a conventional one which might have reached either poet through a variety of sources.[16] Other connections that have traditionally been made between Shakespeare's sonnets and *Astrophil and Stella* have also typically depended on resemblance of motif, such as the comparison of the beloved's eyes to stars, or the situation of the sleepless lover. Indebtedness based only on that kind of evidence is difficult to prove, because of the ways that conventions are typically used in six-teenth-century sonnets, English and continental. They ring endless changes on the same motifs, often, as has been said, retranslating the same models, so that sources can be multiple. At least it is difficult to attribute influence to a single original, a problem compounded by the fact that many conven-tions associated with sonnets were already established in native English poetry. Shakespeare's indebtedness to *Astrophil and Stella* 7, however, can be proved on more grounds than resemblance of motif. For like his other adaptations from Sidney, Sonnet 127 makes at once more inclusive and more detailed uses of its original, pointing to a fuller and more profound attention to Sidney's poetry.

Shakespeare takes over the metaphors which develop the compliment to Stella's black eyes, images of veiled and uncovered faces (resembling those borrowed from Sonnet 22). He also assimilates Sidney's characteris-tic vocabulary for art, and his device of a poem-within-a-poem, not pre-sent in this particular model, but used by Sidney in several other sonnets in *Astrophil and Stella*. Shakespeare's Sonnet 127 is therefore not only modeled on a specific poem of Sidney's, but assimilates what he learned from his familiarity with the whole sequence, and from his evident sym-pathy with Sidney's main preoccupations. For he directs toward them the borrowed motif of black eyes in Sonnet 127, and again in Sonnet 132.

Like the description of Stella rivaling the sun's brightness, *Astrophil and Stella* 7 is a courtly compliment:

> When Nature made her chiefe worke, *Stella's* eyes,
> In colour blacke, why wrapt she beames so bright?
> Would she in beamie blacke, like painter wise,
> Frame daintiest lustre, mixt of shade and light?
> Or did she else that sober hue devise,
> In object best to knit and strength our sight,
> Least if no vaile those brave gleames did disguise,
> They sun-like should more dazle then delight?
> Or would she her miraculous power show,
> That whereas blacke seemes Beautie's contrary,
> She even in blacke doth make all beauties flow?
> Both so and thus, she minding *Love* should be
> Placed ever there, gave him this mourning weed,
> To honor all their deaths, who for her bleed.

The interest for Shakespeare in this model seems to have been partly in
the metaphorical patterns that Sidney associated with black eyes: bare and
hidden faces, brightness behind a veil, openness and disguise. With these
metaphors he also borrowed Sidney's characteristic vocabulary for art—
"colour," "painter," "devise," "show." In Sonnet 7 these terms are made
complimentary to Stella. Yet the multiple combinations of neutral and
suspect meanings inherent in this vocabulary were so frequently exploited
elsewhere by Sidney that they must have suggested possibilities to Shakespeare in this particular model. His recasting of the sonnet points the
motif of black eyes, and its metaphorical associations with disguise and
art toward more radical conclusions than Sidney's here, about the adequacy of poetry to the truth of inward experience, the poet-lover's and his
subject's:

> In the ould age blacke was not counted faire,
> Or if it weare it bore not beauties name:
> But now is blacke beauties successiue heire,
> And Beautie slanderd with a bastard shame,
> For since each hand hath put on Natures power,
> Fairing the foule with Arts faulse borrow'd face,
> Sweet beauty hath no name no holy boure,
> But is prophan'd, if not liues in disgrace.
> Therefore my Mistresse eyes are Rauen blacke,
> Her eyes so suted, and they mourners seeme,
> At such who not borne faire no beauty lack,
> Slandring Creation with a false esteeme,
> > Yet so they mourne becomming of their woe,
> > That euery toung saies beauty should looke so.

Shakespeare begins with a contrast between a former age and contemporary society, which becomes a contrast between poets past and present,
their subjects, and their audiences. As a context for borrowings from
Astrophil and Stella, this contrast makes Sidney a representative figure of
earlier poets and, specifically, his Sonnet 7 an example of an old-fashioned
poem of praise. Astrophil's compliments on Stella's eyes illustrate here for
Shakespeare's poet-lover the lost innocence of an age that is viewed from
a modern perspective as unfallen. In fact Sidney's sonnets were first published only five years after his death, and probably only a few years before
Shakespeare's adaptation was written. His perspective here on his predecessor is therefore partly mythological, a means of heightening his speaker's
sense of distance from an innocent past, a way of evoking a lost pastoral
image. On the other hand, the poem's perspective may have been rooted
in actual social circumstances. For despite how corrupt the court seemed
to Sidney, by all contemporary accounts it became far more vicious in the

last decade of Elizabeth's reign, so that history supports the mythology of Shakespeare's speaker here.[17] In his view the older poet could praise his beloved's eyes as the masterwork of Nature's painting because—in the terms of this sonnet—for a poet of Sidney's age Art's colors are synonymous with Nature's. He could celebrate the beauty of a lady's eyes by associating it with veils and disguises because such coverings in olden times were decorous protections of fairness, like the "fanne's wel-shading grace" in Sonnet 22. He could honor their color by comparing it to mourning dress, because costumes were then dignities appropriate to honor courtly ceremonies. By contrast, Shakespeare's poet-lover can no longer use such compliments uncynically. For he sees himself as living in a society where both beauty and the names to praise it have been "slanderd," "prophan'd," thus bastardizing Sidney's sources of compliment. Poets nowadays have usurped "Natures power," which Sidney's Sonnet 7 defines as "miraculous power" to "show" as truly beautiful what "seemes" ugly. Instead of Nature, it is modern writers who make foulness "seeme" fair, by painting over it with false colors of cosmetics or rhetoric, or disguising it behind masks of "Arts faulse borrow'd face." They therefore participate in the "shame" or "disgrace" of fallen society, which has expelled beauty from its "holy boure." This pastoral image embodies the lost innocence and religious reverence of earlier poetic praise, represented by Sidney's seventh sonnet, in which nature, art, love, the lady's beauty, can be celebrated in a style where words like "miraculous" and "honor" are still used uncynically. Modern poets are not only implicated in the venality of present society. They are even accused of generating it, since corruption is equated with the dislocating or debasing of language, the detachment of names from their true subjects. Poets have created a vicious taste for painted beauty in modern readers of verse, to whom the speaker addresses the sestet of Sonnet 127.

These lines are the poet's own rewriting in tainted modern terms of Astrophil's old-fashioned praise of Stella's eyes. That is, the sestet of Shakespeare's sonnet is a poem-within-a-poem, beginning with a conventional line of compliment: "Therefore my Mistresse eyes are Rauen blacke." The conjunction marks a logical connection with what precedes, which is his declaration that only false faces are praised in poems nowadays. Since this is the case, he will *therefore* celebrate his own mistress in the acceptable modern mode, debasing old-fashioned praise to paint her eyes in the same color as Stella's. They are "suted," meaning matched as well as clothed, in funeral weeds so that their hue suggests mourning. Yet it is not Nature who invents the comparison, as in Sidney's original, but the cynical poet, so that although the lady's eyes "mourners seeme," they actually participate like the poet himself in the deception of "Slandring Creation with a false esteeme." Shakespeare has therefore adapted Sidney's comparison in such a way that it points to the participation of his present-day poet, subject, and reader in modern depravity. This lady's eyes "mourne becomming of their woe," as if wearing a costume or mask that disguises from the world's eye the foulness of her inward nature. The poet invents compliments to their "becomming" appearance which cover insulting truths about her, and hide what is truly in his own heart. The audience for both these performances is also implicated in the same kind of duplicity, for "euery toung saies beauty should looke so." Readers of this poet's verse are so depraved of taste that they mistake painted faces for natural fairness, or would prefer fair faces to wear make-up in order to look like the mistress praised as fair in this fashionable modern poem.

Shakespeare uses Sidney here as a source for the motif and metaphorical design of his own sonnet, and also makes his model a part of his subject as a representative of old-fashioned verse. Such an intricate and intimate relationship between his own sonnet and his predecessor's could result only from having given *Astrophil and Stella* his most sustained attention. Shakespeare's adaptation is appreciative of Sidney's original in this instance explicitly for its differences from his own poem, differences which are paradoxically measured by the calculated resemblances between model and adaptation. By comparison with Drayton's joking quotation of Astrophil's claim to originality in vowing his own, Shakespeare acknowledges a more profound indebtedness. A more bitter comment on his own verse also emerges from such a pattern of connections.

It must also be intentional irony that Shakespeare uses Astrophil to represent the innocence of poet-lovers of the past in a sonnet which borrows motifs, metaphors, vocabulary, and other devices from Sidney's sequence to serve the most cynical ends. His adaptation of the poem-within-a-poem especially illustrates this process. Sidney, the previous chapter has shown, characteristically makes this structure call attention to distinctions between the poet's inward monologue and what he shows of his heart in verse. In Sonnet 80, however, he carries these distinctions further in the direction of Shakespeare's concerns. He follows an octave burlesquing a hyperbolic poem to Stella's "Sweet swelling lip" with a frame in the form of a mock confession:

> Thus much my heart compeld my mouth to say,
> But now spite of my heart my mouth will stay,
> Loathing all lies, doubting this Flatterie is:
> And no spurre can his resty race renew,
> Without how farre this praise is short of you,
> Sweet lip, you teach my mouth with one sweet kisse.

Here Astrophil confesses to manipulating poetic language in the service of desire, and accuses his own heart of promoting lies and flattery. Yet this playful reversal, making the mouth rather than the heart the guardian of truth, allows Astrophil to turn confession into compliment, and compliment back into persuasion. The poet's manipulations of language here are a lover's game; they do not implicate Stella or the reader of the poem-within-a-poem. By contrast, Shakespeare's use of the poem-within-a-poem in Sonnet 127 demonstrates the poet's manipulations in a game which is insulting to both subject and reader. The generalizations of the octave include them in the depravity of modern society. Then the sestet, which is a poem-within-a-poem written in the modern manner, tricks them into accepting it as true praise by conforming to their vulgar, fashionable taste. Sidney's original device is therefore made to contrast what is here viewed as his innocent verse, represented by Astrophil's old-fashioned praise of Stella's eyes in Sonnet 7, with the debased modern version of it in Shakespeare's Sonnet 127.

The position of this poem as the first of the sonnets concerning the dark lady may be intended to introduce the whole group as a sequence in the modern fashion. It uses a subtler version of the strategy of Sir John Davies' "Gullinge Sonnets," circulated in manuscript in the late 1590s, which intend to trick their readers into commending them for the "bastard" styles ridiculed in the poems themselves.[18] The audience for the sonnets focused on the dark lady is identified—for instance, in Sonnet 140—as contemporary in time, and also limited to a world only as wide as rumor can spread:

> Now this ill wresting world is growne so bad,
> Madde slanderers by madde eares beleeued be.

Furthermore, although the sonnets introduced by 127 include imitations of various traditional forms of praise, they do not make any promises to immortalize their subject. That convention occurs often in the sonnets to the young man, and in some instances—Sonnets 54, 104, and 126—in insultingly debased forms which would match the style of address to the dark lady in the concluding group of poems. The omission there of such promises may be explained by the fact that eternizing verse is predicated on the claim that the poem will not only transcend fashion but will miraculously survive change to address generations yet unborn. By contrast, poems in the modern manner, such as those to the dark lady, do not allow the slightest pretensions to escape time; they claim only to have the life span of styles and slander.

The metaphor of black eyes as mourners is used again in Sonnet 132, combined with other borrowings from Sidney, to make his poetry part of Shakespeare's subject. Here, however, the allusions are pointed accusingly. They make Astrophil again a representative of traditional poet-lovers, but they are here attacked for engaging covertly in calculations which are blatant in modern verse, the separation of praise from what is truly felt:

Thine eies I loue, and they as pittying me,
Knowing thy heart torment me with disdaine,
Haue put on black, and louing mourners bee,
Looking with pretty ruth vpon my paine.
And truly not the morning Sun of Heauen
Better becomes the gray cheeks of th' East,
Nor that full Starre that vshers in the Eauen
Doth halfe that glory to the sober West
As those two morning eyes become thy face:
O let it then as well beseeme thy heart
To mourne for me since mourning doth thee grace,
And sute thy pitty like in euery part.
    Then will I sweare beauty her selfe is blacke,
    And all they foule that thy complexion lacke.

This is a persuasion poem of the kind occurring often in Sidney's sequence, but not previously among Shakespeare's own sonnets (perhaps because those addressed to a man cannot use conventional terms to promise poems of praise in return for sexual favors).[19] The sonnet lays heavy stress on the key terms traditional to such persuasions: "pitty," "disdaine," "paine," "grace." This vocabulary, although by no means exclusively Sidney's, is used very often by his poet-lover, beginning prominently in the opening sonnet of his sequence. The term "grace," combining aesthetic, religious, and political connotations with its common meaning of sexual favor, occurs there and in twenty-four other instances in *Astrophil and Stella,* while it appears only seven times in Daniel's sonnets, eight in Drayton's, and eleven in Shakespeare's including in his adaptation of Sidney here in Sonnet 132.[20] Similarly, Shakespeare uses "paine" only here, in three other sonnets to the dark lady, and in Sonnet 38 which is itself also an adaptation of Sidney, whereas Astrophil uses the word fourteen times. The vocabulary of persuasion is therefore a distinguishing feature of his style. Combined with the metaphor of the mistress' black eyes as mourners, another, more specific allusion to Sidney's sequence, this diction makes Astrophil here representative of corrupt persuaders. The associations of him with such a role are especially strong in the second quatrain, in which burlesque of hyperbolic praise, such as Sidney uses in Sonnet 80, is outrageously introduced by "And truly," Astrophil's characteristic kind of mock-disingenuous claim to honesty.[21] The accusation implied by these borrowings and stylistic parallels is that what Shakespeare's speaker blatantly admits in the couplet, with a cynicism breathtaking in its unabashedness, has always been true of poet-lovers like Astrophil. They too, though more covertly, have manipulated praise to win pity and obtain grace, without seeking fit words for what is in the heart, their subject's or their own. Here there are no poets of the past held up as innocent creators of a "holy boure," a sanctified nature which can miraculously preserve love. Instead all poetry is viewed as exploiting a natural world itself perceived to be tainted, where the sun is not a source of celestial brilliance matching the lady's but a cosmetic turning "gray cheeks" to the fashionable hue for conventional blazons. The distance measured by Astrophil, in Sonnets 1 and 2, for example, between what is in his heart and what his verse shows, is recognized but vastly and bitterly widened in Shakespeare's Sonnet 132.

Again by his ways of using Sidney's sonnets, Shakespeare makes his predecessor's verse part of his subject through allusions to it as representative of a traditional kind of poetry. The fact that in Sonnet 127 Sidney's style is viewed as embodying a pastoral innocence lost to Shakespeare's speaker, while in 132 Astrophil is typical of seducers whose persuasions are disguised as poems of praise, shows Shakespeare's careful study of Sidney's sequence. For *Astrophil and Stella* does contain poems at either end of such a spectrum, uncynical compliments and praise acknowledged to be calculated for persuasion. Shakespeare's borrowings in these two sonnets, and in other adaptations, show also his recognition of Sidney's own uneasiness over the proximity of these two types of verse, and the questions raised by it about the relation of poetry to what is in the heart.

Shakespeare's doubts about the adequacy of language to express inward truth become his obsession in the higher-numbered half of his sonnets. There is no fixed point at which a line can be drawn marking a shift in focus away from other concerns. It can be seen, however, that with the exception of Sonnet 21, virtually all Shakespeare's adaptations of specific sonnets by Sidney associate his predecessor's questions about the fidelity of poetry to what is in the heart with his own doubts also about his friend or his mistress. Suspicions about the friend enter the sequence with the comparison of him to the sun masked by clouds in Sonnet 33, and recur elsewhere in the lower-numbered poems, including other adaptations from Sidney. There they involve questions about the friend's appearance of worth and about the morality of praising him as worthy in the poet-lover's verse. These issues then cluster more thickly in sonnets beginning approximately with those after Sonnet 65, the last of the sonnets claiming for poetry a miraculous power to keep the friend's beauty eternally bright. From about that stage in the sequence, the elegiac celebrations of the fading sweets of this world also diminish in number and glamorous force. In Sonnet 67, the poet laments that in the vicious modern world "now nature banckrout is," and from that point on Shakespeare rarely draws untainted imagery from it. The resemblances of his sonnets to those of Daniel and Spenser therefore diminish in the remaining half of the sequence, as the poet-lover ceases to battle with time to rescue his fair young friend from the fate of all other "rarities of natures truth." Correspondingly, resemblances to *Astrophil and Stella* are more extensive and sustained in the higher-numbered sonnets, many more of which take explicitly as

their subject issues about poetry other than its eternizing power. Sidney's
influence is most immediately evident in them. It appears throughout the
second half of the sonnets, not only in shared themes and motifs, however,
but in pervasive habits of language such as Shakespeare's assimilation of
Sidney's vocabulary about art; in his imitation of specific personifications
like a quarrelsome personal Muse, or a neglectful Cupid; in borrowings of
metaphorical designs and structural devices; in adaptations of particular
poems; in echoes of individual lines.[22]

In these adaptations, the cynicism and bitterness are more radical, and
yet not without precedent in Sidneian models, as Shakespeare's borrowings from Sidney in Sonnet 84 illustrate. The sestet opens with another
very precise echo of the metaphor in Sidney's third sonnet for the poet as
a scribe copying what Nature has written in his beloved. The speaker in
Shakespeare's Sonnet 84 debases this metaphor to a recipe for success
offered to any poet wishing his style to be admired by the public:

> Who is it that sayes most, which can say more,
> Then this rich praise, that you alone, are you,
> In whose confine immured is the store,
> Which should example where your equall grew,
> Leane penurie within that Pen doth dwell,
> That to his subiect lends not some small glory,
> But he that writes of you, if he can tell,
> That you are you, so dignifies his story.
> Let him but coppy what in you is writ,
> Not making worse what nature made so cleere,
> And such a counter-part shall fame his wit,
> Making his style admired euery where.
>   You to your beautious blessings adde a curse,
>   Being fond on praise, which makes your praises worse.

Such cynicism as is blatant in Shakespeare's prescription to copy his
subject does not taint Sidney's metaphor in Sonnet 3, where Astrophil's
pose as a humble scribe is playful and complimentary. Yet a cynical point
of view closer to Shakespeare's may be found elsewhere in Sidney's sequence, for example, in Sonnet 35, actually the principal model for Shakespeare's Sonnet 84. The fact that this adaptation also includes in it the
explicit echo of Sidney's third sonnet makes all the more clear Shakespeare's awareness of his predecessor's parallel concerns. He traces them
through Sidney's sequence and then concentrates them in his own poems.

Astrophil in Sonnet 35 openly doubts the possibility of truth in love
poetry, including his own:

> What may words say, or what may words not say,
> Where truth it selfe must speake like flatterie?

Within what bounds can one his liking stay,
Where Nature doth with infinite agree?
    What *Nestor's* counsell can my flames alay,
Since Reason's selfe doth blow the cole in me?
And ah what hope, that hope should once see day,
Where *Cupid* is sworne page to Chastity?
Honour is honour'd, that thou doest possesse
    Him as thy slave, and now long needy Fame
    Doth even grow rich, naming my *Stella's* name.
Wit learnes in thee perfection to expresse,
    Not thou by praise, but praise in thee is raisde:
    It is a praise to praise, when thou art praisde.

Shakespeare's speaker echoes Astrophil's speculations about the morality of praising his subject, but exaggerates their terms. For example, Astrophil links praising with growing "rich," and suggests—by "bounds" as opposed to "infinite"—that the content of truth in a poem can be measured. Shakespeare repeats "rich," and parallels "bounds" with the noun "confine." Then he expands these suggestions. Praise in poetry can be precisely calculated in numerical and monetary terms: "most," "more," "equall," "Leane," "penurie," "lends," "small," "adde." Astrophil, equating the gainful act of writing with mere naming of the beloved, makes the task sound effortless. Shakespeare's speaker uses a metaphor from Sonnet 3 of copying, making the subject a guarantee of literary success and thus eliminating the necessity of invention or effort. Astrophil hints that Stella as well as he may be implicated in the debasement of poetry into flattery, because her inward nature may not be worthy of the praise he heaps on her. To characterize Stella's tyrannical honor he uses ugly words—"possesse" and "slave"—which go beyond the more conventionally acceptable terms *rule* and *servant* in accusing her of cruelly debasing or maddening her lover. The comparable hints by Shakespeare's speaker, when he advises the copier of his subject not to make "worse what nature made so cleere," hide insult behind flattery by exploiting the meanings of "cleere": bright, shining, beautiful, but also evident. Stella is placed in Sonnet 35 in a social world more corrupt than that evoked by such courtly compliments as Sonnets 7 and 22. Here society is more like the tainted world of Shakespeare's higher-numbered sonnets, and of *Hamlet*. Like Astrophil himself, his personifications of Truth, Love, Chastity, Honor, and Fame are courtiers serving self-interest by flattering a tyrant. This pattern of personifications makes "praise" into another such figure: "Not thou by praise, but praise in thee is raisde." The metaphor describes social climbing, not elevation to virtue's throne. The jingling repetition turns Sidney's couplet into burlesque, emptying "praise" of moral content. In Shakespeare's adaptation, the couplet turns burlesque into open insult with the accusation that the friend dotes upon "praise" and falsifies it.

Sonnet 84 belongs to the group concerned with other poets who rival the speaker in praising his subject. They use Sidney's vocabulary for writing—"paint," "show," "inuent"—along with other terms for art that include more sordid, monetary definitions—"affoord," "lends," "spends." Sonnet 84 also borrows Sidney's metaphor of nature as an artist who inscribes in the subject what the poet should copy. Since all the terms for writing used throughout the group of sonnets including 84 carry implications of falseness, then nature as author must be understood here to show in the subject's fair exterior what may not be truly grounded inward in his heart. Or the friend himself may be such an artist, inventing his own "story." This is implied in Sonnet 83, which attaches the vocabulary of writing to the friend's own presentation of himself:

> And therefore haue I slept in your report,
> That you your selfe being extant well might show,
> How farre a moderne quill doth come to short,
> Speaking of worth, what worth in you doth grow.

This vocabulary goes beyond hinting that the subject is hiding particular secrets, or is hypocritical, or a liar. It implies that there is a distinction between what "might show" in his public, social existence, and what he experiences inwardly, comparable to what a poet-lover feels and what he shows in verse. In the second quatrain of Sonnet 84 the subject is said to offer a kind of challenge for those who write about him to "tell, / That you are you." Among many ways to read this, it is paraphrasable: "to discover that you are the unique person that you are, to find out your individual identity." This reading is also supported by line 2, which makes the poet's only task to say "that you alone, are you," adding to other possibilities the interpretation: "you are yourself only when you are alone."[23] Again the subject is implied to have a continuous inward existence, or private identity, apart from his social experience and not readable in his outward show. In this respect he is a figure for whom the relation of inward to outward states is like that which is true for Astrophil solitary in his chamber or alone in company. Yet characteristically this distinction is more radical in Shakespeare's portrayal, and is viewed more cynically. This is true when he focuses on his poet-lover's experience, but especially so when the separation of inward from outward existence is represented by what nature shows in his fair friend, which may or may not make "cleere" what is in his heart.

Shakespeare's association of motifs and metaphors measuring the distance between public and inward existence with Sidney's verse is clearly visible in Sonnet 85. This is a kind of compilation of borrowings from sonnets in Sidney's sequence devoted to the motif of the lover alone in company, which was invented by him, or at least explored in a sustained way by him for the first time in English poetry. Sonnet 85 contains echoes of *Astrophil and Stella* 30, 54, 23, and 27. In all of these some distinction is drawn between the poet-lover's social behavior and his simultaneous preoccupation with a private, inward existence. This compilation of borrowings from several separate sources within Sidney's sequence offers particularly convincing evidence of Shakespeare's deep familiarity with it and his penetration to its most profound implications. For, as has been shown, he studied and adapted many of Sidney's sonnets explicitly focused on the distance between loving and love poetry. His borrowings also from these other sonnets, ostensibly treating a different subject, show that he perceived the network of implicit connections between the two kinds. The nature of his adaptations from *Astrophil and Stella* in Sonnet 85 makes those connections explicit.

Shakespeare introduces the borrowed motif of the poet-lover alone in company in Sonnet 85 by a revision of the couplet from Sidney's Sonnet 30, in which Astrophil distractedly responds to a catalogue of questions plied by curious courtiers:

> I, cumbred with good maners, answer do,
> But know not how, for still I thinke of you.

The identification of outward behavior with manners is the same in Shakespeare's opening line as in Sidney's couplet, and each exploits the same possibilities of *still,* meaning always, nevertheless, but also silent. Both sonnets by these means contrast an existence which is carried on in social acts, gestures, and language, with a simultaneous but distinct unspoken train of thought:

> My toung-tide Muse in manners holds her still,
> While comments of your praise richly compil'd,
> Reserue their Character with goulden quill,
> And precious phrase by all the Muses fil'd.
> I thinke good thoughts, whilst other write good wordes,
> And like vnlettered clarke still crie Amen,
> To euery Himne that able spirit affords,
> In polisht forme of well refined pen.
> Hearing you praisd, I say 'tis so, 'tis true,
> And to the most of praise adde some-thing more,
> But that is in my thought, whose loue to you
> (Though words come hind-most) holds his ranke before,
>   Then others, for the breath of words respect,
>   Me for my dombe thoughts, speaking in effect.

By contrasting his Muse's silence with the praise written by other Muses, Shakespeare identifies the courtly society surrounding his lover by its poetic affectations. (The association of mannered poets with Muses while admitting to owning one himself is a Sidneian device of self-parody, perhaps suggested specifically by *Astrophil and Stella* 3.) This definition of the social world by its literary abuses is close to Sidney's in Sonnet 54, another model here for Shakespeare, where Astrophil contrasts his own reticence in public with the rhetoric and gestures of merely fashionable poet-lovers:

> Because I breathe not love to everie one,
>   Nor do not use set colours for to weare,
>   Nor nourish speciall lockes of vowed haire,
> Nor give each speech a full point of a grone,
> The courtly Nymphs, acquainted with the mone
>   Of them, who in their lips *Love's* standerd beare;
>   'What he?' say they of me, 'now I dare sweare,
> He cannot love: no, no, let him alone.'
>   And thinke so still, so *Stella* know my mind,
> Professe in deed I do not *Cupid's* art;
> But you faire maides, at length this true shall find,
> That his right badge is but worne in the hart:
>   Dumbe Swannes, not chatring Pies, do Lovers prove,
>   They love indeed, who quake to say they love.

Astrophil here lends himself to the conventions of courtly society, as Shakespeare's poet says amen to the idolatrous praises he hears of his friend in company. Also like that speaker, Astrophil meanwhile reserves what is in his mind and heart from the view of those around him, who judge his loving by the same signs as Polonius and Ophelia use to interpret Hamlet's inward state. Neither speaker precisely reveals what is in his heart to the reader either, although Astrophil's playful indirection in including himself among "Dumbe Swannes" tells more than the dubious evasiveness of Shakespeare's speaker when he alludes to "that is in my thought." What "that" may be is ominously unspecified, but its presence within the mind of the speaker is defined metaphorically as a kind of procession arranged by social position, or a race in which contestants are ranked. The sense of continuous sequence and the competitive tenacity implied by "holds his ranke" resemble this metaphor for inward experience to two of Sidney's. In Sonnet 23 Astrophil contrasts what others deem to be his inward preoccupations with this conclusion:

> O fooles, or over-wise, alas the race
>   Of all my thoughts hath neither stop nor start,
>   But only *Stella's* eyes and *Stella's* hart.

In the couplet of Sonnet 27 he describes himself passing blindly and deafly through the social world, "while thought to highest place / Bends all his powers, even unto *Stella's* grace." Continuous anxiety and struggle are associated with inward experience in these metaphors, as in Shakespeare's of the ranked procession or race. All also use language belonging to social life to characterize the lovers' inward existence, which contributes to the sense of it as a life as vivid, detailed, extensive, and continuous as the one in which they act and speak. Both couplets also associate inward experience with a kind of silent expression, acknowledging its paradoxical character by the metaphor of dumbness. Astrophil identifies with the palely elegant "Dumbe Swannes," who do not chatter like vulgar magpies, but who "love indeed," that is, in acts which "prove," or who "quake to say they love." Shakespeare's lover defends his "dombe thoughts" which, unlike the wordiness of poets, deserve respect for "speaking in effect," that is, in fact, in actuality.

Sonnet 85 contains within it a line of development traced in Sidney's sequence. It begins with a distinction between the poet-lover's modest silence and the richly ornamented praise uttered by courtly and conventional invokers of the Muses. That distinction leads to a separation between "thoughts" and "wordes" themselves, which points to a distance between outward behavior, comparable to what shows in poetry, and inward experience, which is "speaking in effect" but not in utterance. The many echoes of *Astrophil and Stella* in this, as in other sonnets, prove that Shakespeare recognized such a line of development in Sidney's sequence, and saw in it the kinds of possibilities he compresses in Sonnet 85. His speaker describes a recurrent situation like the scenes in which Astrophil pictures himself. The occasions are social, governed by conventions common to courtly manners and courtly poetry. The poet-lover hears others talking, he takes some part in the conversation, he is aware of the impression made by his words, gestures, and looks. At the same time, he is conscious of a continuous inward activity which cannot be seen in his social appearance, and cannot be heard in his utterance, although he characterizes it paradoxically as a silent language. The sonnet itself becomes as if it were a kind of private communication, not published in verse or spoken out loud in public. It is like an aside, or like a soliloquy in which the speaker, alone on the stage, gives account to himself of what he experiences within while acting and speaking in company.

Sidney, the previous chapter has shown, was unquestionably interested in rendering this sense of simultaneous inward and outward existence. Characteristically, he associates it with the difference between what the poet-lover shows in verse and what is in his mind and heart. This link suggests that the struggle to write truly is bound up with an effort to include invisible and unspoken experience in his verse. To do so he created the many uses of language marking the distance between

Astrophil's poetry and his inward states. To the same end he also developed new modes for exploring what is in the heart. Shakespeare, in sonnets based on models in *Astrophil and Stella,* shows that he recognized and
expanded on those beginnings.

Some of Shakespeare's adaptations go even beyond imitation of structure and language used to argue the issues about poetry which interested
his predecessor. In some sonnets modeled on Sidney's, he shows that he
absorbed from them fundamental assumptions about human nature which
are new to English poetry in *Astrophil and Stella.* This is true of his sonnets
which follow Sidney's ways of measuring the distance between the poet-
lover's inward and outward states. It is profoundly true of sonnets which
explore that separation as a means of questioning whether invisible and
unspoken experience which is grounded inward in the heart is susceptible
of being interpreted, understood, judged.

Among the poems in which Sidney draws a line, here between octave
and sestet, distinguishing Astrophil's social existence from his inward
state, Sonnet 27 provided the most fruitfully interesting model. Its initial
attraction for Shakespeare may have consisted on the one hand in its
sympathy with the social attitudes prevalent especially in his own higher-
numbered sonnets and in *Hamlet,* for it presents a darker, more dangerous
world surrounding Astrophil than is commonly pictured in Sidney's sequence. On the other hand, this sonnet may have interested Shakespeare
for what it could teach him by its more extended analysis of the lover's
inward state and by the devices used to explore its complex and ambiguous nature:

> Because I oft in darke abstracted guise,
>   Seeme most alone in greatest companie,
>   With dearth of words, or answers quite awrie,
> To them that would make speech of speech arise,
> They deeme, and of their doome the rumour flies,
>   That poison foule of bubling pride doth lie
>   So in my swelling breast that only I
> Fawne on my self, and others to despise:
>   Yet pride I thinke doth not my soule possesse,
> Which lookes too oft in his unflattring glasse:
> But one worse fault, *Ambition,* I confesse,
> That makes me oft my best friends overpasse,
>   Unseene, unheard, while thought to highest place
>   Bends all his powers, even unto *Stella's* grace.

Shakespeare's adaptation in Sonnet 62 expands the lover's confession
of what he sees in his soul so that it fills the whole poem, but he does so
by assimilating Astrophil's judges into himself. He takes a view of his own

sins which is parallel to the outside criticism reported by Sidney's lover in the octave. Shakespeare then copies his model by setting up the remainder of the poem as if it were the speaker's correction of that false judgment. Like Astrophil's glass, this lover's mirror shows him another way of looking at himself, which partially exonerates him from earlier accusations, while shifting to praise of the beloved who preoccupies the speaker's soul. Yet Shakespeare also follows his model in complicating the relationship between sestet and octave, so that apparently contrasting views can no longer be so simply distinguished. He therefore raises questions most certainly suggested here by Sidney about the nature of inward states, how they are to be known, and by what language they may be interpreted:

> Sinne of selfe-loue possesseth al mine eie,
> And all my soule, and al my euery part;
> And for this sinne there is no remedie,
> It is so grounded inward in my heart.
> Me thinkes no face so gratious is as mine,
> No shape so true, no truth of such account,
> And for my selfe mine owne worth do define,
> As I all other in all worths surmount.
> But when my glasse shewes me my selfe indeed
> Beated and chopt with tand antiquitie,
> Mine owne selfe loue quite contrary I read
> Selfe, so selfe louing were iniquity,
>   T'is thee (my selfe) that for my selfe I praise,
>   Painting my age with beauty of thy daies.

In addition to the structure and development described, Shakespeare assimilates patterns of meaning established by Sidney's vocabulary. Sidney's key terms are: "guise," "Seeme," "deeme," and the pun on "lie." Shakespeare's are: "true," "truth," "shewes," and the multiple possibilities of "indeed," all to be found more often throughout *Astrophil and Stella* than in other major English sequences except Shakespeare's. The word *true,* for example, is used four times in Daniel's sonnets, nine in Drayton's and in Spenser's *Amoretti,* twenty-one times by Sidney, and thirty-eight by Shakespeare. Similarly *truth* occurs four times in Daniel's sonnets, once in Drayton's, and twice in Spenser's sequence, but eleven times in Sidney's, and twenty-two in Shakespeare's. The play on multiple meanings of *indeed* is a specialty of Sidney's, who uses it six times while the others employ the word only once, Shakespeare in this adaptation from a sonnet by Sidney. These patterns are also related in both model and adaptation to parallel expressions for the act of interpreting and analyzing such distinctions: Sidney's "I thinke," "I confesse," and Shakespeare's "Me thinkes," "I read."

Also shared by these sonnets are grammatical constructions supporting

words bearing more than one meaning, to create what Stephen Booth
describes as "paradoxically compatible alternatives."[24] These necessarily
demand multiple interpretation. In both poems such ambiguous phrases
are used to invite seemingly contradictory readings of inward experience,
and then to prevent them from being simply in contradiction. Astrophil
reports his critics' view that "only I / Fawne on my self, and others to
despise." This judgment can be read: "I, but not anyone else, fawn on my
self; I do nothing but fawn on my self; I fawn on nothing but my self, not
on anything outside my self." In answer to that accusation, Astrophil
offers an apparently contradictory interpretation:

> Yet pride I thinke doth not my soule possesse,
> Which lookes too oft in his unflattring glasse.

This denial seems at first simply to contradict the charge of narcissism,
but by different means both lines complicate Astrophil's analysis of himself. The first is an instance of Sidney's reversible grammar supporting
double meanings for "possesse." These paraphrases are made possible: "I
think that pride does not own my soul, does not drive it to madness; I
think my soul does not contain pride, does not own it." The next line,
although it uses no ambiguous word order, further complicates interpretation of Astrophil's self-defense. For he makes a claim which simultaneously implies its opposite. What he asserts is: "my soul looks too often
in a glass that is unflattering to be able to possess pride, or be possessed
by it." What he at the same time implies is: "while I think that my soul
does not possess pride, is not possessed by it, it nevertheless looks too
often in an unflattering glass, which is a proud act." The metrical stress
in line 9 is on "thinke," emphasizing the uncertainty of the judgment, the
logical stress is on "I," underscoring its relativity and self-interest. These
ambiguities therefore allow readings which break down the apparent contrast between outside judgments of Astrophil and his own confession. His
soul does seek its own reflection, continually looks at itself, so that while
the mirror does not flatter, the soul's eye (perhaps an implied pun on *I*)
does fawn on itself.[25] Astrophil concedes something like this reading of his
inward state when he confesses his mind to be guilty of ambition worse
than the pride which his breast and soul are accused of harboring. For his
"thought to highest place / Bends all his powers, even unto *Stella's* grace."
At first this does sound like a confession. Then it can be read as a playful
mock confession, exonerating Astrophil by justifying his devotion as aspi-
ration to virtue's throne. Yet the double possibilities in "Bends," meaning
directs but also bows, make the action of his thought also a kind of
fawning. In that sense it is a fault, but why does he call it "worse" than
fawning on himself? Is Stella less worthy than Astrophil, whose pride
should therefore assert itself more? Or does his concentration on her harm

him more than pride, by making him neglect his social world? Is he committing blasphemy, either by aspiring to her heights, or by making her an idol? Astrophil's confession contributes these further ambiguities, complicating interpretation of what is in his heart.

The parallel lines in Shakespeare's Sonnet 62 use similar means to create comparable difficulties of interpretation. The speaker gives a sarcastic account of his self-love matching the accusation by Astrophil's judges:

> And for my selfe mine own worthe do define,
> As I all other in all worths surmount.

The first line may be paraphrased: "I define my own worth instead of letting anyone else define it; I define my own worth for my own benefit, to serve myself." The second line allows the explanation: "I do this since I surmount all others; so that I can surmount all others; as if I surmount all others." Then in apparent negation of all those possible interpretations of his inward state, the lover offers a correction, what he sees "when my glasse shewes me my self indeed." The speaker's alternative view here seems to have a kind of solidity and clarity that begins to dissolve when "indeed" is seen to contain the multiple possibilities of meaning so often exploited by Sidney: in fact, in deed or act, truly. The speaker's view of himself then becomes altogether ambiguous two lines later when he says, "Mine owne selfe loue quite contrary I read." Stephen Booth offers two paraphrases: "my self-love turns to self-loathing," and "my self-love turns out to have been not my own, not love of my *own* self," followed by this comment:

> The roundabout phrasing may have been dictated by Shakespeare's desire to play on the fact that a mirror image is reversed, *contrary.* The phrase *contrary I read* may also have appealed to him because it embodies the reader's and speaker's sense that the speaker's self-image has been exactly contrary to the physical facts of his experience, and because it embodies a capsule description of the poem's process and the reader's experience of it—repeatedly shifting from one kind of truth to another and from one to another basis for perceiving the speaker's position as contrary to truth.[26]

This comment is itself a very precise description of the process of Sidney's sonnet, which Shakespeare assimilated and carried through to a parallel ending in his adaptation. Where Astrophil confesses to a worse fault than he has been judged to have, Shakespeare's lover judges his own sin, and then appears to absolve himself by the claim that the self that he praises is his other self, his friend, whose youthful beauty is the true subject of his praise. Yet judgment and absolution are phrased as ambiguously as Astrophil's confession. For the line "Selfe, so self-loving were iniquity" may be read: "self-loving in this manner, or to this degree, would be sinful," allowing the suggestion that some other kind or degree of self-loving would not be "iniquity." Since that word was synonymous with inequity, inequality, it might exclude moral condemnation by the speaker, and merely point to a sense of disproportion in his self-loving. More cynical are the ambiguities of the couplet, where again multiple readings of "for my selfe" include the ugly possibilities that the lover praises the friend to benefit himself, and also to deceive by "Painting." Added to all Sidney's habitual meanings of that word is Shakespeare's characteristically more tainted suggestion of using cosmetics which disguise and allure. The poet-lover's final confession and absolution are therefore even more murkily ambiguous than Astrophil's. Both speakers, however, are implicated in the corruptions of the world—Astrophil by social climbing, Shakespeare's poet-lover by more vicious flattery and seduction.

The effect of the parallel processes described is to make the confessional mode of these poems a mockery of both judgment and self-revelation. Each speaker appears to correct a false evaluation of himself by baring the truth of his inward state, what is not knowable from readings of his behavior and speech. Yet in each sonnet outside judgments and also private revelations are susceptible of so many simultaneous interpretations that they point to the difficulties of ever reading what is in the heart, even one's own. The ambiguities of the lover's language in each sonnet make it impossible for the reader to know if it is being used to reveal or disguise; if it serves both functions simultaneously; if it works both ways upon the reader and the beloved only, or also on the speaker. It is possible to conclude, however, that Sidney, and Shakespeare following his example here, use such language to widen the distance between what poetry shows and what is grounded inward in the heart. Perhaps its depths may not be known even by self-scrutiny.

Despite use of the confessional mode, neither sonnet seems to be predicated on the assumption, fundamental to most sixteenth-century love poetry, that unseen and unuttered inward experience is nevertheless open and visible to God, and therefore ultimately knowable, or capable of being expressed by its true names. Furthermore, neither speaker here believes that making a confession is any more true a mode of self-knowledge than looking in a mirror, in which one sees only a reflection, even an image which is contrary to fact. Shakespeare's sonnet, after the model of Sidney's, therefore criticizes two of the commonest metaphors in writing of the period for the discovery of what is in the heart.[27]

Another such conventional metaphor, examining account books or making an audit, is explored in one of Sidney's sonnets also chosen by Shakespeare as a model, *Astrophil and Stella* 18:

With what sharpe checkes I in my selfe am shent,
   When into Reason's audite I do go:
   And by just counts my selfe a banckrout know
Of all those goods, which heav'n to me hath lent:
Unable quite to pay even Nature's rent,
   Which unto it by birthright I do ow:
   And which is worse, no good excuse can show,
But that my wealth I have most idly spent.
   My youth doth waste, my knowledge brings forth toyes,
My wit doth strive those passions to defend,
Which for reward spoile it with vaine annoyes.
I see my course to lose my selfe doth bend:
   I see and yet no greater sorow take,
   Then that I lose no more for *Stella's* sake.

Here for the first twelve lines Astrophil is his own critic. Using the measurements of accounting and auditing, he declares himself bankrupt. The terms seem largely unambiguous and unarguable; the language does not invite the kind of multiple interpretation demanded by Sonnet 27. Yet the metaphor of the audit, as it is used here, complicates Astrophil's analysis of what is in his heart by its own somewhat different process.

The terminology of auditing is directed by Astrophil against himself to make judgments which are unequivocal. He calls his accounts "just," which makes them both precise or accurate, and morally right. They all add up to his bankrupcy. Yet there are points in Astrophil's analysis of his inward state where he uses language not numerical or financial, which therefore allows the possibility of interpretations other than judgments based on accurate sums. These possibilities are mostly thickly concentrated in the last lines, where the sonnet form has been shown to invite some such complicating reflection or twist. This effect is especially reinforced by a final couplet, which Sidney uses in this sonnet, as he does in 27 and in the majority of others chosen by Shakespeare as models.

Instances of earlier shifts away from accounting terms prepare for the conclusion. One such occurs at the end of the second quatrain, where Astrophil seems to intensify his self-criticism. Not only has he spent all that he has, but "which is worse, no good excuse can show." Yet excuses, even good ones, do not satisfy financial auditors. They influence only sympathetic listeners who are eager to forgive, like one's self, or who base their interpretations on intentions, motives, mitigating circumstances, conflicting goals, not on numbers that must add up. This language has no place in an audit. It makes Astrophil's self-analysis something other than accounting, his view of his inward state less simple than a column of figures. Similarly, in the third quatrain the lover steps out of his metaphorical role as auditor when he uses language which may be legal or military: "My wit doth strive those passions to defend." There is some magnanimity in the posture of defender, so that Astrophil hints again at other values than numerical justness, while at the same time he continues to criticize himself for acting as defender in a wrong or futile cause. In the last three lines the numerical and financial terms are still used by Astrophil—"lose," "greater," "take," "lose," "more"—but in ways which combine with his self-criticism a much more sympathetic view. For to "lose" one's "selfe" for the "sake" of another, for love, is to have more than a "good excuse." It is to be magnanimous, almost to follow a spiritual imperative to self-sacrifice. Finally, therefore, Astrophil excuses and defends, almost lauds, what he also condemns in himself, so that the sonnet follows the process of his self-analysis. What is in the lover's heart is shown to be undefinable by a single metaphor, however rigorously applied, or kind of vocabulary, however precise in its terms. It even escapes judgment by any one system of values; no counts, though "just," can measure it.

This mode of self-analysis developed in *Astrophil and Stella* 18 is assimilated directly from it by Shakespeare in Sonnet 49:

> Against that time (if euer that time come)
> When I shall see thee frowne on my defects,
> When as thy loue hath cast his vtmost summe,
> Cauld to that audite by aduis'd respects,
> Against that time when thou shalt strangely passe,
> And scarcely greete me with that sunne thine eye,
> When loue conuerted from the thing it was
> Shall reasons finde of setled grauitie.
> Against that time do I insconce me here
> Within the knowledge of mine owne desart,
> And this my hand, against my selfe vpreare,
> To guard the lawfull reasons on thy part,
>   To leaue poore me, thou hast the strength of lawes,
>   Since why to loue, I can alledge no cause.

While in Sonnet 62 Shakespeare transforms his model so that outside judgments become part of the lover's own confession, here he attributes Astrophil's metaphor of auditing accounts to the poet-lover's friend. That is, the speaker imagines that his friend will perform the audit on "thy love"—on his own inward state, and on the speaker's value to him. Yet this shift in its application does not altogether change the use of the conventional metaphor: examination of what is in the heart compared to a financial audit. For Shakespeare's lover, like Astrophil, both recognizes the reasonableness and legality of such an evaluation, and feels its inadequacy. He accepts numerical and financial terms as calculations of his inward worth, even turns Astrophil's military and legal metaphor of defending against himself. Yet at the same time, and far more bitterly than

Sidney's lover, he feels that he deserves to be viewed with more generosity, because his "owne desart" is not simply the sum of his "defects." In the last lines, following their Sidneian model, there emerges the lover's sense of his own true worth, even of his superiority. For, resembling Astrophil, he knows more about loving than anyone who, like his friend, is of the opinion that it can be evaluated simply by numbers and by laws. He has demonstrated this knowledge in the generosity with which he defends his friend's reasoning, even at great cost to himself. He has therefore shown that, like Astrophil, he can lose himself for the sake of another, for love, and like Astrophil he asserts this in the couplet by making financial and legalistic language show their own inadequacy. "To leaue poore me" translates poverty from lack of money into inward deprivation. The metrical stress is on "me," while the logic of the argument emphasizes "poore" (a sophisticated use of meter which, according to John Thompson, Sidney was the first English poet to discover, and which he used in a number of sonnets chosen by Shakespeare as models).[28] The last line also escapes legalism by achieving a generalizing power like the spiritual imperative to self-sacrifice in Sidney's last line. "Since why to loue, I can alledge no cause" opens the question to the nature of love itself, which cannot be defined. The largeness, the vulnerability, and the acceptance in the question defy any sum, reasons, or laws to answer it.

Again Shakespeare assimilates Sidney's exploration of one of the most widely used and accepted metaphors for self-knowledge in sixteenth-century writing, the auditing of one's account books. It is a metaphor on which Shakespeare builds his own Sonnet 146, "Poore soule the center of my sinfull earth." There the speaker puts his soul through such an examination, commanding it to set its financial house in order. In his adaptation of *Astrophil and Stella* 18, however, Shakespeare absorbs Sidney's distrust of the metaphor, which is characteristically not a simple rejection of it for its inadequacy to render the lover's inward state. For Sidney's poet-lover, like Shakespeare's speaker modeled after him in Sonnet 49, recognizes that the conclusion of the audit performed on his inward state is a true account of it, "and yet" not wholly true. Or rather, it is not the complete truth, which somehow escapes conclusions.

The fact that Sidney in these sonnets exposes limits to the metaphors most widely accepted in the period for describing the act of looking in the heart shows these poems to be predicated on other assumptions than those of most sixteenth-century writing. The fullness and power of Shakespeare's adaptations show how profoundly he understood what were Sidney's different assumptions. Uneasiness about the adequacy of such conventions is involved—perhaps simultaneously as both cause and effect—in Sidney's sense that what is in the heart may be unknowable, inexpressible, and that it may therefore defy judgment. His exploration of another metaphor conventional to love poetry of the period, including his own, can trace further the development of his assumptions and of their assimilation by Shakespeare.

One of the commonest metaphors for representing the lover's state in sixteenth-century verse is the comparison of him to a subject ruled by a sovereign mistress. While it had the support of long-established literary tradition, and the encouragement of current fashion in continental poetry, the metaphor also corresponded to the actual situation of the Elizabethan courtier, who paid daily tribute to such a ruler not only in his verses. The language used other than in literary works to address and describe the Queen, while it shares abuses associated with this convention in poetry—triteness and preposterous hyperbole in particular—also shows its richness.[29] For the Queen, as head of both Church and State, was not only in art but in fact a focus for religious and political devotion. She was therefore described in various powerfully charged vocabularies. Furthermore her relation to her subjects was often defined at the same time in much more personal terms than would be appropriate for later rulers governing vastly greater numbers from a far more distant remove.[30] The actual relationship of sovereign to subject therefore supported the poetic metaphor in concentrating within it a wide range of emotional possibilities. Virtually all the worst as well as the best poets of the period worked with these possibilities in their innumerable repetitions of the metaphor.

It is utterly characteristic of *Astrophil and Stella* that Sidney uses a convention effectively while elsewhere in the sequence raising questions, even serious doubts, about its adequacy, or criticisms of its acceptance. Astrophil's allusions to Stella as sovereign mistress ruling over him, her subject, are everywhere. Some are extended metaphorical designs, as in Sonnet 40 in the poem-within-a-poem addressed to her as star, ruler, military conqueror, deity exerting power from the height of virtue's throne. Other references are compressed in a single word made so familiar by conventional repetition that it needs no explanation, such as the "grace" Astrophil seeks to obtain in Sonnet 1. Typically that word gathers religious and political connotations into a compliment to the sovereign lady's beauty, elegance, and high social position, while also being understood as a euphemism for sexual favors.

Sonnet 2 transforms the metaphorical relationship of subject to sovereign into the bondage of slave to tyrant. This is the first of seven occurrences in Sidney's sequence of the word *slave* in its various forms. In almost every instance it is the occasion for much greater bitterness than the resentment that often attaches to the lover's role as subject to a legitimate ruler. This intensity may show personal application for Sidney himself, who was as proud of his high birth and as jealous of his honor as he makes Astrophil of his. The fact that *slave* is in poetic diction quite distant from the predictable terms, variants of *service,* for which it is substituted by Sidney is proved by the absense of the harsher word in any form from the

sonnets of Daniel, Drayton, or Spenser. Shakespeare, however, also uses
it seven times, including once in a sonnet demonstrably borrowing in still
other ways from a Sidneian model.[31]

Sidney seems to make this substitution in order to push the conventional metaphor to the limits of its ugliest implications as a definition of
loving. An example of this practice is *Astrophil and Stella* 47:

> What, have I thus betrayed my libertie?
>   Can those blacke beames such burning markes engrave
>   In my free side? or am I borne a slave,
> Whose necke becomes such yoke of tyranny?
> Or want I sense to feele my miserie?
>   Or sprite, disdaine of such disdaine to have?
>   Who for long faith, tho dayly helpe I crave,
> May get no almes but scorne of beggerie.
> Vertue awake, Beautie but beautie is,
> I may, I must, I can, I will, I do
> Leave following that, which it is gaine to misse.
> Let her go. Soft, but here she comes. Go to,
>   Unkind, I love you not: O me, that eye
>   Doth make my heart give to my tongue the lie.

The brutality in the image of Stella's black eyes burning a brand mark on
Astrophil's side is disturbingly literal, and his humiliation grotesquely
physical as his "necke becomes" a tyrannous yoke, meaning that it suits
such a confinement, but also that it has been deformed so as to be bent
into the shape of a yoke. This description of the lover's debasement into
slavery comes close to destroying the decorum which the wit of the couplet is characteristically designed to preserve. Precisely this indecorous-
ness may have drawn Shakespeare to use the poem as the model for his
own Sonnet 150, in which he also adapts Sidney's motif of black eyes to
assault the conventions of decorous praise:

> Oh from what powre hast thou this powrefull might,
> With insufficiency my heart to sway,
> To make me giue the lie to my true sight,
> And swere that brightnesse doth not grace the day?
> Whence hast thou this becomming of things il,
> That in the very refuse of thy deeds,
> There is such strength and warrantise of skill,
> That in my minde thy worst all best exceeds?
> Who taught thee how to make me loue thee more,
> The more I heare and see iust cause of hate,
> Oh though I loue what others doe abhor,
> With others thou shouldst not abhor my state.
>   If thy vnworthinesse raisd loue in me,
>   More worthy I to be belou'd of thee.

Among the many points of resemblance in structure and verbal detail between these explorations of the lover's enslaved state, one strand of connection traces the way the conventional metaphor is exposed as a euphemism. In each sonnet the lover recognizes that his inward state is ugly, abhorrent, a contradiction of acknowledged fact and value, the very opposite of loving. Astrophil articulates this by his angry denial, "I love you not," Shakespeare's speaker by ringing changes in the sestet on the word "love" (itself a device learned, perhaps, from other sonnets by Sidney), making it mean hate, or perverted taste, or a crude, physiological reflex.[32] Both, however, acknowledge the inadequacy of their own self-scrutiny. Astrophil is forced to take back his denial of "love," for Stella's power over him as her slave "Doth make my heart give to my tongue the lie." Shakespeare's speaker admits to similar might in his mistress "To make me giue the lie to my true sight." Neither can truly name what is in the heart; he can only call it "love," which means everything and nothing. Each therefore uses his examination of his enslaved heart to lead to no conclusion, fulfilling Abraham Fraunce's definition of *aposiopesis,* or *reticentia,* in *The Arcadian Rhetorike* of 1588, which he illustrates with this sonnet of Sidney's: "when the course of a speach begun is in such sort staid, that some part thereof not vttred, is neuertheles perceiued."[33] Or each speaker concludes that the conventional metaphors of love poetry, like the very name "love" itself, are empty disguises for an inward reality that defies definition. For it would be as true and as untrue for either speaker to say *I love you* to the mistress who enslaves him as to say the opposite.

In this sonnet chosen by Shakespeare as a model, Sidney goes beyond questioning the relationship of loving in truth to its show in poetry. For here Astrophil is not struggling to write verse showing what is in his heart, but is trying to describe it truthfully to himself. The broken rhythms of the sestet are signs that this sonnet is intended to represent an internal monologue or a soliloquy, rather than a poem which the lover is laboring to compose (an act signaled in many other sonnets by references to writing, rhetoric, rhymes, numbers, feet, lines, pen, ink, paper). Therefore its language illustrates Astrophil's speech when he is alone, not attempting to persuade anyone except, perhaps, himself. The inadequacy of his internal or private language to escape a "lie" is therefore not principally a commentary here on the relation of poetry to inward truth, but a reflection of Sidney's view that language does not provide a means for discovering what is in the heart.

Shakespeare in Sonnet 58 again imitates Sidney in exposing the ugliness hidden behind the conventional metaphor of the lover in service to a sovereign mistress. Here he carries over the indecorous word "slave" from *Astrophil and Stella* 86, to which his adaptation is also indebted in other ways. The occasion for Astrophil's complaint is a change in Stella's expression, a withdrawal suggesting a newly severe judgment of him:

Alas, whence came this change of lookes? If I
    Have chang'd desert, let mine owne conscience be
    A still felt plague, to selfe condemning me:
Let wo gripe on my heart, shame loade mine eye.
But if all faith, like spotlesse Ermine ly
    Safe in my soule, which only doth to thee
    (As his sole object of felicitie)
With wings of *Love* in aire of wonder flie,
    O ease your hand, treate not so hard your slave:
In justice paines come not till faults do call;
Or if I needs (sweet Judge) must torments have,
Use something else to chast'n me withall,
    Then those blest eyes, where all my hopes do dwell,
    No doome should make one's heav'n become his hell.

The occasion of which Shakespeare's lover complains is his beloved's
absence, or his way of occupying himself when absent from the speaker:

That God forbid, that made me first your slaue,
I should in thought controule your times of pleasure,
Or at your hand th' account of houres to craue,
Being your vassail bound to staie your leisure.
Oh let me suffer (being at your beck)
Th' imprison'd absence of your libertie,
And patience tame, to sufferance bide each check,
Without accusing you of iniury.
Be where you list, your charter is so strong,
That you your selfe may priuiledge your time
To what you will, to you it doth belong,
Your selfe to pardon of selfe-doing crime.
    I am to waite, though waiting so be hell,
    Not blame your pleasure be it ill or well.

Each speaker seizes the occasion to examine his inward state by pushing
to the limits of its implications the convention of the lover in service.

Both poet-lovers make the beloved into a secular power—a judge or a
sovereign lord—who they claim has the right to punish them, while covertly they protest the injustice of their sufferings.[34] Both accept the cruelty
of their torturers: Astrophil when he argues "Or if I needs (sweet Judge)
must torments have," Shakespeare's lover more desperately and more
bitterly exclaiming "Oh let me suffer (being at your beck)." Yet in the end
their justifications and acquiescences are exposed as deceptions—to their
beloveds and to themselves—when each lover calls his bondage "hell."
The vehicle of deception is the metaphor of the lover as slave, pushed here
to bare ugly facts which nevertheless do not fully account for what is in
his heart.

Sidney's transformations in these two sonnets of the lover's conventional role as subject into a metaphor of slavery, and Shakespeare's adaptations of them, trace the development of common concerns. The source of their uneasiness about the convention as a representation of loving is the sense, evident in their Sonnets 47 and 150, that the heart gives the "lie" to such interpretations of it. Following from that is a corresponding notion of the difficulty of understanding and judging either one's self or another. This concern is common to the poems previously discussed which question conventional metaphors for learning to know one's self. It seems also to have been a source of Shakespeare's interest in Sidney's metaphor of loving as slavery in *Astrophil and Stella* 86.

This interest is reflected in Sonnet 58 in a detail borrowed from its Sidneian model. Astrophil argues that if he has indeed, as Stella's severe looks imply, "chang'd desert," then it is the prerogative of his own conscience to be "A still felt plague, to selfe condemning me." The double sense of "still" means that his conscience plagues him continually, but also silently, inwardly. Its workings are unexpressed, and therefore not to be judged. Shakespeare shifts the issue from judgment to exoneration, and the guilty party from the speaker to the beloved, to whom it belongs "Your selfe to pardon of selfe-doing crime." The wording is close enough, and in both lines odd enough—such compounds with *self* are rare in sixteenth-century love poetry—to suggest an echo of Sidney in Shakespeare's phrasing. The "self-doing crime" of the friend may be that done by or to him, or by him to the speaker, ambiguities again embodying the difficulty of clear interpretation, and therefore of true judgment. Shakespeare characteristically pushes the issue to more cynical lengths than Sidney by his speaker's insulting suggestion throughout the sonnet that the friend is indifferent to whether what is in the heart is truly judged, by or of him. Stella's judgments need correction, but Astrophil, in attempting to adjust them, even though by means of a deceptive metaphor, is not wholly cynical. Yet his efforts constitute criticisms of the conventions commonly used in the sixteenth century to show what is in the heart, criticisms on which Shakespeare's assaults are modeled.

What emerges in Shakespeare's sonnets adapted from Sidney is a speaker who cannot be known from his outward show, not because it is a deliberate disguise but because it is so widely distanced from his inward experience. This radical separation then makes utterance incapable of showing truly what is in his heart. Even when he describes his inward state as if in an aside, or reveals it to himself only, in versions of interior monologue or of soliloquy, it defies full expression. In consequence, the speaker in Shakespeare's sonnets is a dramatic creation like Hamlet. His language gives the impression of a figure with a continuous inward existence of which he is himself fully aware, yet cannot show, and even perhaps

cannot interpret. These resemblances between the poet-lover of the
sonnets and Hamlet can be explored in more detail if his first speech in
the play, after his opening aside, is read now in the context of previous
discussions:

> Seemes Maddam? Nay, it is: I know not Seemes:
> 'Tis not alone my Inky Cloake (good Mother)
> Nor Customary suites of solemne Blacke,
> Nor windy suspiration of forc'd breath,
> No, nor the fruitfull Riuer in the Eye,
> Nor the deiected hauiour of the Visage,
> Together with all Formes, Moods, shewes of Griefe,
> That can denote me truly. These indeed Seeme,
> For they are actions that a man might play:
> But I haue that Within, which passeth show;
> These, but the Trappings, and the Suites of woe.[35]

Hamlet's distinction here between "is" and "Seemes," it has been said,
was not in itself a new preoccupation in sixteenth-century verse; it was an
especially common theme in love poetry. For lovers, as represented in
Tottel's miscellany, were typically concerned either to see beneath the
"cloked doublenesse" intended to make them mistake seeming love for
true, as in one of Wyatt's complaints, or, as in one of Surrey's, they strive
to learn "how to hide my harmes with soft dissembling chere, / When in
my face the painted thoughtes would outwardly apere."[36] Equally commonplace in sixteenth-century love poetry are all the visible expressions
of suffering catalogued in Hamlet's opening speech, not only the sighs,
tears, and face of woe, but even his "suites of solemne Blacke" and "Inky
Cloake," which are appropriate to the particular dramatic situation of the
play, but also resemble conventional metaphors of clothing as outward
signs either matching inward states or disguising them. This association
was so strong that *to cloak* was a common verb for the effort of seeming:
Bullokar defines it as "To couer or hide";[37] Puttneham allows the "Courtly
Poet to be a dissembler" insofar as he can "disguise and cloake" his art.[38]
Also associated with this kind of performance was the metaphor Hamlet
uses of play-acting. The word *part* is often rhymed with the favorite
pairing of *heart* and *smart,* as in lines from a song by Wyatt included in
Tottel's miscellany:

> How may a man in smart
> Finde matter to reioyce?
> How may a moornyng hart
> Set foorth a pleasant voice.
> Play who so can, that part:
> Nedes must in me appere:

How fortune ouerthwart
Doth cause my moorning chere.[39]

With similar attention to the distinction between being and seeming, or outwardly appearing, *woe* is coupled with *show* by Sidney in the opening sonnet and four other times in *Astrophil and Stella*. Hamlet's speech is in fact a lover's complaint which, in its vocabulary and metaphors for representing what is in the heart, is virtually identical with Wyatt's and those of other sixteenth-century poets. The impulse behind the choice of this form for the speech can only be guessed. One possibility is that love poetry was the kind traditionally associated with the rendering of inward states, especially the complaint, which was itself catalogued—along with sighs, tears, and sobs—among the modes for expressing them. Another way of accounting for the form of the speech is that Shakespeare's concern with the distance between outward show and what is grounded inward in the heart emerged from his own work in love sonnets, particularly in his adaptations of Sidney's, and was therefore directly associated for him with poems sharing the vocabulary and metaphors of Hamlet's speech.

Some effects of Shakespeare's own work in the sonnet form show in this speech not only in its use of conventions of the complaint, but in more particular aspects of its structure and development. It follows the additive pattern of a catalogue until the last two lines, which are rhymed as in the couplet endings of all Shakespeare's sonnets (in the play there are only two other couplets which do not mark either the entrance or exit of a character, or the close of a scene). Here the couplet makes a kind of complicating reflection on the preceding lines, which is similar to the effect of sonnet endings as they were used by Wyatt and Sidney before Shakespeare himself. As is often true in these sonnets, the complicating effect of the couplet here also depends on the clustering toward the end of the speech, and in the couplet itself, of words exploited for their multiple possibilities of meaning. These, it will be seen, then comment on interpretations of earlier lines.

Beginning with the distinction between seeming and being, the speech predicts a catalogue of contrasts illustrating the difference between false pretenses and what is truly in the heart. The exaggerated phrasing in which Hamlet describes outward expressions of grief—sighs which are the "windy suspiration of forc'd breath," for example—and piles up "all Formes, Moods, shewes of Griefe," encourages the expectation that these signs are superficial appearances. He seems to dismiss them as ostentatious "Trappings" which somehow do not denote him "truly." This reading would make Hamlet's catalogue illustrate the distinction between being and seeming with implications indistinguishable from many treatments in sixteenth-century verse of the theme of dissembling, such as these lines from Tottel's miscellany:

Not euery tricklyng teare doth argue inward paine:
Not euery sigh dothe surely shewe the sigher not to fayne:
Not euery smoke dothe proue a presence of the fire:
Not euery glistring geues the golde, that gredy folke desire:
Not euery wailying word is drawen out of the depe:
Not griefe for want of graunted grace enforceth all to wepe.[40]

As Hamlet's speech develops, however, it proves not to be about dissembling but about sincerity. It is predicated on fundamentally different assumptions about the nature of what is in the heart and its relation to outward expression than those of poems represented by this catalogue of warnings against dissimulation.

Hamlet says of the outward signs that he has listed, "These indeed Seeme." The inserted "indeed," read as an intensive, underscores his dismissal of these mere appearances. Yet at the same time the word can mean in deed, in act, truly (as Sidney's sonnets and one of Shakespeare's adaptations have been shown to use it). This added possibility complicates the relationship between seeming and actually being. Outward signs of woe may seem, may appear, insofar as they are deeds which can be seen; they may nevertheless accord with inward states. Since what is in the heart is invisible, no observer can tell whether or not it is denoted truly in deeds. The same kind of ambiguity is created by other details in the rest of the speech. Hamlet explains that outward signs of grief seem, "For they are actions that a man might play." On the other hand a man might sigh and weep because he truly feels sorrow, as Hamlet does; he might dress in mourning because he is genuinely bereaved, as Hamlet is. The distinction lies only in "that Within" the heart, which cannot be known because it "passeth show." Again the phrasing is ambiguous because of the possible meanings of *show,* used twenty-three times in *Astrophil and Stella,* twenty-two in Shakespeare's sonnets, but only six times in those by Daniel and Spenser, only eight in Drayton's. Its attraction for Sidney and Shakespeare consisted in its ambiguity, for *show* could mean feigned appearance, attaching seeming to outward signs and being to inward states, or it could mean a manifestation. In that sense what is in the heart escapes "showe" because it is inexpressible, or because the truth of its outward expression cannot be judged. Its visible signs, like mourning costume, may match—another meaning for the word *suit* previously shown in the sonnets—its inward being rather than covering it up.

Implied is a much more radical separation of inward from outward experience, the one not knowable from the other, than is suggested by virtually all sixteenth-century poems before *Astrophil and Stella.* They typically dissolve such distinctions between outward signs and inward states, in the manner of the complaining lover in Wyatt's song quoted earlier from Tottel's miscellany:

And in my hart, also,
Is grauen with letters depe
A thousand sighes and mo:
A flood of teares to wepe.[41]

In this view, sighs and tears inevitably denote truly what is in the heart
unless the lover deliberately cloaks these legible signs of grief by calculated
acts of dissimulation. Hamlet, whose sighs and tears are not such actions,
nevertheless knows that their truth cannot be seen or proved. He therefore
declares his sincerity, but offers no demonstration of it. He feels "that
Within" which he does not name. For words, like all outward expression,
are radically ambiguous in their capacity to show what is in the heart. Yet
within him is a private being which, if known, would denote him truly.
Like the speaker in the sonnets, Hamlet therefore casts doubts on the
fundamental assumption that what is hidden in the closet of the heart is
describable by the commonest sixteenth-century term, *secrets*. For this
definition is predicated on assumptions which Hamlet's declaration of
sincerity disavows: that once the key is discovered, the heart may be
unlocked and its contents known by the true names which are engraved
upon it.

♦

5.
Donne

In all of Donne's *Songs and Sonets* there is not one poem which is a sonnet in any stricter sense than would be meant by translating the word to mean little song. Nor indeed are there many songs, poems designed for musical accompaniment or in imitation of sung verse. These omissions are pointed in a group of love poems written at least partially in the 1590s, when songs and sonnets were the type of verse in which the poet-lover most commonly voiced his complaints and praise. Certainly the editor of the second edition of 1635, who imposed the title on Donne's love poems, intended to place the collection in the tradition reaching directly back to Tottel's miscellany, which had been given the same title. Yet Donne deliberately attempted to deny such a simple line of connection in the poems themselves. His minor interest in song forms and strict avoidance of the sonnet are statements about his love poetry. By these among other means he declares it to be different from the verse of the conventional poet-lover, whose absence from Donne's *Songs and Sonets* is another mark of their distinct character.

The speakers in Donne's love poems are almost never identified as poets, neither courtly singers accompanying verses with their lutes, nor courtly writers praising, persuading, complaining, in black ink, on pale papers, in poor rhymes, or sad numbers. Although they are self-conscious in their speech, and often use versions of language conventional to love songs and sonnets, they do not do so explicitly *as poets,* so that they virtually never give attention to the concerns about writing shared by Shakespeare's poet-lover with Astrophil. Even in "The Triple Foole," where Donne's speaker most uncharacteristically identifies himself as both 'loving" and "saying so" in verse, he is not troubled by any distance between his inward state and its expression, but only voices distaste for having both his love and his poems "published."[1] He also puts himself at a humorous distance from the conventional poet-lover by dismissing his own complaints as "whining Poëtry." Such mockery of the conventional figure is characteristic of Donne's lovers, for instance, the speaker in "Loves Growth," who argues:

> Love's not so pure, and abstract, as they use
> To say, which have no Mistresse but their Muse.[2]

This style of mockery resembles Donne's playfulness in a letter of 1616 in which (sounding rather like Sidney in *An Apologie for Poetrie*) he wishes to be known to follow

> a graver course than of a poet, into which (that I may also keep my dignity) I would not seem to relapse. The Spanish proverb informs me, that he is a fool which cannot make one sonnet, and he is mad which makes two.[3]

Before the date of that letter, however, Donne had written more than one sonnet. Perhaps concurrently with his love poems, he wrote half a dozen verse epistles in sonnet form.[4] These characteristically make poetry part of their subject. In one the speaker urges the friend addressed in the sonnet to bestow time upon his Muse.[5] In two the subject is a poet whose songs raise a "lame Ecchoe" in the speaker's own verse, or cause him to blow "Articulate blasts" that will fan into flames the friend's "bright sparkes of Poëtry."[6] Even when the friend addressed is not associated with writing, the speaker nevertheless identifies himself as a poet. Once he apostrophizes his own verse, urging it to deliver pleas for the absent friend's return, as fast as its "lame measure" will allow.[7] In another sonnet on his absense from a friend, his "verse" will be the "strict Map of my misery," while in yet another the poet has absented himself from his friend and also from his mistress.[8] This sonnet "To Mr. C. B.," burlesquing the typical poet-lover who "doth . . . complaine" when "pursu'd with amorous paine," martyred by "scalding sighes," resembles Donne's other epistle sonnets, and also his two dedicatory sonnets, in that the speaker presents himself as a poet.[9] All show that this posture was associated for Donne with the sonnet form. To use it is to create the impression of a writer addressing his audience in a poem as distinct from other forms of utterance. By contrast, in the *Songs and Sonets* many devices are concentrated on contradicting such an effect, being brought to bear instead on creating the impression of a lover talking directly to his lady or to another intimate listener.[10] These differences, it will be seen, are radical in their implications.

All verse epistles of course make some such acknowledgement of their written character, but typically Donne composed his epistles in less restricted forms than the sonnet. He often used pentameter couplets without stanzaic divisions, or stanzas of simple rhyme schemes and no predetermined number. Such verse epistles direct less attention to their formal attributes than the sonnet, which Donne chose to write in its more intricately rhymed pattern, perhaps modeled on some of Sidney's sonnets. The looser epistolary poems are therefore closer approximations to actual letters than are sonnets, and it is perhaps for this reason that Donne used the tighter, more intricate form for those epistles which, almost without exception, are concerned with writing verse. They call attention to themselves as poems by explicit references, and also by their form.

When Donne began to write religious verse is not known. Isaac Walton, in his life of Donne first published in 1640, makes a distinct chronological division between the love poems and the religious verse including the holy sonnets. Such a dividing line would suit the pattern of conversion argued by Walton, and playfully assumed by Donne himself in a letter dated 1619.[11] There speaking of his treatise on suicide, *Biathanatos,* he says that its earlier date of composition identifies it as a "book written by Jack Donne, and not by Dr. Donne." Yet there is no evidence for such a radical distinction in his verse. Helen Gardner dates the linked group of seven sonnets called *La Corona* in July of 1607; all but three of the other nineteen holy sonnets she believes to have been written between 1609 and 1611.[12] There may therefore have been some years in which, writing poems included in *Songs and Sonnets,* Donne had already begun working in religious poetry. Other poets had written in both veins without apparent sense of incongruity. Wyatt and Sidney, for example, translated Psalms presumably in the years when they were also writing love poems, and the great precedent for English poets of the period, Petrarch, mingled the two modes in his collection of sonnets. Even Shakespeare's includes a religious poem, Sonnet 146 ("Poore soule the center of my sinfull earth"), in the midst of the most explicitly sexual sonnets to the dark lady.

Whatever the actual practice of poets, however, there was a conventional view that amorous verse was a youthful endeavor, to be followed if not by penitent devotions, at least by a more sober dedication to sacred subjects. Petrarch's collection tends toward that development in distinctions between poems to Laura in life and in death. A version of this conventional pattern is reflected in the arrangement of Sidney's *Certaine Sonets,* which begins with love poems, but concludes with two sonnets of renunciation, "Thou blind man's marke" and "Leave me ô Love."[13] According to the same convention, one of Sidney's followers, Barnabe Barnes, produced a sequence of love sonnets in 1593 entitled *Parthenophil and Parthenophe.* His *Divine Centurie of Spirituall Sonnets* published two years later opens with a sonnet rejecting his former lustful Muse for inspiration by the Holy Ghost.[14]

Donne was no slave to convention, and the mingling of amorous and religious language in both the *Songs and Sonets* and the holy sonnets—the second of his devout *La Corona* sonnets uses three lines virtually unchanged from his profane satire, "The Progresse of the Soule"—suggests that there would have been no uneasiness for him in writing love poems and devotional verse simultaneously, and that he would have viewed the

shift from one to the other as a natural development rather than a renunciation.[15] In a sermon of 1617, Donne holds up Solomon as an exemplum
of the poet for his authorship of the Canticles, traditionally believed to be
poetry celebrating God's love for the Church. His verse is made to exem-
plify a likeness rather than a sharp division between secular and sacred
writing, an argument made explicit, it will be seen, in Donne's holy
sonnets:

> *Salomon,* whose disposition was amorous, and excessive in the love
> of women, when he turn'd to God, he departed not utterly from his
> old phrase and language, but having put a new, and a spiritual
> tincture, and form and habit into all his thoughts, and words, he
> conveyes all his loving approaches and applications to God, and all
> Gods gracious answers to his amorous soul, into songs, and Epitha-
> lamions, and meditations upon contracts, and marriages between
> God and his Church, and between God and his soul.[16]

It is possible that Donne shaped this portrayal of Solomon to his sense of
his own experience and his development as a poet. In *Essayes in Divinity*
he refers to his youthful bondage in an "Egypt of lust" from which he was
delivered, and in his own holy sonnets he creates speakers who follow
precisely the pattern in poetry ascribed to Solomon, conveying to God all
their "loving approaches and applications" to former mistresses.[17] Whether
or not he identified the figure of Solomon in this passage with himself, it
clearly exemplifies his sense of a continuity between love poems and
religious verse.

Nevertheless there is a distinction between Donne's secular and sacred
poems pertinent to the development traced in previous chapters. For the
pointed absence of sonnets from his love poems, and the use of the form
only in a few verse epistles and dedications, shows that Donne's acceptance of the sonnet as a major form for his religious verse was a deliberate
and significant departure from his practice in the *Songs and Sonets.* This
departure cannot be explained by some special connection between religious matter and the sonnet form which would have made its use in
devotional verse more acceptable or significant for Donne than in love
poetry. He would almost certainly have known some great single examples of religious sonnets, the palinodes of Wyatt and Sidney, and perhaps
Shakespeare's Sonnet 146. Yet he would probably also have known lesser
achievements, such as Barnes' *Divine Centurie,* or the sonnet collections
of William Alabaster and Henry Lok, not much more desirable for association with his own poems than their counterparts among sequences of
love sonnets.[18] A more convincing explanation for Donne's departure
from his practice as a love poet in using the sonnet form for religious
poems has already been suggested by a distinguishing feature of his only
other sonnets, the small group of epistles and dedications. In them, and

in his holy sonnets, the choice of the form seems to have been dictated by his associations of it with the use of a speaker who is identified as a poet. Writing sonnets for Donne, it will be seen, involved the concerns also associated with such a speaker in the sonnets of Sidney and Shakespeare, but excluded from consideration in his own love poems.

Although it is not possible to prove the kinds of explicit adaptations in Donne's sonnets that the preceding chapter demonstrates in Shakespeare's borrowings from Sidney, it is altogether reasonable to assume that Donne had read *Astrophil and Stella*. Sidney was the most famous of sixteenth-century English poets, frequently heading lists like one made by Francis Meres in a work famous for its reference to Shakespeare's "sugared sonets," *Palladis Tamia* of 1598:

> . . . the English tongue is mightily enriched and gorgeouslie inuested in rare ornaments and resplendent abiliments by *Sir Philip Sidney, Spencer, Daniel, Drayton, Warner, Shakespeare, Marlow,* and *Chapman.*[19]

Of all English poems, Sidney's provided the greatest number of illustrations for the compilers of rhetorical treatises, and most often earned him such titles as "Englands Sunne," or "the *Scipio* and the *Petrarke* of our time."[20] Since his sonnet sequence, after circulating quite freely in manuscript, was published in three editions in 1591 and in corrected form with the *Arcadia* in 1598, it could not reasonably have escaped the attention of Donne, who was writing amatory elegies and other forms of love poetry in that period, in London, surrounded by acquaintances themselves interested in poetry. Among them, both Ben Jonson and George Herbert composed poems specifically in response to the opening sonnet of *Astrophil and Stella,* and show familiarity and affinity with Sidney's poems elsewhere in their own verse.[21] Donne himself, while excluding the figure of the poet-lover from his *Songs and Sonets,* creates lovers resembling Astrophil in irreverent cast of mind, and in some verbal practices such as parody and burlesque of conventional styles for talking about love. More specifically he may have learned from Sidney the device of pushing a familiar metaphor to its furthest implications by treating it literally.[22]

It is far less certain, but still possible, that Donne may also have read Shakespeare's sonnets; that their mysteriously untimely publication in 1609, long after the appearance of other major sequences of love sonnets, may have contributed to Donne's interest in the sonnet. In formal characteristics his are in one respect closer to Sidney's, in that they have only two rhymes in the octave, usually in two closed quatrains but, like Shakespeare's, they always rhyme the last two lines. Resemblances to Shakespearean couplets have been noticed in the holy sonnets, and an "introspectiveness" similar to Shakespeare's has been discussed by

Patrick Cruttwell.[23] He locates this shared quality particularly in a comparison of Donne's "Oh, to vex me, contraryes meete in one" with Shakespeare's Sonnet 62, which the previous chapter has shown to be an adaptation of *Astrophil and Stella* 27. Other resemblances can be found, for instance in the rhetorical strategy of boastfully challenging a personified abstraction. Shakespeare's Sonnet 19, "Deuouring time blunt thou the Lyons pawes," and Donne's "Death be not proud" are structured in similar fashion by this device.[24] Both poets expand in comparable ways a traditional metaphor of man's body and soul as a world: Shakespeare in Sonnet 146, "Poore soule the center of my sinfull earth," and Donne in "I am a little world made cunningly." The speaker's admonition to his soul in Sonnet 146 also resembles the authoritative tone of Donne's speaker to his soul in a number of holy sonnets.

In one of Donne's sonnets, "Since she whome I lovd, hath payd her last debt," he does seem to echo Shakespeare's Sonnet 144.[25] Both describe an amorous triangle involving the speaker's soul, a woman whom he calls an angel, and a male figure rivaling the woman in the speaker's love, who is God in Donne's sonnet, and in Shakespeare's a male friend called "my saint." Although Sonnet 144 is a viciously obscene attack on the dark lady, while Donne's sonnet is an elegiac love poem, probably about his late wife to whom he was well known to have been devoted, the poems describe situations which are close enough, and bizarre enough, to suggest imitation by Donne. Even more telling is the model apparently provided by Shakespeare's couplet:

> Yet this shal I nere know but liue in doubt,
> Till my bad angel fire my good one out.

Donne uses the same metaphor, itself not a conventional figure that could be borrowed from any number of sources. He also uses the same rhyme, which is not among the pairs—*heart-smart,* or *disdain-pain,* for example—almost automatic for love poets:

> But in thy tender jealosy dost doubt
> Least the World, fleshe, yea Devill putt thee out.[26]

The evidence does point to a direct borrowing, but nevertheless does not prove that Donne had read Shakespeare's sonnet sequence. For his Sonnet 144 was one of the two from it printed in 1599 in a very similar version in *The Passionate Pilgrim.*[27]

These resemblances do not constitute evidence for the kinds of detailed and profound assimilations made by Shakespeare of his Sidneian models. Yet they do show affinities between Donne's sonnets and those of both Sidney and Shakespeare, which could not be argued simply by virtue of similarities demanded by the form, since such likenesses would not be found between Donne's sonnets and Spenser's or Daniel's. These affinities are most profound in the ways that Donne in a number of his holy sonnets associates the speaker as poet with the same struggle to find a true language for what is in the heart that Shakespeare made the concern of his poet-lover, on the model of Astrophil. Like Shakespeare, Donne saw in this issue implications for a fundamentally different view of both language and inward experience than is characteristic of most poetry of the period, including his own *Songs and Sonets.*

Donne's seven sonnets of the group called *La Corona* are linked in imitation of the title metaphor of the crown, which is a wreath woven by the speaker in his poems. His Muse, he says in the final lines, offers to God the completed circle of sonnets which, if elevated by divine inspiration, is a sanctified garland of "prayer and praise."[28] By this metaphor the activity of Christian petitioner and of poet are equated, an identification made and elaborated in the first sonnet:

> *Deigne at my hands this crown of prayer and praise,*
> Weav'd in my low devout melancholie,
> Thou which of good, hast, yea art treasury,
> All changing unchang'd Antient of dayes,
> But doe not, with a vile crowne of fraile bayes,
> Reward my muses white sincerity,
> But what thy thorny crowne gain'd, that give mee,
> A crowne of Glory, which doth flower alwayes;
> The ends crowne our workes, but thou crown'st our ends,
> For, at our end begins our endlesse rest,
> This first last end, now zealously possest,
> With a strong sober thirst, my soule attends.
> 'Tis time that heart and voice be lifted high,
> *Salvation to all that will is nigh.*[29]

The kind of praying with which the poet's act of praising is identified here is formal, ritualistic, liturgical, public. The speaker moves with no need of explanation from "my" and "mee" to "our" and "all," or omits pronouns altogether so that the individual petitioner is merged into a congregation praying in unison as one body, "'Tis time that heart and voice be lifted high." This is the form of devotion institutionalized by *The Booke of Common Prayer,* and epitomized in the collect which explains its rationale at the conclusion of the litany:

> Almightie God, whiche hast geuen us grace at this tyme with one accorde to make oure commune supplicacions unto thee, and doest promise that whan two or three bee gathered in thy name, thou wylt

graunt theyr requestes: fulfill now, O lorde, the desires and peticions
of thy seruantes, as maye bee moste expediente for them, grauntying
us in this worlde knowlege of thy trueth, and in the worlde to come,
lyfe euerlasting.[30]

This central Anglican assumption was under pressure, if not attack, in
the late sixteenth and earlier seventeenth century, and needed to be defended by such spokesmen of the Church as Donne. Although admitting that private or chamber devotions were sanctioned by Scripture,
they ranked them but 'as almes at the gate," while the true feast is within
the church. Individual prayer could be as dangerous as individual doctrine, and therefore, Donne implies in a sermon, as unacceptable to the
Anglican Church:

> Christ loves not singularity; he called not one alone; He loves not
> schisme neither between them whom he calls.[31]

Forced to allow such prayers, the Church attempted to conform them to
the same uniformity as public worship by issuing collections of private
prayers put forth by authority, which Donne urged his congregation to use
in their chambers:

> Let us . . . not *pray,* not *preach,* not *hear,* slackly, suddenly, unadvi-
> sedly, extemporally, occasionally, indiligently; but let all our speech
> to him, be weighed, and measured in the weights of the *Sanctuary,*
> let us be content to preach, and to hear within the compasse of our
> Articles, and content to pray in those *formes* which the Church hath
> meditated for us, and recommended to us.[32]

Donne insists very often in his sermons on the kind of common prayer
which he imitates in *La Corona.* The liturgy was itself the model for this
style of verse. So were the Psalms, read as they are described in one of
Donne's sermons:

> The Psalmes are the Manna of the Church. As Manna tasted to every
> man like that that he liked best, so doe the Psalmes minister Instruc-
> tion, and satisfaction, to every man, in every emergency and occa-
> sion. *David* was not only a cleare Prophet of Christ himselfe, but a
> Prophet of every particular Christian; He fortels what I, what any
> shall doe, and suffer, and say. And as the whole booke of Psalmes
> is *Oleum effusum* . . . an Oyntment powred out upon all sorts of
> sores, A Searcloth that souples all bruises, A Balme that searches all
> wounds; so are there some certaine Psalmes, that are imperiall Psalmes,
> that command over all affections, and spread themselves over all
> occasions, Catholique, universall Psalmes, that apply themselves to
> all necessities.[33]

Their exemplary, generalizing power is clearly what he values, and is the achievement he attempts in *La Corona*. In that series of sonnets he creates a speaker who represents the collective "heart and voice" of the congregation, praying in the liturgical forms echoed in his circle of poems. They move from celebration of Christ's entrance into "our world" to the invocation of all "Yee" who, raised like the speaker's Muse by the Holy Spirit, behold His glorious ascension.

By such means the sonnets in this group achieve for the most part a deliberate kind of anonymity that a reader of Donne's other poetry must suspect to have been a difficult effort.[34] For in his love poems he characteristically creates speakers who set themseleves apart from other men by their remarkable powers of passion and utterance. Their love is so intense that they know no time or season, as do less impassioned mortals. They are sacred—all other lovers profane—and in possession of holy mysteries. The inclusiveness of their love contains all experience, and they make worlds of their own to control it by their language. Its power is commensurate with the remarkable intensity of what is in their hearts. "The Anniversarie" typifies this tendency when the lover, picturing the state of perfect blessedness enjoyed by souls in heaven, dismisses it indifferently because it will distinguish him and his beloved "no more, then all the rest," whereas on earth they create a kingdom where "none but wee" can reign.[35] To merge heart and voice with all other men in prayer and praise would be an elevation too commonplace for the lovers typical of Donne's *Songs and Sonets,* making the poet of *La Corona,* insofar as he identifies himself with all Christian petitioners, a very different kind of speaker.

He is also distinguishable from Donne's lovers in the significant fact that he identifies his mode of expression explicitly as poetry. He does not claim that the intensity of his inward state alone inspires his speech. For he has a Muse, showing a less immediate identification between passion and utterance than is typically assumed by Donne's lovers. That is, he acknowledges inspiration from a traditional source, which finds expression in a literary form. Also unlike the speakers in the *Songs and Sonets,* the poet of *La Corona* refers to his words as having a separate existence like an object—"this crown"—independent of himself. Sensing their distance, he needs to defend them as a true representation of his inward state when he asks God to "Reward my muses white sincerity" with an immortal crown.

This line marks yet another distinction between the poet in *La Corona* and the speakers in Donne's love poetry. It is a petition to God to differentiate the poet's sanctified praise from profane and therefore insincere and impure poetry, which earns only a fading laurel wreath. Although such a contrast might recall the separation of sacred passion from profane lovemaking in the *Songs and Sonets,* the two kinds of verse are distinguished on the very different grounds of sincerity. That is not a consideration for

Donne's lovers. In the second stanza of "A Valediction: forbidding Mourning," for example, where the speaker entreats the lady to forgo the outward
modes of expression that characterize the complaints of inferior lovers,
his imperatives urge a kind of aristocratic aloofness and privacy, not
sincerity:

> So let us melt, and make no noise,
>   No teare-floods, nor sigh-tempests move,
> 'Twere prophanation of our joyes
>   To tell the layetie our love.[36]

Sacred love here differs from profane in that it does not display itself. It
keeps its mysteries from vulgar view. It does not need to defend itself; the
question of the speaker's sincerity is not at issue here or elsewhere in
Donne's *Songs and Sonets.* His superior powers of passion and utterance
are assumed, and when he urges silence it is only as a gesture of disdain
for vulgar publicity. He knows that his love, once shown to anyone other
than his mistress who is also initiated into its mysteries, would be misun-
derstood. The reason for this is not that its sincerity would be questioned,
however, but rather that the sublunary world is incapable of comprehend-
ing its mysteries. By contrast, the speaker in the first sonnet of *La Corona*
sets himself apart from profane poets on the grounds of his sincerity. His
distinction from them is not that he praises a sacred subject rather than
an idol but that he renders truly in verse what is in his heart.

By defending the sincerity of his Muse, the speaker becomes less a
representative public petitioner there than elsewhere in *La Corona.* For
in that line—"Reward my muses white sincerity"—he claims for himself
a quality of inward experience that is not identifiable with his outward act
of lifting heart and voice in common prayer and praise. His sincerity can
be known only by his private certainty about what is in his heart, which
corresponds to God's understanding of it. Such a concern to defend his
language as true to his inward state is alien to the assumption on which
liturgical prayer is predicated: that the words authorized by God's Church
are themselves acceptable in His sight, although the meditations of the
heart of a single petitioner may be unworthy of them. The members of the
congregation do not search for language true to their inward experience,
or pray that their choice of words be rewarded for sincerity. They petition
God to "clense the thoughts of our hartes" that they may "worthily magnifie
thy holy name" by reciting the liturgy.[37] This is the assumption on which
Donne's arguments for the priority of common prayer are based, as a
passage from another of his sermons defending the position illustrates:

> Whilst thou art a member of that Congregation, that speaks to God
> with a thousand tongues, beleeve that thou speakest to God with all

those tongues. And though thou know thine own prayers unworthy to come up to God, because thou liftest up to him an eye, which is but now withdrawne from a licentious glancing, and hands which are guilty yet of unrepented uncleannesses, a tongue that hath but lately blasphemed God, a heart which even now breaks the walls of this house of God, and steps home, or runs abroad upon the memory, or upon the new plotting of pleasurable or profitable purposes, though this make thee thinke thine own prayers uneffectuall, yet beleeve that some honester man then thy selfe stands by thee, and that when he prayes with thee, he prayes for thee; and that, if there be one righteous man in the Congregation, thou art made the more acceptable to God by his prayers.[38]

Donne's speaker in the first sonnet of *La Corona* ceases to pray with or for other petitioners at the moment when he sets himself apart in the knowledge that his own Muse's language is pure by virtue of its truth to what is in his heart.

In a sense this claim to separateness might liken him to speakers in the love poems, but again there is an all-important difference that he is superior, not in the intensity of his inward state but in his capacity to render it truly in poetry. He defends the sincerity of his utterance precisely because, unlike Donne's lovers, he is a poet conscious of a distance between inward experience and its presentation in verse. He therefore concerns himself explicitly with the struggle to write poetry true to what is in the heart, as Donne's lovers do not, and also with the existence of unexpressed inward experience which the speakers in the *Songs and Sonets* do not dwell on, do not even show particular awareness of. They specialize in knowledge of love and love-making, and revel in their power to articulate what they know to their beloveds. The one exception might seem to be the speaker in "A Valediction: forbidding Mourning," at the moment when he claims to share "a love, so much refin'd, / That our selves know not what it is."[39] Yet in the context, love's mystery here consists in its capacity to transcend the laws of the sublunary world rather than in its inward and unexpressed nature. Throughout the rest of the poem, this speaker is typical of Donne's lovers who claim special knowledge which they keep secret from the world, withholding it from profane eyes. They protect it from publicity, showing it only to their beloveds. Yet what is in their hearts is shared and outwardly, though not publicly, expressed. It can be proved in words and actions, in styles of loving or talking about love, or in deliberate silences which are themselves expressive gestures. There is not in Donne's love poems the sense created in many sonnets by Sidney and Shakespeare that what is in the speaker's heart is so widely distanced from his appearance and utterance that it constitutes a distinct inward existence unknowable from his outward show.

In *La Corona* there is a hint of such awareness at the moment when the speaker steps out of his liturgical performance to claim the adequacy of his verse for the true representation of his inward state. The line "Reward my muses white sincerity" is oddly out of keeping with the rest of the opening sonnet and the group as a whole in the way it violates the expectations of common prayer, for which Donne in his sermons so often argues priority. It is possible only to speculate about the causes for this inconsistency. One surmise is that, although Donne wholly espoused the Anglican liturgy, the nearly anonymous voice of common prayer was a difficult achievement for him, asking suppression of many of his most characteristic interests as a poet. For although there are great examples of liturgical verse—such as two probably known to Donne, Thomas Nashe's "Adieu, farewell earths blisse" and Herbert's "The Sacrifice"—the genre inevitably imposes restrictions.[40] It limits the range of diction and tone, and the elaboration of metaphor, constraints which might have posed difficulties for a poet particularly interested in violations of decorum in vocabulary, tone, and imagery. Another possibility for speculation is that inconsistency in the opening poem of *La Corona* may have resulted from the compelling power of the sonnet form, or more specifically the strength of the associations it had for Donne by the time he chose to write in this form. Such a supposition is encouraged by the fact that in many of Donne's other religious sonnets the speakers, like Astrophil and Shakespeare's poet-lover, are engaged in a struggle to find true language for what is in the heart. Involved in this effort is their preoccupation with inward experience which is invisible and unexpressed, not to be known in outward appearance. At issue, then, is their sincerity. Paradoxically, this preoccupation in some of Donne's holy sonnets is closer to the concerns in love sonnets by Sidney and Shakespeare than to those either in his own love poetry, or in his other religious verse. These interests are predicted by the poet in *La Corona* at the moment when he speaks in a voice not subsumed in common prayer, in the line petitioning God to reward the "white sincerity" of his verse, its fitness to show what is truly in his heart.

Donne's nineteen other religious sonnets differ from *La Corona* in that they are not liturgical poems. In this respect they are also different in kind from most of his religious verse in other forms, where he characteristically uses the style traditional to hymns, meditations, or the liturgy. The speakers in these poems are like the poet—except in one extraordinary moment—in *La Corona,* in that they tend to merge their voices in common prayer, as is, for example, the explicit effort of the petitioner in stanza 23 of "A Litanie":

> Heare us, O heare us Lord; to thee
> A sinner is more musique, when he prayes,
>   Then spheares, or Angels praises bee,

In Panegyrique Allelujaes,
>Heare us, for till thou heare us, Lord
>We know not what to say.
Thine eare to 'our sighes, teares, thoughts gives voice and word.
O Thou who Satan heard'st in Jobs sicke day,
Heare thy selfe now, for thou in us dost pray.[41]

By contrast, in the holy sonnets other than *La Corona* the speakers do not
strive for a representative public voice to utter what is in all hearts. In
choosing for them a different mode, Donne freed their language from the
kinds of constraints imposed by the liturgical style, suggesting that his
restiveness with them may have been a cause of his lapse from common
prayer in the opening poem of *La Corona*. He made possible the use in
these other holy sonnets of speakers who are more like Sidney's and
Shakespeare's in their love sonnets than they are like liturgical petitioners.
Although Donne's speakers do not explicitly identify themselves as poets,
their language evokes in many ways the figure of the poet-lover as it was
developed in the sequences of Sidney and Shakespeare, whose concerns
they share.

In one of Donne's sonnets the speaker spells out a comparison of the
argument he articulates in the poem to a line of persuasion he formerly
used to his "profane mistresses." Such a comparison makes explicit a
whole body of associations built into the history of love poetry, stretching
back through the native and Petrarchan traditions to their common roots
in the conventions of courtly love. These conventions were wholly absorbed into love sonnets, where—numerous examples have shown—it
was habitual to use religious language for describing the devotion of the
lover pleading for grace from his sovereign mistress. It was also a pattern
established in religious poetry as early as Dante's to turn religious language back to sacred subjects by reassimilating the conventions of love
sonnets.[42] Donne's holy sonnet consciously follows this development, also
recalling the model of Solomon's poetry as Donne describes it. For this
speaker actually calls attention to his poem as the redirection of his old
"approaches and applications" from amorous subjects to God:

>What if this present were the worlds last night?
>Marke in my heart, O Soule, where thou dost dwell,
>The picture of Christ crucified, and tell
>Whether that countenance can thee affright,
>Teares in his eyes quench the amasing light,
>Blood fills his frownes, which from his pierc'd head fell,
>And can that tongue adjudge thee unto hell,
>Which pray'd forgivenesse for his foes fierce spight?
>No, no; but as in my idolatrie
>I said to all my profane mistresses,

> Beauty, of pitty, foulnesse onely is
> A signe of rigour: so I say to thee,
> To wicked spirits are horrid shapes assign'd,
> This beauteous forme assures a pitious minde.[43]

The sonnet begins as a sermon in which the speaker admonishes his soul to meditate upon the picture he paints of Christ. In the sestet, however, instead of preaching to his soul, he instructs it by repeating the argument he formerly used to his mistresses to convince them to love him. It is an argument traditional to persuasion poems. Outward beauty is the visible sign of inward beauty, which is goodness; *ergo* the lady who is beautiful must be good, and so will pity her lover, who will in turn honor her in his verse. One of the earliest English sonnets of persuasion, a poem by Surrey, uses this formula. It was undoubtedly known to Donne in Tottel's miscellany under the title "Request to his loue to ioyne bountie with beautie":

> The golden gift that nature did thee geue,
> To fasten frendes, and fede them at thy wyll,
> With fourme and fauour, taught me to beleue,
> How thou art made to shew her greatest skill.
> Whose hidden vertues are not so vnknowen,
> But liuely domes might gather at the first
> Where beautye so her perfect seede hath sowen,
> Of other graces folow nedes there must.
> Now certesse Ladie, sins all this is true,
> That from aboue thy gyftes are thus elect:
> Do not deface them than with fansies newe,
> Nor chaunge of mindes let not thy minde infect:
> But mercy him thy frende, that doth thee serue,
> Who seekes alway thine honour to preserue.[44]

Persuasions, though common among English love sonnets—enriched by a tradition reaching back to Greek and Latin amatory verse—are not numerous in Donne's own love poetry. The few examples there—"The Flea" comes first to mind—tend to avoid the classic argument used by Surrey, preferring more idiosyncratic reasoning.[45] Typically Donne, in some of his love poems, burlesques the conventional formula for persuasion, for example in "Communitie," where it is turned into a kind of nursery rhyme. The speaker, taking the position that some women are neither good nor bad but merely useful, clinches his argument:

> If they were good it would be seene,
> Good is as visible as greene,
>   And to all eyes it selfe betrayes.[46]

The speaker in the holy sonnet, without burlesquing the traditional notion of outward beauty as a sign of inward fairness, associates it with the "picture" of Christ which is in his heart where an idolatrous lover would carry the image of his mistress. He assures his frightened soul that Christ's "beauteous forme" is proof that his mind is beautiful, and therefore that he will "pitty" the soul, and not condemn it to hell. Spelled out this way, the speaker's argument is not unorthodox (Helen Gardner's edition even cites opinions among the Church Fathers about Christ's physical beauty), yet its associations with love poetry are unmistakably worldly, and its application in the sonnet calculatedly indecorous.[47]

The argument that the speaker formerly used to his mistresses was not a disinterested lecture in Platonic philosophy but a persuasion to love. Its high-minded philosophizing was manipulated to serve the self-interest of a lover bent on sexual seduction. It combined flattery of the lady's beauty with veiled threats: had the mistresses persisted in "rigour," he would have been forced to conclude that they were foul or ugly, and perhaps to say so in poetry. If the speaker repeats this seductive argument to his soul, he must be reminding it of how successfully the persuasion worked on those ladies. This comic sexual boasting, with the emphasis on "all" his mistresses, is a form of intimate manly talk that would make the application of the seductive argument to Christ a joke about the speaker's impurities of motive, past and present.

Surprising as this use of the argument may be, it has even more astonishing implications as the terms are worked out more extensively. In the parallel, "as . . . I said . . . so I say," the set of terms intended for comparison seems to be the mistresses to whom he formerly argued, and the soul to whom he now repeats the argument. Actually, however, a closer parallel is between the mistresses whom he flattered for their beauty, and Christ whom he now calls a "beauteous forme." What this set of comparable terms makes clear is that, although the speaker's argument is addressed to his soul, it must be intended to be overheard by Christ, whom the speaker would persuade to love him and his soul, using the language with which he successfully seduced his former mistresses.

Although the speaker seems to reject his past by applying terms of judgment to it like "idolatrie" and "profane," he is actually drawing upon it for his present devotion. Here he repeats his successful persuasion to love partly to allay the fears of his soul, cheering it with jokes and assuring it of future success on the basis of past triumphs.[48] He also uses his well-tried argument as a kind of petition to Christ, such as the speaker in another of Donne's holy sonnets lists among examples of his imperfect devotion: "In prayers, and flattering speaches I court God."[49] This shocking inclusion of a poem of persuasion in a sonnet beginning as a meditation on Christ must be intended to raise questions about the nature of what is in the speaker's heart, and its relation to his language. Such questions, involved in many of Donne's uses of the sonnet, are not at issue in his love poems. This difference can be illuminated if the sonnet is set beside "The Good-morrow," which begins as impudently as the sonnet ends, with as much consciousness of assaulting decorum, but with the all-important difference that the speaker is not in any way identified as a poet. On the contrary, he is placed in a situation—in bed with his beloved—in which it would be ludicrously comical to imagine him in the act of writing a poem. By contrast, the sonnet form, and the uses of the conventions of love poetry in a situation not between lovers, associates Donne's other speaker with writing. A further difference is illustrated by the way the lover in the opening stanza of "The Good-morrow," like the speaker in the sonnet, contrasts his present love-making with his past sexual conquests. He too boasts in ways assertive of his prowess as well as flattering to his mistress:

> But this, all pleasures fancies bee.
> If ever any beauty I did see,
> Which I desir'd, and got, 'twas but a dreame of thee.[50]

Yet unlike the speaker in the sonnet, the lover in "The Good-morrow" does not mention language as his means of seduction, or identify his love-making with his success in argument. He does not therefore raise questions about the relation of his speech to his inward experience, or sense a distance between them. His passions are fully and directly expressed in his utterance, and other outward signs:

> My face in thine eye, thine in mine appeares,
> And true plaine hearts doe in the faces rest.

Typically he uses "true" about his heart as the word is almost always used in Donne's *Songs and Sonets,* to mean constant, faithful. Its opposite would be a heart which is fickle, not one which is insincere. The proof that the lover is in this sense "true" is recognizable by how he "appeares," in his looks, acts, and words. He is not concerned with that within his heart unknowable by outward signs.

The lover in the sonnet, on the other hand, raises questions about his uses of language by admitting to his soul that he has manipulated words in the past for worldly ends. He boasts that he has made the same argument work persuasively on "all" his former mistresses, which is to say he talked so convincingly that they must not have questioned whether his speech derived its power from his true, plain heart or his practiced skill in persuading one lady after another. The conclusion, "so I say to thee," associates these past manipulations of language with his present use of words as well. The reflection which the couplet makes upon the speaker's language is therefore that it has lost none of its calculation; that his present devotion is phrased as much to further self-interest as were his former persuasions to love. This conclusion confirms a view represented, it will be seen, in other sonnets by Donne, that experience is continuous, indivisible into opposing categories like devout and profane, that the speaker's past is dramatically incorporated into his present, that no absolute distinctions divide lover from penitent Christian.

The sonnet as a whole also characteristically comments on the couplet, so that his final exposure of the speaker's manipulations of language at a distance from his inward state is not allowed to remain uncomplicated. Another possible interpretation of them is that, while the speaker uses the seductive argument jokingly, and in full awareness that it exposes his impurities of motive in making it, he nevertheless believes it. The picture of Christ in his heart assures him by its beauty that his argument is true; Christ has a piteous mind, and will accept the speaker's love in all its imperfections. Or Christ will see in the speaker's heart what is not expressed in his words. His freedom to joke about himself in such a controlled and witty way, almost in self-parody, sets his language at a distance from his passions, but in ways which need not insist on their calculation and cynicism. It may be that he can be playful with his argument because he knows that Christ will not misunderstand it, will not judge his heart and soul by his utterance. Implied is a distinction between human judgments by apparent signs, and God's knowledge, similar to that which troubles the speaker in *La Corona* when he begs God to recognize his sincerity, which is not provable in his words.

Here no false judgments are mentioned, nor does the speaker explicitly set himself apart from other men whose outward modes of expression cannot sincerely represent their inward states. Yet his own language shows awareness of theirs, and challenges their misinterpretations of what is in his heart. This stance is shown in the way the speaker's language raises expectations which it then violates. Terms like "idolatrie" and "profane" to judge his past seem here irrevocably to condemn it from the present perspective in which the speaker preaches to his soul a sermon on the Passion. So that when in the sestet he reclaims the language of sexual persuasion as appropriate to use in his relationship with Christ, his outrageous impudence is by no means unselfconscious. It shows full awareness of his assault on conventional expectations associated with poems of persuasion and with situations traditional to prayer. Yet it is not his soul, with whom he jokes in friendly intimacy, who will be shocked, nor Christ, who is intended to overhear, understand, and accept his way of talking. The speaker must therefore be challenging an unacknowledged audience whose right to try his inward state he defies. They will judge him falsely by outward signs which God alone can distinguish from what is in his heart, the picture of Christ, whom he truly loves. They therefore stand in an implied relation to him parallel to that of Astrophil's would-be interpreters, whose failures to guess the nature of his inward state are a measure of its distance from his social appearance.

In another sonnet the assault on expectations raised by the speaker's language makes still clearer his awareness of an audience whose presence is not acknowledged, but whose judgments of his spiritual state he defies in the knowledge of his own sincerity. The sonnet begins with one line evoking the Canticles in a prayer to Christ as the bridegroom of the Church. Here the speaker sounds like a representative Christian, but the expectations for such a voice are immediately violated:

> Show me deare Christ, thy spouse, so bright and cleare.
> What, is it she, which on the other shore
> Goes richly painted? or which rob'd and tore
> Laments and mournes in Germany and here?
> Sleepes she a thousand, then peepes up one yeare?
> Is she selfe truth and errs: now new, now outwore?
> Doth she, 'and did she, and shall she evermore
> On one, on seaven, or on no hill appeare?
> Dwells she with us, or like adventuring knights
> First travaile we to seeke and then make love?
> Betray kind husband thy spouse to our sights,
> And let myne amorous soule court thy mild Dove,
> Who is most trew, and pleasing to thee, then
> When she'is embrac'd and open to most men.[51]

The speaker addresses Christ in his traditional role as the bridegroom of the true Church, but his own relation to that figure, established by his ways of talking, is not that of a petitioner to his Redeemer. Although he uses such a tone in the first line, even its reverence becomes teasingly intimate in the context of what follows. He talks to Christ in tones of mock impatience and incredulity—"What, is it she." He speaks with humorously exaggerated literalness, parodies liturgical formulas, makes a literary joke about chivalric romances, and puns on the word "travaile," all with an offhandedness that implies Christ will catch and appreciate the verbal play. In the last four lines he combines affectionate teasing and elegant compliment, biblical allusions and blunt, sexual joking, in what is again an outrageously applied poem of persuasion to Christ. Here he pushes the convention to its most shocking limits by taking literally the metaphor of the Church as the bride of Christ, and then persuading Him to share her grace, understood as a euphemism for sexual favors, with the speaker.

In this sonnet the speaker addresses Christ in the language of a man of the world talking to someone who recognizes his manner by virtue of friendly intimacy and shared sophistication. He talks with an ease that shows he expects to be understood. Christ will appreciate the way he speaks, and not be shocked or offended. Yet again, as in the other sonnet, the speaker's conscious violation of decorum, turning prayer into a ribald poem of persuasion, shows his awareness that some listeners besides Christ would misinterpret their private conversation. Here his playful questions even define what kind of audience would misunderstand his manner of speaking. For they burlesque the arguments of men capable of theorizing that the true Church sleeps "a thousand, then peepes up one yeare," or that it could "On one, on seaven, or on no hill appeare." Their literal-mindedness and solemn naivete, like that of Astrophil's politically minded interrogators, would make them misjudge him, either as being like themselves or, if unlike, as a blasphemer, an unbeliever. By contrast, his intimate manner shows confidence that Christ understands him and accepts him for what is truly in his heart.

His challenge to other men's false judgments of his inward state is a defense of his sincerity. It is based on awareness, fundamental also to many sonnets by Sidney and Shakespeare, that the truth in the heart is widely distanced from outward appearance, and not to be known by it. Again this concern sharply distinguishes Donne's sonnets from his love poems, as another comparison further illustrates. In the second stanza of "The Canonization" the speaker defies literal-minded judges who complain that his expressions of what is in his heart endanger their property:

> Alas, alas, who's injur'd by my love?
>   What merchants ships have my sighs drown'd?
> Who saies my teares have overflow'd his ground?
> When did my colds a forward spring remove?
>   When did the heats which my veines fill
>   Adde one man to the plaguie Bill?
> Soldiers finde warres, and Lawyers finde out still
>   Litigious men, which quarrels move,
>   Though she and I do love.[52]

What annoys the lover is the refusal of these worldly minded judges to recognize the separation of his sanctified passion from their own mundane concerns. He wishes to preserve the privacy of his sighs and tears precisely because they *are* manifestations of his love. There is no awareness in his protestations that his inward state is unavailable to outward show, or unknowable in apparent signs. Still less is there any concern here or elsewhere in Donne's love poetry that sincerity is difficult if not impossible to distinguish from insincere expression, or that there is an inevitable struggle, such as the speakers in some other sonnets by Donne, enact, involved in the representation of what is in the heart. Unlike those speakers, Donne's lovers do not have to search for language adequate to render inward truth by the Muse's sincerity.

The speakers in these two holy sonnets, while distinct from Donne's lovers in sensing a separation between inward states and modes for expressing them, use the language of persuasions to love with a bravado assertive of their own verbal powers. In defiance of misreadings, they argue with a confidence reminiscent of the lovers in many of Donne's *Songs and Sonets*. In several other holy sonnets, however, the speakers more openly question the adequacy of their own utterance to represent inward truth. By associating their language with the conventions of the complaint, Donne likens them to poet-lovers who struggle uneasily with the capacity of verse to show what is in the heart.

In the last line of one of Donne's sonnets the speaker sets himself apart by virtue of his "true griefe," merely assuming its cause without naming it. Such an assumption is typical of complaining lovers, whose recognizably conventional plight demands no explanation. Although the context actually makes clear that the grief of Donne's speaker is the penitence of a sinner, its association with love poetry is nevertheless not dismissed, but made explicit. For the sighs and tears inevitably used to express the lover's grief in conventional complaints are evoked for comparison with this speaker's "true griefe" earlier in the sonnet:

> If faithfull soules be alike glorifi'd
> As Angels, then my fathers soule doth see,
> And adds this even to full felicitie,
> That valiantly I hels wide mouth o'rstride:
> But if our mindes to these soules be descry'd
> By circumstances, and by signes that be
> Apparent in us, not immediately,
> How shall my mindes white truth to them be try'd?
> They see idolatrous lovers weepe and mourne,
> And vile blasphemous Conjurers to call
> On Jesus name, and Pharisaicall
> Dissemblers feigne devotion. Then turne
> O pensive soule, to God, for he knowes best
> Thy true griefe, for he put it in my breast.[53]

The complaint of Donne's speaker evokes these literary associations not only by his claim to unspecified "griefe" which is "true" in comparison with the sighs and tears of "idolatrous lovers," but also by his use in the couplet of conventional prayer language to plead that the object of his devotion see his "true griefe" where it is hidden in his breast. (Here he uses "true" with the sense it typically has in the sonnets of Sidney and Shakespeare but not in Donne's love poems, to mean sincere more than constant.) Occurring in a sonnet, this language inevitably recalls the petitions

of a poet-lover, who borrows religious vocabulary to plead that his beloved recognize the true devotion in his heart, however imperfectly it is
represented by appearances. In Sonnet 23, for example, Shakespeare's
speaker, confessing to have failed in performance of public worship—
"The perfect ceremony of loues right"—pleads that his friend will interpret in outward signs his unbroken prayers:

> the eloquence
> And domb presagers of my speaking brest,
> Who pleade for loue, and look for recompence,
> More then that tonge that more hath more exprest.
> O learne to read what silent loue hath writ,
> To heare wit eies belongs to loues fine wiht.

The kind of prayer with which Donne's speaker ends his complaint was
also an established convention in religious sonnets, as the prefatory poem
to Henry Lok's *Sundrie Sonnets of Christian Passions* illustrates:

> It is not Lord the sound of many words,
>   The bowed knee or abstinence of man,
>   The filèd phrase, that eloquence affords,
>   Or poet's pen, that heauens do pearce, or can:
> By heauie cheere, of colour pale and wan,
>   By pinèd bodie of the Pharisay,
>   A mortall eye repentance oft doth scan,
>   When iudgement doth on outward shadows stay,
> But Thou—O God—doest heart's intent bewray
> For from Thy sight Lord nothing is conceald;
> Thou formdst the frame fro out the verie clay,
>   To Thee the thoughts of hearts are all reueald,
>   To Thee therefore with hart and minde prostrate,
>   With teares I thus deplore my sinfull state.[54]

Itself a compendium of conventions assimilated from love sonnets, Lok's
poem makes a pointed contrast to Donne's by the way it uses a similar
ending to a very different effect. It follows a Sidneian model such as
Astrophil and Stella 3 by cataloguing false and affected styles, here of
"outward" repentance, which are then contrasted with the true "heart's
intent," exemplified in the poet's different style of grief. Without raising
any questions about the adequacy of the speaker's own language to render
his inward state, as Sidney has been shown to do, Lok turns his Sidneian
model into a contrast between hypocritical display and genuine humility.
His speaker is not troubled by a sense of distance between what is in his
heart and his own modes of outward expression.

Donne, instead of making a simple contrast between his speaker's style
and that of profane lovers, points to their likeness. In doing so he focuses

on the very questions that Lok ignores, but which are raised in his own ways by Sidney. Donne's speaker, because his grief is expressed in precisely the same modes as that of the lovers, fears that it will be indistinguishable from theirs. Like the poet momentarily in the first sonnet of *La Corona,* this speaker defends his sincerity because he is troubled by the separation of what is in his heart from its outward expression. Here that preoccupation fills the entire sonnet. Throughout, the speaker wrestles with his angry sense of discrepancy between what he knows with certainty of his inward state, and what imperfect representations of it appearances will make. They will liken him to other men, from whom his invisible inward states ought truly to distinguish him.

The sonnet begins with the speaker questioning whether the souls of the faithful departed, like his own father, have the same kind of intuitive knowledge as angels, or whether, like the living, they can only reason from how things appear by outward signs. This is orthodox speculation in itself, but the concerns that cause the speaker to raise these questions are not those of a representative Christian saying common prayers. Nowhere, not even in the last three lines where he uses language traditional to prayer, does the speaker lose his sense of the separateness of his inward experience—from that of other men, from the view of souls in heaven, and from outward show.

The speaker describes what angelic intuition would enable his father to "see," his son's spiritual state which is invisible to mortal sight. No appearances could show him as he views himself, straddling the gaping mouth of hell like a Colossus, or like an epic hero, an Odysseus or Aeneas, braving the dangers of the underworld and surmounting them. To the speaker his own knowledge of this inward state is so vivid that he imagines it would, if seen by his father, even add joy to heavenly bliss. Equally vivid, however, is his angry conviction that minds are revealed to other men, even souls in heaven, only in appearances, which render imperfectly, obscurely, or deceptively. Recalling the poet in *La Corona* when he petitions God to "Reward my muses white sincerity," this speaker asks, "How shall my mindes white truth to them be try'd?" This is not a plea, however, but a challenge, a defiant boast. Above all it is an angry protest that he will inevitably be confused with other men whose outward modes for the expression of what is in the heart are indistinguishable from his own. For "idolatrous lovers weepe and mourne" as he does; false believers pray in the same words, using the same forms as he does. His utterance therefore cannot make what is in his mind visible as the "white truth" he sees it to be, or distinguish the "true griefe" in his breast from the complaints of conventional poet-lovers, or from pharisaical devotions.

Only God can know what is in his heart, as he knows it himself. The couplet seems to offer this consolation to resolve the speaker's angry speculations and protests. The tone is calmer, the syntax less tortuous, and

the monosyllabic diction simpler. Compared to earlier rhymes, the final
pair is easy to hear because adjacent and obvious. As in many of Sidney's
sonnet endings, this simple answer makes the speaker's earlier struggles
seem unnecessary, overcomplicated. Like Astrophil's Muse in Sonnet 1,
the speaker himself here finds the truth he has been seeking outwardly
where it has always resided, in his own breast. As has been shown to be
characteristic of the sonnet form, however, the couplet makes a comment
upon preceding lines without negating or canceling their validity, so that
the earlier lines simultaneously reflect on the couplet itself.

When Donne's speaker there uses language associated with the petitions
of both Christian penitents and poet-lovers, he actually offers a resolution
less sure than it sounds, more tentative and troubled.[55] For prayers and
complaints, he has objected, do not always render inward truth. Even to
his own soul he must use modes of expression he knows to be indistinguishable from feigned devotion and profane complaints. No language can
present what is in the heart to men so that it can be truly shown as it is
seen by God. The reasons for this are multiple: that feelings are invisible,
that mortal sight is limited and fallible, appearances difficult to interpret,
and inward states hard to define. Here, for example, the speaker shares
only with God the knowledge of his unspecified but "true griefe." Since
it comes from God, it must be penitent sorrow for his sins. His "mindes
white truth" has led him to recognize failings in himself: hell's mouth
opens beneath him. Yet this admission of sin is not incompatible with
other true feelings about himself; a sense of his own significance, even
impatience at misunderstanding; contempt for less searching honesty than
his own; anger against false righteousness. His "true griefe" is a complex
of inward states which cannot be seen in outward forms, or defined by
language traditional to prayers or complaints. Only God can know it,
whose immediate vision dispenses with appearances, and all other modes
of expression.

Poet-lover's complaints, such as are evoked here and even more directly imitated in two other holy sonnets, are rare among Donne's *Songs and
Sonets*. Since complaining was one of the commonest modes in Tottel's
miscellany and in English sonnet sequences, Donne's shift in preference
sets his love poetry somewhat apart from the tradition, much in the same
way as do his relative lack of interest in persuasions to love, and his
avoidance of love sonnets. More typical in his *Songs and Sonets* are
anticomplaints, such as "The Indifferent," in which the speaker languishes
in the traditional poet-lover's posture— *"Venus* heard me sigh this song"—
in order to bemoan his lady's constancy.[56] Elsewhere the conventions of
complaining are ridiculed by a kind of absurd literalness, as in "The
Computation," where they are used to count years: "Teares drown'd one
hundred, and sighes blew out two."[57] Similarly, in the opening lines of
"Loves Infiniteness" the speaker counts them like money:

If yet I have not all thy love,
    Deare, I shall never have it all;
I cannot breath one other sigh, to move,
    Nor can intreat one other teare to fall.
All my treasure, which should purchase thee,
    Sighs, teares, and oathes, and letters I have spent.[58]

Conventional modes of expression are parodied by a different kind of literalness in the second stanza of "The Canonization," when the lover defends his sighs and tears against the accusations of property owners.[59] There, characteristically, the speaker's impudent assertiveness is not in defense of the sincerity of his own modes of expression. It is a defense of their privacy, and an attack on publicity and display of passion. In "Twicknam Garden," however, Donne burlesques the conventional poet-lover's claim to complain in tears of such purity that they sanctify his grief. The speaker is a caricature of such a figure, "Blasted with sighs, and surrounded with teares," groaning like a mandrake root, weeping perpetually like a fountain:

    Hither with christall vyals, lovers come,
        And take my teares, which are loves wine,
        And try your mistresse Teares at home,
    For all are false, that tast not just like mine.[60]

The mixture of sanctimony and connoisseurship explodes the convention.
    Among Donne's holy sonnets, however, associations with the complaint are used very differently, to raise questions about the nature of inward experience and its relation to expression which are not the concerns of the speakers in Donne's love poetry. One identifies itself with the traditional mode in the first line by evoking "sighes and teares," the inevitable accompaniments of the lover's complaint:

    O might those sighes and teares returne againe
    Into my breast and eyes, which I have spent,
    That I might in this holy discontent
    Mourne with some fruit, as I have mourn'd in vaine;
    In my Idolatry what showres of raine
    Mine eyes did waste? what griefs my heart did rent?
    That sufferance was my sinne, now I repent;
    Because I did suffer I must suffer paine.
    Th'hydroptique drunkard, and night-scouting thiefe,
    The itchy Lecher, and selfe tickling proud
    Have the remembrance of past joyes, for reliefe
    Of comming ills. To (poore) me is allow'd
    No ease; for, long, yet vehement griefe hath beene
    Th'effect and cause, the punishment and sinne.[61]

The sonnet opens with a metaphor as grotesque in its literal descriptive-
ness as any parodies or burlesques of sighing and weeping lovers in Donne's
Songs and Sonets. The speaker wants literally to take back his earlier
complaints. He regrets that he has "spent" them (recalling the financial
audit of sighs, tears, and other stocks by the speaker in "Loves Infiniteness"), the implication being that he has impoverished himself "in vaine."
The octave builds a pattern of contrasts between such previous "waste"
and the hope of "fruit," between earlier sin and his penitence now. The
speaker therefore seems to condemn his sighs and tears, which were the
expressions of his griefs as a profane lover, and by implication therefore
to reject the complaints in which, as a poet, he showed his griefs. This is
the development in the sonnet immediately preceding in Helen Gardner's
arrangement, where the speaker asks for new waters to cleanse his inward
state:

> Drowne my world with my weeping earnestly,
> Or wash it, if it must be drown'd no more:
> But oh it must be burnt; alas the fire
> Of lust and envie have burnt it heretofore,
> And made it fouler; Let their flames retire,
> And burne me ô Lord, with a fiery zeale
> Of thee and thy house, which doth in eating heale.[62]

In another sonnet the speaker also prays that his sinful weeping be washed
away:

> O God, Oh! of thine onely worthy blood,
> And my teares, make a heavenly Lethean flood,
> And drowne in it my sinnes blacke memorie.[63]

Yet in the sonnet of complaint, the terms of the octave in which the
speaker's past expressions of grief seem to be contrasted with his present
actually liken them. Instead of rejecting his former sighs and tears, he
accepts them anew. Rather than asking for their purification, he longs only
for their return. They are not alien to his present condition. He therefore
reclaims them as the speaker in one of the holy sonnets of persuasion has
been seen to redirect to God his past arguments to profane mistresses. The
parallel between the two kinds of reclamation is very close, in that both
speakers insist on associating precisely the same words with the inward
states they nevertheless distinguish as profane and holy. In this penitent's
idolatrous past he "mourn'd"; in his new state of holiness he wishes to
"Mourne" again. Such repetitions are most insistent in the last line of the
octave, "Because I did suffer I must suffer paine." Like Sidney in *Astrophil
and Stella* 5 ("It is most true"), Donne pointedly and repeatedly uses

identical terms for inward experiences which seem to be mutually exclu-
sive, here those of complaining lover and penitent sinner, until the closing
lines explicitly declare them to be indistinguishable:

> To (poore) me is allow'd
> No ease; for, long, yet vehement griefe hath beene
> Th'effect and cause, the punishment and sinne.

His penitent mourning leaves him as impoverished as his love complaints. His wish to take back his former sighs and tears is therefore not
so that he may silence them, but to replenish his store so that he may
spend them again. His profane sufferings seem therefore to be no more
vain, no more wasteful than his "holy discontent." A single phrase, "long,
yet vehement griefe," describes both states, and makes them indistinguishable in kind, duration, intensity, or truth.

This identification of seemingly contradictory or divided states in the
couplet has effects which are multiple and paradoxical. On the one hand
it implies that inward experiences have a continuity and force that gives
them validity. They in turn validate the tears and sighs that express them,
which are themselves as real as "showres of raine." In this view inward
states, by their own truth, also enable poetry, another outward mode of
expression, to show them truly. This is especially so in the complaint. Its
language is capable of rendering the speaker's inward states sincerely, so
that, like his sighs and tears, he can use it again with equal truth now as
in the past. On the other hand, the couplet may be interpreted in an almost
directly contradictory sense to imply that language cannot be commensurate with what is in the heart. For while it may be true of inward experiences that they can simultaneously be the causes and effects of themselves,
or that the same inward condition can be a sin and its own punishment,
those truths contradict the meanings of the words used to state them,
pushing paradox to its limits. Similarly, language to describe inward experiences, using categories like profane and holy which define distinctions
or opposites, cannot render what is in the heart, which is obscure, ambiguous, paradoxical, demanding multiple and contradictory interpretations
simultaneously. These implications of the couplet are worked out elsewhere in the sonnet by ways in which the patterns of contrast, the distinctions, the divisions in the speaker's language are continually disavowed,
rather than validated, by the nature of inward states existing independently, and at a distance from their outward expression.

The closeness of the sonnet as a whole to a poet-lover's complaint itself
raises questions about the speaker's language. Why does Donne use throughout a secular verse model rather than the form of a confession or some
other penitential prayer? Perhaps an answer might be that such forms as

would have been acceptable to Donne tend to merge the individual in the liturgical voice of the representative Christian, and would therefore be inappropriate for this penitent, who sees his plight as unique among sinners. Then why does Donne insist throughout on having the speaker use the same terms for repentance as for thwarted sexual desire? One implication might be that the speaker in his past so fully identified himself with the conventions of the poet-lover's complaint that they determine his inward state rather than being shaped by it. That is the plight of the lover playfully mocked by reversible grammar in *Astrophil and Stella* 6: "His paper, pale dispaire, and paine his pen doth move." If this is the situation of Donne's speaker, although he now desires to "Mourne with some fruit," he cannot. His long and vehement complaining still makes him "poore," impoverished as well as self-pitying. He has no "past joyes," but only sighs and tears to renew him. Therefore his repentance must still take the form of a complaint. In this view, language is not validated by inward states but exists independently from them, moved according to the dictates of its own tyrannical conventions.

Further implications in Donne's use of the complaint can be seen in another of his sonnets. It announces itself to be built on the model of a catalogue of "contraryes" which, with sighs and tears, has been seen to be one of the commonest modes in which sixteenth-century lovers complain:

> Oh, to vex me, contrayes meete in one:
> Inconstancy unnaturally hath begott
> A constant habit; that when I would not
> I change in vowes, and in devotione.
> As humorous is my contritione
> As my prophane love, and as soone forgott:
> As ridlingly distemperd, cold and hott,
> As praying, as mute; as infinite, as none.
> I durst not view heaven yesterday; and to day
> In prayers, and flattering speaches I court God:
> To morrow I quake with true feare of his rod.
> So my devout fitts come and go away
> Like a fantastique Ague: save that here
> Those are my best dayes, when I shake with feare.[64]

This catalogue unmistakably places the speaker in a lineage descending both from Troilus and from Petrarch's poet-lover, as did the sighs and tears in the other holy sonnet of complaint. It especially resembles Petrarch's Sonnet 134 (*Pace non trovo*), probably the most often imitated in English of all his poems, while also recalling complaints in the native tradition, of which Gascoigne's "The passion of a Lover" contains a representative stanza:

My fits are lyke the fever Ectick fits,
Which one daye quakes within and burnes without,
The next day heate within the boosoms sits,
And shivring colde the body goes about.
So is my heart most hote when hope is colde,
And quaketh most when I moste heate behold.[65]

Donne's catalogue of "contraryes," like his other sonnet of complaint, is arranged as a comparison between "prophane love" in the speaker's past and his present "devout" state, a comparison which again actually makes them one. Here this identification seems to run through all eleven lines of the catalogue, so that although the speaker now courts God, rather than a mistress or many mistresses, his inward state is identical with that of his past. He has passions which are as changeable, as self-serving, and even now only intermittently as "true" as those of his past. A further resemblance to Donne's other sonnet of complaint is that again the identification of worldly and sacred inward states, itself multiple in its implications, is given a further complicating twist in the closing lines. Here the speaker compares his "devout fitts," which have already been likened to the contraries of profane love, to a "fantastique Ague" which comes and goes with its fevers and trembling spells, under which he is passive, sinking and recovering in a sickly, dreamlike alternation. This comparison seems to hold true for the contraries of all his experience, past and present, and to summarize them. Yet the speaker himself is not fully satisfied with the truth of his likeness. He makes an exception to it: "save that here / Those are my best dayes, when I shake with feare." His inward states, in other respects like a sick man's, are unlike in that his "best dayes" are those in which he trembles most, whereas to the feverish patient such spells of shaking would mark the returns of the disease. The phrasing makes this more than a witty twist to the logic of the comparison. Like many other sonnet endings, it is a complicating reflection on the speaker's use of language throughout the poem. First it calls in question the comparison of an ague to devout fits by pointing to the limits of its application. Those limits then turn out to extend beyond a single point of difference, because the exception overturns the fundamental parallels between physical and spiritual disease and health. Symptoms of returning sickness in a feverish patient are rightly to be interpreted as marks of improvement in a sinner. That is to say, physical signs are not adequate representations of inward states: "true feare" cannot be distinguished by outward expression, including language such as the speaker has used in his complaint.

His dissatisfaction with it is shown in this pointed way in which he dismantles his own comparison, and in several supporting details. One such detail is the disturbing use of "here," where the reader might expect *now.* For the sonnet consists up through line 11 of a catalogue of past and present contraries, culminating in examples of changes from "yesterday" to "to day" to "To morrow." This pattern might predict the final exception to be that *now* the speaker's experience differs in one respect from his past. No mentions of places, actual or metaphorical, help to locate "here" of line 13, so that it floats ambiguously, hinting at a specific place which is not defined. It may refer to the poem itself, or rather to the particular point in it at which the speaker criticizes his own language, or to the one term of his comparison to which the analogy drawn from sickness is inapplicable. These readings imply that he sees the inadequacy of the complaint as an outward mode of expression for what is in his heart. The last line, then, would be an attempt to render inward truth by different means. Another telling detail in that line supports such an interpretation, the use of "best dayes." The phrase derives from the vocabulary of the sick room where the patient is asked if he is better or worse, if he has had a bad or a good day. In the final line of the sonnet its physiological application is juxtaposed with a moral or theological interpretation. Or rather, the language of the sick room, adequate for rendering outward experience, is translated into another kind of language in an effort to portray the speaker's spiritual state. The effect recalls a device apparently assimilated by Shakespeare in Sonnet 49 from *Astrophil and Stella* 18. In that model and the adaptation of it, both explorations of the metaphor of an audit, the speaker translates the vocabulary of financial poverty into inward deprivation (as Donne uses it in "O might those sighes and teares returne againe"). In all these instances the effort to translate the speaker's terms in this fashion is another way of showing his distrust for the conventional metaphor on which his own poem is built.

The ambiguous word "here," while referring in these ways to points in the speaker's comparison, can also be directed within to his mind, soul, heart, breast, to his inward state which may be unknowable by outward expression. Still another detail in the couplet supports this reading of "here" by another form of translation. For the wording of line 11, "I quake with true feare of his rod," is in the pointedly parallel final phrase translated into a much more reticent statement, "I shake with feare." The speaker there gives no explanation of his cause for fear, or any defense of its sincerity. Only God knows whether or not it is "true," but his knowledge is independent of any outward expression in appearances or utterance. The speaker's reticence is another way of acting upon his sense that what is grounded inward in his heart is at a distance from language used to describe it, which cannot render it truly.

Common to Donne's holy sonnets associated with both persuasions to love and complaints are contrasts which become likenesses between the profane passions of the speaker's idolatrous past and his present devout love. One function of such comparisons, it becomes clear, is to dramatize

in a religious sonnet the conventions of love poetry. That is, the speaker
uses them because the modes conventional to the poet-lover are part of
his own inward experience in the past. And inward experience, these
sonnets insist, is continuous, not divisible into distinct categories but
interwoven, obscure, ambiguous, paradoxical. Therefore the language associated with the poet-lover writing persuasions and complaints is dramatically appropriate—however its conventions are questioned, modified,
or criticized—to the speaker's present rendering of his inward state as a
penitent. The ways in which poetic conventions are tested, translated, or
dismantled contribute to making the speakers in these holy sonnets dramatic creations who are more like Astrophil and the poet-lover in Shakespeare's sonnets than they are like Donne's lovers.

The crucial distinction can now be seen in a comparison of "Oh, to vex
me, contraryes meete in one," where the speaker in the couplet dismantles
his own metaphor with "Loves Infiniteness." In that poem the last stanza
seems to turn in similar fashion on what precedes it, which is an argument
by the speaker developing the conventional metaphor of love as a bargain
in which lovers exchange hearts. In the ending he both criticizes the
metaphor he has spun out, and substitutes a new one:

> Yet I would not have all yet,
>   Hee that hath all can have no more,
> And since my love doth every day admit
>   New growth, thou shouldst have new rewards in store;
> Thou canst not every day give me thy heart,
>   If thou canst give it, then thou never gav'st it:
> Loves riddles are, that though thy heart depart,
>   It stayes at home, and thou with losing sav'st it:
> But wee will have a way more liberall,
>   Then changing hearts, to joyne them, so wee shall
>   Be one, and one anothers All.[66]

An important difference between this final reflection and the sonnet ending is that here the lover, although it is he who had developed the faulty
metaphor of an exchange, had actually disavowed it from the beginning
through his absurdly literal exposition of it. By counting "Sighs, teares,
and oathes, and letters" as if they were money, he consistently dissociates
himself from such a way of thinking about love, so that his pretense of
explicating it can be seen from the start as a vehicle for making fun of it.
His reasons for doing so are not literary, because he is not a poet attacking
the conventions of false and affected verse, but amorous. He apparently
wishes to educate the lady out of her fashionable way of thinking about
their love. In this sense his criticism of the convention is dramatically
incorporated into his experience as a lover, but it does not implicate his
own language in the insufficiency it exposes. It therefore does not point

to any greater distance between what is in his heart and his utterance than is measured by its deliberately burlesque quality. He playfully pretends to use a conventional metaphor for loving, only in order to have his pretense recognized, and in the end he openly acknowledges it by substituting his own "more liberall" metaphor. While there may be some verbal slight-of-hand in such a switch, it signals the lover's witty control of his argument rather than implicating him in the defective qualities of the original metaphor. There is no suggestion that in explicating substitute "riddles" he is continuing to use language at a distance from what is in his heart. On the contrary, he is suiting his argument in a playful fashion to his own way of thinking, assured that it will reveal his true, generous love. His entertaining address to the lady shows that he believes he can articulate what is in his heart, and has confidence that he can educate her to share his understanding of it.

By contrast, in the sonnet the speaker uses, without burlesquing or in other ways ridiculing it, a conventional metaphor drawing terms from outward experience to analyze his inward state. He then points to his own recognition of inadequacy in the metaphor, and attempts to make it true to what is in his heart by translating it from outward to inward reference, stating, "Those are my best dayes, when I shake with feare." This is much the simplest line in the sonnet, composed all of common, monosyllabic words in a poem otherwise crowded with difficult polysyllables, some in the prominent position of rhymes. This simplicity seems to offer release, like the endings of many sonnets by Sidney, while in fact raising new questions about the speaker's language. The line is a statement which for the first time leaves out explanation and evaluation of the speaker's inward state, previously described in a catalogue of contraries. His new reticence signals either that he has come to accept it in all its contradictions, or that he now sees it to be much simpler than he described it to be, or that he is withholding his interpretation of it, perhaps to escape misreading. Or yet another possibility is that he has abandoned all hope of understanding it. His unadorned statement raises these questions of interpretation simultaneously, and resolves none of them.

This sonnet leaves the final impression that the speaker has "here," in his poem and in his heart, inward experience that he cannot name. In this respect he differs from Donne's lovers, whose true, plain hearts are manifest in their utterance and all other forms of expression. He differs also, and in the same respect, from the speakers typical of Donne's religious verse in other forms. For their representative voices use liturgical language which is itself predicated on the assumption that what is in the heart is knowable, and can be truly uttered in the sanctified forms of common prayer. The grounds of the distinctions between Donne's holy sonnets and his other poems are therefore not theological, nor are they derived from a notion of religious matter demanding a special kind of verse. The

distinctions between the sonnets and Donne's other poems, both secular
and religious, emerge instead from the sonnet tradition, and its associations for him with the poet's struggle to find a language that can show truly
what is in the heart, its "white sincerity."

Conclusion:
sincerity

The phrasing in which Donne's speaker in the opening sonnet of *La Corona* defends his "white sincerity" is religious in its associations. For in English verse of this period *white,* when not paired in love poems with *red* to describe the lilies and roses of the beloved's complexion, commonly had the liturgical meaning of purity. Donne uses it this way in his poem "A Litanie" to celebrate "A Virgin Squadron of white Confessors," followed by "The Virgins" in a "cold white snowie Nunnery."[1] With the same connotations his elegiac praises of Elizabeth Drury pay tribute to her "white integrity" and "white innocence."[2] The various grammatical forms of *sincere, sincerely, sincerity* (sometimes *sincereness*) were introduced into English in the sixteenth century, and did occur in other kinds of writing, but most often in religious contexts.[3] All forms appear in the King James verson of the New Testament, most commonly replacing forms of *pure* in earlier English translations.[4] This association may explain the appearance of the word "sincerity" in Donne's holy sonnet, but not in the sequences of Sidney or Shakespeare, despite their concern with the poet-lover's struggle to write sincerely.[5] They rely instead on repetitions of *true* and *truth.*[6] (Sidney uses them a total of thirty-two times, Shakespeare almost twice as many, but Daniel, Drayton, and Spenser in their sequences each fewer than a dozen times.)

The various grammatical forms of sincere were used in the sixteenth century with typical lack of distinctions between their literal and figurative characters, or between their application to outward or inward phenomena. These practices are illustrated in the earliest English dictionary, Cawdrey's of 1604, where "sincere" is defined as "pure, uncorrupt, unmingled, or without dissimulation."[7] For the various forms of the word were used to name tangible or intangible phenomena or qualities of both things and people. When describing physical phenomena, they bore literal meanings: the brain was said to deliver its reports "to the hart sincerely."[8] Colors, particularly, were described as sincere when true in the sense of un-mixed — pure white being a favorite example in which literal and figurative

meanings are interchangeable or indistinguishable. Barnabe Barnes combines them in this fashion in a sonnet celebrating a vision of angels
"arraide in sincere white."[9] *Sincere* was also in use in the sixteenth century
to characterize intangible matters or attributes, here still describing human
qualities or things nonhuman, but with figurative rather than literal meanings. Shakespeare uses it once in this way in the phrase "sincere motions,"
spelling out its metaphorical workings by pairing it with "proofes as cleere
as Founts in *Iuly,* when / We see each graine of grauell."[10] In such uses,
the adjective most often had theological implications. It was, for example,
a term of approval for doctrine thought to be genuine, pure, not perverted,
and for translations of the Bible judged to be correct, exact, true.[11]

When attached to human beings or their attributes, the word in its
various grammatical forms was used without attention to metaphorical
possibilities as synonymous with the more common words: truth, plainness, uprightness. Shakespeare, in his plays, links the adjective form with
inward states, and the adverb to various kinds of utterance: talking, speaking, professing. The noun he associates equally with inward states, utterance, and deeds.[12] In descriptions of human affairs, these words again
occured most commonly in religious contexts: to distinguish "sincere and
faithful professors" from Pharisees, those who wish "truely and sincerely
to serve God" from hypocrites.[13] When used to describe the heart, they
were often attached to inward in some parallel with outward experience,
and then associated with reminders that the secrets of the heart, though
hidden, are nevertheless always open and visible to God. This pattern of
connections is made in *A Briefe and Necessary Catechisme or Instruction*
published in 1582, in a prayer which amply defines "sinceritie of hearte"
by its synonyms and its opposites:

> ... that we may euen from the bottome of our heartes, examine and
> trie our thoughtes, before thy presence, that they bee vpright and
> vnfained, not hypocriticall in outwarde shewe onely and appearance,
> but that euen all corners of our heartes being opened and disclosed
> before thee, wee may euen as though it were openly before the face
> of the whole worlde bring them in shewe, knowinge ... that we haue
> thee to be a viewer of our dooings, a thousand folde more then the
> eyes of man: that thus we may walk as becommeth thy children, not
> onely in outwarde shewe, but also in sinceritie of hearte.[14]

Donne unquestionably shared this generally held notion of inward experience. He heard it similarly described in the opening prayer of the service
of Holy Communion: "Almightie God, unto whom all hartes bee open
and all desyres knowen, and from whom no secretes are hid."[15] In his own
sermons he preached reminders that inward secrets are not hidden from
divine knowledge:

Know, that you do all that you doe, in the presence of Gods Angels;
and though it be in it selfe, and should be so to us, a stronger bridle,
to consider that we do all in the presence of God, (who sees clearer
then they, for he sees secret thoughts, and can strike immediately,
which they cannot do, without commission from him) yet since the
presence of a Magistrate, or a Preacher, or a father, or a husband,
keeps men often from ill actions, let this prevaile something with
thee, to that purpose, that the Angels of God are alwayes present,
though thou discerne them not.[16]

The language of his holy sonnets evokes such orthodox conceptions of
inward experience, for instance when the speaker turns to God who alone
sees the "true griefe" in his breast, or asks Him to reward what cannot be
tried by other men, the "white truth" of his mind, or his "muses white
sincerity."

Yet the sense of what is in the heart which is conveyed side by side with
these orthodox notions in some of Donne's holy sonnets, while not necessarily wholly incompatible with such traditional religious views, actually
resembles more closely the representation of inward experience in the love
sonnets of Sidney or Shakespeare, or in *Hamlet,* than in theological writings like *A Briefe and Necessary Catechisme,* or the Anglican liturgy, or
even Donne's own sermons. For when Donne's speaker in the sonnets
defends his sincerity, he means something more than that he is not a
Pharisee or a dissembler, not an Iago who hypocritically protests his
"sinceritie of Loue, and honest kindnesse."[17] He means something more
than that his thoughts are upright and unfeigned, or that his utterance
truly opens and shows them. He means, that is to say, something more
than the definition of sincerity common especially in religious writing,
represented by the quoted passage from *A Briefe and Necessary Catechisme*: the conformity of outward show to what is truly in the heart.

Donne, in some of his holy sonnets, conveys along with that sense a
different understanding of sincerity. They suggest that his speaker, like
Hamlet, or the poet-lover in Shakespeare's sonnets, or Astrophil, has that
within which escapes show, not because he deliberately cloaks it but
because inward and outward spheres are in themselves radically distinct
and widely distanced. The implications of such a separation are that what
is in the heart cannot be interpreted or judged by outward signs, among
which language is included, even when they are sincere. Inward states
cannot therefore be truly shown, even by the speaker's own utterance in
prayers or poems, cannot be defined by them, even to himself. When he
claims to be sincere, he is therefore asserting the existence of an intrinsic
state of being which he cannot name, cannot precisely know. Yet he
fiercely testifies to its continuous existence and integrity. He is therefore
defending a notion of what is in the heart which is closer to what a modern

writer would call a *real self* or an *inner life* than to its commonest six-teenth-century definition, repeated in Donne's own quoted sermon, as "secret thoughts." For that phrase implies what the sonnets deny, that inward states can ultimately be disclosed and named when the closet of the heart is unlocked and its contents opened to show.

The characteristics of Donne's holy sonnets, as the previous chapter has distinguished some of them from his other religious poetry, point to origins for this sense of inward experience which are themselves also fundamentally literary. Donne's speakers in these sonnets are different from the petitioners in his liturgical verse, who utter what is in the heart and mind of the congregation in the sanctified voice of common prayer. For the speakers in the holy sonnets are involved in efforts to find a language to portray their inward experience, rather than trying to conform it to words whose truth is already established. Such a search is not congru-ent with Donne's many explications—examples from sermons have been quoted—of the nature of prayer. Although there gravely troubled by the difficulty of fixing his mind on the words of his petition, and of purifying his heart to make it worthy to lift up in words of praise, he never questions their ultimate adequacy to render inward states. In this respect the view of language preached in his sermons is predicated on assumptions closer to those of his *Songs and Sonets,* which assume that the true, plain heart appears outwardly, and that its truth can be uttered and recognized. The speakers in the holy sonnets, by contrast, struggle to make that possible in their verse, while doubting their own efforts.

These struggles and doubts derive from a perception that there is an inescapable difference between inward states and their rendering in lan-guage, which is the distinction introduced into English poetry in the open-ing of *Astrophil and Stella,* between matter and form in verse. The shaping force of this distinction—perhaps also of Sidney's influence in defining it—and the strength of its association for Donne with the sonnet is shown by his explorations of it in ways that make some of his holy sonnets fundamentally different from his other writings, both verse and prose. They depart from his concerns, his beliefs, even his most fundamental assumptions there about the nature of inward experience and its relation to language, by following the efforts of Sidney and Shakespeare to render a newly conceived understanding of sincerity. It is a sense of what is in the heart which evolved in the development of the sonnet, from Wyatt's work in the form through the variations and expansions of its uses in the sequences of Sidney and Shakespeare. It is a conception which much later vocabularies, clustered around belief in the existence of a *real self* and an *inner life,* are used to describe, but which in the sixteenth and early seventeenth century was only suggested in the inward language of sonnets, and expanded in *Hamlet.*

Appendix:
other borrowings
by Shakespeare from
Astrophil and Stella

The nature and development of sixteenth-century love poetry previously discussed make it hard to assign specific sources for poems built on matter conventional to the traditions assimilated into Petrarch's sonnet sequence. These difficulties are illustrated in Shakespeare's nocturnal poems — Sonnets 27, 28, 43, 61. We know that in Sidney he had a predecessor particularly interested in the situation of the lover alone in his chamber, made sleepless by his passions, or haunted by dreams of his beloved. In nine sonnets of *Astrophil and Stella,* discussed in Chapter 3, Sidney exploits the possibilities of this situation as a means of exploring the distance between inward experiences, including images and dreams, and outward existence or expression. Chapter 4 has demonstrated that Shakespeare studied *Astrophil and Stella* carefully, shared its central concerns, and often pursued them by means adapted from Sidney. In many instances previously discussed it is possible to point definitively to particular models in Sidney's sequence as sources for sonnets by Shakespeare. Yet his treatments of the nocturnal situation, while resembling Sidney's, do not do so in such specific ways. Rollins, for instance, cites for Shakespeare's Sonnet 43 the possibility of *Astrophil and Stella* 38 as a source, but also Ovid, *Tristia*, III, iii, 18.[1] For Sonnet 27 he records the suggestion of *Astrophil and Stella* 88 and 89 as sources, but also Catullus, XXXI, 7–10, Bartholomew Griffin, *Fidessa* [1596], Sonnet 14, and Petrarch's poems throughout, as well as those of his Italian and French imitators.[2] Booth adds a suggestion from Arthur Golding's translation published in 1567 of *The. xv. Bookes of P. Ovidius Naso, entytuled Metamorphosis,* XV, 188, 208.[3] Virtually no details surely single out Sidney's nocturnal sonnets as sources for Shakespeare's. An exception might be an echo of the play on *ghastly* from *Astrophil and Stella* 96 in Shakespeare's Sonnet 27. (The word occurs elsewhere in the sequences of the five major English sonneteers only once in Drayton's, where it does not describe night's horrors.) The meaning for *ghastly* of ghostlike, spiritlike — as well as terrifying — belongs to the characteristic vocabulary given more stress by both Sidney and Shakespeare than by other sonnet writers: variants of *sprite, shape, shadow, show, shade.*

Other sonnets in which Shakespeare reworks a conventional motif that could have multiple sources nevertheless point more surely to models in *Astrophil and Stella.* One is Sonnet 71, in which the poet-lover disclaims the desire to be remembered in his verse. Shakespeare could have known various models for such a disavowal. While Rollins cites a classical comparison to Tibullus, I, i, 67 f, Petrarch's Sonnet 293 is an example made more familiar by numerous Italian, French, and English variations (Ringler cites Desportes, *Diane,* I, i as well *Astrophil and Stella* 90).[4] There the poet disclaims to have written for fame, disregarding his many promises elsewhere to win immortality for Laura and the laurel crown for himself through the power of his poetry. Astrophil imitates and echoes this Petrarchan model by playfully dissociating himself from other poet's efforts to win fame in Sonnet 90, discussed in relation to its Italian model in Chapter 3:

> *Stella* thinke not that I by verse seeke fame,
>> Who seeke, who hope, who love, who live but thee;
>> Thine eyes my pride, thy lips my history:
> If thou praise not, all other praise is shame.
> Nor so ambitious am I, as to frame
>> A nest for my yong praise in Lawrell tree:
>> In truth I sweare, I wish not there should be
> Graved in mine Epitaph a Poet's name:
>> Ne if I would, could I just title make,
> That any laud to me thereof should grow,
> Without my plumes from others' wings I take.
> For nothing from my wit or will doth flow,
>> Since all my words thy beauty doth endite,
>> And love doth hold my hand, and makes me write.

Whether or not Shakespeare knew Petrarch's original sonnet, or other versions of it in French or English, his immediate model in Sonnet 71 is certainly Sidney's adaptation:

> Noe Longer mourne for me when I am dead,
> Then you shall heare the surly sullen bell
> Giue warning to the world that I am fled
> From this vile world with vildest wormes to dwell:
> Nay if you read this line, remember not,
> The hand that writ it, for I loue you so,
> That I in your sweet thoughts would be forgot,
> If thinking on me then should make you woe.
> O if (I say) you looke vpon this verse,
> When I (perhaps) compounded am with clay,

> Do not so much as my poore name reherse;
> But let your loue euen with my life decay.
>> Least the wise world should looke into your mone,
>> And mocke you with me after I am gon.

The varied nature of the borrowings, and of their transformations, resemble Shakespeare's assimilations from Sidney elsewhere. Astrophil's mock demurrals—"Nor so ambitious am I," "In truth I sweare, I wish not," "Ne if I would"—wittily pretend to dissociate him from precisely the conventional allusions he uses to compliment Stella. Shakespeare's echoing parallels—"Noe Longer mourne for me," "Nay if you read this line," "O if (I say)"—pretend to cherish the friend whom they simultaneously work upon with thinly veiled resentment. The world whose "praise" beside Stella's would count as "shame" to Astrophil is for Shakespeare's poet-lover "vile," mocking, and cynically "wise." His "hand" writes self-pitying reminders of "loue" to his friend which conveniently may be forgotten along with his "poore name." Astrophil's "hand," though humbly denying his right to a "Poet's name," is nevertheless inspired to transcribe beauty at the dictation of "love."

Chapter 4 gives other examples of such transformations by Shakespeare. Playful compliments suited for courtly entertainment are turned into verse in which tribute hints at darker meanings. Chapter 4 also gives examples among the sonnets to the dark lady of poems in which Astrophil's praise of Stella is twisted by Shakespeare into scarcely veiled or even open insult. Another such transformation occurs in Sonnet 137. Rollins cites Lee's description of it as a vituperative poem in the manner of Ronsard and his French and English disciples.[5] An example is *Astrophil and Stella* 11, a compliment wrought out of conventional chiding of the god of love for foolishness, for which Ringler cites a parallel in Guillaume Du Bartas, *Premier Jour de la première Sepmaine,* 155–160:[6]

> In truth, ô Love, with what a boyish kind
>> Thou doest proceed in thy most serious wayes:
>> That when the heav'n to thee his best displayes,
> Yet of that best thou leav'st the best behind.
> For like a child that some faire booke doth find,
>> With guilded leaves or coloured Velume playes,
>> Or at the most on some fine picture stayes,
> But never heeds the fruit of writer's mind:
>> So when thou saw'st in Nature's cabinet
> *Stella,* thou straight lookst babies in her eyes,
> In her cheeke's pit thou didst thy pitfould set,
> And in her breast bopeepe or couching lyes,
>> Playing and shining in each outward part:
>> But, foole, seekst not to get into her hart.

The closeness of Shakespeare's adaptation in the opening quatrain of Sonnet 137 leaves no doubt of his source:

> Thou blinde foole loue, what doost thou to mine eyes,
> That they behold and see not what they see:
> They know what beautie is, see where it lyes,
> Yet what the best is, take the worst to be.

The faults attributed by Astrophil to Cupid are attached here simultaneously to the poet-lover, whose seeing is corrupted, and to the dark lady, whose beauty "lyes":

> If eyes corrupt by ouer-partiall lookes,
> Be anchord in the baye where all men ride,
> Why of eyes falsehood hast thou forged hookes,
> Whereto the iudgement of my heart is tide?
> Why should my heart thinke that a seuerall plot,
> Which my heart knowes the wide worlds common place?
> Or mine eyes seeing this, say this is not
> To put faire truth vpon so foule a face,
>   In things right true my heart and eyes haue erred,
>   And to this false plague are they now transferred.

While in this particular Sidneian model the distinction between Stella's "outward part" and her "hart" is complimentary, it is developed by a vocabulary used elsewhere in *Astrophil and Stella*—and adapted from it by Shakespeare—to mark a distance between inward states and their show: "displayes," "guilded," "colourd," "picture," and the punning word "lyes." Typically, Chapter 4 has shown, Shakespeare is drawn to courtly compliments in *Astrophil and Stella* which are built out of precisely such patterns of vocabulary, or use conceits like that of the book with the "faire" outside. Also typically he alters them to widen the distance between outward and inward, turning playful wit into cynical bitterness.

Like the foolish god of love, the personal Muse is a personification so frequently evoked in sonnet sequences, and in the varied traditions assimilated into them, that sources are hard to single out. Again, however, Sidney seems to have provided a particular model for Shakespeare in *Astrophil and Stella* 70:

> My Muse may well grudge at my heav'nly joy,
> If still I force her in sad rimes to creepe:
> She oft hath drunke my teares, now hopes to enjoy
> Nectar of Mirth, since I *Jove's* cup do keepe.
>   Sonets be not bound prentise to annoy:
>   Trebles sing high, as well as bases deepe:
>   Griefe but *Love's* winter liverie is, the Boy

Hath cheekes to smile, as well as eyes to weepe.
Come then my Muse, shew thou height of delight
In well raisde notes, my pen the best it may
Shall paint out joy, though but in blacke and white.
Cease eager Muse, peace pen, for my sake stay,
I give you here my hand for truth of this,
Wise silence is best musicke unto blisse.

The development of the sonnet by repeated invocations of the Muse—a structure not used in the sequences of the three other major English sonneteers—is imitated by Shakespeare in Sonnet 100. There the Muse is summoned by name in lines 1, 5, and 9: "Where art thou Muse," "Returne forgetfull Muse," "Rise resty Muse," to be given a final command in line 13: "Giue my loue fame." In Sonnet 101 Shakespeare adapts from *Astrophil and Stella* 70 more than this structural design:

Oh truant Muse what shalbe thy amends,
For thy neglect of truth in beauty di'd?
Both truth and beauty on my loue depends:
So dost thou too, and therein dignifi'd:
Make answere Muse, wilt thou not haply saie,
Truth needs no collour with his collour fixt,
Beautie no pensell, beauties truth to lay:
But best is best, if neuer intermixt.
Because he needs no praise, wilt thou be dumb?
Excuse not silence so, for't lies in thee,
To make him much out-liue a gilded tombe:
And to be praisd of ages yet to be.
Then do thy office Muse, I teach thee how,
To make him seeme long hence, as he showes now.

This poet-lover echoes in reverse the commands of Astrophil, whose grudging Muse is invoked first to "shew" and "paint out" his inward state, then to preserve it in "silence." The Muse of Shakespeare's poet-lover, having neglected to celebrate his beautifully "di'd" subject, is imagined inventing an excuse for such "silence" in proverbial terms—"best is best, if neuer intermixt" — that sound like Astrophil's maxim, "Wise silence is best musicke unto blisse." Such wisdom is undercut by more worldly advice which twists Astrophil's desire to "paint out" his inward state. The Muse of Shakespeare's poet-lover is reminded of the power that "lies" in "gilded" verse to make what "showes" now forever "seeme."

Whether or not this adaptation is intended to comment on contradictory sets of attitudes toward inward truth in verse in this Sidneian model or in *Astrophil and Stella* as a whole, it clearly points to them, as do many of Shakespeare's other adaptations from Sidney's sequence. They prove that he recognized its various approaches to the issue of showing in verse what in truth is in the heart.

Notes

Foreword

1. Richard Poirier, "Writing Off the Self," *Raritan* 1 (1981) : 106-33.

Introduction

1. Hyder Rollins, ed., *Tottel's Miscellany,* rev. ed. (Cambridge, Mass.: Harvard University Press, 1965), 1:43–44.

2. Rollins cites allusions to Tottel's volume in *The Merry Wives of Windsor,* 1.1.205–6 and the grave-digger's song in *Hamlet,* 5.1.69 ff. in "Introduction," *Tottel's Miscellany,* 2:121, 285.

3. William Shakespeare, *The Sonnets,* ed. Hyder Rollins, *A New Variorum Edition of Shakespeare* (Philadelphia: J. B. Lippincott, 1944), vol. 1. All quotations from the sonnets are taken from this edition and are cited by number in the text only.

4. Richard Harrier, *The Canon of Sir Thomas Wyatt's Poetry* (Cambridge, Mass.: Harvard University Press, 1975), p. 113. I have consulted the transcript of the Egerton manuscript throughout, but because quotations from it would present many extraordinary difficulties, both for the printer and the reader, I have used such quotations only where the point of my argument demanded. In all other parts of the book except Chapter 2 on Wyatt, I have quoted his poems whenever possible as they were printed in Tottel's miscellany, because these were the versions in which they were known to the other poets discussed in those chapters. Poems not included in Tottel's collection are quoted there from *Collected Poems of Sir Thomas Wyatt,* ed. Kenneth Muir and Patricia Thomson (Liverpool: Liverpool University Press, 1969). This edition is also used for all quotations from Wyatt's poems in Chapter 2. For critiques of this edition see Richard Harrier, *Renaissance Quarterly* 23 (1970): 471–74; H. A. Mason, *Editing Wyatt* (Cambridge: Cambridge Quarterly Publications, 1972).

5. William Shakespeare, *The Tragedie of Hamlet,* in *Mr. Wm. Shakespeares Comedies, Histories & Tragedies,* ed. Helge Kökeritz (New Haven: Yale University Press, 1954), 2.2, p. 754. All quotations from the plays come from this facsimile of the First Folio.

6. Ibid., 1.2, p. 744.

7. Ibid., 5.2, p. 770.

8. Shakespeare's Sonnets 138 and 144 first appeared in William Jagger's miscellany, *The Passionate Pilgrim.* Since the only surviving copy of the first edition is lacking the title page, the date is unknown according to Hallett Smith, *The Tension of the Lyre* (San Marino: Huntington Library, 1981), p. 56. It is dated 1599, the same year as the second edition, by Rollins, *The Sonnets,* 1:353n.

9. Zevedei Barbu, *Problems of Historical Psychology* (London: Routledge and Kegan Paul, 1960), p. 145.

10. Russel Fraser, *The Language of Adam* (New York: Columbia University Press, 1977), p. 215.

11. *Webster's Collegiate Dictionary,* 4th ed., s.v. "new words," pp. xxv–xxxviii. This list was shown to me by Elizabeth Ferry.

12. Shakespeare, *Hamlet,* 1.2, p. 744.

13. Thomas Wythorne, *The Autobiography of Thomas Whythorne,* modern spelling ed., ed. James Osborn (London: Oxford University Press, 1962), p. 35. In quoting from this work I have departed from the practice followed elsewhere in this book of preferring unmodernized texts, because Whythorne wrote his life in his own system of orthography. The fact that he did so is itself revealing of the fluidity of English at that time and of the desire felt by some writers to regularize it. But quotations from the unmodernized version would strain unnecessarily the resources of printer and reader, without being representative of English in that period. I have therefore used that edition only for one quotation from a passage not included in the modernized version, which is abridged. The choice of passages to be excluded from it is itself a reflection of distinctively modern interests: omissions consist principally of moral generalizing.

14. The many studies of treatises on psychology printed in this period reflect simultaneously its elaboration and its lack of development by quoting without chronological argument or distinction from works printed throughout the whole span of the sixteenth century and even well into the seventeenth century. See for example Ruth Anderson, *Elizabethan Psychology and Shakespeare's Plays* (Iowa City: University of Iowa Humanistic Studies, 1927); Herschel Baker, *The Dignity of Man* (Cambridge, Mass.: Harvard University Press, 1947); J. B. Bamborough, *The Little World of Man* (London: Longmans, Green, 1952); Hardin Craig, *The Enchanted Glass* (Oxford: Basil Blackwell, 1950); C. S. Lewis, *The Discarded Image* (Cambridge: University Press, 1967).

15. John Locke, *An Essay Concerning Human Understanding,* ed. Peter Nidditch (Oxford: Clarendon Press, 1979).

16. Michel Foucault, *The Order of Things* (New York: Vintage Books, 1973), pp. 78, 43.

17. Ibid., p. 59. The biblical sanction for this view of language most often cited by writers of the time is Genesis ii, 19, elaborated in representative fashion by Richard Mulcaster, *The First Part of the Elementarie* in *Mulcaster's Elementarie* [1582], ed. E. T. Campagnac (Oxford: Clarendon Press, 1925), p. 188: "For euen God himself, who brought the creatures, which he had made, vnto that first man, whom he had also made, that he might name them, according to their properties, doth planelie declare by his so doing, what a cunning thing it is to giue right names, and how necessarie it is, to know their forces, which be allredie giuen, bycause the word being knowen, which implyeth the propertie the thing is half knowen, whose propertie is emplyed."

18. Timothy Bright, *A Treatise of Melancholie* [1586] (New York: Fascimile Text Society, 1940), p. 47. A brief history of the word *heart* is given by Charles Butler, *The English Grammar* (Oxford, 1633), pp. 29–30: In "ancient writing" and in the "old Bible" the "*heart cor* was most commonly written *hert,*" but in the Homilies "*hart,*" even though "*hart cervus* is so written," for the two had come to be sounded alike. The fact that spelling was thought of as pictoral representation of sound is shown in the title of a work published in 1569 by John Hart, *An Orthographie, conteyning the due order and reason, howe to write or paint thimage of mannes voice, most like to the life or nature,* cited by R. F. Jones, *The Triumph of the English Language* (Stanford: Stanford University Press, 1953), p. 147, n. 10.

19. John Hoskyns, *Direccions for Speech and Style* in *The Life, Letters, and Writings of John Hoskyns,* ed. Louise Osborn (New Haven: Yale University Press, 1937), p. 116. In this and a few other quotations where the text uses marks such as abbreviations which are no longer in existence, I have spelled them out in order not to make unnecessary difficulties for printer or reader.

20. Paul Delany, *British Autobiography in the Seventeenth Century* (London: Routledge and Kegan Paul, 1969), pp. 11–12.

21. Barbu, *Problems of Historical Psychology,* pp. 168–69.

22. George Mead, *Mind, Self and Society* (Chicago: University of Chicago Press, 1955), p. xxiv; Erving Goffman, *The Presentation of Self in Everyday Life* (Edinburgh: University of Edinburgh Social Sciences Research Center, 1956) p. 36; Jacques Lacan, *The Language of the Self* (New York: Delta, 1968); Heinz Kohut, *The Analysis of the Self* (New York: International Universities Press, 1971), pp. xiv–xv, and *The Restoration of the Self* (New York: International Universities Press, 1977), pp. 311, 306. For discussions of the word *self* in ordinary language and in the technical language of sociologists and psychologists, see Henry Johnstone, *The Problem of the Self* (University Park: Pennsylvania State Press, 1970), pp. 31–42; R. D. Laing, *The Self and Others* (London: Tavistock Publications, 1961), pp. 116–25.

23. Georges Gusdorf, *La Découverte de Soi* (Paris: Presses Universitaires de France, 1948), p. 23. Montaigne's chief competitor for the credit of being the earliest representative of the modern self is Petrarch. See for example Robert Durling, *The Figure of the Poet in the Renaissance* (Cambridge, Mass.: Harvard University Press, 1965), p. 87; Thomas Greene, "The Flexibility of the Self in Renaissance Literature," *The Disciplines of Criticism,* ed. Peter Demetz, Thomas Greene, and Lowry Nelson (New Haven: Yale University Press, 1968), p. 246. A list of beginnings credited to Petrarch, and their attributors, is given by Arnaud Tripet, *Pétrarque ou La Conaissance de Soi* (Geneva: Librairie Droz, 1967), p. 10. The "modern conception of the self" is traced to Descartes' "discovery of the *cogito*" by Risieri Frondizi, *The Nature of the Self* (New Haven: Yale University Press, 1953), p. 3.

24. Jonathan Culler, *Structuralist Poetics* (Ithaca: Cornell University Press, 1976), pp. 30, 28.

25. Stephen Greenblatt, *Renaissance Self-Fashioning* (Chicago: University of Chicago Press, 1980).

26. See the following representative remarks: that Wyatt "introduced the introspective note into English poetry," Raymond Southall, *Literature and the Rise of Capitalism* (London: Lawrence and Wishart, 1973), p. 23; that "Sidney's poetry, more than the work of any other Elizabethan, demands attention for its persistent tone of personal revelation," Dorothy Connell, *Sir Philip Sidney* (Oxford: Clarendon Press, 1977), p. 52; that Shakespeare's contribution to poetic tradition was a language "equal to the most demanding kind of close psychological analysis," Douglas Peterson, *The English Lyric from Wyatt to Donne* (Princeton: Princeton University Press, 1967), p. 223; that the poetry of Shakespeare and Donne embodies a new impulse toward more searching "self-examination," more "individualist criticism," an "obsessive yet dramatic introspection," Patrick Cruttwell, *The Shakespearean Moment* (New York: Vintage Books, 1960), pp. 12, 21, 49.

27. Sir Thomas More, *The confutacyon of Tyndales answere,* eds. L. Schuster, R. Marius, J. Lusardi, and R. Schoek, in *The Complete Works of St. Thomas More* (New Haven: Yale University Press, 1973), 8.1.202.

28. Ezra Pound, *Gaudier-Brzeska* (New York: New Directions, 1970), p. 85. This quotation was located for me by Professor Frank Bidart of Wellesley College.

29. William Empson, "Donne and the Rhetorical Tradition," *Elizabethan Poetry,* ed. Paul Alpers (New York: Oxford University Press, 1967). p. 73.

30. More, *The confutacyon of Tyndales answere,* 8.2.742, 749–50.

31. Ibid., 8.2.751.

32. Ralph Palmer, ed., *Seneca's "De Remediis Fortvitorvm" and the Elizabethans* (Chicago: Institute of Elizabethan Studies, 1953), p. 21.

33. Sir Thomas Wyatt, *Tho. Wyatis Translatyon of Plutarckes Boke of The Quyete of Mynde* in *Collected Poems,* pp. 442, 447. Three of the commonest terms for what we would call feelings are treated as synonymous by Thomas Wright, *The Passions of the minde in generall* (London, 1604). p. 7: "Those actions then which are common with vs, and beastes, wee call Passions, and Affections, or perturbations of the mind." Other writers distinguish among these terms, for instance Ralph Lever, *The Arte of Reason* [1573] (Menston: Scolar

Press, 1972): "Some take passions for any affection, be it great or small: but in our English speeche we use this terme, when wee would expresse a vehement pang, eyther of the bodie, or of the minde."

34. *The First and Second Prayer Books of Edward VI* (London: Everyman's Library, 1968). p. 212.

35. Samuel Daniel, *Delia* in *Poems and A Defence of Ryme*, ed. A. C. Sprague (Cambridge, Mass.: Harvard University Press, 1930), p. 28.

36. Sir Philip Sidney, *Astrophil and Stella* in *The Poems of Sir Philip Sidney*, ed. William Ringler (Oxford: Clarendon Press, 1962). All quotations from Sidney's poems are taken from this edition. Those from *Astrophil and Stella* are cited by number in the text only.

37. Robert Cawdrey, *A Table Alphabeticall of Hard Usual English Words*, ed. Robert Peters (Gainesville: Scholars' Facsimiles and Reprints, 1966), p. 114. The development of an "introspective" attitude toward feelings in early seventeenth-century vocabulary is discussed by Owen Barfield, *History in English Words* (New York: George H. Doran, n.d.), pp. 158–59.

38. Lionel Trilling, *Sincerity and Authenticity* (Cambridge, Mass.: Harvard University Press, 1974), p. 23.

39. Sister Miriam Joseph, *Shakespeare's Use of the Arts of Language* (New York: Columbia University Press, 1949), p. 14.

40. Rosemond Tuve, *Elizabethan and Metaphysical Imagery* (Chicago: University of Chicago Press, 1967), p. 351.

41. Ibid., p. 334.

42. Ibid., pp. 351–53.

43. Peter Ramus, *The Logike of the Most Excellent Philosopher P. Ramus Martyr*, ed. Catherine Dunn, trans. Roland Mac Ilmaine (Northridge: San Fernando Valley State College, 1969). For extensive discussions of this rhetorical revolt, see W. S. Howell, *Logic and Rhetoric in England, 1500–1700* (Princeton: Princeton University Press, 1956); Walter Ong, *Ramus, Method, and the Decay of Dialogue* (Cambridge, Mass.: Harvard University Press, 1958).

44. This argument is made by Daniel Javitch, *Poetry and Courtliness in Renaissance England* (Princeton: Princeton University Press, 1978), p. 36.

45. The point is made by David Kalstone, *Sidney's Poetry* (Cambridge, Mass.: Harvard University Press, 1965), p. 105. It is expanded in rhetorical and metrical analyses by Neil Rudenstine, *Sidney's Poetic Development* (Cambridge, Mass.: Harvard University Press, 1967), p. 168 and throughout.

46. Jerome Mazzaro, *Transformations in the Renaissance Lyric* (Ithaca: Cornell University Press, 1970), p. 101.

47. Richard Harrier, "Invention in Tudor Literature: Historical Perspectives," *Philosophy and Humanism*, ed. Edward Mahoney (Leiden: E. J. Brill, 1976), p. 374. For some other recent rhetorical explanations of changes in later sixteenth-century poetry, see Thomas Sloan and Raymond Waddington, eds., *The Rhetoric in Renaissance Poetry* (Berkeley: University of California Press, 1974); Russell Fraser, *The Dark Ages and the Age of Gold* (Princeton: Princeton University Press, 1973); G. K. Hunter, "Drab and Golden Lyrics," *Forms of Lyric*, ed. Reuben Brower (New York: Columbia University Press, 1970), pp. 1–18; Michael Murrin, *The Veil of Allegory* (Chicago: University of Chicago Press, 1969).

48. For discussions of the sonnet form, see Stephen Booth, *An Essay on Shakespeare's Sonnets* (New Haven: Yale University Press, 1969), pp. 29–30 and throughout; Paul Fussell, *Poetic Meter and Poetic Form* (New York: Random House, 1965), pp. 113–33; John Crowe Ransom, "Shakespeare at Sonnets," *The World's Body* (New York: Charles Scribner's Sons, 1938), pp. 270–303; Colin Williamson, "Structure and Syntax in *Astrophil and Stella*," *Review of English Studies* 31 (1980): 271–84. A historical account of the development of the sonnet form between 1220 and 1250 is given by Ernest Wilkins, *The Invention of the Sonnet and Other Studies in Italian Literature* (Roma: Edizioni di Storia e Letteratura, 1959), pp. 14–39.

49. Robert Durling, "Introduction," *Petrarch's Lyric Poems* (Cambridge, Mass.: Harvard University Press, 1976), p. 9. Because there is no sixteenth- or early seventeenth-century translation of the whole of Petrarch's sequence, I have used Durling's translations and the Italian text on which they are based throughout. All quotations from poems in this edition in both Italian and English translation are cited by number in the text only.

50. Discussions of Petrarch's influence on Wyatt's sonnets, including detailed comparisons of Wyatt's translations with their Petrarchan originals, are numerous. For extended examples see the following books: Sergio Baldi, *Sir Thomas Wyatt,* trans. F. T. Prince (London: Longmans, Green, 1961), pp. 30–35; Otto Heitch, *Die Petrarcaübersetzungen Sir Thomas Wyatts* (Stuttgart: Wilhelm Braumüller, 1960), pp. 76–124; J. W. Lever, *The Elizabethan Love Sonnet* (London: Methuen, 1956), pp. 20–35; H. A. Mason, *Humanism and Poetry in the Early Tudor Period* (London: Routledge and Kegan Paul, 1959), pp. 188–98; Kenneth Muir, *Life and Letters of Sir Thomas Wyatt* (Liverpool: Liverpool University Press, 1963), pp. 228–31; Raymond Southall, *The Courtly Maker* (Oxford: Basil Blackwell, 1964), pp. 78–91; Patricia Thomson, *Sir Thomas Wyatt and His Background* (Stanford: Stanford University Press, 1964), pp. 179–90.

51. The fullest discussion of Petrarch and Sidney is in Kalstone, *Sidney's Poetry,* especially pp. 105–32.

52. This quality in Petrarch's sonnets is discussed by Durling, "Introduction," *Petrarch's Lyric Poems,* p. 13.

53. *Tottel's Miscellany,* 1:169–70.

54. Michael Drayton, *Ideas Mirrovr* in *The Works of Michael Drayton,* ed. J. W. Hebel (Oxford: Basil Blackwell, 1931), 1:96; *Zepheria* in *Elizabethan Sonnets,* ed. Sidney Lee (New York; E. P. Dutton, n.d.). 2:755.

55. Christopher Marlowe, "The Passionate Shepherd to his Love," *The Complete Works of Christopher Marlowe,* ed. Fredson Bowers (Cambridge: University Press, 1973), 2:537.

56. This convention of disguise and Sidney's uses of it are discussed by Jean Robertson, "Sir Philip Sidney and his Poetry," *Elizabethan Poetry,* Stratford-Upon-Avon Studies 2 (London: Edward Arnold, 1960), pp. 115–16. The argument that Sidney gives a name to Astrophil in order to dissociate himself from him is made by Alan Sinfield, "Sidney and Astrophil," *Studies in English Literature* 20 (1980): 28.

57. George Pettie, "The Letter of G. P. to R. B. Concerning This Woorke," *A Petite Pallace of Pettie His Pleasure,* ed. Herbert Hartman (London: Oxford University Press, 1938), p. 5. This passage is cited as an illustration of the common tendency to make veiled allusions in narratives by C. T. Prouty, *George Gascoigne* (New York: Benjamin Blom, 1966), p. 193.

58. Evidence that Sidney's contemporaries made these identifications is discussed by Robertson, "Sir Philip Sidney and his Poetry," pp. 117–18. For other discussions of such contemporary identifications, see J. G. Nichols, *The Poetry of Sir Philip Sidney* (Liverpool: Liverpool University Press, 1974), pp. 65–67. Surrey is imagined visiting the chamber where Geraldine was born and writing a sonnet in praise of it by Thomas Nashe, *The vnfortunate Traueller* in *The Works of Thomas Nashe,* ed. Ronald McKerrow (London: A. H. Bullen, 1904–8), 2:270.

59. *Tottel's Miscellany,* 1:38, 34.

60. Ibid., 1:136, 25, 147.

61. Ibid., 1:44, 51.

62. Ibid., 1:37.

63. Ibid., 1:67.

64. Ibid., 1:45. The relation of this translation to its model, Poem 360 in Petrarch's sequence, is discussed in Chapter 2.

65. Ibid.,1:77.

66. Ibid.

67. Ibid., 1:199, 170, 160.

68. Ibid., 1:81, 12.

69. George Gascoigne, "Gascoignes woodmanship," *The Complete Works of George Gascoigne,* ed. John Cunliffe (Cambridge: University Press, 1907), 1:348–51.

70. *Tottel's Miscellany,* 1:80.

71. D. D. Carnicelli, "Introduction," *Lord Morley's "Tryumphes of Fraunces Petrarke"* (Cambridge, Mass.: Harvard University Press, 1971), p. 31.

72. Daniel, "To the right Honourable the Ladie *Mary,* Countesse of Pembroke," *Poems,* p. 9.

73. Ibid.

74. Thomas Watson, *Passionate Centurie of Love* in *Poems,* ed. Edward Arber (London: J. and W. Rider, 1870), p. 23.

75. Watson, "To the frendly Reader," *Passionate Centurie,* p. 21.

76. Giles Fletcher, "To the Reader," *Licia* in *The English Works of Giles Fletcher, the Elder,* ed. Lloyd Berry (Madison: University of Wisconsin Press, 1964), p. 78.

77. Ibid., p. 80.

78. Sir Philip Sidney, *An Apologie for Poetrie* in *Elizabethan Critical Essays,* ed. G. G. Smith (Oxford: Oxford University Press, 1950), 1:20.

79. Along with her main argument that in the sixteenth and seventeenth centuries the "critical question of 'sincerity' is neglected in favor of the poetic problem of efficacy through credibility," Rosemond Tuve notes that "Sincerity is sometimes commented on, by both theorists and poets, as a prerequisite for writing credibly." To illustrate she cites *Astrophil and Stella* 1, *Elizabethan and Metaphysical Imagery,* p. 182.

80. The autobiographical references in *Astrophil and Stella* 33 are noticed in Ringler, "Commentary," *The Poems of Sir Philip Sidney,* p. 472; A. C. Hamilton, *Sir Philip Sidney* (Cambridge: University Press, 1977), p. 95. Neither comment distinguishes this kind of autobiographical poem from the sonnets alluding to actual names and events such as Sonnet 20, to which 33 is specifically likened by Hamilton.

81. Wyatt, *Collected Poems,* p. 5. This poem did not appear in Tottel's miscellany, probably because the content was dangerous, whether or not it alludes to autobiographical facts.

82. Ibid., pp. 212–13.

83. Arguing against the view represented by C. S. Lewis that sonnet sequences are essentially "more like an erotic liturgy than a series of erotic confidences," C. L. Barber claims that "Many of Shakespeare's sonnets are drastic (and unparalleled) exceptions to this rule: they refer to complicated and very private relations," "An Essay on the Sonnets," *Elizabethan Poetry,* ed. Alpers, p. 302. For the view that a sonnet sequence is like "public prayer" see C. S. Lewis, *English Literature in the Sixteenth Century* (Oxford: Clarendon Press, 1954), p. 491.

84. The possibility that "hate away" in line 13 of Shakespeare's Sonnet 145 is a pun on the name Hathaway is discussed by S. Schoenbaum, *William Shakespeare: A Compact Life* (Oxford: Oxford University Press, 1978), p. 91.

85. *Tottel's Miscellany,* 1:3.

Chapter 1

1. This quotation is from the second poem on the death of Wyatt, entitled "Of the same," *Tottel's Miscellany,* 1:28; "The Printer to the Reader," Ibid., 1:2.

2. George Puttenham, *The Arte of English Poesie,* ed. Gladys Willcock and Alice Walker (Cambridge: University Press, 1970), p. 60.

3. Sidney, *An Apologie for Poetrie,* p. 196. A similar view is expressed by William Webbe, *A Discourse of English Poetrie* [1586] in *Elizabethan Critical Essays,* 1:239: "I know no memorable worke written by any Poet in our English speeche vntill twenty yeeres past,"

followed two pages later by highest praise for Chaucer, "Though the manner of hys stile may seeme blunte and course to many fine English eares."

4. Rollins, "Introduction," *Tottel's Miscellany,* 2:65–66. Lack of interest in distinguishing the contributors from one another is suggested by the comment on Wyatt and Surrey by Puttenham, *The Arte of English Poesie,* p. 62: "betweene whom I finde very little difference."

5. Wyatt, *The Quyete of Mynde,* p. 440. He mentions Latin because his own translation is of a Latin version of the Greek original.

6. Mulcaster, *Elementarie,* p. 102.

7. F. W. Bateson, *English Poetry and the English Language* (New York: Russell and Russell, 1961), p. 31. For other discussions of the growth of English in this period, see Jones, *The Triumph of the English Language*; J. L. Moore, *Tudor-Stuart Views on the Growth, Status and Destiny of the English Language* (Halle: Niemeyer, 1910).

8. The need of other languages to borrow from English "be nothing so often, as ours to vse theirs" according to Mulcaster, *Elementarie,* p. 173.

9. Ibid., pp. 172–76. The quotation is from the title page of Cawdrey, *A Table Alphabeticall.* For accounts of the earliest English dictionaries see James Murray, *The Evolution of English Lexicography* (Oxford: Clarendon Press, 1900); Dewitt Starnes and Gertrude Noyes, *The English Dictionary from Cawdrey to Johnson* (Chapel Hill: University of North Carolina Press, 1946).

10. John Bullokar, "To the Courteous Reader," *An English Expositor* (Menston: Scolar Press, 1967).

11. The most comprehensive and influential study representing this view is Lawrence Stone, *The Family, Sex and Marriage in England, 1500–1800* (New York: Harper and Row, 1977).

12. Trilling, *Sincerity and Authenticity,* pp. 24–25.

13. Thomas Elyot, *Dictionary,* ed. R. C. Alston (Menston: Scolar Press, 1970); Thomas Cooper, *Theasaurus Lingvae Romanae et Britannicae* [1565] (Menston: Scolar Press, 1969).

14. Bullokar, *An English Expositor.*

15. Pierre Charron, *Of Wisdome,* trans. Samson Lennard (London, 1608), p. 61. This pairing translates the French of Pierre Charron, *De la Sagesse* (Bovrdeaus, 1601), p. 141: *en particulier & indiuidu.*

16. St. Augustine, *The Confessions of the Incomparable Doctour S. Avgvstine,* trans. Toby Matthew (London, 1620), p. 51. The original word *incolumitatem* is translated "being" by William Watts [1631], *St. Augustine's Confessions,* Loeb Classical Library (Cambridge, Mass.: Harvard University Press, 1950), 1:59.

17. Thomas Tusser, "The Authors Life," *Five Hundred Points of Good Husbandry,* ed. E. V. Lucas (London: James Tresgaskis, 1931), pp. 202–12; Thomas Churchyard, *A Tragicall Discourse of the Unhappy Mans Life* in *Biographical Miscellanies,* ed, Philip Bliss (Oxford, 1813), pp. 14–39. For discussion of these and other early lives see Wayne Shumaker, *English Autobiography* (Berkeley: University of California Press, 1954), pp. 1–19.

18. Sir James Melville, *Memoirs of his own life, 1549–1593* (Edinburgh: J. Ballantyne, 1827).

19. Sir Thomas Bodley, *The life of Sir Thomas Bodley, written by himself* (Chicago: A. C. McClurg, 1906).

20. Simon Forman, "Forman's Autobiography," "Forman's Diary, 1564–1602," *Simon Forman,* ed. A. L. Rowse (London: Weidenfeld and Nicolson, 1974), pp. 267–99.

21. Henry Machin, *The Diary of Henry Machin,* ed. John Nichols (London: Camden Society, 1968), pp. 63, 283, 272, 143–44.

22. Sir Fulke Greville, *Life of Sir Philip Sidney* [1652], ed. Nowell Smith (London: Folcroft Library Editions, 1971), pp. 6, 69.

23. James Osborn, *The Beginnings of Autobiography in England* (Los Angeles: University of California Clark Memorial Library, 1959), pp. 23–24.

24. Whythorne, *Autobiography,* p. 1.

25. Ibid., p. 87.

26. For discussion of the difference between the preoccupation of modern autobiographers with their "unique selves" or "inner lives," and the generic character of early autobiographies, see Jonathan Goldberg, "Cellini's *Vita* and the Conventions of Early Autobiography," *Modern Language Notes* 89 (1974): 71–83.

27. Whythorne, *Autobiography,* pp. 103–4.

28. Ibid., pp. 112–13.

29. Hoskyns, *Direccions for Speech and Style,* p. 148.

30. Ramus, *Logike,* p. 33.

31. Helen White, *The Tudor Books of Private Devotion* (Madison: University of Wisconsin Press, 1951), pp. 166–67.

32. Thomas Becon, *The Pomander of Prayer* in *Prayers and Other Pieces of Thomas Becon,* ed. for the Parker Society by Rev. John Ayr (Cambridge: University Press, 1844), pp. 74–85.

33. Stephen Guazzo with Bartholomew Young, *The Civile Conversation of M. Steeven Guazzo,* ed. Sir Edward Sullivan (London: Constable, 1925), 1:1.

34. Sir Toby Matthew, "The Preface to the Reader," *Confessions of S. Avgvstine,* p. 37.

35. *A Booke of Christian Exercise* (London, 1596), p. 254. This work is attributed to R. P., "Perused by" Edmund Bunny, and published with *Boore* misprinted for *Booke* on the title page, which is corrected in the edition of 1621.

36. Osborn, *The Beginnings of Autobiography,* p. 24.

37. Whythorne, *Autobiography,* p. 175.

38. Wyatt, *Collected Poems,* p. 119.

39. Edmund Spenser, *Amoretti* in *The Minor Works,* ed. C. G. Osgood and H. G. Leitspeich, *The Works of Edmund Spenser,* ed. E. Greenlaw, C. G. Osgood, F. M. Paddelford, R. Heffner (Baltimore: Johns Hopkins Press, 1947), 2:196. The equation of "our selves, that is to say, our bodies" is made in a translation by Philemon Holland of Plutarch, *The Philosophie, commonlie called, The Morals* (London, 1603), p. 313. Knowledge of self is equated with knowing one's "owne temperature" in a translation by John Hales of *The preceptes of Plutarche for the conseruation of good healthe* (London 1543).

40. *Prayer Books of Edward VI,* p. 40.

41. Butler, *The English Grammar,* p. 40.

42. Sidney, *An Apologie for Poetrie,* p. 150.

43. For example Wright, *The Passions of the minde,* p. 14: "Selfe-love then may bee defined, an inordinate inclination of the soule, affecting too much the pleasures of the body against the prescript of right reason"; Charron, *Of Wisdome,* p. 229: "selfeloue presumption, and foolish dotage of our selues."

44. Greville, *Life of Sidney,* p. 19.

45. William Lily and John Colet, *A Short Introduction of Grammar* [1549] (Menston: Scolar Press, 1970).

46. Wyatt, *The Quyete of Mynde,* p. 454. The words *nosce te ipsum* surely "proceded of god" according to Sir Thomas Elyot, *The Boke Named The Gouernour,* ed. H. H. S. Croft (London: Kegan Paul and Trench, 1883), 2:204; Wright, *The Passions of the minde,* title page.

47. John Calvin, *The Institvtion of the Christian Religion,* trans. Thomas Norton (London, 1574), p. 1.

48. Martin Luther, *A Commentarie of M. Doctor Martin Lvther Vpon The Epistle of S. Paul to the Galathians,* trans. Thomas Vautroullier (London, 1575), p. 61.

49. John Frith, *A Myrrour or glasse to know thy selfe* in *The Whole Workes of W. Tyndall, John Frith, and Doc. Barnes* (London, 1573), p. 83.

50. Sir Philip Sidney, "Sidney's Letter to Edward Denny" in Appendix 5 of James Osborn, *Young Philip Sidney* (New Haven: Yale University Press, 1972), p. 538.

51. Sir Philip Sidney, *The Correspondence of Sir Philip Sidney and Hubert Languet,* trans. Steuart Pears (London: William Pickering, 1845), p. 143.

52. Elyot, *The Gouernour,* 2:203.

53. Ibid., 2:204–6. For discussion of the Stoic contention that the "true self . . . is in every man the same," see Ludwig Edelstein, *The Meaning of Stoicism* (Cambridge, Mass.: Harvard University Press, 1966), p. 42.

54. Charron, *Of Wisdome,* pp. 223–24.

55. Levin Lemmens, *The Touchstone of Complexions,* trans. Thomas Newton (London, 1581), pp. 2–3.

56. Peter de la Primaudaye, *The French Academie,* trans. T. B. (London, 1586), p. 12.

57. Cicero, *Marcvs Tullius Ciceroes thre bookes of duties,* trans. Nicholas Grimald (London, 1558), p. 50.

58. Charron, *Of Wisdome,* p. 4.

59. Michel de Montaigne, *The Essayes of Montaigne,* trans. John Florio (New York: Modern Library, 1933), pp. 121, 361.

60. Ibid., p. 298.

61. Ibid., p. 47. The term *rolle* occurs in the corresponding French passage in *Essais de Messire Michel, Seignevr de Montaigne* (Paris, 1587), p. 75: *Mais a ce denier rolle de la mort & de nous il n'y a plus que feindre, il faut parler bon Francois, il faut monstrer ce qu'il y a de bond & de net dans le fond du pot.*

62. Montaigne, *Essayes,* p. 565.

63. Cicero, *Epistolae,* lib. 6, ep. 4 is cited as an example of the use of *conscientia* by Frondizi, *The Nature of the Self,* p. 35, n. 5.

64. Wyatt, *The Quyete of Mynde,* pp. 447, 461.

65. Thomas Nashe, from *Strange News, or Four Letters Confuted* in *Elizabethan Critical Essays,* 2:241; the *O.E.D.* cites Ben Jonson, *Poetaster,* 5.1.130–31. Both passages are cited by George Gordon, *Shakespeare's English* (Oxford: Clarendon Press, 1923), pp. 259–61. Ben Jonson, "My Picture Left in Scotland," *The Poems* in *Complete Critical Edition of Ben Jonson,* ed. C. H. Hereford, P. and E. Simpson (Oxford: Clarendon Press, 1954), 8:149–50.

66. The earliest use in England of consciousness meaning "the apprehension by the self of its own operations and states" is traced to the Cartesians and then to Locke by Frondizi, *The Nature of the Self,* p. 35, n. 5. He notes that Locke's uses of it, with only one exception, are concentrated in chapter 27 of *An Essay Concerning Humane Understanding,* which was added to the second edition, published in 1694.

67. William James, "The Stream of Thought," *The Principles of Psychology* (New York: Henry Holt, 1890), 1:224–90.

68. The "Reines or Kidneis" are equated by John Rider, *Bibliotheca Scholastica* [1589], ed. R. C. Alston (Menston: Scolar Press, 1970). Sidney in his translations of the Psalms uses the phrases "my inward reynes" and "my reines, and inmost of my heart," *Poems,* pp. 288, 305. A variant, "heart and entrailes," is used by Florio translating Montaigne, *Essayes,* p. 916.

69. Stephen Batman, trans., *Batman vppon Bartholome, his Booke De Proprietatibus Rerum* (London, 1582), p. 15; Charron, *Of Wisdome,* p. 46.

70. *A Booke of Christian Exercise,* p. 53.

71. St. Augustine, *The Confessions of S. Avgvstine,* p. 377. For the Latin original see *St. Augustine's Confessions,* 1:442: *interioris domus meae, quam fortiter excitaveram cum anima mea in cubiculo nostro, corde meo.*

72. Francis Petrarch, "The Epistolare Preface" to book 2, *Physicke against Fortune,* trans. Thomas Twyne (London, 1579), p. 162; Wright, *The Passions of the minde,* p. 212; Charron, *Of Wisdome,* pp. 6 (the translation, by pairing terms, underscores the original metaphor in Charron, *De La Sagesse,* p. 8: *en son priué*), 137; Daniel, *A Defence of Ryme,* p. 154.

73. *The Holy Bible, an Exact Reprint of the Authorized Verson* (Oxford: Oxford University Press, 1833). All quotations from the Bible are taken from this reprint, unless a different translation is specified, and are cited by book, chapter, and verse in the text only.

74. Geoffrey Chaucer, *The Book of Troilus and Criseyde*, ed. R. K. Root (Princeton: Princeton University Press, 1945), p. 244.

75. Ibid., p. 114.

76. Stone, *The Family, Sex and Marriage*, pp. 223-25 and throughout.

77. Henry Parker, Lord Morley, "To his posterity," *Poetry of the English Renaissance*, ed. J. W. Hebel and H. H. Hudson (New York: F. S. Crofts, 1940), p. 44.

78. Chaucer, *Troilus and Criseyde*, pp. 243-44.

79. *Tottel's Miscellany*, 1:39.

80. For examples see Whythorne, *Autobiography*, pp. 87-88; George Gascoigne, *A discourse of the aduentures passed by Master F. I.* in *A Hundreth sundrie Flowres* (London, 1573), pp. 234, 268. For comparison of these works as autobiographical writings see Rudolph Gottfried, "Autobiography and Art: An Elizabethan Borderland," *Literary Criticism and Historical Understanding*, ed. Phillip Damon (New York: Columbia University Press, 1967), pp. 109-34. The influence of Gascoigne's work on Whythorne's is suggested by James Osborn, "Introduction," *The Autobiography of Thomas Whythorne*, unmodernized ed. (Oxford: Clarendon Press, 1961), p. liv.

81. William Roper, *The Lyfe of Sir Thomas Moore, Knighte*, ed. James Cline (New York: Swallow Press, 1950), pp. 30-31.

82. Montaigne, *Essayes*, p. 746.

83. Mark Girouard, *Life in the English Country House* (New Haven: Yale University Press, 1978), p. 76.

84. *A Booke of Christian Exercise*, pp. 11-12.

85. John Florio, *Second Frutes* [1591]. ed. R. C. Simonini (Gainesville: Scholars' Facsimiles and Reprints, 1953), p. 125.

86. Edmund Spenser, *The Faerie Queene Book III*, ed. F. M. Padelford in *Works*, p. 24. The size and placing of mirrors can be learned from such details as the commands of a woman "rising in the morning," described by Peter Erondell, "The French Garden," *The Elizabethan Home*, ed. M. St. Clare Byrne (London: Frederick Etchells and Hugh Macdonald, 1925), p. 43: "Why doe you not set my great looking glasse on the table? It is too high, set the supporter lower."

87. Shakespeare, *Hamlet*, 3.4, p.760.

88. Ibid.

89. Queen Elizabeth, *The Mirror of the Sinful Soul*, ed. Percy Ames (London: Asher, 1897). This translation of a French poem by Queen Margaret of Navarre was made by Elizabeth at the age of eleven.

90. "Of Common prayer and Sacramentes," *Certaine Sermons* (London, 1595).

91. More, *The confutacyon of Tyndales answere*, 8:1:208.

92. William Tyndale, *An aunswere vnto Syr Thomas Mores Dialogue* in *The Whole workes*, pp. 254, 264-65.

93. Ibid., p. 249.

94. Ibid., p. 284.

95. "Of Common prayer and Sacramentes," *Certaine Sermons*.

96. John Donne, *The Sermons of John Donne*, ed. George Potter and Evelyn Simpson (Berkeley: University of California Press, 1953-62), 8:292.

97. Lady Margaret Hoby, *Diary of Lady Margaret Hoby*, ed. Dorothy Meads (London: George Routledge, 1930).

98. Rev. W. K. Clay, ed., *Private Prayers Put Forth By Authority During the Reign of Queen Elizabeth*, Parker Society vol. 43 (Cambridge: University Press, 1851). This volume contains *The Primer*, 1559; the *Orarivm*, 1560; the *Preces Privatae*, 1564; *A Booke of Christian Prayers*, 1578.

99. Guazzo, *The Civile Conversation*, 1:28.

100. Ibid., 1:xciii.

101. The phrase occurs, for example, in the heading of the ceremony "Of Them That Be Baptized in Priuate Houses In Tyme Of Necessitie," *Prayer Books of Edward VI*, p. 242.

102. *Private Prayers*, p. 442.

103. Whythorne, *Autobiography*, unmodernized ed., p. 154. This passage, omitted from the abridged modernized version, echoes the "generall Confession," *Prayer Books of Edward VI*, p. 224: "we knowledge and bewaile our manyfold synnes and wyckednes, which we from tyme to tyme, most grevously haue committed."

104. "Of Common prayer and Sacramentes," *Certaine Sermons*.

105. Martin Luther, *A Commentarie Vpon the Fiftene Psalmes*, trans. Henry Bull (London, 1577), pp. 108, 67.

106. Chaucer, *Troilus and Criseyde*, p. 29.

107. This work is quoted by White, *The Tudor Books of Private Devotion*, p. 157.

108. Donne, *Sermons*, 7:205.

109. Theodore Beza, *A briefe and pithie some of the christian faith*, trans. R. F. (London, 1566), "The Epistle Didacatorie."

110. Greville, *Life of Sidney*, p. 41.

111. William Shakespeare, *The Tragedie of Romeo and Juliet*, 1.1, p. 652.

112. The *O.E.D.* cites for *privacy* only one use (in a religious work dated 1450) before Shakespeare, who is cited as using it in the sense of retirement from public action in *Troilus and Cressida* 3.3,190–91.

113. Guazzo, *The Civile Conversation*, 1:48.

114. Shakespeare, *Hamlet*, 1.2, p. 744.

115. Charron, *Of Wisdome*, p. 203; a similar pairing, "privie thoughts and secret conceits," is used by Henry Peacham, *The Garden of Eloquence* [1593], ed. W. G. Crane (Gainesville: Scholars' Facsimiles and Reprints, 1954), "To the Right Honorable Sir Iohn Pickering."

116. Baldassare Castiglione, *The Book of the Courtier*, trans. Sir Thomas Hoby (London: J. M. Dent, 1948), p. 108.

117. Sidney, *An Apologie for Poetrie*, p. 64.

118. John Woolton, *The Christian Manual*, ed. for the Parker Society (Cambridge: University Press, 1851), p. 95.

119. *Prayer Books of Edward VI*, p. 212.

120. *A Booke of Christian Exercise*, p. 53.

121. *The Geneva Bible* [1560] (Madison: University of Wisconsin Press, 1969), p. 245.

122. *Prayer Books of Edward VI*, p. 253.

123. Whythorne, *Autobiography*, p. 1.

124. Charron, *Of Wisdome*, p. 162.

125. Cawdrey, *A Table Alphabeticall*, p. 17, where the spelling is "apparant."

126. Lemmens, *The Touchstone of Complexions*, p. 22.

127. Guazzo, *The Civile Conversation*, 1:177–78.

128. de la Primaudaye, *The French Academie*, p. 403.

129. Wright, *The Passions of the minde*, pp. 105, 27.

130. Ibid., p. 212.

131. Charron, *Of Wisdome*, p. 4.

132. Ibid., p. 6. For similarly contradictory assumptions, both held by a single author, see Montaigne, *Essayes*, pp. 68, 566: "How often doe the forced motions and changes of our faces witnesse the secretest and most lurking thoughts we have, and bewray them to by-standers?" "They see not my heart, when they looke upon my outward countenance."

133. Lemmens, *The Touchstone of Complexions*, p. 22.

134. William Perkins, "Of the nature and practice of Repentance," *Two Treatises* (Cambridge, 1597), p. 9. In addition to all the other meanings discussed in this chapter, *inward*

was sometimes used with the sense of intimate, as it is meant in Montaigne, *Essayes,* p. 523: "inward and familiar acquaintance."

135. Charron, *Of Wisdome,* p. 202. The English version underscores the architectural metaphor in the definition of the private life, translating from Charron, *De la Sagesse,* p. 271: *l'vne priuée d'vn chacun au dedans & en sa poitrine.*

136. Charron, *Of Wisdome,* pp. 202–3. Here the English follows closely the categories of the French from Charron, *De La Sagesse,* p. 273: *interne, domestique, publique.*

137. Sidney, *An Apologie for Poetrie,* p. 180.

138. Spenser, *Amoretti,* pp. 213–14.

139. Batman, *Batman vppon Bartholome,* p. 12; St. Augustine, *The Confessions of S. Avgvstine,* p. 786; Woolton, *The Christian Manual,* pp. 70–71.

140. Lemmens, *The Touchstone of Complexions,* p. 22.

141. Bright, *A Treatise of Melancholie,* p. 47.

142. Batman, *Batman vpon Bartholome,* p. 12. A similar lack of distinction between references to literal and figurative inward parts is shown in an exhortation to the contemplation of God's blessings by William Kempe, *The Education of Children* in *Four Tudor Books on Education,* ed. Robert Pepper (Gainesville: Scholars' Facsimiles and Reprints, 1966), p. 215: "how can you but be feruently moued with heart and will and all the veynes of your bodie."

143. Wyatt, *Collected Poems,* p. 114.

144. Watson, Sonnet 68, *Passionate Centurie,* p. 104; Shakespeare, *Hamlet,* 3.2, p. 757.

145. Ben Jonson, *The English Grammar,* ed. Alice Waite (New York: Sturgis and Walton, 1909), p. 78: "In our English speech we number the same parts as the Latins. *Noun, Pronoun, Verb, Participle, Adverb, Conjunction, Praeposition, Interjection.* Only we add a ninth, which is the article."

146. William Bullokar, *Pamphlet for Grammar* in *The Works of William Bullokar,* vol. 2, ed. J. R. Turner (Leeds: University of Leeds, 1980), pp. 1–2; Paul Greaves, *Grammatica Anglicana* (Menston: Scolar Press, 1969), p. 6; Butler, *The English Grammar,* pp. 33–36.

147. Butler, *The English Grammar,* p. 36. The adjective was not defined as a part of speech until the eighteenth century according to Josephine Miles, "Major Adjectives in English Poetry," *University of California Publications in English* 12 (1946): 309. She notes, however, that Elizabethan rhetoricians define the figure of Epitheton, or the Qualifier, as giving "a quality by way of addition."

148. The *O.E.D.* gives 1565 for the date of this quotation from Bishop Jewel.

149. Daniel, *A Defence of Ryme,* p. 154.

150. Wyatt, *Collected Poems,* p. 110.

151. Sidney, *Poems,* p. 150.

152. Ibid., p. 38.

153. Sir Thomas Elyot, *The Castel of Helth* [1541] (New York: Scholars' Facsimiles and Reprints, 1936), pp. 11, 68.

154. Ibid.,p. 85.

155. "A short declaration of the true, liuely and Christian fayth," *Certaine Sermons.*

156. "Of Common prayer and Sacramentes," ibid.

157. Edward Dering, "A confession of sinnes with faith and repentaunce," *A Briefe and Necessary Catechisme or Instruction* (London[?], 1572[?]).

158. This defense of Lok's poetry from the 1593 edition of his sonnets is quoted by Lily B. Campbell, *Divine Poetry and Drama in Sixteenth-Century England* (Cambridge: University Press, 1959), p. 131.

159. Lemmens, *The Touchstone of Complexions,* p. 36.

160. This passage from Thomas Gataker, *A Good Wife Gods Gift* is quoted by Carroll Camden, *The Elizabethan Woman* (Mamaroneck: Paul P. Appel, 1975), p. 201. The passage is based on 1 Peter iii, 3–5, which is also the source of the admonition to wives at the close of the marriage ceremony, *Prayer Books of Edward VI,* p. 258: "whose apparell let it not bee

outwarde, with broyded heare, and trymming about with golde, either in putting on of gorgeous apparell: But leat the hyd man which is in the hearte, be without all corrupcion. . . .For after this maner (in the olde tyme) did the holy women, which trusted God, apparell themselues."

161. *Tottel's Miscellany,* 1:44.

162. Bullokar, *An English Expositor.* "Expression" is defined "A squeezing or pressing out" by Henry Cockeram, *The English Dictionarie* [1623] (Menston: Scolar Press, 1968). Wyatt uses the verb with a characteristic lack of distinction between literal and figurative in a poem in *Tottel's Miscellany,* 1:42:

> Oft ye riuers, to hear my wofull sounde,
> Haue stopt your cours, and plainely to expresse,
> Many a teare by moisture of the grounde
> The earth hath wept to hear my heauinesse.

Chapter 2

1. "The Printer to the Reader," *Tottel's Miscellany,* 1:2.

2. The exception is Nicholas Grimald, who was not a courtly maker. Of his forty contributions to Tottel's volume, only the first three concern love.

3. Stone, *Family, Sex and Marriage,* pp. 103–4.

4. Wyatt, "To the most excellent and most vertuous princess Katheryn", *The Quyete of Mynde,* p. 441. For the most influential discussion of the interchange between the motifs of literature and of courtly life, see J. Huizinga, *The Waning of the Middle Ages* (New York: Doubleday Anchor, 1956), especially pp. 242–64.

5. Wright, *The Passions of the minde,* p. 57. The essential connection between love and poetry is explained in greater physiological detail by Juan Huarte, *Examen de Ingenios. The Examination of mens Wits,* trans. Richard Carew (London, 1594), pp. 312–13: "when a man beginneth to entreat of amorous matters, sodainly he becommeth a Poet. . . .And the reason is, because these workes appertaine to the imagination, which encreaseth and lifteth it selfe vp from this point, through the much heat, accasioned in him by this amorous passion. And that loue is an hot alteration, sheweth apparently, through the courage and hardinesse, which it planteth in the louer, from whom the same also reaueth all desire of meat, and will not suffer him to sleep."

6. Puttenham, *The Arte of English Poesie,* p. 45.

7. *Tottel's Miscellany,* 1:121.

8. Ibid., 1:184.

9. Mulcaster, *Elementarie,* p. 167. This passage is quoted by Walter Ong, "Historical Backgrounds of Elizabethan and Jacobean Punctuation Theory," *PMLA* 59 (1944): 355. For discussion of the shift from oral to silent reading habits, see Walter Ong, *The Barbarian Within* (New York: Macmillan, 1962), p. 175.

10. Wyatt, *Collected Poems,* pp. 3–4.

11. Ibid., pp. 83–84.

12. Ibid., pp. 17–18.

13. *Tottel's Miscellany,* 1:41–42.

14. Wyatt's translation, quoted and discussed in the following pages, is "If amours faith," *Collected Poems,* p. 12. The looser adaptation is "If waker care," ibid., p. 78.

15. Watson, headnote to Sonnet 40, *Passionate Centurie,* p. 76.

16. Catullus, 85, *The Poems of Gaius Valerius Catullus,* trans. F. W. Cornish in *Catullus Tibullus and Pervigilium Veneris,* Loeb Classical Library (Cambridge, Mass.: Harvard University Press, 1956), p. 162.

17. Wyatt, *Collected Poems,* p. 22.

18. Watson, Sonnet 40, *Passionate Centurie,* p. 76.

19. Wyatt, *Collected Poems*, p. 22. This kind of syntactical ambiguity is different from the *double entendre*, a poem or speech in which a phrase may attach to what precedes or follows it, a device which is likened to other verbal games such as riddles, anagrams, acrostics, rebuses by John Stevens, *Music and Poetry in the Early Tudor Court* (Lincoln: University of Nebraska Press, 1961), p. 162.

20. Wyatt, *Collected Poems*, pp. 12-13.

21. Ibid., pp. 5-10. The model is Petrarch's Poem 360.

22. Ibid., pp. 79-82. The model is Petrarch's Poem 37.

23. Chaucer, *Troilus and Criseyde*, p. 22. An exception to Wyatt's practice is his translation of Petrarch's Sonnet 199 into a poem of five six-line stanzas, "O goodely hand," *Collected Poems*, pp. 65-66.

24. Wyatt, *Collected Poems*, p. 23.

25. For examples of *trust* used in poems other than sonnets, see ibid., pp. 17, 52, 59, 62, 72, 79.

26. Ibid., p. 3.

27. *Tottel's Miscellany*, 1:8.

28. Wyatt, *Collected Poems*, p. 24.

29. Ibid., p. 14.

30. *Tottel's Miscellany*, 1:121, 122.

31. Ibid., 1:170.

32. Joost Daalder, ed., *Sir Thomas Wyatt Collected Poems* (London: Oxford University Press, 1975), p. 18, n. 9.

33. Wyatt, *Collected Poems*, p. 88.

34. Ibid., p. 36; Harrier, *The Canon of Sir Thomas Wyatt's Poetry*, p. 142; *Tottel's Miscellany*, 1:211.

35. This reading is suggested by Richard Harrier, "A New Biographical Criticism of Wyatt, "*Notes and Queries* 204 (1959): 189.

36. Wyatt, *Collected Poems*, pp. 212-13.

37. Stevens, *Music and Poetry in the Early Tudor Court,* especially pp. 154-94; Whythorne, *Autobiography*, pp. 31-32.

38. Whythorne, *Autobiography*, p. 40.

39. Wyatt, *Collected Poems*, p. 9.

40. Ibid., pp. 19, 194, 45.

41. Ibid., p. 26.

42. Ibid., p. 42.

43. Ibid., p. 20.

44. Ibid., p. 53.

45. Ibid., p. 59.

46. Ibid., p. 27.

47. Ibid., pp. 4, 16.

48. Ibid., p. 2.

49. Ibid., p. 69.

50. Ibid., p. 2.

51. The associations of color with art, rhetoric, and dissimulation are often made, for example in such treatises as Dudley Fenner, *The Artes of Logike and Rhetorike* [1584] in *Four Tudor Books on Education,* p. 176: "Sophistrie is the feined Art of Elenches, or coloured reasons. A colourable reason, or Elenche, is a shewe of reason to deceiue withall."

52. *Tottel's Miscellany*, 1:56.

53. Wyatt, *Collected Poems*, pp. 257-58.

54. Ibid., p. 231.

55. This traditional metaphor is discussed by Thomson, *Sir Thomas Wyatt and His Background,* p. 162.

56. Wyatt, *Collected Poems*, p. 59.

57. Ibid., pp. 83, 17.

58. Ibid., p. 16.

59. Ibid., pp. 21-22.

60. Ibid., pp. 19-20.

61. Lamenting the inconsistencies of English spelling, in which some writers follow new pronunciations while others follow the old for antiquity's sake, Butler chooses Wyatt's punning word as an instance where pronunciation should dictate different spelling in *The English Grammar*, p. 29: "*Dear* [*charus*] (wer' of coometh dearling) differs from *deer'* [*carus* and *dama*,] as wel in voice as writing." The proximity of *dear-deer* was often chosen to make this point because it was a very common pun, for example the one used most often of all by Shakespeare, according to M. M. Mahood, *Shakespeare's Wordplay* (London: Methuen, 1957), p. 51. The play on *heart-hart* is among his next most common puns, with *grace, will, light, lie, crown, sun-son, color, use, shape.*

62. Wyatt, *Collected Poems*, p. 5.

63. Ibid., pp. 3-4.

64. Ibid., p. 18.

65. For uses of *alas* in sonnets, see Wyatt, *Collected Poems*, pp. 20, 23, 24, 238. Functions of the apostrophe are discussed by Jonathan Culler, *The Pursuit of Signs* (Ithaca: Cornell University Press, 1981), pp. 135-54.

66. Wyatt, *Collected Poems*, p. 3.

67. Both literal and figurative references to forests elsewhere in Petrarch's poems are noted by Muir and Thomson, "Commentary," *Collected Poems*, p. 265.

68. Wyatt, *Collected Poems*, pp. 18, 51.

69. Ibid., p. 16.

70. Ibid., p. 73.

71. The affinity between Wyatt's metaphor of the "hertes forrest" and both the forests of courtly romances, such as those of Malory and Ariosto and also Dante's *selva oscura*, is discussed by Thomson, *Sir Thomas Wyatt and His Background*, p. 174.

72. Wyatt, *Collected Poems*, p. 21.

73. Ibid., pp. 11-12.

Chapter 3

1. Sidney, *An Apologie for Poetrie*, p. 196.

2. Sidney, *Poems*, pp. 41, 38.

3. Ibid., pp. 75-76. Another example of a song form within a fourteen-line poem is Poem 24 in ibid., pp 43-44. Lines 1, 4, 7, 10, 13 begin "Leave of my sheepe," while lines 3, 6, 9, 12 parallel complaints of the sun's cruelty or departure.

4. Ibid., p. 74.

5. *Tottel's Miscellany*, 1:50.

6. Harrier, *The Canon of Sir Thomas Wyatt's Poetry*, p. 125.

7. *Tottel's Miscellany*, 1:39.

8. Ibid., 1:39. A link between Wyatt and Sidney may have been provided by Ronsard, according to H. W. Richmond, "Ronsard and the English Renaissance," *Comparative Literature Studies* 7 (1970): 141-60. His argument is that Ronsard, who taught Sidney ways of evoking a "sense of subjective personality through his verse," may have learned this from Wyatt.

9. The body of English sonnets published between 1557 and 1582, said to be almost three times the number included in Tottel's collection, is discussed by William Harris, "Early Elizabethan Sonnets in Sequence," *Studies in Philology* 68 (1971): 451-69.

10. George Gascoigne, *Certayne Notes of Instruction Concerning the Making of Verse or Ryme in English* in *Elizabethan Critical Essays*, 1:55.

11. Daniel, *A Defence of Ryme*, p. 138.

12. Sidney, *Poems*, pp. 161-62.

13. *Tottel's Miscellany*, p. 1:69.

14. Sidney, *Poems*, p. 161.

15. John Thompson, *The Founding of English Meter* (London: Routledge and Kegan Paul, 1961), pp. 152-53.

16. Harris, "Early Elizabethan Sonnets in Sequence," pp. 457-58.

17. George Watson, *The English Petrarchans*, Warburg Institute Surveys 3 (London: Warburg Institute, 1967), p. 2.

18. A. Lytton Sells, *The Italian Influence in English Poetry* (Bloomington: Indiana University Press, 1955), p. 105; Carnicelli, "Introduction," *Lord Morley's "Tryumphes of Fraunces Petrarke,"* p. 18.

19. Sidney, *Poems*, p. 144.

20. A catalogue of English translations of Sonnet 134 and other poems by Petrarch is printed in Watson, *The English Petrarchans*, pp. 15-41.

21. Ibid., p. 2.

22. For an account of this ceremony, see Morris Bishop, *Petrarch and his World* (Bloomington: Indiana University Press, 1963), pp. 160-71.

23. Whythorne, *Autobiography*, p. 40.

24. Sidney, *An Apologie for Poetrie*, p. 195.

25. Ibid., p. 206. The absence of the promise to immortalize Stella in verse is discussed by Nichols, *The Poetry of Sir Philip Sidney*, pp. 10-11.

26. Sidney, *An Apologie for Poetrie*, p. 207.

27. For discussions of anti-Petrarchan conventions within the Petrarchan tradition among continental writers, and Sidney's connections with them, see John Nelson, *Renaissance Theory of Love* (New York: Columbia University Press, 1958), pp. 220-30; Mario Praz, *The Flaming Heart* (New York: Doubleday Anchor, 1958), pp. 264-86. On Astrophil's claims as poet in Sonnet 90 and elsewhere, see Jacqueline Miller, " 'Love doth hold my hand': Writing and Wooing in the Sonnets of Sidney and Spenser," *ELH* 46 (1979): 541-47.

28. *Tottel's Miscellany*, 1:34.

29. Ibid., 1:85-87. The association of monosyllables with the speech of plain Englishmen is implied in Wyatt's satire by the identification of the speaker as a Kentish gentleman. It is made more bluntly by George Gascoigne in the Preface to *The Poesies* [1575], cited by Fraser, *The Language of Adam*, p. 220: "The more monosyllables that you use, the truer Englishman you shall seem."

30. Murrin, *The Veil of Allegory*, p. 169: "Sidney considered the invocation to be the poet's way of indicating that what he made was fiction and not truth."

31. Wyatt, *Collected Poems*, p. 74.

32. Sidney, *An Apologie for Poetrie*, p. 202.

33. The verb *to paint* in *Astrophil and Stella* has some meanings which overlap with, and some which are distinct from, the metaphor of poetry as a "speaking picture," which Sidney uses in ibid., pp. 158, 165. For discussion of Sidney's interest in this metaphor, see Forrest Robinson, *The Shape of Things Known* (Cambridge, Mass.: Harvard University Press, 1972), pp. 137-204.

34. For comments on rhetorical "masks" in *Astrophil and Stella*, see for example Hamilton, *Sir Philip Sidney*, p. 12; Richard Lanham, "*Astrophil and Stella*: Pure and Impure Persuasion," *English Literary Renaissance* 2 (1972): 101; Nichols, *The Poetry of Sir Philip Sidney*, p. 151. The term *mask*, along with *role-playing*, is now often coupled with or substituted for the term *persona*, which came into prominence in discussions of Sidney with the appearance of an essay by Theodore Spencer, "The Poetry of Sir Philip Sidney," *ELH* 12 (1945); 251-78.

35. Sidney uses *skill* in *An Apologie for Poetrie*, pp. 151, 154, 157, 161, 206.

36. For uses of *show* and *paint* see Sidney, ibid., pp. 155, 157, 172; 159, 168, 176, 202.

37. *Tottel's Miscellany,* 1:99.

38. Ibid., 1:141.

39. For some discussions of sixteenth-century attitudes toward art as suspect, see for example Murray Bundy, " 'Invention' and 'Imagination' in the Renaissance," *Journal of English and Germanic Philology* 19 (1930): 535–45; Russell Fraser, *The Dark Ages and the Age of Gold* (Princeton: Princeton University Press, 1973); William Rossky, "Imagination in the English Renaissance: Psychology and Poetic," *Studies in the Renaissance* 5 (1958): 49–73.

40. *Tottel's Miscellany,* 1:188.

41. Ibid., 1:5.

42. Discussions of *Astrophil and Stella* 45 from a variety of points of view may be found in Rosalie Colie, *Paradoxia Epidemica* (Princeton: Princeton University Press, 1966), pp. 94–95; Nichols, *The Poetry of Sir Philip Sidney,* pp. 151–52; Richard Young, *English Petrarke* in *Three Studies in the Renaissance* (New Haven: Yale University Press, 1958), pp. 8–9.

43. Sidney, *An Apologie for Poetrie,* p. 154.

44. For uses of *tale* and *fable,* see Sidney, ibid., pp. 152, 160, 166, 169, 172, 175, 183.

45. *Tottel's Miscellany,* 1:87. The most influential discussion of the plain style is Ivor Winters, "The 16th Century Lyric in England," *Elizabethan Poetry,* ed, Alpers, pp. 93–125. See also Peterson, *The English Lyric from Wyatt to Donne.*

46. Parody in *Astrophil and Stella* has been noticed, for instance, by Rudenstine, *Sidney's Poetic Development,* p. 204; Young, *English Petrarke,* p. 14. Sidney's use of parody is also discussed by Ronald Levao, "Sidney's Feigned *Apology,*" *PMLA* 94 (1979): 223–33.

47. Astrophil is called "th'arcadian shepheard" by Barnabe Barnes in Sonnet 95, *Parthenophil and Parthenophe,* ed. Victor Doyno (Carbondale: Southern Illinois University Press, 1971), p. 54.

48. Identifications of Sidney with Philisides by Spenser and Ludovic Briskett are mentioned by Robertson, "Sir Philip Sidney and his Poetry," p. 115n.

49. Astrophil's use of more than one style leads to different conclusions in other discussions such as Lanham, "*Astrophil and Stella*: Pure and Impure Persuasion," pp. 100–115; Robert Montgomery, *Symmetry and Sense* (Austin: University of Texas Press, 1961), especially pp. 77–99.

50. Daniel, *A Defence of Ryme,* p. 143.

51. The device of a frame itself was not Sidney's invention, but was used in other types of poems, for example in the lengthy narrative entitled "The louer here telleth of his diuers ioyes and aduersities in loue and lastly of his ladies death," *Tottel's Miscellany,* 1:137–45. In such poems, however, the device was not used to the ends it serves in Sidney's sonnets.

52. This instance in Sonnet 34 of a poem-within-a-poem is noticed by Barbara Herrnstein Smith, *Poetic Closure* (Chicago: University of Chicago Press, 1968), pp. 149–50.

53. An example of this conventional metaphor occurs in *Astrophil and Stella* 39, line 7: "O make in me those civill warres to cease."

54. The contest in Sonnet 58 is described, apparently without recognition of the contrast between Astrophil's composition and Stella's recitation, as a debate between Aristotelian and Augustinian views of poetry by Geoffrey Shepherd, "Introduction," *An Apology for Poetry* (New York: Harper and Row, 1977), pp. 56–61.

55. Sidney, *An Apologie for Poetrie,* p. 154.

56. The Seventh song in *Astrophil and Stella* opens:

Whose senses in so evill consort, their stepdame Nature laies,
That ravishing delight in them most sweete tunes do not raise.

57. The importance of the pun on *lie,* although not specifically for Sidney, is discussed by Christopher Ricks, "Lies," *Critical Inquiry* 2 (1975): 121–42.

58. *Tottel's Miscellany,* 1:34.

59. For discussion of the link between psychological and literary conceptions of the image-making faculty, see Rossky, "Imagination in the English Renaissance," pp. 49–73.

60. For uses of *charm* to describe the power of poetry, see Sidney, *An Apologie for Poetrie,* pp. 151, 154, 187.

61. Ibid., pp. 154, 156.

62. Direct indebtedness of *Astrophil and Stella* 99 to Petrarch's Sonnet 164 and Ronsard's version of it (*Or que le ciel*) is claimed by William Kennedy, *Rhetorical Norms in Renaissance Literature* (New Haven: Yale University Press, 1978), p. 67.

63. Chaucer, *Troilus and Criseyde,* p. 266.

64. The "dramatic contrasts" between Astrophil's "inner life and the external world in which he continues to exist" are noted by G. K. Hunter, "Spenser's *Amoretti* and the English sonnet tradition, "*A Theatre for Spenserians,* ed. Judith Kennedy and James Reither (Toronto: University of Toronto Press, 1973), p. 129.

65. Sir Philip Sidney, "To Sir Francis Walsingham," *The Prose Works of Sir Philip Sidney,* ed. Albert Feuillerat (Cambridge: University Press, 1968), 3:167.

66. These readings of "ungratefulnesse" in Sonnet 31 are suggested by David Kalstone, ed., *Sir Philip Sidney Selected Poetry and Prose* (New York: Signet, 1970), p. 138n.

67. This common view of the endings of Sidney's sonnets is represented by the remarks on the closing of *Astrophil and Stella* 71 by Smith, *Poetic Closure,* p. 214.

Chapter 4

1. Sidney, *An Apologie for Poetrie,* p. 156. Its influence on Shakespeare's plays is the thesis of Alwin Thaler, *Shakespeare and Sir Philip Sidney* (Cambridge, Mass.: Harvard University Press, 1949). Lack of concern with mutability in Sidney's sonnet sequence is discussed by Connell, *Sir Philip Sidney,* pp. 49–50, citing Kalstone, *Sidney's Poetry,* p. 122; A. C. Hamilton, "The 'mine of time': Time and Love in Sidney's *Astrophil and Stella,*" *Mosaic* 13 (1979): 81–91.

2. For extended discussions of the promise to immortalize the friend in Shakespeare's sonnets, see Ferry, *All in War with Time,* pp. 3–63; J. B. Leishman, *Themes and Variations in Shakespeare's Sonnets* (New York: Hillary House, 1961); Lever, *The Elizabethan Sonnet,* pp. 246–72.

3. The widely noticed influence of Daniel's *Delia* on Shakespeare's sonnets is discussed by Paul Ramsey, *The Fickle Glass* (New York: AMS Press, 1979), pp. 52–62.

4. Spenser's sonnets, often discussed as influencing Shakespeare's, are said to be "mysteriously closer to Shakespeare's than to those of any other Elizabethan" by F. T. Prince, "The Sonnet from Wyatt to Shakespeare," *Elizabethan Poetry,* Stratford-upon-Avon Studies 2, pp. 23–24.

5. Among many discussions of Italian and French influences on English sonneteers see Janet Scott, *Les Sonnets Élisabéthains* (Paris: Librairie Ancienne Honoré Champion, 1929); Sells, *The Italian Influence in English Poetry;* D. G. Rees, "Italian and Italianate Poetry," *Elizabethan Poetry,* Stratford-upon-Avon-Studies 2, pp. 53–70.

6. Drayton, *Ideas Mirrovr,* p. 96.

7. Ibid., p. 104.

8. William Drummond, *Poems* in *The Poetical Works of William Drummond,* ed. L. E. Kastner (Manchester: University Press, 1913), 1:3.

9. Fulke Greville, *Cælica* in *Poems and Dramas of Fulke Greville,* ed. Geoffrey Bullough (New York: Oxford University Press, 1945), 1:86. For comparisons between poems by Sidney and Greville, see J.M. Purcell, "Sidney's *Astrophil and Stella* and Greville's *Cælica,*" *PMLA* 50 (1935): 413–22.

10. Barber, "An Essay on the Sonnets," p. 302.

11. Resemblances between Shakespeare's Sonnet 21 and Sidney's attitudes toward love poetry, both in *Astrophil and Stella* an *An Apologie for Poetrie,* have often been noted, for example by Rosalie Colie, *Shakespeare's Living Art* (Princeton: Princeton University Press, 1974), p. 115; Kenneth Muir, *Shakespeare's Sonnets* (London: George Allen and Unwin, 1979), p. 55. The fullest discussions of these resemblances are Inga-Stina Ewbank, "Shakespeare's Poetry," *A New Companion to Shakespeare Studies,* ed. K. Muir and S. Schoenbaum (Cambridge: University Press, 1971), pp. 101–4; Joan Grundy, "Shakespeare's Sonnets and the Elizabethan Sonneteers," *Shakespeare Survey* 15 (Cambridge: University Press, 1962): 41–49.

12. Stephen Booth, "Commentary," *Shakespeare's Sonnets* (New Haven: Yale University Press, 1978), p. 169.

13. *Tottel's Miscellany,* 1:85–87.

14. Booth, "Commentary," *Shakespeare's Sonnets,* p. 197.

15. Echoes of Constable's *Diana* are discussed along with the influence of Marlowe's *Hero and Leander* by Ramsey, *The Fickle Glass,* pp. 115, 36–41.

16. The common notion that Shakespeare's Sonnet 127 is indebted to Sidney for the motif of black eyes is cited by Rollins, *The Sonnets,* 1:323n. The sonnet's resemblance to Sidney's playful debunkings of conventional praise is discussed by Carol Neely, "Detachment and Engagement in Shakespeare's Sonnets: 94, 116, and 129," *PMLA* 92 (1977): 90. The conclusion that since the motif of black eyes was an established convention, it constitutes no evidence of direct borrowing by Shakespeare from Sidney is reached by T. W. Baldwin, *On the Literary Genetics of Shakespeare's Poems and Sonnets* (Urbana: University of Illinois Press, 1950), p. 324.

17. Lawrence Stone, *The Crisis of the Aristocracy 1558–1641* (Oxford: Clarendon Press, 1965), p. 490.

18. Sir John Davies, *Gullinge Sonnets* in *The Poems of Sir John Davies,* ed. Robert Krueger (Oxford: Clarendon Press, 1975), p. 163. These and others of Shakespeare's sonnets to the dark lady also cynically exploit the rhetorical figure associated with "blasphemous Poets" in Pettie's translation of Guazzo, *The Civile Conversation,* 1:68: "who using the figure Antiphrasis, and speaking by contraries, will give in mockage, the name of faire to a woman that is foule, and of honest, to one that is an harlot, and will commend the eyes of one which looketh a squint."

19. The fact that addressing love poems to a man was cause for nervousness is shown by the example of Richard Barnfield, discussed by Colie, *Shakespeare's Living Art,* p. 98. Barnfield published in 1594 a volume of such poems, *The Affectionate Shepheard. Containing the Complaint of Daphnis for the loue of Ganymede* in *The Poems of Richard Barnfield* (London: Fortune Press, n.d.), pp. 1–24. He dissociated himself from his poet-lover in the prefatory letter to his next volume of 1595, *Cynthia With Certaine Sonnets, and the Legend of Cassandra* in ibid., p. 46: "I will vnshaddow my conceit: being nothing else, but an imitation of *Virgill,* in the second Eglogue of *Alexis.*" The official view held by Church and State was embodied in the act of 1533, reissued in 1563, making male homosexuality punishable by death. There is no evidence whether this law was ever enforced, according to Stone, *The Family, Sex and Marriage,* p. 492.

20. Here and in all other instances where the precise numbers of occurences of words in sonnet sequences are cited, I am indebted to Herbert Donow, *A Concordance of the Sonnet Sequences of Daniel, Drayton, Shakespeare, Sidney, and Spenser* (Carbondale and Edwardsville: Southern Illinois University Press, 1969).

21. Shakespeare's use in Sonnet 132 of conventional comparisons to degrade the lady is noticed by Philip Edwards, *Shakespeare and the Confines of Art* (London: Methuen, 1968), p. 25.

22. Borrowings by Shakespeare from Sidney other than those discussed in this chapter and in the Introduction are considered in the Appendix.

23. Booth, "Commentary," *Shakespeare's Sonnets,* pp. 283–84.

24. Ibid., p. 243. This is one among many instances where Booth's descriptions of Shakespeare's characteristic habits of language precisely fit those which he learned directly from Sidney.

25. The spellings of *eye, I,* and *aye* were sometimes interchangeable, making available such a pun in Shakespeare's Sonnet 62, according to Booth in ibid., p. 242.

26. Ibid., p. 243.

27. For studies of interpretations in Shakespeare's plays of the imperative to know oneself, see Paul Jorgensen, *Lear's Self Discovery* (Berkeley: University of California Press, 1967); Rolf Soellner, *Shakespeare's Patterns of Self-Knowledge* (Columbus: Ohio State University Press, 1972).

28. Thompson, *The Founding of English Meter,* p. 140.

29. An example of hyperboles suitable to describe Queen Elizabeth is given by John Florio, *Florio His firste Fruites* (London, 1578), p. 11: "As for the queene, to tel you the plaine truth, no tongue is sufficient to prayse her ynough." The plaine truth is then amplified by nine nouns naming virtuous qualities belonging solely to her, that "shee may rather be called celestiall, then terrestrial," followed by twelve adjectives of praise, seven negatives of vices she has not, and four more categories of praise, so that "I can not neither tel, neither expresse, neither almost thinke the great vertues wherewith shee is adorned." In conclusion she is lauded for keeping a sumptuous court, loving strangers, and speaking eight languages.

30. Elizabeth's speeches typically combine majesty and intimacy suggestive of the special nature of her relationship to her subjects. This is illustrated, for example, by the exchange between the Commons and the Queen described and quoted from J. E. Neale, *Queen Elizabeth I* (New York: Doubleday Anchor, 1957), p. 122.

31. The literalness of the treatment of the metaphor of slavery in Shakespeare's Sonnet 133 and in *Astrophil and Stella* 2 is noted by Booth, "Commentary," *Shakespeare's Sonnets,* p. 460. Shakespeare's habit of forcing the literal implications of a metaphor is noted by Colie, *Shakespeare's Living Art,* p. 59.

32. Shakespeare's "twistingness of repetition" of the word *love* in Sonnet 40 is said to represent a practice "unique" in his verse by Ramsey, *The Fickle Glass,* p. 102.

33. Abraham Fraunce, *The Arcadian Rhetorike,* ed. Ethel Seaton (Oxford: Basil Blackwell, 1950), p. 80.

34. The kind of equivocation described here as characteristic of Shakespeare's Sonnet 58 is found in the closely related preceding sonnet by Philip Martin, *Shakespeare's Sonnets* (Cambridge: University Press, 1972), pp. 71–72.

35. Shakespeare, *Hamlet,* 1.2, p. 744.

36. *Tottel's Miscellany,* 1:6, 52.

37. Bullokar, *An English Expositor.*

38. Puttenham, *The Arte of English Poesie,* p. 302.

39. *Tottel's Miscellany,* 1:49.

40. Ibid., 1:204–05.

41. Ibid., 1:48.

Chapter 5

1. John Donne, "The Triple Foole," *Songs and Sonnets* in *The Elegies and The Songs and Sonnets,* ed. Helen Gardner (Oxford: Clarendon Press, 1966), p. 52.

2. Donne, "Loves Growth," *Songs and Sonnets,* p. 76.

3. John Donne, "To Sir Henry Goodyer," *The Life and Letters of John Donne,* ed. Edmund Gosse (New York: Dodd, Mead, 1899), 2:79.

4. The suggestion that the twenty-eight lines "To Mr. B. B.," which also contain references to poetry, are not a single poem but a pair of sonnets is made by W. Milgate, "Commentary," *The Satires, Epigrams and Verse Letters* (Oxford: Clarendon Press, 1967), p. 220.

One sonnet, "To Mr. T. W.," refers to a plague, which suggests a date of composition between 1592 and 1594, according to Milgate, "Commentary," ibid., p. 213. He finds other references which also indicate that the sonnets were written in the 1590's. For discussion of Donne's sonnets in the epistolary tradition, see D. J. Palmer, "The Verse Epistle," *Metaphysical Poetry,* ed. Malcolm Bradbury and David Palmer (Bloomington: Indiana University Press, 1971), pp. 73–99.

5. Donne, "To Mr. I. L.," *Verse Letters,* p. 67.

6. Donne, "To Mr. R. W.," "To Mr. S. B.," ibid., pp. 66, 67.

7. Donne, "To Mr. T. W.," ibid., p. 60.

8. Donne, "To Mr. T. W.," "To Mr. C. B.," ibid., pp. 62, 63.

9. Donne, "To Mrs. Magdalen Herbert: of St. Mary Magdalen" preceding *La Corona* and "To E. of D. with six holy Sonnets" preceding the 1633 *Divine Meditations* in *The Divine Poems,* ed. Helen Gardner (Oxford: Clarendon Press, 1966), pp. 1, 5–6. All quotations from Donne's holy sonnets are taken from this edition and are cited by page in the notes rather than by number in the text because there are different traditions of numbering followed in other editions.

10. For discussion of the implications in Donne's avoidance of the figure of the poet-lover in his *Songs and Sonets,* see Ferry, *All in War with Time,* pp. 67–125.

11. Isaac Walton, *The Life of Dr. John Donne* in *The Complete Angler and The Lives of Donne, Wotton, Hooker, Herbert and Sanderson* (London: Macmillan, 1925), p. 220; Donne, "To Sr. R. Ker," *Life and Letters,* 2:124.

12. Gardner, "General Introduction," *The Divine Poems,* pp. xxi, n. 2, pp. xxxvii–l. Her dating of the holy sonnets depends in large part on the argument that, while at least one of the three separate sonnets in the Westmoreland manuscript must be dated after the death of Donne's wife in 1617, since it is presumed to be an elegy on Anne Donne, the other sixteen are a group of meditations which must have been composed at the same time but not necessarily with the separate three. For another schematic arrangement of Donne's holy sonnets with which this chapter also disagrees, see Douglas Peterson, "John Donne's *Holy Sonnets* and the Anglican Doctrine of Contrition," *Essential Articles for the Study of John Donne's Poetry,* ed. John Roberts (Hamden: Archon Books, 1975), pp. 313–23. For discussion of the dating of *La Corona,* see David Novarr, *The Disinterred Muse* (Ithaca; Cornell University Press, 1980), pp. 85–93.

13. Sidney, *Poems,* pp. 161–62.

14. Barnabe Barnes, *A Divine Centurie of Spirituall Sonnets* in *The Poems of Barnabe Barnes,* ed. Alexander Grosart (Manchester: Charles Simms, 1875), p. 161.

15. The repetition of lines from stanza 8 of "The Progresse of the Soule" in lines 2 to 4 of the second sonnet of *La Corona* is noted by Gardner, "Commentary," *The Divine Poems,* p. 57.

16. Donne, *Sermons,* 1:236.

17. John Donne, *Essays in Divinity,* ed. Evelyn Simpson (Oxford: Clarendon Press, 1952), p. 75.

18. William Alabaster's devotional sonnets are considered in relation to Donne's by Louis Martz, "The Action of the Self: Devotional Poetry in the Seventeenth Century," *Metaphysical Poetry,* pp. 101–21; Henry Lok's sonnets are discussed by Campbell, *Divine Poetry and Drama in Sixteenth-Century England,* pp. 130–33.

19. Francis Meres, *Palladis Tamia,* ed. D. C. Allen (New York: Scholars' Facsimiles and Reprints, 1930), p. 280.

20. Thomas Nashe, "The Preface to Sidney's Astrophel and Stella," *Elizabethan Critical Essays,* 1:224; Sir John Harrington, "Notes to Book XVI," *Orlando Furioso,* cited by Robertson, "Sir Phillip Sidney and his Poetry," p. 117.

21. Jonson, "On Lvcy, Countesse of Bedford," *Poems,* p. 52; George Herbert, "Jordan II," *The Works of George Herbert,* ed. F. E. Hutchinson (Oxford: Clarendon Press, 1941), pp. 102–3.

22. Shakespeare's adaptation from Sidney of this device of treating conventional metaphors literally is discussed in the introduction and in Chapter 4. For examples of this practice in Donne's love poetry, see "The Legacie" and "Loves Infiniteness," *Songs and Sonnets,* pp. 50, 77.

23. Patrick Cruttwell, *The English Sonnet* (London: Longmans, Green, 1966), p. 28.

24. Resemblances in the couplets of Donne's "Death be not proud" and Shakespeare's Sonnet 146 ("Poore soule the center of my sinfull earth") are noted by Hallet Smith, *The Tension of the Lyre,* p. 67. The likeness to a Shakespearean couplet of the ending of Donne's sonnet, "If faithfull soules be alike glorifi'd," is observed by M. E. Grenander, "Holy Sonnets VIII and XVII: John Donne," *Essential Articles for the Study of John Donne's Poetry,* p. 326.

25. If Donne's sonnet, "Since she whome I lovd, hath payd her last debt," has been assumed correctly to be an elegy on his wife, who died in 1617, he could certainly by that date have known the 1609 edition of Shakespeare's sonnets.

26. Donne, "Since she whome I lovd, hath payd her last debt," *The Divine Poems,* p. 15.

27. The couplet of the version of Shakespeare's Sonnet 144 in *The Passionate Pilgrim,* although different in other details, uses the same metaphor and rhyme words as the 1609 version:

> The truth I shall not know, but liue in dout,
> Till my bad Angell fire my good one out.

This version in its entirety is printed by Rollins, *The Sonnets,* 1:368n.

28. Donne, "7. Ascension," *La Corona* in *The Divine Poems,* p. 5. The meditative structure of *La Corona* is analyzed by Louis Martz, *The Poetry of Meditation* (New Haven: Yale University Press, 1955), pp. 107–12.

29. Donne, *La Corona* 1, *The Divine Poems,* pp. 1–2.

30. *Prayer Books of Edward VI,* p. 235.

31. Donne, *Sermons,* 2:280.

32. Ibid., 2:50.

33. Ibid., 7:51.

34. The unavailability of the "weighty impersonality of true liturgical utterance" for Donne in "A Litanie" is discussed by Wilbur Sanders, *John Donne's Poetry* (Cambridge: University Press, 1971), p. 122.

35. Donne, "The Anniversarie," *Songs and Sonnets,* pp. 71–72.

36. Donne, "A Valediction: forbidding Mourning," *Songs and Sonnets,* p. 63.

37. *Prayer Books of Edward VI,* p. 212.

38. Donne, *Sermons,* 7:233.

39. Donne, "A Valediction: forbidding mourning," *Songs and Sonnets,* p. 63.

40. Thomas Nashe, "The Song," *Svmmers Last Will and Testament* in *Works,* 3:282–84; Herbert, "The Sacrifice," *Works,* pp. 26–34.

41. Donne, "A Litanie," *The Divine Poems,* p. 24.

42. The relation of Donne's sonnets to this mixed tradition of religious and amorous verse is discussed by Booth, *An Essay on Shakespeare's Sonnets,* pp. 178–79.

43. Donne, "What if this present were the worlds last night," *The Divine Poems,* p. 10.

44. *Tottel's Miscellany,* 1:12.

45. Donne, "The Flea," *Songs and Sonnets,* p. 53.

46. Donne, "Communitie," ibid., p. 34.

47. Gardner, "Commentary," *The Divine Poems,* p. 71.

48. The speaker's bragging in this sonnet is noticed but condemned as bad taste by Martz, *The Poetry of Meditation,* p. 84.

49. Donne, "Oh, to vex me, contraryes meete in one," *The Divine Poems,* p. 16.

50. Donne "The Good-morrow," *Songs and Sonnets,* p. 70.

51. Donne, "Show me deare Christ, thy spouse, so bright and cleare," *The Divine Poems,* p. 15.

52. Donne, "The Canonization," *Songs and Sonnets*, p. 74.

53. Donne, "If faithfull soules be alike glorifi'd, "*The Divine Poems*, p. 14.

54. Henry Lok, *Christian Passions and Extra-Sonnets: 1597* in *Miscellanies of the Fuller Worthies Library*, ed. Alexander Grosart (Blackburn, 1871), 2:150.

55. The precariousness of the resolution in the couplets of many of Donne's sonnets is noted by Martz, "The Action of the Self," p. 108.

56. Donne, "The Indifferent," *Songs and Sonnets*, pp. 41–42.

57. Donne, "The Computation," ibid., p. 36.

58. Donne, "Loves Infiniteness," ibid., p. 77.

59. Donne, "The Canonization," ibid., p. 74.

60. Donne, "Twicknam Garden," ibid., pp. 83–84.

61. Donne, "O might those sighes and teares returne againe," *The Divine Poems*, pp. 13–14.

62. Donne, "I am a little world made cunningly," ibid., p. 13.

63. Donne, "If poysonous mineralls, and if that tree," ibid., p. 8.

64. Donne, "Oh, to vex me, contraryes meete in one," ibid., pp. 15–16.

65. Gascoigne, "The passion of a Lover," *Complete Works*, 1:41. The resemblance of Donne's sonnet to Petrarch's Sonnet 134 is discussed by Colie, *Paradoxia Epidemica*, p. 138. "Oh, to vex me" is called "Petrarchan in structure" by Robin Skelton, "The Poetry of John Donne," *Elizabethan Poetry*, Stratford-Upon-Avon Studies 2, p. 219.

66. Donne, "Loves Infiniteness," *Songs and Sonnets*, p. 78.

Conclusion

1. Donne, "A Litanie," *The Divine Poems*, p. 20.

2. John Donne, "A Funerall Elegie," "The Second Anniversarie," *The Epithalamions, Anniversaries and Epicedes*, ed. W. Milgate (Oxford: Clarendon Press, 1978), pp. 37, 44.

3. Donne, in a secular context, writes of the "sincerity" of his "heart" in a letter "To Sir Henry Goodyer," *Life and Letters*, 1:169.

4. The Tyndale, Coverdale, and Geneva versions of Titus ii, 7 use "wholesome worde" where "sinceritie" occurs in the authorized version; the Tyndale and Coverdale versions of 1 Peter ii, 2 have "reasonable mylke" where the authorized version has "sincere milke." See William Tyndale, *The New Testament of Our Lord and Saviour Jesus Christ* [1526], ed. J. P. Dabney (Andover, 1837); Myles Coverdale, *The Holy Scriptures* [1535] (London, 1838); *The Geneva Bible*.

5. Although *sincerity* in its various forms was not conventional to the vocabulary of love sonnets, the speaker professes his "sincere love" in Sonnet 4 of William Smith, *Chloris* [1596] in *Elizabethan Sonnets*, 2:326. Both Sidney, in *Astrophil and Stella* 28, and Shakespeare, in Sonnet 66, use "simplicitie," closely related to *sincerity* in its sixteenth-century meanings, even perhaps deriving from the same root. This proximity is indicated by an entry in Elyot, *Dictionary*, where *simplex* is translated "that is not double, syncere or playne, without deceipt," compared with the definition of "sincere" as "plaine" by Bullokar, *An English Expositor*, and Cockeram, *The English Dictionarie*.

6. The importance of *true* and related words in Shakespeare's sonnets is discussed by James Winny, *The Master-Mistress* (New York: Barnes and Noble, 1968), pp. 121–28.

7. Cawdrey, *A Table Alphabeticall*, p. 115. Since in his definitions "or" does not usually indicate a distinctly alternative meaning, its use here does not mark a distinction between literal and figurative uses of *sincere*.

8. Bright, *A Treatise of Melancholie*, p. 93.

9. The *O.E.D.* cites Barnes, *Divine Centurie*, Sonnet 48.

10. William Shakespeare, *The Famous History of the Life of King Henry the Eight*, 1.1, p. 543.

11. An example cited in the *O.E.D.* is the title of a work of 1583, *A Defense of the sincere and true translations of the holie Scriptures into the English tong.*

12. In Shakespeare's plays four uses of *sincere,* three of *sincerely,* six of *sincerity* are listed in Marvin Spevack, *The Harvard Concordance to Shakespeare* (Cambridge, Mass.: Harvard University Press, 1973), p. 1150.

13. Woolton, *The Christian Manual,* p. 56; Donne, *Sermons,* 1:190.

14. Dering, "A confession of sinnes with faith and repentanunce," *A Briefe and Necessary Catechisme.*

15. *Prayer Books of Edward VI,* p. 212.

16. Donne, *Sermons,* 3:154.

17. William Shakespeare, *The Tragedie of Othello,* 2.3, p. 11.

Appendix

1. Rollins, *The Sonnets,* 1:12ln, 122n.

2. Ibid., 1:78n, 79n.

3. Booth, "Commentary," *Shakespeare's Sonnets,* p. 178.

4. Rollins, *The Sonnets,* 1:186n; Ringler, "Commentary," *The Poems of Sir Philip Sidney,* p. 487.

5. Rollins, *The Sonnets,* 1:35ln.

6. Ringler, "Commentary," *The Poems of Sir Philip Sidney,* p. 464.

Index